This book is dedicated to Our Lady of Walsingham
and to my geometry teacher Professor Keith Critchlow

First published 2023

Copyright © Tom Bree 2023

Published by The Squeeze Press
an imprint of Wooden Books Ltd
Red Brick Building, Glastonbury, BA6 9FT

A CIP catalogue record for this book is available
from the British Library

ISBN-13: 978-1-906069-21-6

Designed and typeset by Tom Bree
and Wooden Books Ltd, UK.

Printed and bound by Dream Colour Printing, China

www.woodenbooks.com

the
SQUEEZE
PRESS

THE COSMOS IN STONE

TOM BREE

CONTENTS

Foreword   viii

Preface   ix

Introduction   xi

Part I

THE 12TH-CENTURY CLIMATE OF WISDOM AND THE CENTRALITY OF JERUSALEM

1. THRONE OF WISDOM.   1

1.1 The Virgin Mary and Lady Philosophy as   2
    images of Sophia.
1.2 The Virgin Mary and the number seven.   9
1.3 Wisdom surrounded by the Seven Liberal   12
    Arts.
1.4 The Seven Liberal Arts as a preparation for   17
    Philosophy and Theology.
1.5 The Gnostic ascent symbolism of Sophia –   20
    seven steps to the Ogdoad.
1.6 Ascent symbolism in the 12th century and   24
    its perceived origins in biblical, Greek and
    Gnostic sources.

2. REVELATION AND THE DESCENT OF   27
   THE HEAVENLY CITY.

2.1 The end of the Bible and the end of time.   28
2.2 The cube at the centre of the world – the   30
    earthly squaring of the heavenly circle.
2.3 A medieval English coronation – the circular   39
    crown, the cuboid stone and the ladder that
    joins them.

3. THE KINGDOM OF JERUSALEM.   41

3.1 Reaching the centre of the world.   42
3.2 The visual depiction of Jerusalem's centrality. 45
3.3 The familial connections between the   49
    monarchs of Jerusalem and England.

4. THE ENGLISH GOTHIC CATHEDRAL   51
   AS AN IMAGE OF THE HEAVENLY AND
   EARTHLY JERUSALEM

4.1 The emergence of the Gothic style in the era   52
    of the Kingdom of Jerusalem.
4.2 Wells Cathedral as an image of both the   55
    Heavenly and earthly Jerusalem.
    - Palm Sunday at the Golden Gate of Jerusalem 55
      and the great west door at Wells.
    - The cathedral design's emulation of the   57
      Temple Mount's topographical layout –
      a Templar connection?

Part II

THE COSMOLOGICAL AND GEOMETRIC DESIGN ELEMENTS OF THE FIRST ENGLISH GOTHIC CATHEDRAL

5. THE LADY CHAPEL AS AN IMAGE OF   63
   THE MORNING STAR.

5.1 Planet Venus – the Morning and Evening   64
    Star.
5.2 Lady chapels at the east ends of English   66
    Gothic cathedrals.
5.3 The Pentagram and the Octagram of Venus.   68

5.4 The Morning Star in the design of the Wells   71
     Cathedral Lady chapel.

5.5 The Risen Christ as the Bright Morning Star.   75

5.6 Jerusalem – 'established by Planet Venus'.   82

6. THE VIRGIN MARY AS THE ROSE   83
     AND THE STELLA MATUTINA

6.1 The Virgin Mary and the five-fold rose of   84
     Eden.

6.2 The rose in fairy tales and the return to Eden.   88

6.3 The association of the rose with planet Venus.   91

6.4 The Rosary beads as a talisman of the   92
     Morning Star.

6.5 Rosary symbolism in Wells Lady chapel.   94

6.6 The Octaeteris, the Venus pentagram and the   96
     ninety-nine Moons.

6.7 The crescent moon and the star.   97

6.8 The cosmological resemblance of the Virgin   98
     Mary and Fatimah Zahra.

     - The Tasbih of Fatimah and the ninety-nine   98
       beads.

     - The Hand of Fatimah and the number five.   99

6.9 Ascent to the Rose of Divine Love.   100

7. PYRAMID GEOMETRY AND   103
     THE SIZE OF THE EARTH

7.1 The Great Pyramid's cosmic mythos.   104

7.2 The pyramid triangles.   109

     - Golden ratio polygon geometry in the   113
       Golden Pyramid Triangle.

     - The Golden Pediment Triangle.   117

     - The Fibonacci Pyramid Triangle.   119

7.3 John Michell and the Earth-Moon pyramid   120
     diagram.

7.4 The lunar cosmology of the 5–12–13 triangle.   132

7.5 The pyramid angle as the latitude of   134
     Woodstock, Oxford, Cressing Temple and
     Temple Cowley.

8. THE USE OF PYRAMID GEOMETRY IN   139
     GOTHIC CATHEDRAL DESIGN

8.1 Pyramid geometry in the design of Wells   140
     Cathedral

     - The Lady chapel and the retroquire.   140

     - The quire and the chapter house.   144

     - The west front and the nave.   155

9. THE OCTAGONAL CHAPTER HOUSE   161
     AS AN IMAGE OF THE MOON,
     THE EIGHTH HEAVEN AND WISDOM

9.1 The Earth-Moon diagram at Wells, York and   162
     Southwell.

9.2 The Moon and the magic square in the   166
     chapter house staircase at Wells.

9.3 The lunar inclination angle in the York and   174
     Southwell chapter houses.

9.4 The lunar inclination angle at the doorway   176
     that leads inwards.

9.5 The Eye of Providence and the three seats   184
     with an all-seeing view.

9.6 Harran – city of the moon and the mystery   192
     to the north.

9.7 The Virgin and the rose in the east end rose   197
     window at Laon.

10. THE WELLS BISHOP'S PALACE   201

10.1 Northern Dean and Southern Bishop.   202

10.2 The moat walls at Wells and the Great   204
     Pyramid in Egypt.

10.3 The overall layout in relation to Wells   208
     Cathedral.

11. THE CATHEDRAL NAVE AS AN   211
     IMAGE OF PLANET EARTH.

11.1 The equator–ecliptic angle and the Saltire of   212
     St Andrew.

11.2 Seven by three and thirty by thirteen. 216
11.3 The extremities of Cancer and Capricorn and the equinoctial middle way. 217
11.4 The Orthodox cross of St Andrew. 219

Part III

THE ARITHMETICAL AND MUSICAL DESIGN ELEMENTS OF THE FIRST ENGLISH GOTHIC CATHEDRAL

12. THE MEASUREMENT UNITS. 221

12.1 The reconciliation of Heaven and Earth via the 'incarnation' of number. 222
12.2 Three foot-units, one cubit and their common micro-unit. 225
12.3 The musical relationships of the three foot-units. 230
 - The use of means, multi-layered grids and micro-variations throughout the ground plan. 232

13. THE NAVE AND THE MUSICAL NUMBERS OF PLANET EARTH. 233

13.1 The two measurement grids and the 'earthly' ratio 365:364. 234
13.2 The lunar year of twelve synodic moons. 239
 - The number 33 and the cosmic Christ. 240

THE CHAPTERS 14 TO 17 are listed in these contents pages although they do not appear in this printed book. They are available as a free downloadable pdf from the web address **www.tombreegeometry.com**
A selection of diagrams from these chapters are shown in the nine unnumbered pages following page 240

14. THE GREAT PYRAMID, THE EARTH-MOON DIAGRAM AND THE MASTER DIAGRAM OF WELLS CATHEDRAL. 241

14.1 The master diagram and the size of the Earth and the Moon. 242
 - The use of the ratio 56:55. 245
 - The quire and chapter house area. 246
 - The west front. 249
 - The nave. 252
14.2 The latitude geometry of St Andrews Cathedral in Scotland. 258

15. THE QUIRE AS THE CENTRAL PLACE ON EARTH. 261

15.1 The Solomonic quire and the musical measures of Magnesia. 262
15.2 The pyramid rhomb diagram in the design of the Tabernacle. 266
15.3 Pi and Three in the Molten Sea. 268
15.4 The golden section in the sacristy's two doorways. 269

16. THE OCTAGONAL CHAPTER HOUSE AND TREASURY. 279

16.1 The chapter house. 280
16.2 The treasury/undercroft. 284
16.3 The prevalence of the number 3 on the north side of Wells Cathedral. 286
16.4 The lunation triangle numbers in the chapter house staircase. 292

17. THE RETROQUIRE AND LADY CHAPEL. 295

17.1 The number 55,440 in relation to the Great Pyramid. 296
17.2 The eastern end of the cathedral. 298
17.3 Micro-variations in the pyramid Geometry of the Bishop's Palace Moat walls. 313
17.4 The latitude geometry of the Great Pyramid. 314

Part IV

THE COSMOS IN STONE AND THE INITIATIC JOURNEY OF THE SOUL

18. THE CHRISTIAN ROOTS OF FREEMASONIC SYMBOLISM   317

18.1 The Cosmological Design Symbolism of Wells Cathedral and the Layout of a Freemason Lodge Room.   318
- The west door – the beginning of the equinoctial/paschal axis.   322
- The nave – the tropics and the equator in the point-within-the-circle diagram.   322
- The cathedral crossing as the centre of the world.   324
- The Temple of Solomon, the spring equinox, computus and Holy Week.   325
- Jachin and Boaz.   327
- The solstitial saints and their chapels in the northeast and southeast corners.   329
- The resurrection of the Bright Morning Star in the Lady chapel.   331
- Where is the north? – one striking difference from a modern-day Freemason lodge room.   333

19. THE MIDDLE PATH OF INITIATION   337

19.1 The Middle Path - A linear expression of centrality.   338
19.2 The Morning Star – both Risen Christ and Fallen Angel.   341

20. TRACES OF MEDIEVAL CHRISTIAN COSMIC INITIATION.   355

20.1 The soul's return journey to itself.   356
- The war within the soul.   359
- The pentagram of Solomon and Gawain.   363
- The initiatic descent of the Moon into the Earth.   365
- The initiatic cave.   367
- Ascent to the heavenly female.   370
- Dante, the Templars and Love.   371
- The Eternal Spring in Paradise Lost.   373
- The mountain 'on the farthest sides of the north'.   375
- The doctrine of correspondences, the golden ratio and the tetraktys walk.   377
- The sacristy in Wells Cathedral.   384

21. FINAL POINTS.   391

21.1 Palm Sunday to Pentecost and the synodic period of Venus.   392
21.2 The latitude geometry of Jerusalem and Hermopolis.   393
21.3 The Golden Pediment Triangle in the design of the Great Pyramid?   395
21.4 But who designed Wells Cathedral?   397
21.5 The use of Revelation 22:16–17 in the design of the east end.   399

EPILOGUE   401

What this study suggests in relation to the current climate of atheistic materialism, environmental destruction and cosmological colonialism.

ACKNOWLEDGEMENTS   404

IMAGE CREDITS   405

INDEX   407

FOREWORD

An introduction written by Keith Critchlow (1933–2020), formerly Professor at the Prince's School of Traditional Arts, for a slideshow talk that Tom Bree gave in 2018. The talk was delivered to the Temenos Academy at the Royal Asiatic Society in London on the evening of Thursday 22nd March. In Professor Critchlow's absence the introduction was read out by his friend and student Mrs Barbara Clauson.

"Tom Bree first came to our school in 2001 and very soon showed himself to be an accomplished geometer. Not only this but he soon became a very skilled parquetry craftsman.

Tom has developed into a master of the oral tradition – having discovered the profound relationship between imagery and the imagination.

Tom has also worked tirelessly on the deeper symbolism of Christian pointed architecture – in particular the underlying meaning of the cathedral at Wells, a town where he has chosen to make his home.

Without heroes like Tom we might never have realized the hidden meaning of our greatest architectural monuments. All of these hold not only the geometric and number secrets inherent in the Christian faith but also the wisdom of learning about the ladder of consciousness that leads to Wisdom itself – a value so urgently needed in our time.

I hold the greatest regard for Tom Bree and the work he is unfolding and feel honoured to have been his Tutor. All I ask for this audience is to carefully listen and concentrate, as Tom is an oral teacher of great value."

PREFACE

THE MATERIAL CONTAINED in this book is the fruit of ten years of research that took place mostly between 2010 and 2020. The research continues, but there is now more than enough to form the various storylines that are described within these covers.

This particular area of research became apparent to me when I was just under the pivotal age of forty. But its origin can, in a certain sense, be traced all the way back to the spiritual awakening that I experienced aged twenty-two. Back then I was attempting to become a pop star, but the awakening gave me a wider view, and an immense desire to travel around many of the world's great religious centres. The awakening was spontaneous and didn't occur as a result of my following any particular religion, teaching or teacher. However, it was very much centred around a relationship with nature and the wider cosmos, along with a recognition of the transcendent unity of all religious traditions. This awakening then fuelled my various travels in Europe, Asia, Africa and Central America between the ages of twenty-four and thirty. It is really what still fuels me to this day.

I embarked on these travels on the summer solstice in 1996. A few months later I happened to be in Ephesus in Turkey around the feast of the Virgin Mary's Assumption. After a failed attempt to spend seven days travelling around the modern-day centres of the Seven Churches of the Apocalypse, I walked up the mountain to the House of Mary (Meryemana), on what would have been the eighth day, and took part in the annual celebration of the Assumption that takes place there. This formed one of the many impromptu mini pilgrimages that I followed while on these travels. But it would only be seven years hence that the significance of this particular event would become apparent.

Apart from the many experiences – both good and bad – that my travels presented me with, the key thing that they brought forth was my continuing interest and involvement in geometry: as an art form, but also primarily as a contemplative focus within the Spiritual Imagination. One of the primary features of my awakening was the spontaneous emergence of geometric forms in the visual imagination while contemplating particular spiritual ideas.

On my thirtieth birthday it was my very great fortune to begin a two-year practical art MA at the Prince's Foundation with Professor Keith Critchlow as my sacred geometry teacher. This was the perfect 'next step' after all of my travels, and prepared me for the next stage of my life's journey.

Immediately after finishing the MA, I went on holiday to meet a friend in northern Cyprus. The cheapest route I could find involved a flight to Athens followed by boats through the Aegean and then overland through Turkey to the boat for Cyprus. While en route I happened to end up in Ephesus, again around the feast of the Virgin Mary's Assumption – seven years after my first time there. This unplanned yet synchronous 'conjunction' led to me deciding, there and then, that I would visit Meryemana every seven years on seven occasions going into the future, to ascend the mountain with its beautiful views and memorable smell of pine trees. But again it was only seven years hence that the significance of this particular event became apparent to me.

Immediately after returning home from northern Cyprus I went on a summer geometry course with Professor Critchlow. The thematic focus of the course was the number seven. I had the very great fortune of meeting someone called Helen on this course who I eventually became married to. She is a stained-glass conservator here in the small city of Wells, and this led to me leaving London aged thirty-three and setting up home in the 'smallest city in England'.

Before I moved to Wells, Helen had been boarding with Patricia Young in Fenny Castle – just to the west of the city. Patricia's father Donald Matthews was the Treasurer of the Friends of Wells Cathedral between the 1960s and 1980s. It was his copy of a ground plan drawing of Wells Cathedral that Patricia offered to me in late 2009, knowing of my interest in sacred geometry in art and architecture. This is where the story of this book begins.

In 2010, my third trip to Meryemana was beckoning. But by this time Helen and I had a son and therefore not much extra money or time. I looked more locally for Marian shrines, and was immediately presented with Walsingham. My third pilgrimage accordingly 'came home' from the House of Mary near Ephesus to her Holy House in Walsingham.

Along with Christian tradition the main celebration at Walsingham was on the eve of the Assumption. So I ended up travelling back to Wells on the day of the Assumption itself. Back in Wells I spent many hours poring over the ground plan of Wells Cathedral – which unbeknown to me was slowly drawing me into her cosmos. In the early hours of the following morning, I made an intriguing discovery in the form of an underlying geometric relationship within the ground plan. The relationship was governed by a particular isosceles triangle with a base of 11 and a height of 7. However, it was just over a month later, on a day that the full moon coincided with the autumn equinox, that it became apparent that this significant triangle was part of an underlying geometric design that used a renowned cosmological diagram involving a significant relationship between the Earth and the Moon. This particular diagram was devised or rather (re)discovered in the early 1970s by a maverick friend of Professor Critchlow called John Michell.

But it was seven years hence, while researching my fourth Marian pilgrimage, that I became aware of the fact that the equinoctial full moon of my discovery seven years earlier had also been the eve of the feast of Our Lady of Walsingham to whose Holy House I had just made a pilgrimage. Such is the reason behind this book's dedication.

The equinoctial full moon in 2010 accordingly became the symbolic gateway into the research presented in this book. The particular area of the cathedral's design that this cosmological diagram governs is, in symbolic terms, the cathedral's 'highest point'. It would turn out to be another equinoctial full moon, in spring 2019, that would form the symbolic gateway out of the research through the discovery of the very 'lowest point' of the cathedral – 'the lowest depths of the pit', no less. So, having abseiled down from the highest point to the lowest, I now have the rest of my time to attempt the climb back up again.

May the Mother of God – the Stella Maris – accompany me and guide me along the way!

INTRODUCTION

THE USE OF GEOMETRY as a language of spiritual symbolism lies at the heart of this book. To perceive geometry in this way is not new, but rather something that goes far back into the ancient world within many different cultures across the globe. One of the reasons for looking at geometry in such a way is that it reflects and embodies the eternal and unchanging reality of number. Whatever culture or historical era we are living in, indeed whichever 'spherical' planet we reside on, the same laws of number apply to each and every one of us. One of the ways in which we come into direct physical contact with these 'divine numerical thoughts' is through their manifestation in pattern. Such numerical patterns can be experienced temporally through music and spatially through geometry.

An understanding of this was approached in the medieval world through a study known as the Quadrivium. The four subjects of the Quadrivium, which were studied in the medieval European universities, concerned number and its manifestation in geometry, music and cosmology. The heavenly vault overhead was looked upon as an image of the Divine Mind in which the cyclical movements of the heavenly spheres marked out number patterns that could act as a reminder of the Divine Harmony, which ultimately lies beyond anything that can be seen or heard. In the words of Plato, 'time is a moving image of eternity', and in this sense it can be understood that the hands of a clock, which mark out time, are merely externalising the knowledge of the clock's hub, which itself remains stationary and thus outside of the cycle of time – yet also at the very heart of it.

To look at the cosmos in such a way is to attempt to align oneself with the Divine Harmony. But until we are reminded of such things, we can fall into a forgetfulness of them – or worse still, only focus upon their purely technical usefulness so as to exploit them for some kind of personal material gain. To remember the Divine Harmony, in all of its truth and beauty, is to remember the Good. To remember the Good is to remember the One ... and to remember the One is to remember one's True Self.

Sacred art and architecture is specifically designed to act as both a mental and a physical reminder of the Divine Harmony, and this book focuses in on various examples of this. Accordingly, the central theme is Wisdom, and how such Wisdom involves a symbolic ascent of the soul from the earthly realm of the senses up to the heavenly realm of the Divine Mind, and how such a journey became embodied in the medieval designs of Gothic cathedrals – each one a great cosmos in stone. It is often asked whether it is possible for the modern mind to understand the medieval mind, and in a certain sense such a historical knowledge might be seen as impossible. But to contemplate the Divine Mind through a study of the Quadrivial arts is to be in the same state of soul as the learned men and women of medieval Christendom, and in this sense the human soul of any era can attempt to orientate its vision towards its True Self through a spirit-centred philosophical study of the Quadrivial arts and their application in sacred architecture.

The City of Wells, the Dowry of Mary
New Year's Day 2021

Part I

The 12th century

climate of Wisdom and

the centrality of Jerusalem

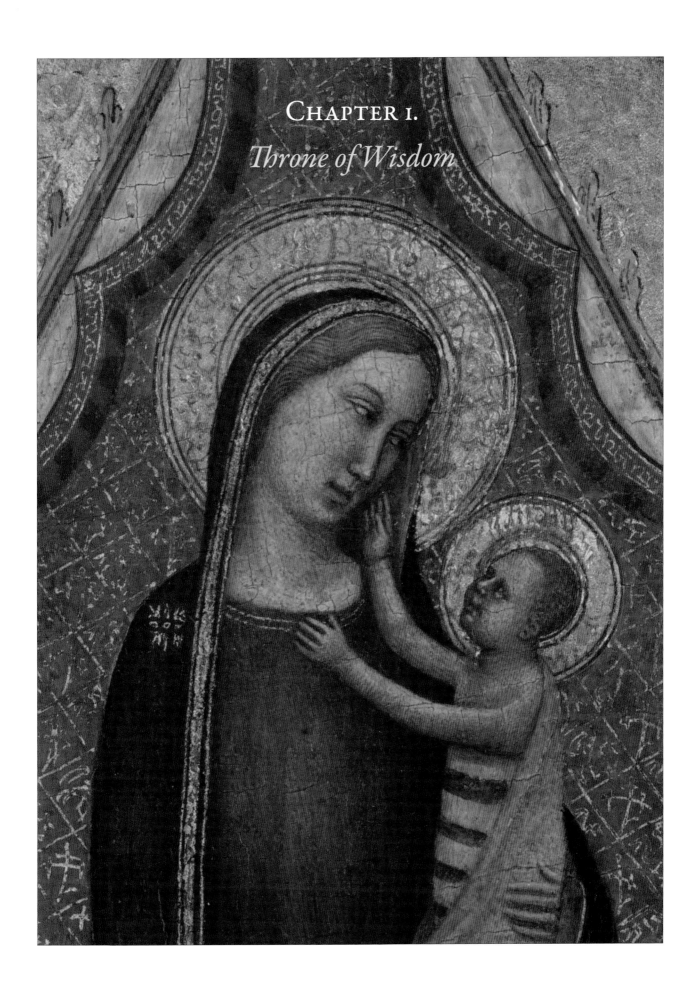

CHAPTER I.
Throne of Wisdom

1.1 THE VIRGIN MARY AND LADY PHILOSOPHY AS IMAGES OF SOPHIA

IN 12TH-CENTURY CHRISTENDOM Sophia, or 'Wisdom', was often depicted in the form of a female sitting on a throne or seat. Sophia can also be thought of as an archetype who presents herself in more than one identity. Two such identities in the culture of the 12th-century Roman church were the Virgin Mary and Lady Philosophy.

Lady Philosophy is a character in *The Consolation of Philosophy* – a written work by the Christian-Platonist philosopher Boethius. This was one of the most widely read books during the medieval Christian era, yet it contains not a single mention of the biblical storyline. This is not to say that is a non-Christian or even an un-Christian work as such, but rather that Wisdom – the book's key theme – was of central concern to an educated medieval Christian in their religious life. To orientate the soul's vision towards Wisdom was to move closer to God, because the Wisdom in question was Holy Wisdom – the Wisdom of God.

Boethius wrote *The Consolation of Philosophy* while imprisoned and awaiting execution. His crime was simply to have fallen out of favour within the grimy world of politics. But as he languished in his prison cell, a ladder of escape presented itself to him. Or more correctly, a ladder presented 'herself' to him because the ladder in question was none other than Lady Philosophy.

'While I was thus mutely pondering within myself, and recording my sorrowful complainings with my pen, it seemed to me that there appeared above my head a woman of a countenance exceeding venerable. Her eyes were bright as fire, and of a more than human keenness; her complexion was lively, her vigour showed no trace of enfeeblement; and yet her years were right full, and she plainly seemed not of our age and time. Her stature was difficult to judge. At one moment it exceeded not the common height, at another her forehead seemed to strike the sky; and whenever she raised her head higher, she began to pierce within the very heavens, and to baffle the eyes of them that looked upon her. Her garments were of an imperishable fabric ... On the lower-most edge [of these garments] was inwoven the Greek letter Π ["p" or "pi"], on the topmost the letter ϑ ["th" or "theta"], and between the two were to be seen steps, like a staircase, from the lower to the upper letter.

Lady Philosophy - north rose window at Laon Cathedral

So the ladder that appeared to Boethius was not one by which he could climb over the physical stone walls of his prison, but rather a consolatory inward ladder of ascent leading from his earthly immersion in grief and sorrow up towards Divine Wisdom. Such an ascent was effected through philosophy because the letter Theta – written at the top of the ladder – is understood to stand for *theoria*, the contemplation of Divine Wisdom. The word 'philosophy' itself also relates to Wisdom, or rather a loving friendship with Wisdom as expressed through the Greek words *philia* and *sophia*. It was this Heaven-sent friendship with Sophia – in the form of Lady Philosophy – that was to become Boethius' consolation within his tragic predicament.

As to the Greek letter pi, written at the bottom of Lady Philosophy's ladder, this is usually associated with the word *praxis* – a practical engagement in the physical world of the senses. Sometimes also with the word *politikos* – the earthly world of politics with all its fluctuating fortunes of glory and ignominy.

A distinction between *praxis* and *theoria* immediately speaks of Boethius' love of Platonist philosophy, in which a central theme is the distinction between the practical involvement in the earthly world of the senses, and the contemplative *theoria* of the intelligible world that is approached through an ascent beyond the senses.

As to the 'political' in relation to the 'theorial', this carries a certain Christian Gnostic overtone that perceives the suffering of a corrupt earthly realm below, in which the soul is imprisoned, as opposed to the certainties and freedom of the unchanging heavenly realm above.

As will become clear, these two influences of Platonism and early Christian Gnosticism are both prominent within the 12th-century Christian imagery of the Wisdom tradition.

The Virgin Mary is another Sofianic figure who in the 12th century was depicted on a throne. But in this particular depiction of Sophia, the baby Jesus is on Mary's lap, and so henceforth she is the *Sedes Sapientiae* – the Seat of Wisdom. In this sense the Holy Wisdom is Christ – the Logos – although the enthroned image of Mary appears to suggest that Wisdom has given birth to herself.

The image shown above is from the tympanum of the southern west door of Chartres Cathedral. Chartres is much renowned for its medieval cathedral school, in which there was an open embracing of various pre-Christian wisdom traditions that were viewed as being concordant in varying degrees with Christian

Madonna and Child Enthroned by Bernardo Daddi

3

beliefs. Plato's philosophy was particularly prominent in the learning of the Chartres school as was the Hermetic philosophy that was understood to be an ancient Egyptian wisdom tradition transmitted to Plato when he was in Egypt.[1] The lineage of ancient knowledge was accordingly looked upon as having its origins in ancient Egypt, and then having moved from Egypt to Greece and then from Greece to Rome.[2]

With ancient Egypt in mind, they had their own renowned image of an enthroned female with a baby on her lap. It is often pointed out that the Christian image of Mary and Jesus bears much resemblance to the ancient Egyptian image of Isis and Horus.

Isis with Horus on her lap

Interestingly the name Isis also means 'seat' or 'throne', and so she is the seat of Horus in a similar way to the Virgin Mary being the seat of Christ – the *Sedes Sapientiae*. Another interesting correlation is that in the early church Jesus was understood to have been born at the winter solstice,[3] which is the same 'corner' or

'turning point' in the four-fold annual cycle on which Horus was born. Such similarities should not be misunderstood to be one religion actively and conspiratorially stealing the forms of another religion that existed prior to it. It could rather be described as the recurrence of a perennial archetype in which the movement 'upwards' from the darkest point in the annual cycle towards the lightest is marked by the emergence of a divine incarnation who embodies heavenly light. In this sense such a solstitial storyline is as Christian as it is ancient Egyptian. There may have even been a degree of conscious recognition on the part of the later tradition of the influence of the earlier tradition. In his writings on Christian doctrine St Augustine uses the metaphor of gold and silver that has been mined by a previous religious tradition as also being of value to Christians, because gold and silver are of value to all. So archetypal principles themselves – with their universal value of gold and silver – stand prior to all traditions and are not the invented or 'patentable' property of any of them, because the value of such 'mined' principles is perennial and forever recurring in each new era of human culture.

Such symbolic ways of seeing appear to have characterised the outlook of places such as the Chartres Cathedral school, which was part of a great opening up to the knowledge of the pre-Christian ancient world in the era described as the '12th-century Renaissance'.

Returning to the Sofianic image of the enthroned Virgin Mary with Christ, her status in England during the medieval era was such that England was known as *The Dowry of Mary* owing to the very great devotion that the English had to the Virgin. A Marian apparition had taken place in the English village of Walsingham in 1061, and the site of this apparition would go on to become a very significant pilgrimage centre for king and pauper alike.

---

1. See *Mathematical Theologies*, David Albertson, Oxford University Press, 2014, chapter 4, page 99
2. For instance in the words of Hugh of St Victor: *Egypt is the mother of the arts and thence they came to Greece and thence to Italy*, in Didascalicon, bk 3, ch 2.
3. See the early Christian treatise, *On the Solstices and Equinoxes, the Conception and Birth of our Lord Jesus Christ and John the Baptist.*

Our Lady of Walsingham is depicted in the form of the *Sedes Sapientiae*, and interestingly she also resembles Boethius' description of Lady Philosophy because of what she is holding in her hands. The long-stemmed lily that she holds in one hand for instance resembles Lady Philosophy's sceptre. But whereas Lady Philosophy holds a book in her other hand, Our Lady of Walsingham's other hand is supporting Christ – the 'Word' made flesh – who is himself holding a book.

Our Lady of Walsingham

Our Lady of Walsingham's throne stands between two pillars, much like the pillars Jachin and Boaz that stood on either side of the eastern doorway of the temple of the wise King Solomon. Indeed the Virgin Mary is symbolically associated with the temple doorway in the east as it is described in chapter 43 of Ezekiel's vision. A description of this symbolism appears in an old sermon by St Aelred – a 12th-century English Cistercian abbot who was a contemporary of St Bernard of Clairvaux.

'Ezekiel says, "He brought me to the gate which looks towards the east and it was shut." The most holy Mary is this eastern gate. For a gate which looks towards the east is the first to receive the rays of the sun. So the most blessed Mary, who always looked towards the east, that is towards the brightness of God, received the first rays or rather the whole blaze of light of that true Sun ...'

Our Lady's Dowry, Reverend T. E. Bridgett. [+]

Such a description of the Virgin and her relationship to the sunrise in the east inevitably speaks of another of her titles – *Stella Matutina* (Morning Star). The planet Venus is the Morning Star, and her rising in the east just prior to sunrise heralds the coming of the divine light of the Sun. She is illuminated by the Sun, hence our capacity to see her in the dawn sky, reflecting the solar light down to us here on Earth before the Sun's supernal light itself emerges above the horizon – illuminating our world and revealing all that was hidden in the darkness of the night. So henceforth, as St Aelred suggests, Mary 'is the first to receive the rays of the sun'. We shall look in more detail at this particular Marian title later on, as well as Christ's own use of a similar epithet – the Bright Morning Star – as a description of himself within the closing lines of the Book of Revelation.

The 12th-century focus on Wisdom was closely associated with King Solomon. In Gothic-era depictions of the *Sedes Sapientiae* the Virgin's throne was directly associated with the throne of King Solomon, whereby it rested on two lions in emulation of the biblical description of the throne. Such perceptions of Solomon's wisdom derive from the Jewish origins of Christianity, in which the Wisdom tradition is also very much associated with King Solomon via various biblical writings such as the Book of Proverbs. The opening verses of chapter 1 say as much.

'The proverbs of Solomon the son of David, king of Israel; To know wisdom and instruction; to perceive the words of understanding;

To receive the instruction of wisdom, justice, and
judgment, and equity ...'

Another significant Jewish Wisdom text is the *Book of Wisdom*, which is also known as the *Wisdom of Solomon*. One of the various beautiful written tracts about Wisdom and her qualities is chapter 7. Here it is recorded in full.

'I also am mortal, like everyone else,
a descendant of the first-formed child of earth;
and in the womb of a mother I was molded into flesh,
within the period of ten months, compacted with blood,
from the seed of a man and the pleasure of marriage.
And when I was born, I began to breathe the common
air, and fell upon the kindred earth;
my first sound was a cry, as is true of all.
I was nursed with care in swaddling cloths.
For no king has had a different beginning of existence;
there is for all one entrance into life, and one way out.
'Therefore I prayed, and understanding was given me;
I called on God, and the spirit of wisdom came to me.
I preferred her to scepters and thrones,
and I accounted wealth as nothing in comparison with her
Neither did I liken to her any priceless gem,
because all gold is but a little sand in her sight,
and silver will be accounted as clay before her.
I loved her more than health and beauty,
and I chose to have her rather than light,
because her radiance never ceases.
All good things came to me along with her,
and in her hands uncounted wealth.
I rejoiced in them all, because wisdom leads them;
but I did not know that she was their mother.
I learned without guile and I impart without grudging;
I do not hide her wealth,
for it is an unfailing treasure for mortals;
those who get it obtain friendship with God,
commended for the gifts that come from instruction.
'May God grant me to speak with judgment, and to have
thoughts worthy of what I have received;

for he is the guide even of wisdom
and the corrector of the wise.
For both we and our words are in his hand,
as are all understanding and skill in crafts.
For it is he who gave me unerring knowledge of what
exists, to know the structure of the world and the activity
of the elements; the beginning and end and middle of
times, the alternations of the solstices and the changes of
the seasons, the cycles of the year and the constellations of
the stars, the natures of animals and the tempers of wild
animals, the powers of spirits and the thoughts of human
beings, the varieties of plants and the virtues of roots;
I learned both what is secret and what is manifest,
for wisdom, the fashioner of all things, taught me.
'There is in her a spirit that is intelligent, holy,
unique, manifold, subtle, mobile, clear, unpolluted,
distinct, invulnerable, loving the good, keen,
irresistible, beneficent, humane, steadfast, sure,
free from anxiety, all-powerful, overseeing all,
and penetrating through all spirits that are intelligent,
pure, and altogether subtle.
For wisdom is more mobile than any motion;
because of her pureness she pervades and penetrates
all things.
For she is a breath of the power of God,
and a pure emanation of the glory of the Almighty;
therefore nothing defiled gains entrance into her.
For she is a reflection of eternal light,
a spotless mirror of the working of God,
and an image of his goodness.
Although she is but one, she can do all things,
and while remaining in herself, she renews all things;
in every generation she passes into holy souls
and makes them friends of God, and prophets;
for God loves nothing so much as the person who lives
with wisdom.
She is more beautiful than the sun,
and excels every constellation of the stars.
Compared with the light she is found to be superior,
for it is succeeded by the night,
but against wisdom evil does not prevail'.

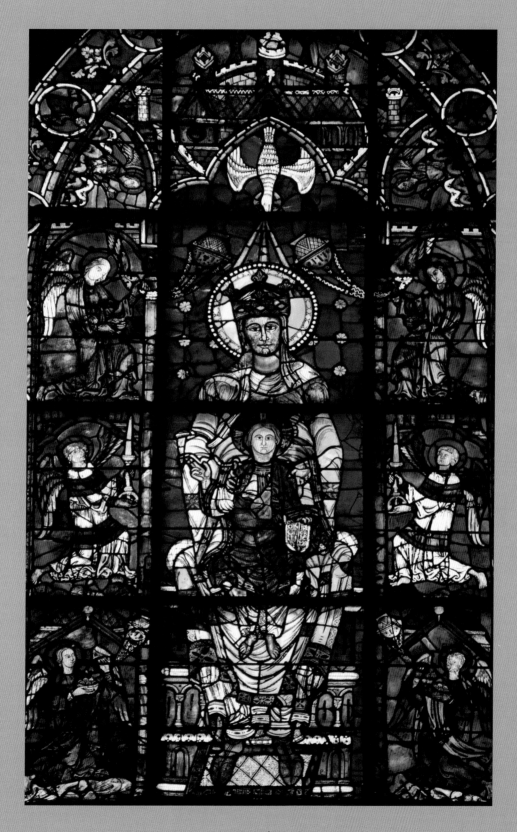

'Notre-Dame de la Belle Verrière' in Chartres Cathedral

Lady Philosophy from The Consolation of Philosophy - depicted on the central pillar between the two doors of the great west door at Notre Dame in Paris

"She was of awe-inspiring appearance, her eyes burning and keen beyond the usual power of men..........it was difficult to be sure of her height, for sometimes she was of average human size, while at other times she seemed to touch the very sky with the top of her head, and when she lifted herself even higher, she pierced it and was lost to human sight. Her clothes were made of imperishable material, of the finest thread woven with the most delicate skill... on the bottom hem could be read the embroidered Greek letter Pi, and on the top hem the Greek letter Theta. Between the two a ladder of steps rose from the lower to the higher letter.....There were some books in her right hand and in her left hand she held a sceptre."

The Consolation of Philosophy - Book I Chapter I

8

1.2 THE VIRGIN MARY AND THE NUMBER SEVEN

ANOTHER FEATURE of the pillars on the throne of Our Lady of Walsingham is their seven rings. Four of these rings are around one of the pillars, with three around the other. These rings are associated with the seven sacraments as well as the seven gifts of the Holy Spirit. But the number seven is also directly associated with the Virgin herself, as can be seen through various sevenfold descriptions such as her *Seven Joys*, *Seven Sorrows* and her *First Seven Steps* as a young child. A visual example of this numerical association is the Abingdon Labyrinth, which commemorates her Assumption and is formed of seven circles.

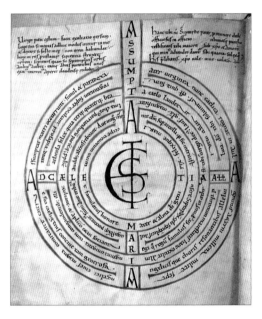

The Abingdon Labyrinth

The labyrinth exists in a manuscript copy of Boethius' *The Consolation of Philosophy* which was produced in Abingdon in the early 11th century - just a few decades prior to the aparition at Walsingham. Above the labyrinth is a description of it which includes the words *'Wisdom has structured this city, which a sevenfold*

circle surrounds'. So accordingly this Marian quality of sevenness is also directly associated with Wisdom.[5] This is related to the description in the Book of Proverbs of the house that Wisdom built with seven pillars. The sevenness of Mary also mirrors the sevenness of the gifts of the Holy Spirit via another of her many titles, namely the *Spouse of the Holy Spirit*. This particular title refers to the interaction between 'uncreated divinity' and 'created humanity' within the conception of Christ – the Holy Wisdom. Such interaction speaks of Christ's dual nature, in which there is both divinity and humanity at the same time.

Another instance of sevenness that involves both the Holy Spirit and the Virgin Mary occurs in relation to the feast of Pentecost. The calendrical calculation of Pentecost is such that it takes place seven weeks (i.e. 7 × 7 days) after Easter Sunday. Its iconographical depiction shows Mary at the centre of the twelve apostles, who are encircled around her as the Seven Gifts of the Holy Spirit descend onto those who were gathered in the upper room. Her presence forms a central pillar – an *axis mundi*, or ladder – that connects the heavenly vault above with the sacred earth below her feet, and in doing so she reflects the unity of the Holy Spirit flowing between the two worlds of the Father above and the Incarnate Son below.

The Seven Gifts of the Holy Spirit are derived from the Book of Isaiah, and interestingly the first and greatest of the gifts is again Wisdom herself.

'And there shall come forth a rod out of the stem of Jesse, and a Branch shall grow out of his roots:
And the spirit of the LORD shall rest upon him, the spirit of wisdom and understanding, the spirit of counsel and might, the spirit of knowledge and of the fear of the LORD;

---

5. The division of the seven rings on Our Lady of Walsingham's throne into three and four also reflects the words written on the pathways of the Abingdon Labyrinth about the inhabitant of this 'sevenfold heaven' who is 'three-fold four-fold blessed'. See p141 of *Through the Labyrinth* by H Kern, Prestel, 2000.

And shall make him of quick understanding in the fear of the LORD: and he shall not judge after the sight of his eyes, neither reprove after the hearing of his ears'

Isaiah 11:1–3

From this particular quote are derived the spiritual qualities of 1. Wisdom, 2. Understanding, 3. Counsel, 4. Fortitude (i.e. courage), 5. Knowledge, 6. Piety and 7. Fear of the Lord (i.e. fear as in 'awe' or 'wonder'). The repetition in the above quote of the word 'fear' is interpreted first as piety and then as fear itself.

The Virgin's association with the number seven is also reminiscent of the beliefs of the pre-Christian group known as the Pythagoreans (c 6th-century BC), who are said to have described the number seven as 'the number of the virgin'.

The Pythagoreans were a spiritual fraternity gathered around the mathematician Pythagoras. They could be described as contemplative mathematicians in that they saw number as being expressive of a spiritual realm of unchanging truths – Wisdom beyond words, as it were. The decad (i.e. the numbers from 1 to 10) was their central focus, and their depiction of it took the form of a triangular arrangement of ten dots which is known as a *'tetraktys'*. They would swear an oath over this

geometric form as part of their initiation because it was understood to embody various aspects of symbolic meaning within the Pythagorean philosophy.

The prefix 'tetra' derives from the Greek word for the number four. This relates to the *tetraktys'* hierarchy of four levels in which the arrangement of its ten dots can be understood to embody $1 + 2 + 3 + 4 = 10$. This arrangement expresses a descent or emanation from divine unity to the fourfoldness of materiality. This is also geometrically understood through the unfolding of the dimensions of space. The single dot at the top of the tetraktys symbolises the invisible origin because a single point is dimensionless. The 'flowing' of this point in one direction creates a line which is the first dimension. The two points - one at either end of the line - are then symbolised by the two dots in the *tetraktys'* second level. Three points form the three corners of a two-dimensional triangular plane and finally, with four points, a three dimensional solid can be produced in the form of a tetrahedron - a pyramid shape with four corners.

In this sense the *tetraktys* numerically symbolises an unfolding of the hidden origin, or the 'One', down to the visible and embodied fourfoldness of the material world. The tenfold totality of all the dots in the *tetraktys* are accordingly a muliplicitous and all-encompassing image of the unity or the 'One' from which they derive.

The Pythagorean Tetraktys

A tetraktys-shaped tracery window in the Lady chapel of Wells Cathedral. Nine angels look up towards the 'One' - who is depicted as God the Father.

There is also a musical dimension to the *tetraktys* that is understood through the arrangement of two number sequences. These sequences are described in Plato's *Timaeus* dialogue in relation to the World Soul. Elsewhere they are referred to as the *lambda* because their arrangement forms the shape of the Greek letter lambda which then resembles the right and left-hand sides of a *tetraktys*. Both sequences begin from the number 1 which coincides with the single dot at the top of the *tetraktys*. The left-hand side then proceeds as 2-4-8 and the right side as 3-9-27. These powers of 2 and 3 reflect a movement through the dimensions as described above. Lines with lengths of 2 and 3 beget squares with areas of 4 and 9 which then beget cubes with volumes of 8 and 27. The interactions of the lambda numbers create musical relationships in the form of ratios such as 2:1, 3:2, 4:3 and 9:8.

$$1$$
$$2 \qquad 3$$
$$4 \qquad\qquad 9$$
$$8 \qquad\qquad\qquad 27$$

Returning to the Pythagorean description of the number seven as 'the number of the virgin', the reasoning behind this symbolic title drew from the fact that it doesn't 'give birth', and also has no parents. This particular numerical symbolism relates to a multiplication process involving all of the numbers within the decad. In *The Theology of Arithmetic* – a work attributed to Iamblichus – the process is described in the following way:

'... *by mingling [the number seven] with any of the numbers within the decad, it does not produce any of the numbers within the decad, nor is it produced by the intercourse of any of the numbers within the decad ...*'

So the number seven is the only number that doesn't appear within the 'procreative' processes of the decad. Within a multiplication process there are the 'parents' (i.e. the two numbers that are multiplied together) and the offspring (i.e. the result of the multiplication process), so for instance if the numbers 2 and 3 are the parents then the number 6 will always be their offspring. With this in mind the number 7 is the only number within the decad that doesn't feature in any multiplication sequence involving parents or offspring that also appear in the decad. This can be demonstrated as follows:

$$2 \times 2 = 4 \qquad 2 \times 3 = 6 \qquad 2 \times 4 = 8$$
$$2 \times 5 = 10 \qquad 3 \times 3 = 9$$

First of all the number 1 does not appear because the Pythagoreans didn't look upon it as a number, but rather the principle of all number. If 1 is multiplied by itself it remains unchanged in itself because $1 \times 1 = 1$. Something similar applies for every other number in that the multiplying of any number by 1 will leave the number unchanged in its being. So 1 is beyond the generative numbers that follow it – and which together generate outwards into multiplicity. Henceforth the multiplication processes shown above begin with the number 2, which can be multiplied by itself as well as by the numbers 3, 4 and 5, and in each case their offspring will also be a number contained within the decad. However if 2 was to then be multiplied by 6, the offspring would be 12, which is outside of the decad – even if its parents are within it. The only other procreative relationship that can take place beyond those already mentioned is the multiplication of 3 by itself, which gives birth to 9. So henceforth the five multiplication processes shown above are the only ones with both parents and offspring that remain within the decad. On closer inspection it also then becomes clear that the only number within the decad that doesn't feature as a parent or an offspring is the number 7. Consequently, it is a virgin and has no parents. As Iamblichus puts it:

'*They called the heptad [i.e. the number seven] "Athena" ... because it is a virgin and unwed just like Athena in myth and is born neither of mother (i.e. of even number) nor of father (i.e. odd number), but from the father of all (i.e. from the monad, [the number 1] the head of number).*'

The medieval Christian perception of Pythagorean number symbolism, and its use as a way of engaging in spiritual contemplation, is something that lay at the heart of a 12th-century Christian education. It formed part of a sevenfold system of learning known as the 'Seven Liberal Arts'. Indeed the 12th-century depiction of Wisdom as an enthroned female was often surrounded by depictions of the Seven Liberal Arts in female form.

1.3 WISDOM SURROUNDED BY THE SEVEN LIBERAL ARTS

'Wisdom hath builded her house, she hath hewn out her seven pillars ... She hath sent forth her maidens: she crieth upon the highest places of the city'

Proverbs 9:1 & 3

THE THREE EXAMPLES of Wisdom surrounded by the Seven Liberal Arts shown here all date from the second half of the 12th century. The image to the right is an illumination from the encyclopedia *Hortus Deliciarum* 'Garden of Delights'. The image below shows the Tympanum of the southwest portal of Chartres Cathedral and the image on the next page shows a very early rose window from the north side of Laon Cathedral.

In the image from the *Hortus Deliciarum* Philosophia is on her throne surrounded by seven females who are enacting the seven arts. The philosophers Plato and Socrates are sitting immediately below her. She has seven streams springing forth from her. These streams symbolise the Seven Liberal Arts and, much like the rings on the pillars of the throne of Our Lady of Walsingham, three of the streams (i.e. the Trivial Arts, or Trivium) are on one side of her whereas the four streams of the Quadrivium are on the other side. They also flow forth from the same region of her body, as where the

seven rings on the pillars of the Walsingham throne are located (i.e. the torso area). So visually there is a natural correspondence between the two images.

The image of the southwest door of Chartres Cathedral shows the same doorway tympanum from the earlier image of the Virgin Mary with Christ on her lap. But this image also includes the figures that surround her, nearly all of whom are representative of the Seven Liberal Arts. Some of the statues are females enacting the arts themselves, whereas the other statues are renowned historical

figures associated with particular arts. Pythagoras for Music, Euclid for Geometry, Ptolemy for Astronomy, Boethius for Mathematics, Priscian for Grammar, Cicero for Rhetoric and Aristotle for Dialectic.

The north rose window from Laon is centred upon Lady Philosophy as the ladder (shown close-up in 1.1). She is surrounded by the Seven Liberal Arts and Medicine. The Liberal Arts were depicted in female form, which suggests they are all aspects of Sophia – or Wisdom's 'maidens' as mentioned in the quote from the Book of Proverbs at the beginning of this section. Wisdom is female in the Hebrew tradition as well as the Greek tradition, and so there is a natural correspondence between these two great streams of spiritual tradition that together lie at the root of Christianity. The female depiction of the seven arts also recalls the seven bridesmaids in Martianus Capella's written work *On the Marriage of Philology and Mercury*. This influential Latin work from the 5th century describes the marriage in Heaven of Philology (a learning through words) and Mercury (intelligence) in a wedding within which the Seven Liberal Arts act as Philology's bridesmaids. After the first and second chapters – 'The Betrothal' and 'The Marriage' – the remaining seven chapters are then each devoted to describing one of the Seven Arts.

'Rhetoric' - north rose window at Laon

The Seven Liberal Arts were divided up into two different stages of learning. The Trivium was studied first, followed by the Quadrivium. Thierry of Chartres was the pivotal 12th-century figure in the study of the Seven Arts, and he produced an encyclopedia about them. Whereas he looked upon the Quadrivium as something for the intellect, he saw the Trivium as forming the student's capacity to express the knowledge of the intellect. However, the Trivium came first and was then followed by the Quadrivium because in this way the Trivium prepared the soul for the receipt of the intellectual illumination that was inherent to both the Trivium and the Quadrivium. It is standard for a spiritual path to consist of an initial stage of preparation prior to a stage of illumination. So in this way the Trivium consisted of studies concerned with developing and refining a student's capacity for engaging with learning, as well as then having the capacity for its expression. The three subjects of the Trivium were Grammar, Dialectic (logic) and Rhetoric. These studies of language, thinking and speaking were an essential training for the microcosmic soul to prepare it for an engagement with the quadrivial study of numerics that consisted of studies concerning both the macrocosm and microcosm together.

The Quadrivial Arts were Arithmetic, Music, Geometry and Cosmology. The first two dealt with 'multitude'. If Arithmetic deals with number itself, then Music deals with 'numbers in relationship' – i.e. musical ratios such as 2:1, 3:2 and 4:3. Rather than studying musical performance or composition, the study of Music concerned its mathematical formulation and expression through ratios, a study historically associated with Pythagoras.

The other two quadrivial subjects concerned 'magnitude'. These two studies were Geometry – which deals with 'magnitude' itself, and Cosmology – which concerns 'magnitudes in motion', i.e. the periodic cyclical movements of the stars and planets.

The study of the Quadrivium was associated with Boethius (c 477-524), who actually coined the term when he wrote about it in works such as *De Institutione Arithmetica*. The essential nature of Quadrivial studies was described by Boethius in the opening lines of this particular work.

'Among all men of ancient authority who, following the lead of Pythagoras, have flourished in the purer reasoning of the mind, it is clearly obvious that hardly anyone has been able to reach the highest perfection of the disciplines of philosophy unless the nobility of such wisdom was investigated by him in a certain four part study, the Quadrivium, which will hardly be hidden from those properly respectful of expertness. For this is the wisdom of things which are, and the perception of truth gives to these things their unchanging character.'

A few paragraphs later his words become even more earnest.

If a searcher is lacking knowledge of these four sciences, he is not able to find the true; without this kind of thought nothing of truth is rightly known. This is the knowledge of those things which truly are; it is their full understanding and comprehension. He who spurns these, the paths of wisdom, does not rightly philosophise. Indeed if philosophy is the love of wisdom, in spurning these, one has already shown contempt for philosophy.'

Such works expressed the significance of the Quadrivium in no uncertain terms. But perhaps most importantly they described the significance of Quadrivial studies in relation to philosophy. In a world of perpetual change and movement the unchanging forms of number become an essential focus for the soul when contemplating the unchanging and eternal nature of Spirit.

One of the non-Christian wisdom texts that the learned 12th-century churchmen and women took an interest in was the Latin *Asclepius* dialogue between the mythical sage, Hermes Trismegistus, and Asclepius. Hermes is even more hardline than Boethius in his critique of those who use the Quadrivial Arts for anything other than supports for the contemplation of God:

'HERM: Philosophy is nothing else than striving through constant contemplation and saintly piety to attain to knowledge of God; but there will be many who will make philosophy hard to understand and corrupt it with manifold speculations.

ASCL: How so?

HERM: In this way Asclepius; by a cunning sort of study in which philosophy will be mixed with unintelligible sciences such as arithmetic, music and geometry. Whereas the student of philosophy undefiled, which is dependent upon devotion to God, and on that alone, ought to direct his attention to the other sciences only so far as he may thereby learn to see and marvel how the returns of the heavenly bodies to their former places and halts in pre-ordained positions, and the variations of their movements, are true to the reckonings of number; only so far as, learning the measurements of the earth, the depth of the sea, the force of fire, the properties, magnitudes, workings and natures of all material things, he may be led to revere, adore and praise God's skill and wisdom. And to know the science of music is nothing else than this – to know how all things are ordered, and how God's design has assigned to each its place; for the ordered system in which each and all by the supreme Artist's skill are wrought together into a single whole yields a divinely musical harmony sweet and true beyond all melodious sounds. I tell

'Geometry' - north rose window at Laon

you then that the men of after times will be misled by cunning sophists, and will be turned away from the pure and holy teachings of true philosophy. For to worship God in thought and spirit with singleness of heart, to revere God in all his works, and to give thanks to God, whose will, and his alone, is wholly filled with goodness, – this is philosophy unsullied by intrusive cravings for unprofitable knowledge.'

Hermetica, edited and translated by W. Scott

The Christian mystical philosopher and mathematician Nicholas of Cusa was to express a similar sentiment in the 1400s in his written work *On Learned Ignorance*. For him the study of number was essentially a contemplation of Spirit.:

'Did not Pythagoras, the first philosopher both in name and in fact, consider all investigation of truth to be by means of numbers? The Platonists and also our leading thinkers followed him to such an extent that our Augustine and after him Boethius, affirmed that, assuredly, in the mind of the Creator number was the principle exemplar of the things to be created ... Proceeding on this pathway of the ancients, I concur with them and say that since the pathway for approaching divine matters is opened to us only through symbols, we can make quite suitable use of mathematical signs because of their incorruptible certainty.'

'Astronomy' - north rose window at Laon

One name mentioned in Nicholas of Cusa's quote who has himself not yet been quoted here is St Augustine (354-430). So the final word shall be left to him who, along with Boethius, St Dionysius and various others, was one of the most important transmitters of Platonism into the early church. In his theological text *De Doctrina Christiana* (On Christian Doctrine) he expounds on the value of Quadrivial studies while at the same time warning against an approach to learning that treats the knowledge of the four arts merely as a materialistic acquisition – in other words, knowledge for its own sake – rather than as a tool or a way of contemplating the Creator through a study of the numerical basis of Creation. Unfortunately this seems to be advice that much of the modern educational world pays little attention to.

'Coming now to the science of number, it is clear to the dullest apprehension that this was not created by man, but was discovered by investigation. For, though Virgil could at his own pleasure make the first syllable of Italia long, while the ancients pronounced it short, it is not in any man's power to determine at his pleasure that three times three are not nine, or do not make a square, or are not the triple of three, nor one and a half times the number six, or that it is not true that they are not the double of any number because odd numbers have no half. Whether, then, numbers are considered in themselves [i.e. Arithmetic], or as applied to the laws of figures [Geometry], or of sounds [Music], or of other motions [Cosmology], they have fixed laws which were not made by man, but which the acuteness of ingenious men brought to light.

'The man, however, who puts so high a value on these things as to be inclined to boast himself one of the learned, and who does not rather inquire after the source from which those things which he perceives to be true derive their truth ... [and also] ... does not strive to make all things redound to the praise and love of the one God from whom he knows that all things have their being – the man, I say, who acts in this way may seem to be learned, but wise he cannot in any sense be deemed.'

De Doctrina Christiana, Book 2, Chapter 38

I.4 THE SEVEN LIBERAL ARTS AS A PREPARATION FOR PHILOSOPHY AND THEOLOGY

IN THE 12TH CENTURY cathedral schools the Seven Liberal Arts were understood to act as a necessary prelude to the study of Philosophy and Theology. In the words of the 12th-century monk and theologian Hugh of St Victor,

'... the ancients, in their studies, especially selected seven [arts] to be mastered by those who were to be educated. These seven they considered so to excel all the rest in usefulness that anyone who had been thoroughly schooled in them might afterward come to a knowledge of the others by his own inquiry and effort rather than by listening to a teacher. For these, one might say, constitute the best instruments, the best rudiments, by which the way is prepared for the mind's complete knowledge of philosophic truth. Therefore they are called by the name Trivium and Quadrivium, because by them, as by certain ways, a quick mind enters into the secret places of wisdom.'

So a loving friendship with Sophia required a preparatory seven steps, and this reflects the imagery of Sophia surrounded by the Seven Arts. But these seven steps were also associated with the ascent of Lady Philosophy's ladder. The image on the right is from a 13th-century manuscript of *The Consolation of Philosophy*. Lady Philosophy's ladder has seven steps, and on each rung is written the name of one of the Seven Liberal Arts. So the seven-step journey to Philosophy was one that required an ascent of the soul to a higher clime.

An interesting addition to all of this is the fact that the seven arts were also symbolically associated with the seven planetary spheres of ancient cosmology, and were thus effectively seven rungs on a cosmic ladder leading upwards to Divine Wisdom in the eighth heaven.

The seven planets of ancient cosmology are the seven moving objects that the naked eye can see in the sky, which move against the fixed stars. The word 'planet'

Lady Philosophy's ladder of the Seven Liberal Arts

derives from the Greek word meaning 'wanderer', in the sense of those celestial objects that 'wander' along their own courses rather than in accord with the fixed stars. They are the Sun and Moon and all the planets between Mercury and Saturn (minus Earth). These seven 'planets' were seen as existing on concentric spherical shells that surrounded Earth, which was at the centre of all of the spheres.

The order of the planets is as follows. Moving upwards (or outwards) from Earth the first planet, or 'planetary sphere', is the Moon, followed by Mercury and then Venus. Then comes the Sun followed by Mars, Jupiter and finally Saturn. Beyond Saturn lies the eighth sphere of the fixed stars. In Plato's *Timaeus* dialogue he refers

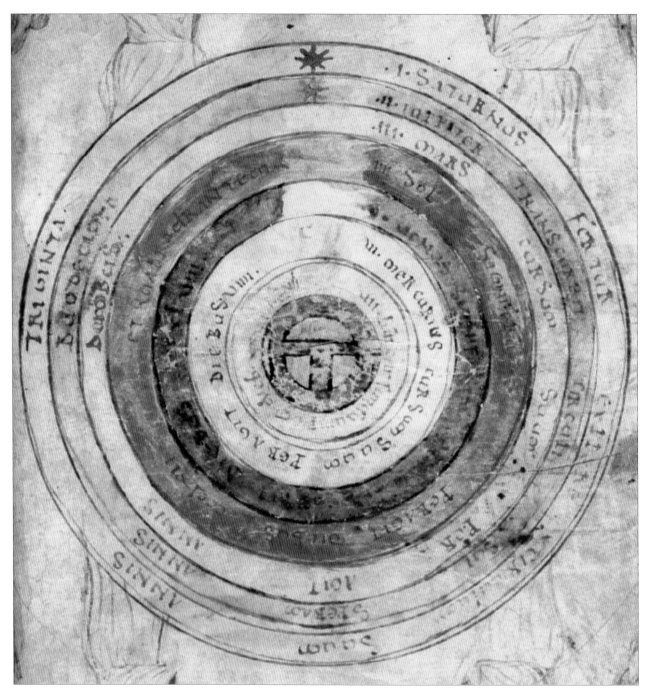

Mappa Mundi 2 from Bede, De natura rerum. Depicting the seven planetary spheres around the Earth which is itself symbolised by the green 'T' inside the 'O'. The 'O' is the Earth and the 'T' is its tripartite division into Asia (above), Europe (bottom left) and Africa (bottom right). Jerusalem is where the three of them meet.

to the seven spheres as 'the Different' and the eighth sphere as 'the Same' and the 'X' shape that their circles together create – the equator and the ecliptic – he associated with the World Soul.

Returning to the Seven Liberal Arts and the seven planets, a 12th-century Englishman called Alexander Neckam is one of the people who made a symbolic connection between them in writing. Alexander Neckam was born in 1157 on the same day as another baby called Richard, who would grow up to become King Richard I of England – the renowned Crusader King, Richard the Lionheart. As a result of this shared birthday Neckam's mother was enlisted to act as a wet nurse for the future king, and so consequently – as *frères de lait* – Neckam and Richard were in close proximity to one another as children, feeding from the same mother. But whereas Richard grew up to become the King of England, Neckam grew up to be an educated teacher and churchman who wrote various works on the sciences.

In his written work *De naturis rerum* Neckam made a connection between the Seven Liberal Arts and the seven planets, in which he associated the qualities of each art with a planet in such a way that mostly reflected their usual orders of hierarchy. Grammar, the first subject of the Trivium, he associated with the Moon – the first planetary sphere. But instead of then moving on to the usual second planetary sphere of Mercury, he went straight on to the Sun – usually the fourth sphere – which he associated with the second Trivial art, Dialectic. Then he moved back to the usual running order of the arts and the planets, whereby he associated Mercury with Rhetoric, Venus with Arithmetic, Mars with Music, Jupiter with Geometry and finally Saturn with Cosmology. This placing of the Sun in second position within the planetary order instead of fourth reflects Plato's description of the order of the spheres in his Myth of Er, in the Republic

In another chapter from the same work, Neckam also made a connection between the Seven Liberal Arts and the seven gifts of the Holy Spirit, and indeed there is also a long tradition of associating the seven planets with the seven gifts of the Holy Spirit which was taught by St Irenaeus as far back as the 2nd century.[6]

The Italian poet Dante Alighieri was born just over a hundred years after Neckam in the 1260's, and he too wrote about the Seven Liberal Arts in relation to the seven planets. He made an association between them in his *Convivio* – a work he wrote just a few years prior to his famous poem about cosmological ascent, *The Divine Comedy*.

In chapter 13 of the *Convivio* he wrote the following:

'*... the seven heavens nearest to us are those of the planets; next come two heavens above them, which are in motion, and one above them all, which is still. To the first seven correspond the seven sciences of the Trivium and the Quadrivium, namely Grammar, Dialectics, Rhetoric, Arithmetic, Music, Geometry, and Astrology.*'

So if these seven 'educational steps' could be looked on as seven rungs on a cosmological ladder of ascent, what then lay beyond the seventh rung in the three remaining heavens?

'*To the eighth sphere, namely the Starry Heaven, corresponds natural science, which is called Physics, and the first science, which is called Metaphysics; to the ninth sphere corresponds Moral Science; and to the still heaven corresponds Divine Science, which is called Theology.*'

Henceforth the 'ascent' through the Seven Liberal Arts subsequently lead to Physics and Philosophy in the eighth and ninth heavens, which then culminated in the tenth heaven of Theology. These ten levels later featured in Dante's cosmological ascent described in *Paradiso* – the third and final section of his poem *The Divine Comedy,* or *Commedia*.

With all of this in mind we will now turn our attention to the early Gnostic traditions of Christianity, in which there were believed to be seven levels that led up to an eighth level – the Ogdoad – which was the abode of the Sophia herself.

6. See *The Lost Knowledge of Christ*, Dominic White, Liturgical Press, 2015, page 43. Also see St Irenaeus' *The Demonstration of Apostolic Preaching*. Section 9.

1.5 THE GNOSTIC ASCENT SYMBOLISM OF SOPHIA - SEVEN STEPS TO THE OGDOAD

THE GNOSTIC CHRISTIANS flourished in the Mediterranean region during the first couple of centuries after Christ. They emerged out of Jewish and Judeo-Christian groups in the aftermath of the fall of Jerusalem in the 1st century, and there were many different groups among them with many differing beliefs, although there were some core beliefs shared by many of them.

The word gnostic means 'to know' or 'to have knowledge', and the type of knowledge in question is inner spiritual wisdom such as that written about in the Jewish/Christian books of Wisdom and Proverbs, as well as Ecclesiastes, Job, Sirach and some of the Psalms.

The emphasis of the Gnostics was to develop their innate but buried capacity for inner Wisdom so as to be able to free themselves from the 'prison' of the material world – a world which various of the Gnostics looked on as being corrupt and evil.

This negative view of the world necessitated another key feature of various of the Gnostic groups – the idea of escape from the corrupt material world via an ascent through seven levels up to an eighth level called the Ogdoad, or the abode of Sophia – the Great Mother of all. These seven levels reflected the seven planetary spheres of ancient cosmology, leading up to the eighth sphere of the fixed stars. The re-ascent was made possible by Christ, who had been sent down to Earth by the Godhead in the form of the man Jesus. He brought the gnosis required by souls for their re-ascent out of the material and physical world back up to the spiritual domain.

The Gnostic Sofia was looked upon as the maternal origin of the seven levels that lay below the Ogdoad. She was described by St Irenaeus in his written work *Against heresies.*

'This mother they also call Ogdoad, Sophia, Terra, Jerusalem, Holy Spirit, and, with a masculine reference, Lord.'

Against heresies, book 1, Chapter 5 – 3

In some of the Gnostic beliefs Sophia was described as having fallen from the Pleroma (literally 'fullness') – an ideal spiritual realm of divine life. But she was still understood to be an emanation of the Godhead – albeit the lowest one. As a result of her fall she gave birth to an evil son known as the Demiurge, who subsequently created the corrupt material world including the seven levels below the Ogdoad. So in this way Sophia was located between the higher spiritual domain from which she had fallen and the lower material realm of which she was the maternal origin. As St Irenaeus described it,

'her place of habitation is an intermediate one, above the Demiurge indeed, but below and outside of the Pleroma.'

Against heresies, book 1, Chapter 5 – 3

In this sense the Gnostic Sophia bears a certain degree of resemblance to the Virgin Mary through being a *mediatrix* between the earthly and heavenly worlds in the way that the Virgin is the 'intercessor' between humanity and Christ. But whereas the Gnostic Sophia is looked upon as having fallen into her mediatory position, the Virgin Mary is understood as having been raised into hers.

Interestingly, the Virgin Mary is also symbolically associated with the ladder via an Orthodox tradition that takes place on the feast of her nativity. The three readings at Vespers on this particular feast are all from the Old Testament, though they are allegorically understood via New Testament-style Marian interpretations. The first of the three is the story of Jacob's ladder. The Virgin is associated with Jacob's ladder in the sense of her being the one who links Heaven and Earth. It is through her that Christ climbed down into Incarnation, and equally it is through her that there is the possibility of the climb back up from whence Christ came. In the words of St Athanasius:

'For the Son of God became man so that we might become God'

The other two readings at this particular Marian Vespers have both been quoted above. They are Ezekiel's description of the eastern door of the temple – (quote in 1.1 by St Aelred), and the description from the Book of Proverbs about the house built by Wisdom with seven pillars (beginning of 1.3).

Another Marian storyline that resembles Gnostic themes is that of Mary's first seven steps as a child. The story is from the Protoevangelium of James, which despite not being part of the Bible has been widely accepted during various eras of Christian history – including the 12th century. The story describes Mary's first seven steps that lead to the breast of her mother Anne. Such numerics inevitably reflect the seven planetary steps up to 'mother' Sofia in the eighth clime.

'Day by day, the child grew stronger. When she was six months old, her mother set her on the ground to test whether she could stand. And after walking seven steps, she came to her mother's breast. And her mother picked her up, saying, "As the Lord my God lives, you will not walk on this earth again until I take you to the temple of the Lord.'

Chapter 6:1–3

Yet another interesting Marian concordance can be seen in the form of another of her titles – *Stella Maris* (Star of the Sea), a title much used in the medieval church. This cosmological epithet – also an ancient title of Isis – is a description of the celestial north pole, which is effectively the central pivot of the circular movement of the stars in the eighth heaven and thus again associates the Virgin with the abode of the Gnostic Sophia. We will look more closely at this particular Marian title later on.

Bearing in mind the association of the Virgin Mary with the Holy Spirit, it is also of interest that one of the Gnostic Sophia's titles and roles was that of Holy Spirit. Alongside this, one of Sophia's main symbols is the dove – the Christian symbol of the Holy Spirit. Another numerical correlation is the Christian perception of the Holy Spirit as being the source of seven qualities (i.e. the Seven Gifts), and how this numerically resembles the Gnostic Sophia being the maternal origin of the seven planetary spheres. Such a connection is again reflected in the Christian analogy between the Seven Gifts and the seven planets. However, the Seven Gifts of the Holy Spirit are understood to be blessings that descend from above rather than a corrupt and cursed invention of the Gnostic Sophia's son, the Demiurge, that sink downwards from the Ogdoad into increasing material darkness.

The first seven steps of the Virgin Mary - Mosaic in Chora Church, Istanbul

Returning to both the Gnostic storyline and *The Consolation of Philosophy* it appears that there is a thematic resemblance between the two of them. The story of Boethius in his prison cell and the coming of Lady Philosophy in the form of a ladder resembles the Gnostic storyline of ascent out of the corrupt earthly world that imprisons the soul. Boethius is imprisoned in his earthly predicament and suffering torment as a result. But he is then offered a ladder of 'escape', which consists of an ascent to the higher world of *theoria* and is made possible through a loving friendship with Wisdom, i.e. 'Philia-Sophia'.

However, Boethius appears not to possess the same hatred for the world that led to some of the Gnostic groups being criticised by the Early Church Fathers as well as Platonist philosophers such as Plotinus, who felt that some of the Gnostics had subverted Plato's philosophy. Plotinus actually put his critique into philosophical writing in the ninth tractate of his second Ennead which was entitled 'Against Those that Affirm the Creator of the Cosmos and the Cosmos Itself to be Evil'. Plato had also described a character called the Demiurge in his *Timaeus* dialogue and, much like the Gnostic Demiurge, Plato's character is described as creating the world. However he is not an evil character such as the Demiurge came to be perceived in various of the Gnostic storylines. In this way Boethius was clearly a Platonist rather than a world-negating Gnostic.

There appears to be a similar echo of Gnosticism in the 12th-century depiction of the Sofianic throned female surrounded by the Seven Liberal Arts. The idea that the seven arts are streams that issue forth from Sophia again resembles the Gnostic perception that Sophia is the maternal origin of the seven spheres. The 12th-century educational practice of studying the Seven Liberal Arts as a prelude to Philosophy and Theology also carries a similar Gnostic overtone in that the student's capacity to enter into the wisdom required for Philosophy and Theology is followed by an 'ascent' through seven subjects of study – first the Trivium and then the Quadrivium – themselves associated with the seven planetary spheres.

With all of this we can see something in the 12th-century Christian wisdom tradition that distinctly resembles some of the early Gnostic symbolism, albeit without the heretical perceptions of the 'evil' earthly world which in themselves spoke of a diabolical [7] fissure within the Gnostic soul. The mainstream of 12th-century Christianity didn't espouse a world-negating view.

During the first half of the 12th century, possibly the most significant individual in the Roman Catholic church was St Bernard of Clairvaux, and he was much renowned for his love of the Virgin Mary as well as his love for the natural world in all its spiritual profundity. One well-known expression of this comes from a letter that Bernard wrote to a fellow Cistercian in 1125.

'Trust my experience: One learns more among the trees of the forest than from books. The trees and rocks will teach you a wisdom you cannot hear from teachers.'

From a letter to Henry Murdach [8]

To find another 12th-century Christian concentration on the spiritual beauty of the natural world one need look no further than a Gothic cathedral with its grove-like appearance. Pillars like tree trunks that ascend towards the heavenly crossed ribbed vault of tree canopies; Christ crucified on a green vine tree bursting forth with its Eucharistic grapes; carved leaf forms everywhere with verdant green men looking downwards, reminding the Christian of the exuberance and resurrection of life that greens the world around every Easter-tide on the first Sunday following the first full moon after the spring equinox. Such a sentiment was expressed by St Augustine in one of his sermons on the subject of springtime and Easter.

---

7. Literally 'to throw apart'.
8. See page 118 of *Scripture And Pluralism: Reading the Bible in the Religiously Plural Worlds of the Middle Ages and Renaissance*, Brill, 2005.

'The whole of nature, which till this moment had the semblance of death [i.e. winter], celebrates the Resurrection together with her Lord. The enchanting loveliness of the trees, as they put forth their leaves and are set about, as with gems, by their blossoms ... Sol [i.e. the Sun], the kindling of all the stars, lifts up his face and lets it shine [i.e. the increasing daylight hours of springtime], and, like a king in his glory, sets on his head the diadem of the stars ... Luna [i.e. the Moon], who sets herself farther away from her rising each day, decks herself for Easter with her full raiment of shining light [i.e. the paschal full Moon].'

St Augustine

The idea of 'greenness' was emphasised by another learned 12th-century Christian, who is also much renowned for her focus on Sophia. Hildegard of Bingen was another lover of the earthly world – a world that she viewed as being essentially theophanic. She would often use the term *viriditas* ('greenness') as a symbol of the divine presence in the surrounding world. She also spoke of the relationship between Creator and Creation in terms of a marriage, rather than with the Gnostic language of divorce.

*'Creation is allowed in intimate love
to speak to the Creator as if to a lover'*

Hildegard is also renowned for her focus on Sophia. In her musical work *Symphonia Armonie Celestium Revelationum (Symphony of the Harmony of Celestial Revelations)* there is the following antiphon for Divine Wisdom, which again describes a Sofianic middle realm by which Sophia is able to join the above with the below.

*'Sophia!
You of the whirling wings,
Circling encompassing
Energy of God
You quicken the world in your clasp
One wing soars in heaven
One wing sweeps the earth
And the third flies all around us.
Praise to Sophia!
Let all the earth praise her!'*

Sophia - Hildegard of Bingen

23

1.6 ASCENT SYMBOLISM IN THE 12TH CENTURY AND ITS PERCEIVED ORIGINS IN BIBLICAL, GREEK AND GNOSTIC SOURCES

IN THE 12TH-CENTURY CHURCH, the Bible was understood to have four levels of meaning. The lowest of the four was the literal/historical level that dealt with the actual biblical storyline – and which therefore concerned the past. Then came the typological or allegorical level, which dealt with seeing the Old Testament allegorically reflected in the New Testament, and so accordingly this looked at the past in relation to the present. Then came the moral level, which concerned the living of one's life in the present time. Finally, the highest level was the anagogical, which concerned what lay, symbolically speaking, in the future – or rather 'at the end of time'. The anagogical level concerns what might be described as the mystical understanding of the scripture which brings us back to the ladder of ascent, because the Greek word *anagogical* means 'to climb' or 'to ascend'.

The 12th century was a time of return to the allegorical storylines of late antiquity, including various examples that dealt with the idea of the soul's mystical ascent. The purpose of such an ascent was to re-orientate the soul's vision away from transient earthly things towards its heavenly origin situated in an unchanging realm that was, symbolically speaking, 'above'. This focus on ascent saw the return of some of the older storylines that included this theme, such as *The Consolation of Philosophy* with its description of Lady Philosophy's ladder, and *The Marriage of Philology and Mercury* involving the ascent up to the marriage in Heaven. Another older text concerning cosmic ascent that became very popular was *The Dream of Scipio* by Cicero, which the 12th-century scholars studied indirectly through Macrobius' commentary on it. All of these storylines were influenced by Plato, whose description of the Myth of Er concerned a journey to the Spindle of Necessity, which was effectively a spindle of light about which turned the seven planets along with the eighth sphere of the stars. Another ascent theme is found in Plato's *Symposium* dialogue, which is on the subject of love. This involves the ladder of love that leads upwards and away from carnal worldly love (*Aphrodite Pandemos*) and on to heavenly or divine love (*Aphrodite Urania*).

Two significant cosmic ascent narratives were actually written by Christians in the high Middle Ages itself. The lesser-known one is a poem called *Cosmographia* by Bernard Silvestris, which was written in the first half of the 12th century. It was very much a part of the culture of the school of Chartres, and was even dedicated to

The Ladder of Divine Ascent - St Catherine's Monastery in Sinai, Egypt

Thierry of Chartres himself. It is renowned as having been read to Pope Eugene III, who as the first Cistercian pope was closely connected to St Bernard of Clairvaux. The storyline concerns the creation of the Megacosm (the cosmos) and then the Microcosm (the human) and involves a descent of the human soul through the planetary spheres under the guidance of *Urania* (the heavens) and *Natura* (nature). Again, the whole storyline has a very Chartrian Platonist flavour.

The other medieval Christian ascent narrative is *The Divine Comedy* by Dante. This epic poem first involves a descent into the centre of the Earth, followed by an ascent up the mountain of Purgatory. Then a cosmic ascent through the seven planetary spheres followed by the eighth sphere of the stars, and the transparent ninth sphere – the *Primum Mobile* – and finally the *Empyrean*, where Dante is taken direct to God by St Bernard of Clairvaux as a result of his praying to the Virgin Mary for her intercession.

Such ascent symbolism very much pervaded medieval Christianity through its interest in Platonism. But there were already similar storylines contained within the Bible itself.

An old Testament example is Ezekiel's vision in which God places him on the top of a high mountain from where he is able to see God's Temple and a new Jerusalem.

A New Testament example is the storyline in 2 Corinthians 12, in which St Paul describes an ascent to the third and highest heaven. He speaks in the third person, although it is generally assumed that he is talking about himself.

'I know a man in Christ who fourteen years ago was caught up to the third heaven – whether in the body or out of the body I do not know, God knows. And I know that this man was caught up into paradise – whether in the body or out of the body I do not know, God knows – and he heard things that cannot be told, which man may not utter.'

Another biblical story of ascent is that of Jacob's ladder in the Book of Genesis. This particular story describes

a dream that Jacob experiences when on the road between Beersheba and Harran in which he witnesses a ladder stretching between Heaven and Earth.

'And he dreamed, and behold a ladder set up on the earth, and the top of it reached to heaven: and behold the angels of God ascending and descending on it.'

Genesis 28:12

Jacob's Ladder

Another storyline of ascent that the 12th-century Christians would have come into contact with is an Islamic one. It is centred on the Temple Mount in Jerusalem, and is architecturally represented by the Dome of the Rock – an Islamic shrine that commemorates the ascent itself. This Islamic tradition (the *Miraj* or *Night Journey*) involves the Prophet Mohammed first travelling to Jerusalem and then ascending from the Temple Mount up through the seven planetary spheres, within which he meets various Islamic prophets. Interestingly, the story of Jacob's ladder became associated with the Dome of the Rock when the building was temporarily converted into a church during the 12th-century Kingdom of Jerusalem.

So, within the High Middle Ages there was a particular focus within theology, scriptural studies, philosophy

Jacob's Ladder ascending into a cloud - west front of Bath Abbey

'And when we have received with an unearthly and unflinching mental vision, the gift of light ... let us then ... be restored again to its unique splendour. For this never loses its own inherent unity [but] remains firmly and solitarily centred within itself in its unmoved sameness; and elevates, according to their capacity, those who aspire to itself, and makes them one after the example of its own unifying Oneness.'

Celestial Hierarchies, Chapter 1

and the arts on the symbolic storylines of the soul's ascent from Earth up to Heaven. But despite all of these 'physical' descriptions of ascent, it is essential to recognise that such journeys were primarily understood as inward ascents of the soul back to its divine origin. A purely literal understanding of the ascent storyline would be to only engage in the lowest of the four levels used in the medieval interpretation of scripture, i.e. the literal aspect of a storyline, whereas the anagogical understanding of 'climbing' involves a return of the soul up the ladder on which it originally descended into the created world. Such a (re)ascent is described by St Dionysius at the beginning of his *Celestial Hierarchies*.

Considering the 12th-century Christian emphasis upon cosmic ascent, it is perhaps of little surprise that such a symbolic storyline also appears to have been central to the symbolic meaning of the Gothic cathedral designs of the era. Such an ascent could in one sense be described as beginning from the west door, the dark place of the setting Sun – and leading up to the church's east end – the place of the rising Sun and the Bright Morning Star, both of which are cosmological images of the risen Christ. But the very verticality and soaring nature of the Gothic style is in itself an architectural expression of the soul's irresistible desire to remember its true identity through climbing up to a reunification with its divine origin. The ascent symbolism found within the designs of Gothic cathedrals is a central theme of this book. But before moving directly on to considering the cathedral design studies themselves, we will look at another important guiding theme within Gothic cathedral design – namely the descent of the Heavenly Jerusalem in the Book of Revelation. This vision involves the ascent of St John the Divine to a very high place from where he then witnesses the descent of the Heavenly Jerusalem – and it is this Heavenly City that could be described as one of the prototypes of the Gothic cathedral.

CHAPTER 2.

Revelation and the Descent of the Heavenly City

2.1 THE END OF THE BIBLE
AND THE END OF TIME

IN THE FINAL BOOK of the Christian New Testament, St John the Divine describes a dramatic vision that he saw while on the Greek island of Patmos. It is an 'eschatological' vision, which means that it concerns the end of time. The storyline itself – known as the Apocalypse – has a dream-like quality, although for much of it the word 'nightmare' might be a more suitable description as there is much death and destruction prior to what eventually becomes the final resolution at the end of the vision. As a result of this, the word *apocalypse* has come to be associated with death and destruction and the end of the world, when in actual fact it is simply the Greek word for 'revelation' in the sense of 'the raising of a veil'. The storyline involves the revealing of things that will happen at the 'end of time'.

There have been many attempts to interpret the storyline of Revelation, but the book's descriptions are perhaps so otherworldly that any kind of final and conclusive interpretation is just too elusive, and the reader is forever left with a certain sense of mystery in relation to its meaning. However, one of the most notable things about the vivid images contained in the writing is the frequent use of numerical description. Interestingly, there is also a direct association made between Wisdom and the capacity to discern and understand such numerical symbolism.

Bearing in mind the 22/7 pi measurement of a circle, the book's 'twenty-two' chapters describe the unfolding of various sets of 'seven' stages. There are seven descriptions of seven churches; the opening of seven seals on a scroll; seven angels blowing seven successive trumpet soundings that bring forth seven destructive forces and seven angels that bring forth seven plagues. Indeed, the number seven is mentioned on as many as sixty occasions within the book in relation to these various sets of seven. Mention is also made of seven golden lamp stands, seven stars, seven flaming torches, seven horns, seven eyes, seven spirits of God, seven angels, seven thunders and seven thousand people killed in an earthquake. Again, with pi in mind, there is a particularly significant point within the twenty-two chapters which takes place once the seventh chapter has been completed. It involves the opening of the seventh seal, after which there is first half an hour of silence, then all hell appears to be let loose.

The number four is also particularly prominent in the text. It is mentioned on around thirty occasions in relation to four living creatures, four angels, four winds, four horns and the four corners of the Earth. Along with the numbers seven and four there are also many other numbers that are included in the text and often repeated on more than one occasion.

As mentioned earlier, there are two examples within the text in which an understanding of such numerical symbolism is directly associated with Wisdom. The word 'wisdom' itself actually appears on four occasions within the text, and on the first two occasions it is used as a description of a divine quality possessed by God and the Lamb of God. On the other two occasions it is specifically described and called upon as a quality that is required to be able to discern a description involving number symbolism. In chapter 13 for instance there is the infamous description of the number 666:

'This calls for wisdom: let the one who has understanding calculate the number of the beast, for it is the number of a man, and his number is 666.'

Then a little later there is a description of the Whore of Babylon and the seven-headed red dragon upon which she is seated:

'This calls for a mind with wisdom: the seven heads are seven mountains on which the woman is seated.'

There is another apparent sevenness, albeit one that is not explicitly mentioned, and that is the seven-step cosmic ladder of the planetary spheres. It appears to form part of a description of a female who has come to be associated with the Virgin Mary:

'And there appeared a great wonder in heaven; a woman clothed with the sun, and the moon under her feet, and upon her head a crown of twelve stars: And she being with child cried, travailing in birth, and pained to be delivered.'

Revelation 12:1–2

In terms of cosmological symbolism the woman can be understood to be the Virgin Mary, as the planetary ladder down whom Christ climbs into his incarnate form. The first and lowest planetary sphere is the Moon, and this is what the woman has below her feet. Above and beyond the seventh planet is the eighth sphere of the fixed stars with its twelve zodiacal constellations, and this resembles the crown of twelve stars. Indeed the central point among these constellations is the celestial north pole, or *Stella Maris* - a Marian title, and this point could be said to be located on or just above the physical crown of the woman's head. In the middle of

the planetary ladder is then the predominant planet, which is also the only one of the seven planets that is visible in the daytime. Its very presence in the heavens brings about the light of the daytime itself, and it is this light of the Sun in which the woman is clothed. It could also be said to be the light of the Sun of Righteousness to whom she is giving birth. This is all reminiscent of the Marian ladder symbolism mentioned in the previous chapter.

However, it is the description of the geometric shape of the Heavenly City that is of particular interest in terms of geometric number symbolism.

'And the city lieth foursquare, and the length is as large as the breadth: and he measured the city with the reed, twelve thousand furlongs. The length and the breadth and the height of it are equal.'

Rev 21:16

Henceforth the Heavenly Jerusalem is described as being cube-shaped ... and so it is to the cube that we shall now turn our attention.

'A woman clothed with the sun'

2.2 THE CUBE AT THE CENTRE OF THE WORLD – THE EARTHLY SQUARING OF THE HEAVENLY CIRCLE

FOR MANY CENTURIES the holy city of Jerusalem has been understood to be the centre of the Jewish and Christian worlds. This originates from a Jewish tradition which was then inherited by Christianity via the story of Christ's Passion and Resurrection, which is also centred in Jerusalem. In terms of geometric symbolism this 'centrality' is presented in the form of a cube. Such cubic symbolism has been applied to both the Heavenly Jerusalem and also to the Jewish temple on the Temple Mount, and this will shortly be described in more detail.

The cube has various interesting qualities. For instance, it could be described as the transmuted form taken on by a sphere when it is turned 'inside out', as it were.[1] If a sphere is cut along three of its circular planes that coincide with the three axes of the three dimensions of space, the sphere becomes divided into eight equal parts. This process of dividing the sphere in half three times in a row reflects the mathematical process of $2 \times 2 \times 2 = 8$, or in other words '2^3' (2 'cubed'). If a sphere is cut in half it becomes two hemispherical pieces. If those two pieces are both cut in half they become a total of four tetartospherical pieces, and if these four parts are each then cut in half again there becomes a total of

eight ogdospherical pieces. If these eight equal parts are all then inverted in their axial orientation they together take on the form of a cube.

The eight corners of this cube together formed the undivided centre of the sphere at the beginning of the process, but they subsequently divided from one another and became the eight points that are furthest removed from the centre of the cube. The process thus began from that which is most internal, centrally unified and hidden, but terminated in that which is most external and revealed or 'outwardly realised'.

However, this transmutation from unity to eightness occurs via the sevenness of a three-dimensional cross. This cross is naturally present as a result of the intersections of the three circular planes by which the sphere was divided into eight. These are the three planes mentioned above that coincide with the three axes of the three dimensions of space. Clement of Alexandria describes the three-dimensional cross in his *Stromateis*:

'From God "Heart of the Universe" issue all the directions of space, each indefinite in extent, one upwards, one downwards, one to the right, one to the left, one forwards and one backwards; turning his gaze in these six directions, none of which extends further than the others, He accomplishes the world; He is the beginning and the end (the alpha and the omega); in Him the six phases of time are accomplished and from him they receive their indefinite extensions; herein resides the secret of the number seven.'

Symbolism of the Cross, René Guénon [2]

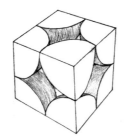

---

1. See René Guénon, *The Reign of Quantity and the Signs of the Times* (Sophia Perennis, 2004), chapter 20, 'From Sphere to Cube'.
2. (Luzac and Company, Ltd, 1975), chapter IV, page 15.

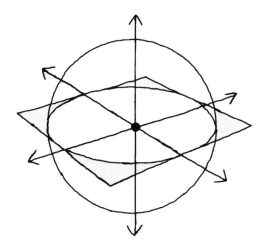

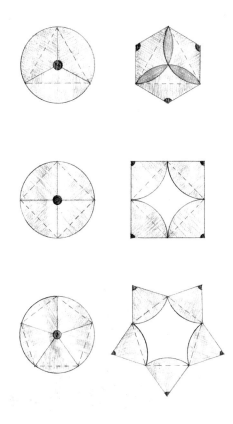

(Above) Diagram of a three-dimensional 'six-armed' cross

Three-dimensional cross on the dome of St George's church in Cairo, Egypt

Circles divided into 3, 4 and 5 and then inverted into
1) A hexagon 2) A square and 3) A five-pointed Star

Henceforth the final eightness of the cube is realised via a seven-fold journey in a similar way to the eighth note of a musical scale being a reflection and a repetition of the first note, albeit in a different form or at a different level.

This is but one example of a set of symbolic geometric processes that can be referred to as 'the squaring of the circle'. The circle or sphere is the geometric symbol of Heaven – and thus that which is most internal and 'hidden'. Whereas the cube or square is the symbol of Earth – that which is most external and revealed.

A similar result arises when a two-dimensional circle is cut into four equal quarters and then turned inside out to form a square. This is the only example of such a process of regular division of the circle followed by inversion, in which a regular polygon is produced that has the same numerical symmetry as the initial division of the circle. The three-fold division of the circle inverts into a hexagon rather than a triangle, and every division from five onwards inverts into a polygon star.

So, in this sense, there is a natural inverse relationship between the circle and square. Their geometric intermediary is the four-fold cross, owing to the role that it plays in the transmutation of one into the other. It is the cross that effectively creates the four 90° right-angles that are, at first, conjoined at the circle's centre, but which then turn outwards to form the square. The fact that the square is the only regular polygon with corners that together contain a total of 360° – the total number of degrees in a circle – is the mathematical indication of this inverse relationship between circle and square.

The process in which the circle becomes squared is a symbolic one by which the geometer enacts a movement from Heaven 'down' to Earth – or from the 'internal' outwards to the 'external'. An important point to remember here is that all such symbolic processes within a practice of sacred geometry are essentially external physical actions or outward supports by which the artist contemplatively seeks to encourage and effect an inward transformation of the soul. Without such an inner dimension to the work, the outward practice of geometry can become a meaningless or purely materialistic exercise.

The tools by which the geometer enacts the symbolic process of squaring the circle are themselves associated with the heavenly circle and the earthly square. They are the compasses or dividers, which symbolise Heaven, and the ruler or set-square, which symbolises Earth. The Heaven-Earth symbolism of these tools is prominent in Freemasonry, although they also appear at a much earlier date within ancient Chinese philosophy. The two following quotes are from Mengzi (4th century BC), a Confucian philosopher who was considered second only to Confucius himself:

'A Master Mason, in teaching apprentices, makes use of the compasses and the square. We who are engaged in the pursuit of Wisdom must also make use of the compasses and the square.'

'The compass and square produce perfect circles and squares. By the sages, the human relations are perfectly exhibited.'

Another interesting polarity present within the relationship between the two tools is that the ruler and set-square actually resemble the geometric forms they help to bring forth – the straight line or right angle – whereas the compasses do not resemble a circle. This is expressive of the polarity of 'heavenly activity' as opposed to 'earthly passivity', because the ruler and set-square bring about their linear forms through remaining still and passive whereas the compasses obtain the circle through the activity of turning. So to recognise the circle within the compasses they need to be viewed in their active capacity, that is when they are turning in a circular motion and thus drawing the circle. Interestingly this circularity is most ideally observed if the turning compasses are viewed vertically from the 'Heaven's-eye view' – from directly above the compasses.

The triangular form of the opened compasses can be looked upon as an image of the 'Holy Mountain'. This triangular form of the mountain has a single summit at the top – the location at which the two legs of the compasses meet and are joined as one. It then has a horizontal earthly base down below that is marked out by the horizontal circular plane drawn by the pencil. The other leg of the compasses contains the sharp point that is rooted in the horizontal 'earthly plane', and through its stationary turning movement it symbolically represents a 'spine' – an unchanging vertical or 'ontological' axis of the mountain. These two relationships of 'togetherness' (the 'unity' from which the two compass legs descend) and 'separation' (the proximity between the compasses' point and pencil) in turn reflect, on the one hand, the circle's singular

central point and, on the other, the two points – one at either end of the circle's horizontal linear radius.

As already mentioned, the circle does ultimately become apparent through the active turning of the compasses when viewed from directly above. From this Heaven's-eye view, the sharp point of the compasses remains stationary yet turning, while the pencil externally marks out the turning movement of the stationary point with a visible circumference that could be described as an outward reflection of the circle's still and dimensionless central point.

Returning to the cube that was mentioned earlier as having been derived from the sphere, one of the mathematical differences that becomes apparent between these two geometric forms is that of the proximities between their respective centres in relation to the various points on their peripheries. The sphere can be described as having a radius of 1, and indeed it accordingly embodies unity because every point on its periphery is radially equidistant from its central point. The cube on the other hand embodies different distances between its centre and its three main peripheral extremities. These three differing distances bring forth the numbers 1, 2 and 3 in the form of their square roots. The three differing measurements within the cube that embody this are:

1. From the centre of the cube to the centre of each square face.

2. From the centre of the cube to the middle of each edge.

3. From the centre of the cube to each of its eight corners. (See diagram in the next column)

These three measurements relate to one another respectively as $\sqrt{1}$, $\sqrt{2}$ and $\sqrt{3}$.

But in this journey from sphere to cube the pi measurement of a circle/sphere still actually reflects itself in the relationship between $\sqrt{1}$, $\sqrt{2}$ and $\sqrt{3}$. This can be seen in the fact that if $\sqrt{1}$ is equal to 1 – which in mathematical terms it actually is – then the addition of $\sqrt{2}$ to $\sqrt{3}$ gives

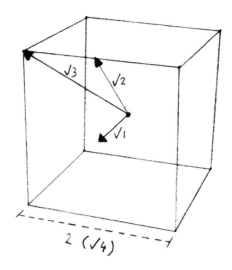

A cube with three measurements marked within.
From the cube's centre to the centre of each square face measures $\sqrt{1}$,
to the mid-point of each of the cube's edges is $\sqrt{2}$,
and to each of the cube's corners is $\sqrt{3}$.
The edge-length of the cube is 2 – which is also $\sqrt{4}$.

a very close approximation of pi at 3.146 (i.e. 1.414 + 1.732 = 3.146).

Returning to the fact that the sphere has a single uniform measurement between its centre and its periphery – unlike the cube, which has its three different measurements – there is in fact a uniform measurement within the cube as well, which accordingly reflects the uniform measurement of the sphere. But whereas the sphere's uniform measure is its radius of 1, the cube's uniform measure is present in its edge-lengths of 2.

So the movement from sphere to cube also embodies a movement from 1 to 2, or from 'unity to duality', in such a way that the duality is a kind of dual reflection of the original unity. However, this twoness is still encompassed by the original sphere in the sense that each pair of oppositional radii in the sphere together form a diameter which also measures 2.

As was just mentioned, the movement from the sphere's radius of 1 to the cube's edge-length of 2 takes place via $\sqrt{2}$ and $\sqrt{3}$. But the number 2 is actually the same as $\sqrt{4}$. So ultimately the movement from sphere to cube begins from $\sqrt{1}$, which begets $\sqrt{2}$ followed then by √3 and finally √4, and it is in this fourth and final stage that the One shows itself in a complete cuboid form. This also reflects the four-fold unfolding of the tetraktys from the 'heavenly One' at the summit down to the 'earthly four' at the base.

There is another example of such an unfolding of fourness, which shows itself in the dimensional unfolding of the cube within the following four stages:

1. A dimensionless point

2. A dimensionless point flowing forth to produce a one-dimensional line (length)

3. A line moving sideways to produce a two-dimensional square plane (breadth)

4. A square plane moving downwards or upwards to produce a three-dimensional cube (depth).

This four-fold process is also symbolically associated with the tetraktys in the sense that the point, line, plane and solid respectively require the same numbers of points that are found in the four levels of the tetraktys.

Another interesting quality embodied by the cube is that it contains the three primary musical ratios. These three ratios are the building blocks of the diatonic musical scale, because their various interactions bring about the octave scale of eight notes. This musical eightness could then be said to be numerically reflected by the eight corners of the cube. The three ratios are associated with Pythagoras and appear in stories concerning his experimental studies with music. They are numerically described as 2:1 (octave), 3:2 (fifth) and 4:3 (fourth) and the way in which this shows itself in the form of the cube is as follows.

The cube has six square faces, eight corners and twelve edges.

So the ratio 2:1 is present in the relationship between the cube's edges and faces, i.e. 12:6;

... the 3:2 ratio can then be seen in the relationship between the edges and corners – 12:8;

... and finally the ratio 4:3 can be seen in the relationship between the corners and faces – 8:6.

These three fundamental musical ratios are also mentioned in Plato's *Timaeus* dialogue. So too are the so-called 'Platonic solids', which are the five primary ways of dividing the periphery of a sphere into regular polygons. The cube is one of these five solids because it divides the periphery of the sphere up into six square faces. Plato associates these five three-dimensional solids with the four earthly elements – fire, air, water and earth – plus a 'quintessential' fifth element about which he says less. But again, in relation to the cube, Plato describes it as symbolising the element of earth.

More generally, in various traditional cultures around the world, the square and the cube are described as symbolising the Earth. A linguistic example of the description of Earth's squareness is still present within the term 'the four corners of the Earth'. Such square/cubic symbolism is also prominent in the architectural forms of various religious traditions. For instance, a dome surmounting a rectilinear cuboid base is an architectural feature in various religious traditions, and usually contains a symbolism concerning 'the place where Heaven and Earth meet'. The dome is Heaven, whereas the cuboid base is Earth and the human presence within the building – with head up in Heaven and feet down on Earth – bears 'microcosmic' witness to the joining of the

Tomb of the Samanids in Bukhara, Uzbekistan

two worlds through an embodied participation in the prayer or meditation that is characteristic of that particular place of religious observance.

Within all three of the Abrahamic religious traditions of Judaism, Christianity and Islam, the centre of the world is cube-shaped. The most visually obvious example of this is the Kaaba in Mecca – the centre of the Islamic world. The word *kaaba* literally means 'cube'. The Kaaba is the cuboid building in Mecca that all Muslims effectively turn towards when they pray – regardless of which region of the world they happen to be praying in. If a Muslim is able to go on a pilgrimage (*Hajj/Umrah*) to Mecca, one part of the pilgrimage entails an encircling of the Kaaba seven times in an inward spiralling movement known as the *Tawaaf* (circumambulation).

The Kaaba in Mecca

This anticlockwise movement – which reflects the anticlockwise motion of the stars overhead around the celestial north pole – gradually leads the pilgrim closer and closer to the Kaaba, which for Muslims is the earthly pole. The 'eight-cornered' cube is then finally reached after the seventh circumambulation. This resembles the Prophet's Miraj in which he ascended through the seven planetary spheres.

The centrality of Jerusalem is symbolically associated with the cube, and this can be seen within the Jewish and Christian traditions of centrality. Interestingly Muslims also used to pray towards Jerusalem before the eventual

institution of the Kaaba in Mecca as the central geographical point of the Muslim world.

The cube at the centre of the Jewish world features in the descriptions of both of the former Jewish temples that were situated on the Temple Mount in Jerusalem. These two temples – usually referred to as the Temple of Solomon and Herod's temple – are both described as having a cubic Holy of Holies that measured 20 × 20 × 20 cubits.[3] Jerusalem is thus seen as being the centre of the Jewish world; the Jewish temple is then the centre of Jerusalem; the cubic Holy of Holies the centre of the temple. In Rabbinic literature it is described in the following way:

'Just as the navel is placed in the middle of a man, so is the Land of Israel the navel of the world, as it says "those who sit on the centre of the land" (Ezekiel, 38:12). The land of Israel sits in the middle of the world, and Jerusalem in the middle of the land of Israel, and the Temple in the middle of Jerusalem, and the palace [the Holy of Holies] in the middle of the Temple, and the ark in the middle of the palace and the Foundation stone before the palace from which the world was founded.'

Midrash Tanchuma, Kedoshim 10

Jerusalem is also the centre of the Christian world, and as mentioned earlier the description of the Heavenly Jerusalem in the Book of Revelation again describes the shape of a cube:

'And the city lieth foursquare, and the length is as large as the breadth: and he measured the city with the reed, twelve thousand furlongs. The length and the breadth and the height of it are equal.' 21:16

Titus Burckhardt describes how this cubic shape relates to the 'heavenly' numeric of the number twelve in relation to the City's gates:

'The heavenly Jerusalem is in fact the "squaring" of the heavenly cycle, its twelve gates corresponding to the

---

3. This resembles the multiplication of *two-cubed*, i.e. 2 × 2 × 2 = 8. So the cubic Holy of Holies in Jerusalem's temple has a volume of 8,000, i.e. 20 × 20 × 20.

The Heavenly Jerusalem by Jacobello Alberegno

The trees of the four seasons i.e. three months per tree like
the three gates on each of the four sides of the Heavenly City.
Window designed and made by Helen Bree.

*twelve months of the year ... Upon the walls of the heavenly
city are seen twelve angels, who are the guardians of the
gates, and under each gate is portrayed one of the twelve
apostles, whose names are written on the city's foundations.
Under the gates there are also represented twelve circles or
spheres with inscriptions referring to the twelve precious
stones garnishing the foundations of the wall.'*

Titus Burckhardt, *Mirror of the Intellect* 4

There is a quadripartite division of these twelve gates
whereby there are three of them on each of the four sides
of the city, which themselves face in the four directions
of north, south, east and west. Having three gates on
each of the city's four sides reflects the three months
within each seasonal quarter of the annual cycle.

The four-fold layout of the twelve doorways also allegorically reflects the four-fold layout of the twelve tribes
of Israel encamped around the Tabernacle in the desert,

with three tribes encamped in each of the four directions. This earthly 'four-cornered' layout in turn reflects
the circular heavenly order of the circle of the Zodiac
which is divided into four quarters by the solstices and
the equinoxes.

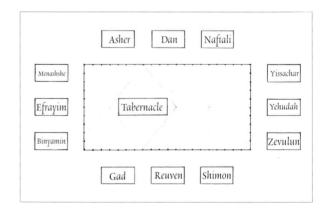

The twelve tribes of Israel encamped around the Tabernacle

---

4. (Quinta Essentia, 1987), pages 102–3.

But the square ground plan of the Heavenly City is also marked out up in the eighth heaven of the fixed stars by way of the correspondence between the four living creatures, mentioned in both Revelation and Ezekiel, and the four zodiacal signs which lie at the midpoints between the solstices and equinoxes. The ox-headed creature is Taurus the bull, the lion-headed creature Leo the Lion, the eagle, Scorpio,[5] and the human-headed creature, Aquarius the water-carrier. As the diagram shows, these zodiacal signs – centred on the midpoints between the solstices and equinoxes – form the four corners of a square that fits around the solstitial/equinoctial cosmic cross of the constellations. All of this reflects the traditional layout of a city in which there is a cruciform arrangement of streets that all lead out of the city's central square.

That which was hidden at the beginning of the process becomes fully revealed in 'earthly' terms because the eight corners of the cube were united as one at the centre of the sphere at the beginning of the process, but they became the eight most far-removed points from the centre when the 'heavenly' sphere was turned inside out to form the 'earthly' cube.

The process by which this transmutation takes place involves a seven-fold journey in the form of a three-dimensional cross that emanates outwards in the six directions of space from a seventh central point. These six directions reflect the orientations of the six square faces of the cube, which in turn reflect both the heavenly and underworld realms as well as the four-foldness of the Earth.

The four Zodiacal signs marked by the four corners of the square - Taurus, Leo, Scorpio and Aquarius - correspond to the four living creatures that are mentioned in the books of Revelation and Ezekiel

The starry mosaic vault of the Mausoleum of Galla Placidia in Ravenna. The positions of the four living creatures correspond with the four Zodiacal signs as shown in the diagram to the left. The cross is orientated to the spring equinox.

So, therefore, a symbolic understanding of the cubic shape of the Heavenly City is that it is the earthly form taken on by the heavenly sphere at the end of time. This marks the end of the process of transmutation of the sphere into a cube, or in other words the turning of the sphere inside out whereby it forms a cube.

This results from the fact that the four sides of the cube together face in the four horizontal directions of north, south, east and west – towards the four corners of the Earth – whereas the top and bottom faces look vertically upwards to the heavens and downwards to the underworld. So the cube is the central place where the

5. In the Hebrew Zodiac Scorpio is an eagle. See *Architecture, Time and Eternity*, Adrian Snodgrass, Aditya Prakashan, 2014, chapter 26, page 295.

ontological (the vertical) and the cosmological (the horizontal) meet. Henceforth it is the meeting-place where the marriage between these two worlds is effected and finalised at the 'end of time', and accordingly the Heavenly City is 'prepared as a bride adorned for her husband'. But rather than being a particular moment located within time – a moment that will occur at some future date – this final moment of union at the 'end of time' is a perpetual reality, revealing Itself to the soul with eyes that can see.

'And I heard a great voice out of heaven saying, "Behold, the tabernacle of God is with men, and he will dwell with them, and they shall be his people, and God himself shall be with them, and be their God. And God shall wipe away all tears from their eyes; and there shall be no more death, neither sorrow, nor crying, neither shall there be any more pain: for the former things are passed away."'

Revelation 21:3–4

The Heavenly Jerusalem by Maius - Beatus de Morgan, commantaire sur l'apocalypse de Beatus de Liébana

2.3 A MEDIEVAL ENGLISH CORONATION -
THE CIRCULAR CROWN, THE CUBOID STONE
AND THE LADDER THAT JOINS THEM

THE SYMBOLISM OF MONARCHY is closely connected to the establishment of a relationship between Heaven and Earth. In the Chinese language, for instance, the written character for the word 'king' is a vertical line that has three horizontal strokes drawn through it – one at the top, one in the middle and one at the bottom. These three lines symbolise Heaven, Man and Earth, and the vertical line that unites them geometrically symbolises the ontological establishment of a connection between these three worlds.[6]

The English Coronation Chair and the Chinese character for 'King' (Wang)

Such archetypal symbolism also appears to be present in the medieval traditions of the coronations of English monarchs through objects that are still used up to the present time. This symbolism specifically relates to the medieval design of the English Coronation Chair.

The Coronation Chair was originally made in the late 13th century for the coronation of Edward I. It was made specifically to contain an ancient Scottish coronation stone that Scottish kings had been crowned on for centuries. The stone was taken from the Scots by the English as a spoil of war and was thereafter used in the English coronation ritual. The Coronation Chair was designed in such a way that the stone could be positioned directly below the seat of the monarch who was being crowned (*see image on left*). As will soon become clear, such a geometric arrangement appears to reflect the establishment of a connection between Earth and Heaven.

The stone is cuboid in form and would appear to symbolise the Earth, or in another sense the foundation stone at the navel of the Earth. It has various names, the most common one being the *Stone of Destiny*. The word 'destiny' is etymologically derived from the Latin word *destinare*, which means to 'make firm' or 'establish', and so such a word inevitably speaks of the stability of the fixed square Earth on which there is the possibility of something becoming established. The word 'destiny' is also related to the word 'destination', which brings to mind the movement from 'the above' down to 'the below' – from the circle 'down' to the square – whereby the Heavenly State becomes established once having reached its 'destination' here on the earth.

---

6. See René Guénon, *The Great Triad* (Quinta Essentia, 1991), chapter 17, page 117. Also, the pictorial etymology for this Chinese character derives from an image of an axe, an object associated with the Creator God Pangu, whose swing of an axe divides Heaven (yang) from Earth (Yin). The handle of an axe is also associated with the so-called 'marriage go-between', much like the king who effects the marriage between Heaven and Earth.

There is another name that is often used for the stone, and this particular name draws our attention upwards, as it were, towards that which is above and beyond the stone. The name in question is 'Jacob's Pillow', which is a direct reference to the stone upon which Jacob rested his head as he slept, and had the dream of a ladder that reached upwards to Heaven:[7]

'Now Jacob went out from Beersheba and went toward Haran. So he came to a certain place and stayed there all night, because the sun had set. And he took one of the stones of that place and put it at his head, and he lay down in that place to sleep. Then he dreamed, and behold, a ladder was set up on the earth, and its top reached to heaven; and there the angels of God were ascending and descending on it.'

Genesis 28:10–12

With the coronation ceremony in mind, moving directly upwards from the cuboid stone one eventually finds ones way up to the circular diadem or headband of the crown that is placed upon the monarch's 'spherical' head. So henceforth the coronation ceremony itself appears to microcosmically enact the joining together of the two worlds of the circle/sphere – that is situated 'above' – and the cuboid 'down below'. Indeed the whole ceremony takes place at the centre of a beautiful four-fold Cosmati pavement in Westminster Abbey which itself geometrically reflects the four-foldness of the Earth. But the reference to Jacob's pillow also speaks of the ladder that *'was set up on the earth, and its top reached to heaven'*. In terms of the coronation symbolism, if the stone of destiny is at the foot of the ladder then the ladder itself would appear to be symbolised by the body of the monarch because it physically unites the heavenly crown above with the earthly stone of destiny below. Such a microcosmic ladder of ascent and descent is symbolically reminiscent of a process that the Indian Tantric tradition refers to as Kundalini – a spiritual practice that consists of an energetic ascent of seven levels up through the body

from the bottom of the spine up to the crown of the head. This in turn bears an inevitable microcosmic resemblance to the ancient macrocosmic storyline of the soul's ascent through seven planetary spheres. The Cosmati pavement on which the coronation ceremony traditionally takes place becomes a physically experienced centre-of-the-world for the duration of the ceremony for all of those who are its witness. Similarly, the Kaaba is the physically experienced centre of the world for the Muslim on Hajj, and likewise the Temple Mount for the Jew at Jerusalem's Western Wall. The following words of St Cyril of Jerusalem speak of a similar centrality in wider Christian terms:

'Christ opened his arms on the Cross to embrace the whole World, because Golgotha stood at the centre of the World.'

When the soul turns towards 'the centre of the world' it physically enacts an inner process of transition in which it turns inward towards its own centre. But all of these many centres – both inward and outward – can be described as images of a supreme transcendent centre that is ultimately beyond all of the many centres of this world despite manifesting its quality of 'centrality' in each one of them. Such a centrality symbolises the meeting-place of Heaven and Earth that exists within each one of us – for we all perpetually stand at the centre of a circular horizon at which the heavenly blue sky meets the earth. However, this meeting of sky and earth is merely an outward appearance – as is any visible circumference – of a circle's invisible central point, which symbolises the perpetual and unchanging location of the human heart.

'Don't you know that you yourselves are God's temple and that God's spirit dwells in your midst?'

1 Corinthians 3:16

We shall now turn our attention to one particular medieval Christian example of an inwardly experienced and outwardly-realised geographical centrality – namely the 12th-century Kingdom of Jerusalem.

---

7. This Judeo-Christian name for the stone appears to have its origin in a story about St Colomba in which he saw angels when on his death bed – a death bed which had the stone as its pillow. (*The Coronation Stone*, William Forbes Skene, page 25.)

Chapter 3
The Kingdom of Jerusalem

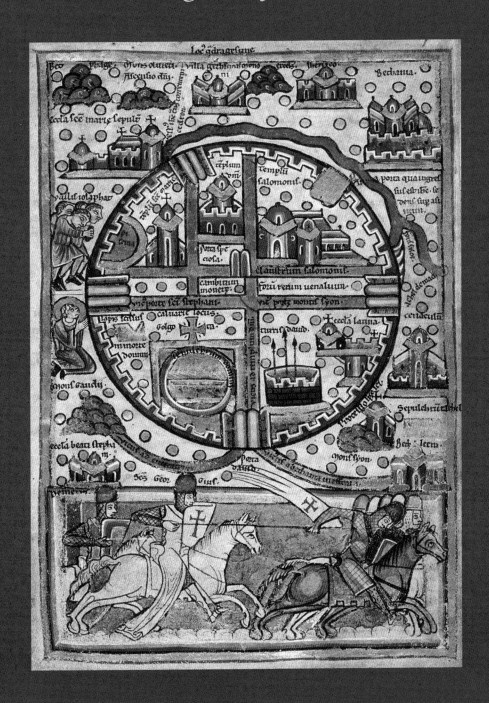

3.1 REACHING THE CENTRE OF THE WORLD

'Thus saith the Lord God; This is Jerusalem: I have set it in the midst of the nations and countries that are round about her.'

Ezekiel 5:5

'Come from the four winds, O breath, and breathe upon these slain, that they may live. So I prophesied as he commanded me, and the breath came into them, and they lived, and stood up upon their feet, an exceeding great army. Then he said unto me, "Son of man, these bones are the whole house of Israel: behold, they say, Our bones are dried, and our hope is lost: we are cut off for our parts. Therefore prophesy and say unto them, Thus saith the Lord GOD; Behold, O my people, I will open your graves, and cause you to come up out of your graves, and bring you into the land of Israel.'

Ezekiel 37: 9–12

THE KINGDOM OF JERUSALEM existed for a little under 200 years. It was established soon after the Crusaders took Jerusalem in 1099, and it came to an end in 1291. It is generally understood to have consisted of two eras, which are sometimes referred to as the first kingdom and second kingdom. The first kingdom was based in Jerusalem between 1099 and 1187, and the second in Acre from 1192 to 1291.

Jerusalem and kingship are intimately connected within the Judeo-Christian tradition. Not only was Jerusalem the place where kings David and Solomon reigned in the Old Testament era, but it was also the place where Christ 'the King' brought forth the era of the New Covenant between God and humanity through his death on the cross followed by his Resurrection and Ascension. Kingship in Jerusalem is also intimately connected to messiahship. In Jewish beliefs the Messiah is actually referred to as the 'King Messiah' (*melekh mashiach*), and also understood to be in the family line of King David.

As we saw in the last chapter, the understanding of Jerusalem's centrality is one of Christianity's many inheritances from Judaism. It seemed to become particularly significant in the 12th century in relation to the establishment of the Crusader Kingdom. A coronation ritual takes place at the perceived centre of the world because the 'central place' is the one and only location where the ladder of ascent and descent is set up and climbable. However, this 'one and only location' could be said to exist in many different places and contexts.[1]

A characteristic of many religious traditions is the recognition of a centre – or usually various centres and focalities. A significant religious activity is to then prayerfully focus upon these physically experienceable centres/focalities as a way of contemplating the world of Spirit. In medieval English Christianity it may have been a geographical place of pilgrimage such as Jerusalem, Rome, Canterbury or Walsingham, or a cosmological direction such as the sunrise on the eastern horizon towards which a church building is orientated. It could even be a focal object such as a crucifix or icon, towards which prayer is orientated. Or it could be a church's altar or a sacred well, or even

---

1. This is artistically symbolised by the centring of the clay on the potter's wheel, which is the necessary starting point before the form of the pot can ascend upwards through the throwing process.

a reliquary through which the incarnate presence of the pilgrim can enter into actual physical proximity to a trace of the incarnate presence of a saint.

In terms of the wider cosmos, the recognition of a centre is far more overtly geometric, in the sense that a planetary system of spheres all contemplate their spherical light source through orbiting it over and over again for millions of years at a time. In this sense we could be said to be part of a cosmos that is perpetually embodying an uncountable number of contemplative prayers, each of which orientates the cosmic soul's vision towards the One through geometrically circumnavigating a multitude of central gravitational points.

However, the soul's journey of return to its origin is one that can often consist of great trials and hardships. If the circle is understood to be an overhead image of the Holy Mountain, whereby the central point of the circle is the mountain's summit and the circumference its base, it becomes apparent that the radius is actually a steep path of ascent upon which passage is not so straightforward. To reach the summit of a mountain one must get through the densely forested slopes, where is it easy to lose one's way. Then there is the climbing of the craggy rock faces, from which one can easily fall. There is also the extreme change of temperature the higher one goes up the mountain, for which the wayfarer might not have brought suitable apparel on their first attempt at reaching the summit.

Planet Earth in 'orbital prayerfulness'

Ascending the Holy Mountain

To prayerfully focus upon a centre or focality of any sort is to outwardly enact an inner state of contemplation in which there is a turning inwards toward one's own centre. To outwardly enact such a turning inwards is to externally live the inner life in which the soul fixes its gaze purely upon its origin, in much the same way that a geometer contemplates the One through the physical act of drawing a circumference that outwardly reflects the dimensionless centre from which it was effectively born. It is a state of being in which the soul could be described as in the world but not of the world.

But such hardship is part of the life experience that encourages the soul to grow in wisdom through realising what is most important, as opposed to what is fleeting and impermanent.

With such reflections in mind it may be possible to have some sense of the spiritual conviction on the part of the Crusaders who went on an eastward journey of great penitential suffering and sacrifice to the centre of the world. Today there is a phenomenon called Jerusalem Syndrome, in which people experience a spiritual crisis through becoming psychologically intoxicated and overawed as a result of actually visiting the Holy Centre 'itself' – rather than just focusing upon it from afar. The 'Holy Centre' in question here is of course not just the geographically definable city of Jerusalem, but also – more importantly – what could be described as the soul's 'Inner Jerusalem', or 'the centre of the being'. This direct beholding of the supernal light of the Sun could be said to lead to a temporary 'dazzling and blindness', which modern psychiatric medicine describes as a psychotic episode. The pilgrim generally revives a few weeks later, although one would assume that such a pilgrimage remains etched on the memory for quite some time. One wonders if the 12th-century Crusaders experienced a similar extreme of exuberance and awe, in no small part due to the first Crusade having taken Jerusalem just a few months before the dawning of a new century. It has been suggested that the dawning of the previous century in 1000 AD had contained millenarian expectations on the part of some for the second coming of Christ, and with it the establishment of the New Jerusalem. Such suggested millenarianism is associated with chapter 20 in the Book of Revelation:

'Then I saw an angel coming down from heaven, having the key to the bottomless pit and a great chain in his hand. He laid hold of the dragon, that serpent of old, who is the Devil and Satan, and bound him for a thousand years; and he cast him into the bottomless pit, and shut him up, and set a seal on him, so that he should deceive the nations no more till the thousand years were finished. But after these things he must be released for a little while.'

From a spiritual perspective this makes the perception of Jerusalem's centrality a profound experience on the part of those who 'took up the cross' and joined the Crusade. It would naturally make the reaching and taking of Jerusalem a very spiritually charged event, even if also a rather horrific and violent one. To recognise a remote geographical place as the holy centre of

The Maccabees (depicted as medieval Crusader knights) - travelling to Jerusalem to free the temple from 'foreign' rule. The story of the Maccabean revolt to free Jerusalem became allegorically associated with the medieval Christian Crusades.

the world is one thing, but to then actually go on a journey to that place – a journey which involves much hardship and sacrifice – and for the journey's completion to result in the establishment of a Christian Solomon-esque monarchy, could be looked upon as ordaining the eschatological conditions required for the return of the Messiah at the end of time. The old Jewish belief that the Messiah will enter Jerusalem on a donkey having descended the Mount of Olives is one that Christ dramatically enacted on Palm Sunday. As will become clear, this monumental event would become significant again in the 12th-century Kingdom of Jerusalem as well as at the great west doors of English cathedrals. This commemoration of Christ's entry into Jerusalem would also become a foreshadowing, or indeed an enactment, of the entry into the Heavenly Jerusalem at the end of time.

3.2 THE VISUAL DEPICTION OF JERUSALEM'S CENTRALITY

THE MEDIEVAL WESTERN European perception of Jerusalem's centrality appears to have been expressed symbolically in a variety of depictions. The foremost of these is the Mappa Mundi. There are various of these medieval maps that depict the known world, and on many of them Jerusalem is clearly marked as the central place on Earth. Interestingly the oldest map in existence that overtly displays this particular geographical feature dates back to 1109, which is just a decade after the Crusaders reached Jerusalem. Bearing in mind that the map would have taken time to research and produce, this pushes the date of its inception back even closer to the establishment of the Kingdom of Jerusalem in 1099. This in itself shows a European perception that understands the Crusades as having reached the central place on Earth.

Another Christian geometric symbol of centrality that relates to Jerusalem is the seal of the Crusader Kingdom itself. The Jerusalem cross clearly expresses a quincuncial image of 'the centre and the four corners' via the arrangement of its five crosses. There is one large central cross with four smaller crosses in the four quarters - a layout that appears to be Armenian in origin. In geometric terms it is much like the typical Islamic garden, which also symbolises the fourfold Earth with

its central fountain and four streams running therefrom in the four directions. These four streams are an image of the four rivers that ran out of Eden, and they demarcate the garden's four quarters, each of which is often also divided into four quarters. Similarly, the symbolism of the Jerusalem cross would appear to express the idea that Jerusalem is at the centre of the four corners of the Earth. It would also relate to a symbolism in which the four Gospel writers are understood to have taken Christ's ministry from Jerusalem to the four corners of the Earth. The image below shows a plan view of the Taj Mahal and the four-fold garden, at the northern head of which this famous mausoleum stands. It is the typical layout of an Islamic garden with a water source in the centre and four streams running outwards in the four directions. The image below on the left depicts a Jerusalem cross which later became the seal of the Crusader Kingdom. Note the large central cross with another smaller cross in each quarter, and its resemblance to the four-fold layout of an Islamic garden.

The Jerusalem Cross - seal of the Crusader kingdom

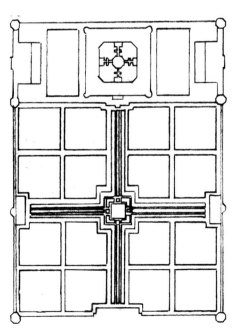

Ground plan of the fourfold garden containing the Taj Mahal mausoleum

Interestingly there could also be said to be a 'micro-cosmic' equivalent of the Jerusalem cross, which shows itself in the depiction of the Five Wounds of Christ. These are the wounds that were inflicted on Christ's body during the Crucifixion, which itself took place in Jerusalem. These wounds are also depicted in a quincuncial arrangement much like the five crosses that form the Jerusalem cross, and so again there is an image of a 'square with a centre'. The four corners of this square show Christ's wounded hands and feet and, much like the four corners of the Earth that represent the four most extreme regions of the 'square Earth', the wounded hands and feet are the four extremities of the human body. The symbolic centre or 'heart' of the human body is the corporeal heart, and accordingly it is the pierced heart of Christ that contains the fifth wound, which is thus depicted centrally between the four-fold arrangement of hands and feet. So the Sacred Heart of Christ is accordingly associated with Jerusalem – the heart of the world.

Christ's five wounds on Bishop Beckynton's tomb in Wells Cathedral

Another centrally orientated form that is associated with Jerusalem is an architectural one. The round churches that have come to be so closely associated with the Knights Templar appear to have been influenced by the design of two circular/polygonal buildings in Jerusalem. The first of these two 'centrally planned'

Temple Church in London. A circular church built by the Knights Templar.

buildings (i.e. with a circular or polygonal ground plan) is the Holy Sepulchre, which commemorates Christ's Crucifixion and Resurrection. The second is the Dome of the Rock, which is an Islamic shrine that was built to commemorate Prophet Mohammed's Night Journey (Miraj). This domed building was also considered to be on the site of Solomon's Temple as well as Mount Moriah, on which Abraham nearly sacrificed his son. The Dome of the Rock was turned into a church during the Kingdom of Jerusalem, and was referred to as the Temple of the Lord. It lay directly next door to the headquarters of the Knights Templar in the Al-Aqsa Mosque, which itself came to be known as the Temple of Solomon. The ground plan of the Dome of the Rock is octagonal, whereas the sepulchre area (Anastasis) within the Church of the Holy Sepulchre is circular – although it effectively embodies a twenty-fold symmetry in relation to its pillars. Within Templar church architecture both circular and octagonal ground plans are used – as well as a few other polygonal shapes, although the octagon is the most common.

The ground plan of a centrally planned building inevitably emphasises a single focal point rather than a linear axiality. A single focal point implies stillness, whereas the axiality of a line could be described as embodying a movement that leads from a *beginning point*, at one end of the line, to an *end point of culmination* at the other end. So for example the usual orientation and layout of a church embodies such an axial movement, which begins from the western end of the church

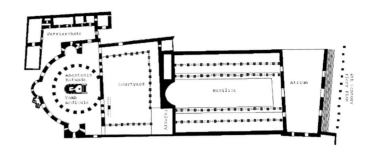

The dome of the Anastasis rotunda - located at the western end of the ground plan of the Church of the Holy Sepulchre

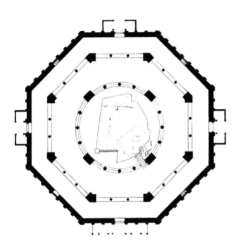

The Dome of the Rock with its octagonal ground plan

and then moves eastwards towards the place of the rising Sun, which is a cosmological image of Christ 'the Risen Son'. Indeed, to even speak of a church's 'orientation' is to speak of the east, because the orientating of oneself involves turning to face the orient (i.e. the east). The words 'orient' and 'origin' both derive from the Latin word *oriri* meaning 'rise', in the sense of the Sun rising in the orient at the origination of the day. So with this in mind an axial movement through a church from west to east doesn't emphasise a single central focal point in the way that a centrally planned building does. However, the culminatory eastern end

of a church is, in a certain sense, a central point that is reached as a result of the eastward 'ascent' of the church. So a church's east end is effectively the summit at the top of the holy mountain to which the pilgrim ascends, and from an overhead view the summit of a mountain is centrally located. Such a 'centrality in the east' is sometimes geometrically expressed, particularly in the French Gothic cathedrals, in the way that the eastern end of the cathedral is polygonal: its geometric shape is accordingly derived from the 'heavenly' circle, unlike the 'earthly' four-cornered rectangular bays that form the rest of the building.

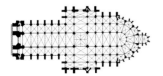
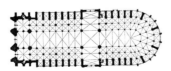
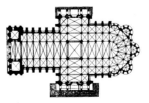

Ground plans of the cathedrals in Amiens, Paris and Chartres. Mostly composed of 'earthly' rectangular bays, apart from their 'heavenly' circular east ends.

Such symbolism of an eastward ascent to a centrally located point is seemingly also present in the famous description of the Kingdom of Jerusalem by Fulcher of Chartres.

'Consider, I pray, and reflect how in our time God has transferred the West into the East, For we who were Occidentals now have been made Orientals. He who was a Roman or a Frank is now a Galilaean, or an inhabitant of Palestine. One who was a citizen of Rheims or of Chartres now has been made a citizen of Tyre or of Antioch. We have already forgotten the places of our birth ...'

Fulcher's description clearly utilises a spiritual/cosmological language of symbolism that fits a cosmic Christian liturgical mindset. This movement of the Western European Crusaders to 'the east' embodies the eastward movement within a church towards the place of the rising Sun/Son. So as well as being centrally located, Jerusalem is also in the east, and in this sense both 'the centre' and 'the east' symbolise an extremity or culmination in relation to a particular movement that starts from a beginning point and which leads to a final end point. A biblical example of such eastern centrality is implied by St Peter's description of inward spiritual illumination, and resurrection, in which *'the morning star rises in your hearts'* (2 Peter 1:19). The heart is symbolically central, whereas the Morning Star is a symbol of the emergence of light in the east.

Returning to centrally planned architecture, it was mentioned a little earlier that, in geometric terms, a centrally planned church emphasises 'the point' and thus it could be said 'stillness', whereas the more standard axial church layout emphasises 'the line' and accordingly the movement from one end of the line to the other. Having said this, the 'centrality' of a centrally planned church could actually be viewed as embodying an axial movement, albeit a vertical one. In this sense the singular central point on the floor of the building denotes the beginning of a vertical ascent toward the building's vault, which symbolises the heavens. Such would appear to be the case with the centrally planned design of the Dome of the Rock for instance, bearing in mind that it commemorates Prophet Mohammed's ascent through the planetary spheres. So it is also of interest that in the era of the Crusader Kingdom, when this building was briefly Christianised, it became a focal shrine for commemorating the story of Jacob's ladder despite the fact that this Old Testament story is not traditionally understood to have taken place in Jerusalem. Even the Holy Sepulchre would appear to indirectly contain such ascent symbolism, because it is based on the old Roman mausolea architecture that is expressive of the ascent of a deceased soul back up through the planetary spheres. But the Holy Sepulchre itself could actually be said to symbolise a vertical movement, albeit a downward one, in which Christ descends into Sheol for the Harrowing of Hell.

Returning to the symbolism of point and line, if the still-point could be said to symbolise 'Being' then the axial movement from one end of a line to the other could be said to symbolise 'Becoming'. The way to view these two principles in one diagram is to say that the still-point of Being is situated at one end of the line of Becoming. So a movement from the beginning of the line to the end of it is a movement of Becoming that culminates and resolves in Being. With this kind of metaphysical principle in mind, the symbolism of centrality *in the east* that the 12th-century Roman Christians associated with Jerusalem could be looked upon as a very high one, in which there is a perception that a final destination has been reached. Having reached this central place the only possible movement left is a vertically orientated one, either upwards or downwards, upon what could be described as an 'ontological axis'. This in turn resonates with an eschatological millenarian state of mind which has made the final preparations for the descent of the Heavenly Jerusalem and the second coming of Christ.

A highway shall be there, and it shall be called the Holy Way; the unclean shall not travel on it, but it shall be for God's people; no traveller, not even fools, shall go astray ... And the ransomed of the Lord shall return, and come to Zion with singing; everlasting joy shall be upon their heads; they shall obtain joy and gladness, and sorrow and sighing shall flee away.'

Isaiah 35:8 & 10

3.3 THE FAMILIAL CONNECTIONS BETWEEN THE MONARCHS OF JERUSALEM AND ENGLAND

THROUGHOUT THE 12th century the kingdoms of Jerusalem and England were both in the hands of the same few extended families of Frankish nobles.

The Kingdom was established in the year that Jerusalem was taken by the Crusaders. In the year 1099 Godfrey de Bouillon became the first ruler of Jerusalem. He is said to have rejected the diadem and title of 'King', preferring to take on the humbler role of 'Defender and Advocate of the Holy Sepulchre'. This was apparently due to his belief that only Christ could be described as the King of Jerusalem.

However, Godfrey did not last long and had died by the middle of the following year. He was succeeded by his brother Baldwin, who was then crowned King Baldwin I – and thus Baldwin was the first actual Crusader 'King' of Jerusalem. He was crowned in Bethlehem – the city of King David. It was this Davidic connection that had actually caused Bethlehem to be the birthplace of Christ eleven centuries earlier. Baldwin's coronation took place on Christmas day in the year 1100, which speaks volumes of how the Crusader culture viewed itself. Precisely 1100 years to the day after the birth of Jesus Christ, the Crusaders were crowning a monarch to be the king of the centre of the world in the very same city where Christ 'the King' had been born. Baldwin's crowning also took place precisely 300 years to the day after the crowning, in St Peter's Basilica in Rome, of Charlemagne as the Holy Roman Emperor. So this coronation must surely have been experienced as a profoundly meaningful moment.

These first two rulers of Jerusalem – Godfrey de Bouillon and King Baldwin I – were both uncles of Matilda of Boulogne, the wife of King Stephen of England, who later reigned from 1135 to 1154. Stephen had succeeded his uncle – Henry I – who came to the English throne in the same year that Baldwin I was crowned as the first King of Jerusalem – AD 1100.

Baldwin I was then succeeded by Baldwin II, who is described as being his cousin although the precise familial relationship has never been fully understood. Baldwin II's coronation took place in 1118, which was the same year as the consecration in Seborga of the Poor Fellow-Soldiers of Christ – or the Knights Templar, as they came to be known. It was Matilda of Boulogne's close familial connections to the first few rulers of Jerusalem that helped to bring about the granting of the first English manor of land to the Templars in 1136 at Cressing Temple in Essex. This was then followed a few years later by the addition of some land at Temple Cowley in Oxford. The Templar expert Helen Nicholson points out that:

'... it was Matilda's generosity to the [Templar] order that laid the foundations of a long and close relationship between the Templars and the kings of England.' [2]

Baldwin II was succeeded in 1131 by his daughter Melisende, and the renowned Crusader Fulk - Count of Anjou - to whom she had recently become married. Fulk was the grandfather of Henry II of England (1154–1189), who succeeded King Stephen. Fulk was also very closely connected to the Knights Templar almost from their inception, and it was actually during his reign that Matilda of Boulogne granted Cressing Temple to the Templars. Fulk was then succeeded by his son Baldwin III in 1143, who jointly ruled with his mother Melisende until she died in 1161.

2. *A Brief History of the Knights Templar*, Helen Nicholson, Robinson Publishing, 2010, chapter 6.

Baldwin was succeeded by his brother Amalric I in 1163. Amalric died in 1174 and was succeeded by his son, who became Baldwin IV.

Back in England, 1174 is also the year that Reginald de Bohun (or Fitz Jocelin) became the Bishop of Bath. It is thought that Reginald then instigated the building of the first English Gothic cathedral in the following year, 1175. This building, in the new (i.e. Gothic) style, started to be built in the small city of Wells alongside the older Saxon minster (church) of St Andrew.

So Wells Cathedral would have been designed at some point during all of these familial successions in England and Jerusalem. Wherever it was designed and whomever it was designed by, the period of time in which it was designed happens to coincide with a cultural era in which the same noble Frankish extended families were in power in both Western Europe and the Holy Land.

A final point to make here is the apparent association of Bishop Reginald of Bath with the culture of the Crusades. First, it was Reginald who was one of the two bishops that flanked the Crusader King Richard 'Lionheart' in his coronation ceremony at Westminster Abbey. Reginald's eventual election as Archbishop of Canterbury also occurred as a result of the closeness that he and his relative Savaric had with Richard I.[3] Indeed Savaric even accompanied King Richard on the third Crusade in 1190 and was then subsequently elected as Reginald's successor as Bishop of Bath very soon thereafter.

There is also an intriguingly brief mention of Bishop Reginald by Walter Map – a 12th-century chancellor and precentor of Lincoln. In his satirical work *De Nugis Curialium* (Of the Trifles of Courtiers), he very briefly mentions Reginald during a few chapters involving

The coronation of Fulk and Melisende [4]

stories about the Templars and the Crusades. He first mentions the poverty and nobility of the Templars in their early days, but then moves on to saying how such poverty and nobility didn't necessarily last once the Templars had become wealthy. In the middle of these descriptions he suddenly, and very briefly, digresses to accuse Bishop Reginald of paying the Pope so as to become the Bishop of Bath. Having made this short accusatory digression he returns to mention the Templars again, as if suggesting that the Templars and Bishop Reginald of Bath were in some way all part of the same element of perceived corruption. Map's writing is satirical and has a tone of gossip about it. So the fact that he mentions De Bohun becoming the Bishop of Bath, in the same sentences as the Templars, makes for an interesting insinuation of an association.[5]

Whatever the moral state of Bishop Reginald de Bohun of Bath, he is a significant figure in the history of Gothic architecture because he is the bishop who instigated the building process of the Cathedral of St Andrew in Wells – the first English Gothic cathedral.

3. See *The Social Politics of Medieval Diplomacy: Anglo-German Relations* (1066–1307), Joseph Patrick Huffman, University of Michigan Press, 2009, p151-2.
4. Note the cosmic symbolism in this coronation image which relates to *the-union-of-opposites*. The bishop is the 'ontological axis' uniting the Above with the Below (note his mitre touching the top frame of the image). From this 'central place' he is able to unite the Masculine (Fulk) with the Feminine (Melisende). The figure behind Melisende wears the same colours as Fulk whereas vice versa with the figure behind Fulk (much like the Yang in Yin and the Yin in Yang). All five figures wear brown but only the Bishop wears sky blue. Fulk's raised right hand faces inwards whereas Melisende's right hand faces outwards. Their thrones are coloured inversely.
5. For this brief mention of Bishop Reginald in *De Nugis Curialium*, see the chapter entitled 'Concerning the Old Man of the Assassins'.

Chapter 4.

The English Gothic Cathedral as an Image of the Heavenly and Earthly Jerusalem

4.1 THE EMERGENCE OF THE GOTHIC STYLE IN THE ERA OF THE KINGDOM OF JERUSALEM

The Lay Brothers Refectory at Fountains Abbey

THE MEDIEVAL GOTHIC style of Christian architecture is characterised by pointed arches, ribbed vaults and external flying buttresses, which allow for there to be bigger windows that let in more light. This architectural style developed in 12th-century France out of the Romanesque style of architecture, which only used semicircular arches. The development of the pointed arch and the ribbed vault in the Christian Gothic style appears to have been influenced by Middle Eastern styles of architecture, within which such pointed architectural forms had already been used for over four hundred years in Islamic buildings. This suggests that builders from Western Europe visited the Middle East – presumably for the purposes of research as well as for pilgrimage – because an artist rarely learns their practice from the written word rather than through direct involvement in an artistic practice. The evidence of this could be said to be 'written' in the very pointed arches and ribbed vaults themselves rather than in any actual written words. However, it is also documented that master masons and craftsmen from Western Europe visited the Middle East during the era of the Crusades.[1]

With this in mind, it is inevitably of interest that the European Gothic style developed within a few decades of the establishment of the Kingdom of Jerusalem. Spain and Sicily were other places where contact had been taking place between Christian and Islamic cultures, although the great emphasis that Gothic cathedral design appears to place on Jerusalem suggests more of an influence coming in from pilgrim-architects who had spent time in the Holy Land. Such an architectural development appears to suggest a 'bringing home' to Western Europe of some of the holy essence of the eastern kingdom, in the sense of emulating the architectural appearance that had been experienced at first-hand by such pilgrim-architects.

The first completed example of Gothic architecture is the eastern end of the abbey of St Denis in Paris, which was started in 1135, and finished and dedicated in 1144. However, the first Gothic cathedral was built to the southeast of Paris in Sens. Like St Denis in Paris, the building work for St Stephen's Cathedral in Sens started in the 1130s, although the sanctuary wasn't consecrated until 1164. Sens Cathedral was built very much under the influence of St Bernard of Clairvaux, who was a close friend of the Archbishop of Sens – Henry Sanglier. Archbishop Sanglier was also a close friend of Abbot Suger, who oversaw the Gothic building work at St Denis in Paris. St Bernard had a close association with the Kingdom of Jerusalem through his patronage of the Knights Templar, who had only just returned to France in 1127 after nine years in Jerusalem. Bernard was also very significant for the Crusades through his preaching of the Second Crusade at Vezelay in 1146.

The Gothic style started to spread throughout France and beyond as the 12th century proceeded. It reached England in the 1170s, where William of Sens designed

---

1. For example see *Wells Cathedral – A History*, ed. L.S. Colchester (Open Books, 1996), chapter 3, page 58.

Pointed arches in the mosque of Ibn Tulun in Cairo, Egypt (started 876AD)

the quire and the east end of Canterbury Cathedral.[2] Having said this, there is some very early Gothic vaulting at Durham Cathedral, which began to be built around 1130. Interestingly, this is a very similar time to when the Cistercians and the Templars began to make connections in England, such as with the establishment, in 1128, of the first English Cistercian abbey at Waverley in Surrey. The Grand Master of the Templars, Hugues de Payens, is also known to have visited England and Scotland for the first time in 1128.

Early pointed arches in the vault of Durham Cathedral

(above) Sainte-Chapelle (below) Le collège des Bernardins - both in Paris

2. The ground plan of the east end Corona Chapel at Canterbury clearly resembles the ground plan of the east end of St Stephen's cathedral in Sens, as indeed both were designed by William of Sens. But the fact that the name Stephen means 'crown' suggests an interesting possibility in symbolic terms that requires further study. The east end of Canterbury is a corona chapel that is specifically at the 'crown' of the cathedral, and associated with the physical head-crown of Thomas à Becket. Could there be any similar coronal association with the east end chapel at St Stephen's in Sens?

But the first English Gothic cathedral was built in the small city of Wells in Somerset. The work on the Cathedral Church of St Andrew started around 1175 and was completed in its ground plan by the early to mid 1300s. This cathedral is described as being the first English Gothic cathedral, as well as the first 'fully' Gothic cathedral in the world, in the sense that it was the first cathedral built with the pointed arch throughout. It is also renowned to this day as being one of the most beautiful Gothic cathedrals in England. The quadrivial design of Wells Cathedral also happens to be the main architectural study within this book, and there will be a close focus on the design theory, measurements and symbolism of the cathedral's ground plan, although various aspects of other English Gothic cathedrals will be approached as well. With the previous chapters in mind, we will begin the study of Wells Cathedral at what appears to be the most appropriate place, which is the entrance at the great west door. On the one hand this door marks the beginning of an eastward journey of 'ascent'. At the same time it is also an image of the entrance to both the heavenly and the earthly Jerusalem.

The west front of Wells Cathedral - an image of both the Heavenly and earthly Jerusalem

4.2 WELLS CATHEDRAL AS AN IMAGE OF BOTH THE HEAVENLY AND EARTHLY JERUSALEM

Palm Sunday at the Golden Gate of Jerusalem and the great west door at Wells

'The great enterprise that is about to be undertaken requires an inner disposition, a state of grace, on the part of the builder. The mystical vision of harmony can become a model for the artist only if it has first taken possession of his soul and become the ordering principle of all its facilties and aspirations.' 3

> Abbot Suger on the builders of the Gothic east end of the Abbey of St Denis in Paris

THE GOTHIC CATHEDRAL is often described as a symbol of the Heavenly Jerusalem. So to enter the cathedral is to enter into the ideal state at the end of time – the 'cubic' earthly establishment of the ideal 'spherical' heavenly order. In his book *The Foundations of Christian Art* Titus Burckhardt draws on the natural formation of the cubic crystal system as a symbol of the cubic finality of the Heavenly City.

'The Heavenly Jerusalem is really a crystal, not only because of its transparent, incorruptible and luminous substance, but also because of its crystalline form. It is the "crystallisation", in the eternal present, of all the positive and essentially indestructible aspects of the temporal or changing world.'

Such symbolism of entry into the ideal state is still liturgically enacted on Palm Sunday at Wells Cathedral to this day, where the liturgy begins outside the great west door. At the appropriate moment the amassed congregation follows the procession of clerics and the Vicar's Choral into the cathedral through the great west door, as if to re-enact the historical event of Christ's entry into Jerusalem through the Golden Gate on the first Palm Sunday. However, this symbolism of passage is also expressive of an entry into the Heavenly City at the end of time, and so as a result of the liturgical enactment Wells Cathedral becomes an earthly image of the Heavenly Jerusalem. But certain architectural features seem to suggest that it was intentionally designed to also be a 'heavenly image' of the earthly Jerusalem, and one example of this is the architectural design of the west door itself. Like many other Gothic cathedral doors, the great west door of Wells contains two doors. So it is inevitably of interest that Jerusalem's Golden Gate also contains two doors – and is the only gate of Jerusalem's old city to possess such a feature. The Muslims even have specific names for the two doors, which translate as the Gate of Mercy and the Gate of Repentance. The Golden Gate was periodically unblocked from the very early 12th century onwards, soon after the Crusaders had taken Jerusalem, and the same type of Palm Sunday procession used to pass through the Golden Gate every year, as is recorded in the written accounts of various European pilgrims. In 1170 John of Würzburg wrote in his *Description of the Holy Land*:

'This gate, moreover, in pious remembrance of our Lord's divine and mystic entrance when He came up from Bethany over the Mount of Olives to Jerusalem, is closed within, and blocked up with stones without, and is never opened to anyone except on Palm Sunday, on which day every year, in memory of what there took place, it is solemnly opened to a procession and to the whole people, whether they be citizens or strangers. After the patriarch has

3. See *The Gothic Cathedral, Otto Georg von Simson*, Princeton University Press, 1988, page 127.

The west door of Wells Cathedral

The two doors of Jerusalem's Golden Gate - where Christ entered the Holy City on Palm Sunday

preached a sermon to the people at the foot of the Mount of Olives, when the service for that day is over, it is closed again for a whole year as before, except on the day of the Exaltation of the Holy Cross, upon which also it is opened.' [4]

A German monk called Theoderich was writing his own *Description of the Holy Places* at a similar time, and he actually mentions the two separate doorways of the Golden Gate along with a Palm Sunday tradition that is associated with them:

'He [Christ] arrived at the Golden Gate, which is twofold. As He approached it, one of the doors opened of itself, for the bolt fell out, and, violently drawing out its ring, made the other door fly open with a loud noise: wherefore a chapel has been consecrated in honour of it, wherein this ring, which is covered with gilding, is regarded with great reverence. The gate itself is never opened except on Palm Sunday and on the day of the Exaltation of the Cross.' [5]

So the Palm Sunday liturgical tradition at Wells possibly has its origin in the Jerusalemic culture of the Crusader Kingdom. As mentioned above, the first Kingdom of Jerusalem existed from 1099 to 1187, and this happens to be the very same few decades in which Wells Cathedral would have been designed.

In relation to the biblical description of the Heavenly Jerusalem, there appears to be another significant element of design informing the west doors of Gothic cathedrals, and this would seem to associate the cathedral with the Heavenly City as well as the earthly one. The three doorways on the front of a Gothic cathedral reflect the three doorways on each side of the Heavenly Jerusalem as described in the Book of Revelation. So accordingly, the west doors of Gothic cathedrals afford a symbolic entry into both the Heavenly and the earthly Jerusalem at one and the same time. This also demonstrates an apparent analogy of some kind, in the perceptions of 12th-century Christendom, of the Heavenly Jerusalem with the Frankish Crusader Kingdom of Jerusalem.

---

4. The feasts of both Palm Sunday and the Exaltation of the Holy Cross occur within close proximity to the two equinoxes – Palm Sunday in spring, and the Holy Cross in autumn. A cosmic feature of this, in relation to the Golden Gate, is that an eastern-facing congregation of worshippers, i.e. who are facing a patriarch preaching a sermon at the foot of the Mount of Olives, would be in a position to witness the Sun rising directly over the Mount of Olives at either of these festivals, because the Holy Mountain is directly to the east of the Golden Gate and the Sun rises from the eastern point of the horizon on the equinoxes. So the Sun would effectively shine its rays of golden light through the Golden Gate on these two feast days.

5. These written accounts by John of Würzburg and Theoderich are both available from the online library for the Palestine Pilgrims' Text Society.

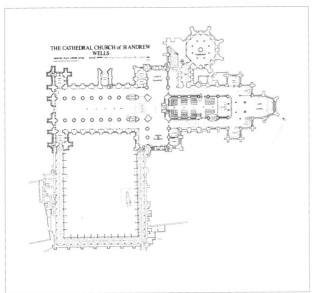

Wells Cathedral architectural plan

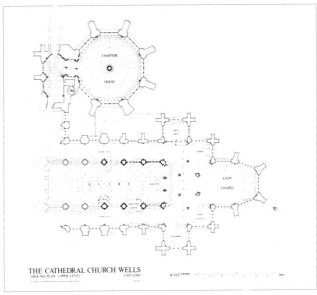

Close up: Octagonal chapter house to the north of the 'Solomonic' quire

THE CATHEDRAL DESIGN'S EMULATION OF THE TEMPLE MOUNT'S TOPOGRAPHICAL LAYOUT – A TEMPLAR CONNECTION?

VENTURING FURTHER EASTWARDS into Wells Cathedral, through the nave and up as far as the quire, there is another interesting design feature. It bears a resemblance to a specifically 12th-century Christian understanding of the layout of Jerusalem's Temple Mount.

The quire – as it now stands with six bays – is the same size as the biblical description of the Temple of Solomon. Each of the six bays has an east–west measurement of 10 cubits, which emulates the 60-cubit east–west length of the temple as it is described in the Bible. Looking at the architectural plan of this part of the cathedral, it also becomes clear that directly to the north of this 'Solomonic' quire there is a 'centrally planned' octagonal building, which contains the chapter house as well as a room below that was used as a treasury. Such an architectural layout is reminiscent of the Temple Mount in Jerusalem, where the octagonal Dome of the Rock is situated directly to the north of the Al-Aqsa Mosque.

As mentioned in the previous chapter, during the first Kingdom of Jerusalem the Al-Aqsa Mosque was the headquarters of the Knights Templar, and the building was actually referred to by the Crusader culture as the Temple of Solomon. So the fact that the Wells quire is the same size as the biblical description of the Temple of Solomon, as well as being immediately to the south of an octagonal chapter house, seems to fit with a symbolic layout that emulates the topography of the 12th-century Temple Mount.

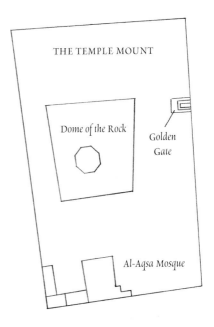

The layout of the Temple Mount in Jerusalem's Old City

57

The Crusader culture referred to the Dome of the Rock as the Temple of the Lord, and it was converted into a church during the first kingdom. Within the mindset of a 12th-century cathedral designer, who may or may not have visited Jerusalem, one would assume that these two Islamic buildings would have been looked upon as entirely Christian, and not in any way Islamic even if there was an awareness of their Islamic origin. So to use them in a design would be to incorporate significant elements of 'Christian Jerusalem' into the design of an English cathedral church.

Interestingly, the octagonal form of the Dome of the Rock has seven archways in a row on each of its outside walls, and this resembles the interior walls of the Wells chapter house – on which, again, there are seven arches per wall.

The octagonal Dome of the Rock - seven arches on each outer wall

The octagonal chapter house at Wells – seven arches on each inner wall

The apparent underlying geometric design of Wells Cathedral also suggests a very direct relationship between the quire and the chapter house. This relationship is not a liturgical one, and indeed the chapter house is not even a consecrated area within the cathedral. However, one of the pyramid triangles used in the design has its baseline running east–west through the middle of the quire, with its apex at the centre of the chapter house. The rectangle that governs the size of the 'Solomonic' quire is then derived from this pyramid triangle via a ten-pointed polygon star that is made up of two opposing pentagrams.

The pentagram star is associated with King Solomon in medieval Christian symbolism, and this appears to originate from a much older storyline within which the very building process of Solomon's temple itself is associated with the pentagram star. There will be more about the use of pyramid geometry in the design of Wells Cathedral in chapters 7 and 8.

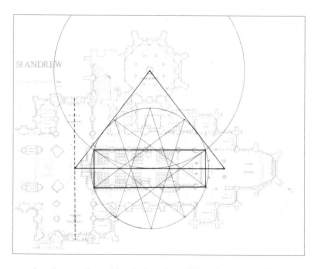

The red rectangle marking the boundary of the quire is derived from a decagram star which is itself derived from the green pyramid triangle

Returning to the Golden Gate and its association with the west door of Wells (and other Gothic cathedrals), this gate is in the eastern wall of the old city immediately before the Mount of Olives. There is an old Jewish belief that the Messiah will one day come down the Mount of Olives on a donkey and enter Jerusalem through this gate – in the Jewish tradition the gate is called the Gate of Mercy. The gate leads straight onto the Temple Mount, and in this sense it is the door that leads onwards and inwards to the temple. The west door of Wells Cathedral has a similar function to the Golden Gate in that it opens the way on to the path that leads directly up to the 'holy enclosure' – and in the case of Wells the quire appears to have been designed to replicate the dimensions of the Temple of Solomon. So despite the easterly position of the Golden Gate and the westerly position of the west door at Wells, they have the same symbolic function as the gateway inwards that leads to the holy enclosed area. The inverse location of the doorways is due to the inverse orientation of the temple in relation to a church building. The doorway to the Temple of Solomon was in the east, with the Holy of Holies in the west, whereas a cathedral generally has a main entrance in the west and a quire further to the east. However, in both cases such a portal is the symbolic threshold between the outer and inner worlds. In passing through such a doorway the soul physically enacts an inner process of transition in which it enters inwards towards the Central Place.

There is a similar analogy here – of an architectural temple relating to what might be described as an 'inner temple' – within Hindu and Buddhist mandalas such as the Sri Yantra, and Tibetan thangka mandalas. Such images essentially depict overhead views of architectural temples, and the architectural image is a visual tool that becomes the meditative focus for the inward and upward movement of the religious devotee to the Holy of Holies at the centre and summit of the 'inner temple'. Existing temples in Asia such as the Angkor Wat and Borobudur take the analogy even further, by effectively being three-dimensional architectural mandalas within which the religious adherent experiences and embodies involution and ascension.[6]

Returning to King Solomon and his temple, the Palm Sunday storyline does also appear to contain a regal Solomonic dimension in relation to Jesus riding on the colt of a donkey. The biblical description of Christ's mode of carriage recalls Zechariah's prophetic description of Kingship:

'Rejoice greatly, O daughter of Zion; shout, O daughter of Jerusalem: behold, thy King cometh unto thee: he is just, and having salvation; lowly, and riding upon an ass, and upon a colt the foal of an ass.'

Zechariah 9:9

Zechariah's words are sometimes understood as a reference to the description of Solomon's coronation in the Book of Kings which also appears to be significant in relation to Christ's 'regal' status within the 'Heavenly City'.

'And king David said, Call me Zadok the priest, and Nathan the prophet, and Benaiah the son of Jehoiada. And they came before the king. The king also said unto them, Take with you the servants of your lord, and cause Solomon my son to ride upon mine own mule, and bring him down to Gihon: And let Zadok the priest and Nathan the prophet anoint him there king over Israel: and blow ye with the trumpet, and say, God save king Solomon.'

1 Kings 1

So we are left with various questions. Did the designer of Wells Cathedral intentionally emulate the 12th-century layout of Jerusalem's Temple Mount along with the biblical description of Solomon's Temple? If so, does the design of Wells Cathedral originate from the Knights Templar themselves, because the position of the quire within the design – the heart of the whole cathedral no less – would appear to symbolically equate to the 12th-century Templar presence at the Temple of Solomon (i.e. the Al-Aqsa Mosque)? Or is the design more generally expressive of the culture and surroundings of the first Kingdom of Jerusalem, and an architectural attempt to 'bring home' to Western Europe a reminder of the glory of the 'oriental' Christian kingdom situated at the centre of the world?

6. Involution as viewed from an aerial (i.e. vertical) view, and ascension as viewed from a terrestrial (horizontal) view.

The painting here by Jean Fouquet shows a late 15th-century depiction of the building of the Temple of Solomon, in which the temple very clearly resembles a French Gothic cathedral. Such an association inevitably suggests an analogy within medieval Christian perceptions between these two architectural edifices. Whatever the facts of the matter, it can at least be said that the beating heart of Wells Cathedral, the place that still hosts the daily offices and prayers, is composed of measurements that are the same as the Temple of Solomon. So it can accordingly be suggested that, through the layout of medieval Islamic architecture on the Temple Mount, the design of Wells Cathedral presents an imaginal Christian image of the central Jewish place into which Christ entered during Holy Week as both Messiah and King in the line of David.

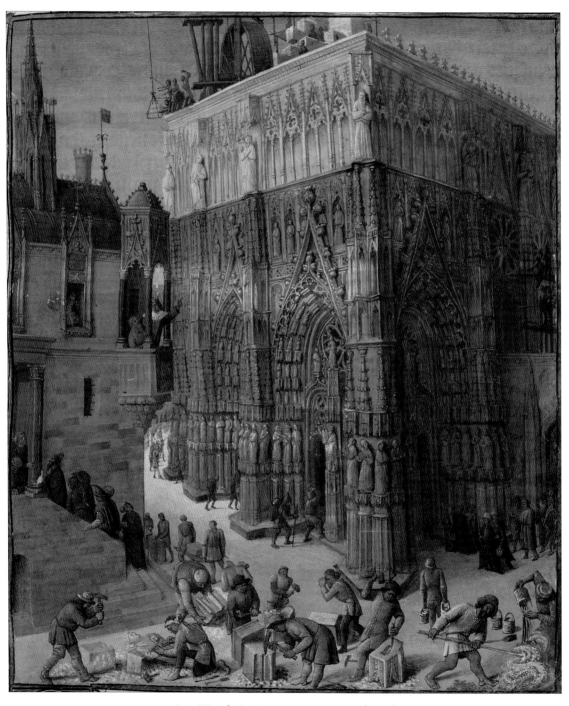

The Building of Solomon's Temple by Jean Fouquet (c 1465)

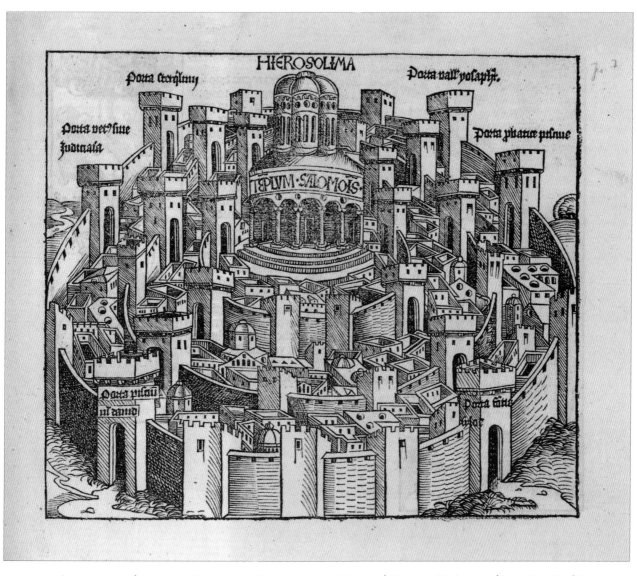

HIEROSOLIMA

Porta ttrōlmi;

Porta vall' yoſaphſt.

Porta vet' ſiue iudiciala

Porta pbancē priſiue

TĒPLVM·SALOMŌIS·

Porta piſau ul dauid

Porta ſãtē ſtof

Some 15th century images of Jerusalem would depict a centrally planned and domed 'Temple of Solomon' i.e. like the Dome of the Rock / Temple of the Lord

The three portals found on many Gothic cathedral west fronts architecturally embody a symbolic image of the three gates on each side of the Heavenly Jerusalem

Part II

The Cosmological

and Geometric Design Elements

of the First English Gothic Cathedral

CHAPTER 5.

The Lady Chapel as an Image of the Morning Star

5.1 PLANET VENUS –
THE MORNING AND EVENING STAR

In one of the final sentences of the Book of Revelation Christ proclaims his Davidic family lineage, which is one of the necessary significations of Jewish messiahship. In the same sentence he also describes himself as 'the Bright Morning Star'. It is to this particular cosmological epithet – also used for the Virgin Mary – that we shall now turn our attention

VENUS IS ONE OF THE two planets in our solar system that is closer to the Sun than Planet Earth. Earth is the third planet out from the Sun, whereas Venus is the second. Planet Mercury is then the closest. This diagram of concentric circles represents the Sun surrounded by the circular orbital pathways of Mercury, Venus and Earth.

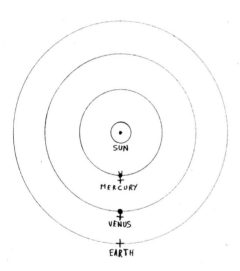

Venus and Mercury's closer orbital proximity to the Sun presents an interesting cosmological phenomenon when viewed from a geocentric (Earth-centred) perspective. Looking at the diagram, we first need to imagine ourselves located somewhere (anywhere) on Earth's circular orbital path. It then becomes possible to recognise that if we look in the direction of any part of the orbital circles of Venus and Mercury, we are looking – at least roughly – in the direction of the Sun. The furthest that Venus ever appears to stray from the

Sun is around 46° in any direction. The fact that these two planets are in closer proximity to the Sun means that they should regularly be on view to us during the daytime when the Sun is also in our sky.

However, the Sun's supernal light 'bleaches out' the starry sky, and this accordingly renders the two planets invisible during daylight hours. However, just before the Sun rises and just after it sets it is sometimes possible to see the two planets, because then the Sun is not above the horizon and thus not entirely obscuring our view of the starry sky. It is for this reason that both planets have been referred to as the Morning Star and the Evening Star. However, these titles are much more commonly associated with the planet Venus, and have now been for thousands of years.

From our geocentric viewpoint, when Venus is to the left of the Sun she is the Evening Star and accordingly visible just after sunset. Whereas when she is to the right of the Sun she is the Morning Star and henceforth visible just before the sunrise. When she passes in front of the Sun or behind the Sun she is again invisible to us due to the Sun's glare. Another significant aspect of her movement, as we see her from Earth, is that when she is in the eastern sky just before sunrise she is rising – much like the Sun. Whereas when she is in the western sky just after sunset she is descending and setting – again like the Sun. It is for this reason that the symbolism of Planet Venus is inextricably associated with the emergence and recession of light, and accordingly she is both the Morning and Evening Star.

In practical cosmological terms, the reason we can see her at all is because she reflects the light of the Sun down to us, and so we can see her illuminated body from here on Earth. But when she reflects the light of the Sun down to us the Sun itself is still hidden from our vision below the horizon. So in this sense, when Planet Venus is the Morning Star, she is the herald of the rising Sun.

The synodic period of Planet Venus takes around 584 of our Earth days to complete, which is effectively 1.6 years. This is the amount of time between inferior conjunctions, which is when a straight line is formed by the respective positions of the Sun, Venus and Earth. Put more simply, Venus orbits the Sun more quickly than Earth, so every 584 days Venus catches up and passes between Earth and the Sun, which causes an inferior conjunction between them.

As mentioned above, when Venus is to the right of the Sun she is the Morning Star. This occurs for around 263 days in a row. Then she disappears for 50 days as she passes behind the Sun. She then appears again as the Evening Star for around 263 days – having moved on to the left side of the Sun. She finally disappears again for around 8 days as she passes in front of the Sun. She is then reborn as the Morning Star for another 263 days.

263 days + 50 days + 263 days + 8 days = 584 days.

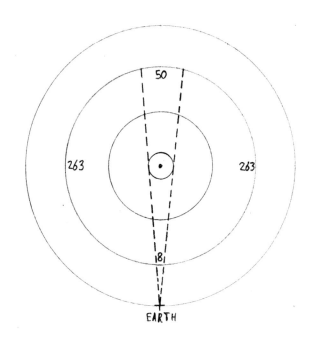

The Crescent Moon and the Morning Star in the eastern sky at dawn

5.2 LADY CHAPELS AT THE EAST ENDS OF ENGLISH GOTHIC CATHEDRALS

THERE IS A SYMBOLISM relating to the Virgin Mary in which she is the first to receive the rays of the Sun. This accords with her symbolic association as the eastern door of Solomon's temple as it is described in Ezekiel's vision – i.e. an eastern door is the first to receive the rays of the Sun when it rises in the east. The other important point about Ezekiel's description of the temple's eastern door is that it is shut, and this is understood in Christian thought to symbolise Mary's virginity. However, the shining of the Sun's rays through the window into an enclosed place is present in the symbolism of the Annunciation, in which the room or walled garden in which Mary is situated is enclosed and non-enterable by a human being. The light that shines through the window is the ray of light of the Holy Spirit by Whom the Virgin conceives the Light of the World. Interestingly, there was also an early Christian understanding that the Annunciation was the spring equinox, which in the Roman calendar was on 25 March. So again there is a symbolism here concerning the emergence of light – a primary vernal quality – and also of the east, because the spring equinox, by analogy, is associated with the eastern point of the compass.[1]

Another dimension of the Marian symbolism of eastern solar light can be seen in her title Stella Matutina – 'Morning Star'. As mentioned above, the Morning Star is specifically associated with the cosmological ascension of light in the east. In relation to Marian symbolism it is generally a reference to the idea that she reflects the light of Christ into the world, in a similar way to the Morning Star reflecting the light of the Sun into our world. There is also the accompanying idea that she precedes her son in a similar way to the Morning Star preceding the rising of the Sun, but is then eclipsed by his supernal light when he does finally arise into human vision.[2] There is also a connection with the Virgin's role as Intercessor in the sense of her having a direct line of vision towards the solarity of Christ, in contrast to humanity down here on Earth for whom the Sun is still below the horizon. In this sense the Virgin Mary, as the Intercessor, is a personification of the Edenic summit of the human soul that is in a perpetual face-to-face relationship with the light of Christ. So henceforth it is towards this summit of its own being that the soul orientates its vision when praying to the Virgin for her Intercession.

Such symbolism of emergent cosmological light from the east would appear to be one of the primary reasons why Lady chapels are found at the eastern end of English Gothic cathedrals. In effect they are architectural images of the Morning Star rising in the east. As already mentioned, the Virgin Mary as Stella Matutina could be described as a personification of the Edenic summit of the human soul, and so it is symbolically appropriate that the Lady chapel is similarly at the 'summit' of the English Gothic cathedral. As it is the part of the cathedral that is nearest to the rising of the Sun in the east, the Lady chapel is the first to receive the rays of the Sun.

Another dimension of this symbolism can be seen in the very common medieval image of the Coronation of the Virgin as Queen of Heaven. The very title 'Queen of Heaven' is itself one that has histori-

---

1. Winter is thus the 'dark and cold' northern point of the compass, summer is the sunny and warm south point, and autumn's receding light is like that of the sunset in the west.

2. A similar title, 'Bright Morning Star', is used in relation to John the Baptist who, as the forerunner of Christ, is the herald of his coming.

cally been used for various pre-Christian deities who are associated with the planet Venus though particularly for Inanna – the Sumerian Venus – who was regularly referred to by the title. Returning to the specifically Christian Marian understanding of the title, it is her crown that appears to correlate with the Lady chapel, in the sense of the Lady chapel itself being the 'crown' of the cathedral.

A similar symbolic association of east end chapels with the 'crown' is also present in a completely non-Marian form at the east end of Canterbury Cathedral, which is actually named the Corona Chapel (literally the 'crown chapel'). It is in this particular chapel that the severed head-crown of Thomas à Becket was kept as a commemoration of his martyring in 1170. The whole cathedral can accordingly be looked upon as an image of his transfigured body.

So the east end location of Lady chapels in English Gothic cathedrals appears to be related to the cosmological emergence of light in the east, and specifically to the rising of Planet Venus – the Morning Star. However, as we have seen, the rising of the Morning Star in the east is inextricably associated with the rising of the Sun, which is an image of Christ – the Light of the World – preceded by his mother the Virgin Mary as the Stella Matutina.

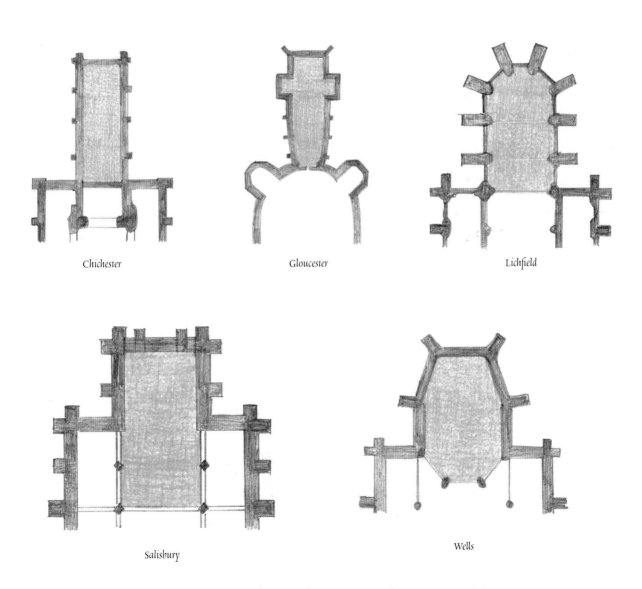

Chichester

Gloucester

Lichfield

Salisbury

Wells

A variety of English Lady chapels (shaded green) all at the east-ends of their respective cathedrals

5.3 THE PENTAGRAM AND
THE OCTAGRAM OF VENUS

A REMARKABLE GEOCOSMIC fact about the planets Earth and Venus is that they together create an almost perfect fivefold geometric symmetry through their relative movements. But even more remarkable is that, as well as forming fivefold symmetry, their relationship also produces a near-perfect eightfold symmetry. These two cosmological geometries are generally referred to as the Venus Pentagram and the Venus Octagram[3] because it is specifically these two polygon stars that the planetary relationship produces.

 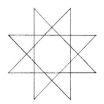

If the pentagram is a geometric embodiment of the number 5, and the octagram that of the number 8, we are accordingly also presented with two consecutive Fibonacci numbers. Indeed the Fibonacci number 13 that follows on after 5 and 8 is also present in the Earth-Venus relationship, because the amount of time it takes for the pentagram and octagram to occur is an eight-year cycle, and a period of eight Earth years (2,922 days) is virtually identical to a period of thirteen Venus years (2,921.1 days). A relationship between the Fibonacci numbers 5 and 8 can also be seen in the 584-day synodic cycle of Venus because, as explained earlier, 584 days are equal to 1.6 years, and the Fibonacci calculation 8 ÷ 5 is equal to 1.6. So accordingly, the relationship of 584 to 365 is the same as the relationship of 8 to 5. These two numbers are also seen in the fact that the planet Venus is both the Morning Star and the Evening Star for five separate synodic periods of time each over the course of an eight-year cycle.

This presence of Fibonacci numbers points in the direction of the golden ratio, and sure enough the reason for the existence of this cosmic geometry is that the orbital periods of Venus (224.7 days) and Earth (365.25 days) approximate the golden ratio of 1 to 1.618 ... Their actual relationship is 1 to 1.6255 (i.e. 365.25 days ÷ 224.7 days = 1.6255), which is virtually identical to the Fibonacci relationship 13/8 (i.e. 13 ÷ 8 = 1.625).

These Venusian geometries are possible to recognise both from a heliocentric (Sun-centred) perspective,[4] as well as from a geocentric perspective. This means that they are very likely to have been known about for millennia, because astronomers are known to have been in possession of some very sophisticated astronomical knowledge going far back into antiquity. The usual Babylonian depiction of Planet Venus – who the Babylonians called Ishtar – was quite simply an octagram star, which clearly suggests that they were aware of the Venus Octagram relationship.

'Ishtar' on the stele of King Melishipak I

3. See *A Little Book of Coincidence*, John Martineau, Wooden Books, 2000.
4. See the author's YouTube film *The Pentagram Dance of Earth and Venus*.

As for the Venus Pentagram, it occurs in the following way. Venus moves around her orbital path faster than Earth, and this means that she periodically catches up and passes Earth by. At this point of passing there is a linear relationship between Earth, Venus and the Sun. As mentioned earlier, this linear relationship is known as an inferior conjunction. This type of conjunction occurs around every 584 days. Over a period of eight years these conjunctions together gradually plot out the coordinates of a pentagram star. The diagrams to the right show two concentric circles that represent the orbital paths of Earth and Venus. The green dot is Venus and the blue dot is Earth. The diagrams sequentially show the whereabouts of these inferior conjunctions that take place every 1.6 years. The diagram also shows a gradually forming pentagram star, which follows the conjunctions in their particular order of occurrence.

The Venus Octagram works in a different way. Bearing in mind that there are eight years in this particular cosmological cycle, an octagram star will inevitably develop one of its eight stellations per year. So in this sense the diagrams below demonstrate the fact that whenever Earth returns to its starting point in an orbital cycle the positions of Venus will – year by year – gradually plot out the coordinates of an octagram star.

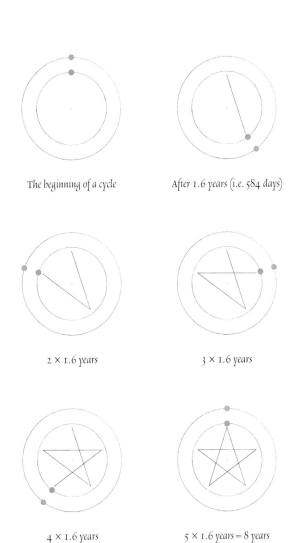

The beginning of a cycle

After 1.6 years (i.e. 584 days)

2 × 1.6 years

3 × 1.6 years

4 × 1.6 years

5 × 1.6 years = 8 years

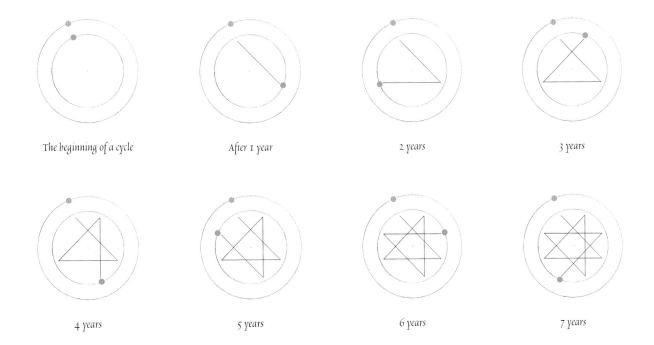

The beginning of a cycle

After 1 year

2 years

3 years

4 years

5 years

6 years

7 years

69

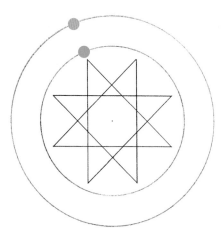

The full 8-year cycle

After a period of eight years Earth and Venus return back almost to the same positions in relation to one another, having plotted out both pentagram and octagram stars. All of the diagrams above show this phenomenon from a heliocentric perspective. However, the generation of both geometric stars can also be observed from a geocentric perspective. When viewed geocentrically, the coordinates of the geometry are effectively plotted out on the dark canvas of the starry vault overhead. This means that an Earth-bound viewer can observe the phenomenon without any need for modern technology. So it is reasonable to suggest that the ancients were aware of this heavenly display of geometric light. But for now, we will look at an apparent medieval example of such cosmological knowledge in a chapel dedicated to the Virgin Mary herself.

The Lady chapel, at the east end of Wells Cathedral

5.4 THE MORNING STAR IN THE DESIGN OF THE WELLS CATHEDRAL LADY CHAPEL

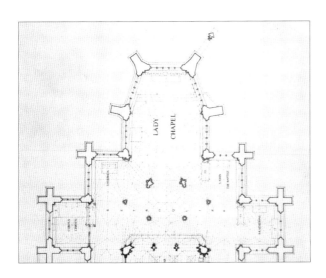

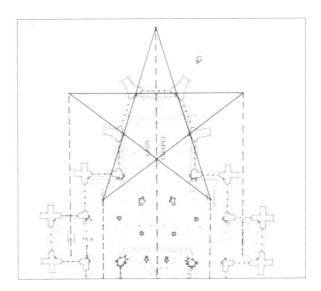

IT IS OFTEN NOTED that the ground plan of the Lady chapel at the east end of Wells Cathedral is a slightly unorthodox shape. It has been described as a stretched or elongated octagon, because its eight sides don't exhibit the more standard symmetry of a regular octagon. On closer inspection, however, it starts to become clear that this peculiarity of shape is due to the fact that the chapel's outline is actually formed by a fusion of two regular polygons – a pentagon and an octagon.

The three eastern walls of the Lady chapel are orientated in such a way that they produce three edges of a pentagon within the ground plan. Similarly the five western walls – three of which are arched entrances – form five edges of an octagon. First of all, this displays a simple Fibonacci relationship (i.e. 3 of 5 and 5 of 8 – in other words, three edges of a fivefold polygon and five edges of an eightfold polygon). More significantly, it traces out the two geometric symmetries that are associated with the movements of Planet Venus – the Morning and Evening Star.

The full extent of this correlation is made apparent when it becomes clear that the two polygons are actually the central areas of pentagram and octagram stars

which the designer has used to govern wider aspects of the design of the cathedral's east end. In the following image, for instance, the pentagon has been extended into a full pentagram star, and the dotted lines then demonstrate the axial relationships that this star has with the shape of the whole east end area of the cathedral.

The central axis of the pentagram star inevitably coincides with the central axis of the whole cathedral. The feet of the pentagram also fall along the middle axes of the side aisles, and mark the central axes of these aisles. Indeed the feet of the pentagram themselves fall around the midpoints of the two east end, side aisle chapels. The outer dotted lines then mark the central axes of the two transept chapels.

The pentagram star embodies the golden ratio, and one such example of this in the design theory depicted above can be seen in the differing distances between these dotted lines. The distance between the outer dotted lines and the side aisle dotted lines is smaller in comparison to the distance between the side aisle dotted lines and the central dotted line. These two distances – a smaller one and a larger one – embody the golden ratio of 1 to 1.618.

This pentagram star in the Lady chapel's design is generated from a larger, overarching geometric diagram that covers the whole east end area. The whole diagram will be shown in more detail in chapter 8, entitled 'The Use of Pyramid Geometry in Gothic Cathedral Design'. For now, let it just be said that the pentagram is generated through being inscribed within a particular size of circle. With this in mind, there is an interesting geometric relationship between pentagram and octagram stars that becomes apparent if they are inscribed within circles the same size as one another. This is shown in the diagram below.

Having drawn the two stars within the same size of circle, let the pentagon at the centre of the pentagram star be contained within a smaller circle. Then let the octagon at the centre of the octagram star have a circle contained within it. These two circles are very similar in size to one another.[5] If the container circle for both stars has a radius of 1, then the smaller circle that contains the pentagon has a radius of 0.382, whereas the smaller circle contained in the octagon has a radius of 0.383.

This relationship of similarity is then used to inform the design of the Wells Lady chapel, (see diagram on following page) whereby the two smaller circles are overlapped to form a Vesica Pisces arrangement, and their particular relationships with the pentagon and octagon are then used to create the overall shape of the chapel.

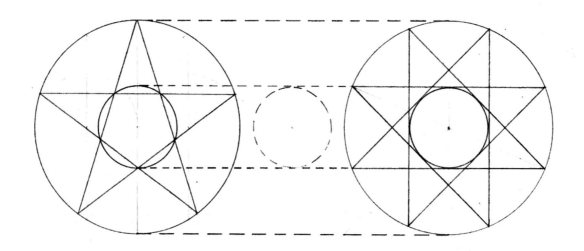

The circle that contains the pentagon is almost the same size as the circle contained within the octagon

5. See page 16 of *Sacred Geometry*, Miranda Lundy, Wooden Books, 2002, section entitled 'The Canon'.

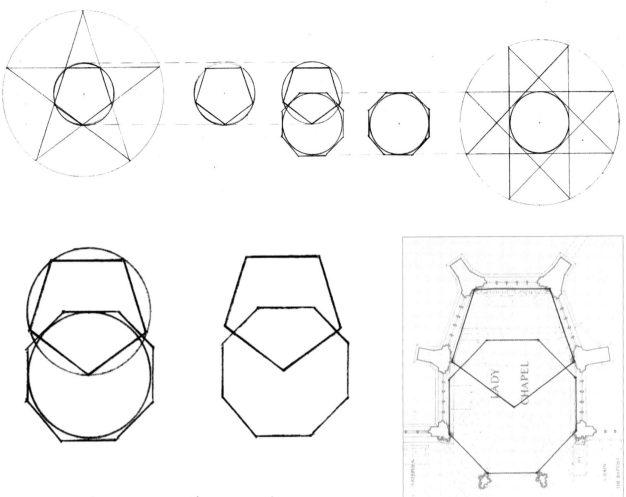

The shape of the Lady chapel as derived from pentagram and octagram stars

The fact that the shape of the Wells Lady chapel appears to be generated from a pentagon and an octagon, that have been derived from the central areas of pentagram and octagram stars, suggests even more strongly that the designer of the Wells Lady chapel used cosmological symbolism relating to the Morning Star. This particular shape of east end Lady chapel is unique to Wells, although this should not detract from the design theory proposed here. Every Gothic cathedral is unique in its design and appearance, and so to suggest that there is a uniform design symbolism and set of measurements used in all cathedral designs would seem unreasonable. However, it is very common for a Lady chapel to be located specifically at the east end of an English Gothic cathedral – although again, there is not a single Lady chapel that looks like any other.

What will also become clear as this book proceeds is that there appears to be a particularly prominent cosmological symbolism at Wells Cathedral that for some reason is not present to the same degree at any other English Gothic cathedral.

One of the most renowned features of the Wells Lady chapel is the starburst dome that crowns the chapel. This heavenly vault displays an eight-pointed star, much like the octagram star of Ishtar. But despite the Wells Lady chapel being dedicated to the Virgin Mary, the crowning image at the centre of the starburst dome is one of Christ. It is specifically an image of the risen and ascended Christ 'in Glory', although unlike most 'Glory' images here Christ is also showing his five wounds.

The Star-burst dome that crowns the Lady chapel at the east end of Wells Cathedral

This number of Christ's crucifixion wounds is the primary symbolic association that he has with the number five. So again, with an eightfold starburst dome that is centred on Christ's five wounds there is a numerical concentration upon five and eight – the two numbers that are so closely associated with the heavenly activity of the Morning and Evening Star.

Alongside this there is a whole layer of Morning Star symbolism specifically associated with Christ rather than the Virgin Mary. This symbolism chronologically precedes the Virgin's association with the Morning Star, and it relates to the paschal symbolism of Christ's death and Resurrection. It is to this that we will now turn our attention.

5.5 THE RISEN CHRIST
AS THE BRIGHT MORNING STAR

IN THE FINAL FEW VERSES of the Book of Revelation Christ uses a cosmological epithet to describe himself.

'I, Jesus, have sent my angel to give you this testimony for the churches. I am the Root and the Offspring of David, and the Bright Morning Star.'

There is no immediate indication as to what he means by the title 'Bright Morning Star', although in the medieval Roman Catholic proclamation known as the Exsultet the symbolism is quite clearly related to Christ's Resurrection, as symbolised by the cosmological re-emergence of light. The Exsultet is recited at the beginning of the Easter Vigil, specifically in close relational proximity to the newly lit paschal candle, which is an image of the light of the Risen Christ. The final few lines of this proclamation are as follows:

'May this flame be found still burning
by the Morning Star:
the one Morning Star who never sets,
Christ your Son,
who, coming back from death's domain,
has shed his peaceful light on humanity,
and lives and reigns for ever and ever.'

So the Bright Morning Star can be understood symbolically in relation to the re-emergence of light that becomes apparent through the Resurrection of Christ on Easter Sunday. Another New Testament use of the term 'Morning Star' is in Peter's second epistle:

'We also have the prophetic message as something completely reliable, and you will do well to pay attention to it, as to a light shining in a dark place, until the day dawns and the morning star rises in your hearts.'

2 Peter 1:19

This particularly beautiful use of cosmological symbolism, as a description of inward spiritual experience, again suggests that the Morning Star symbolically relates to the emergence of light through the rising of it into the world – or in this particular case, the inward emergence of spiritual illumination in the human heart.

As mentioned earlier, the planet Venus is specifically associated with the light of the Sun, and this occurs as a result of the planet always being in apparently close proximity to the Sun. As also mentioned, when visible to us Venus is either rising in the east just before sunrise or setting in the west just after sunset.

Returning to the Exsultet and its description of Christ's Resurrection, there is another significant idea appearing on two occasions, and that is Christ's rising out of the underworld:

'This is the night,
when Christ broke the prison-bars of death
and rose victorious from the underworld.'

A few lines later there is a similar refrain:

'O truly blessed night,
worthy alone to know the time and hour
when Christ rose from the underworld!'

This rising of Christ out from the underworld is a reference to the Harrowing of Hell, which is an early story associated with the non-biblical *Gospel of Nicodemus*. It is also mentioned in the Apostles' creed as well as the Athanasian creed, which places it at the heart of Christian belief. The Athanasian creed describes it in the following way:

'For as the reasonable soul and flesh is one man; so God and Man is one Christ; Who suffered for our salvation;

The ceiling boss at the centre of the star-burst dome in the Wells Lady chapel containing an image of the risen and ascended Christ.

descended into hell; rose again on the third day from the dead. He ascended into heaven, he sitteth on the right hand of God the Father Almighty, from whence he will come to judge the living and the dead.'

These paschal descriptions of descent and resurrection are significant in Christianity, but they also reflect an ancient cosmological myth that involves the descent, death and resurrection of Planet Venus – or rather 'Inanna', as she was known in ancient Sumeria.

The Descent of Inanna is an ancient storyline thought to date back to at least the third millenium BC. It describes Inanna's descent through seven levels into the underworld. Having reached the underworld she is then judged by seven judges and found to be guilty of hubris, which results in her being condemned to death. Her deathly state lasts for three days and three nights, and is then followed by her resurrection and ascension back up into Heaven from whence she came. In cosmological terms her descent is associated with the setting of the planet Venus in the west as the Evening Star, and her resurrection is associated with the rising of Venus as the Morning Star in the east.[6]

At this point it is important to remember that Inanna is Inanna and Christ is Christ. They are not the same figure and their storylines are not identical to one another, and so to suggest that Christianity has somehow conspiratorially stolen the clothes of an older religion is to again fall into the trap of mistaking perennially meaningful cosmythology for the invented property of one religious tradition over another. One could say that such storylines of death and resurrection are as Christian as they are ancient Sumerian, because a deeper symbolic understanding and experience of 'death-followed-by-resurrection' is inherent to the human experience of inward transformation. Whether it be the initiations into the mysteries that existed in the ancient world, or the Christian experience of being 'born again', *the death* of an old, more worldly, existence is an essential stage of initiatic transition prior to being

reborn in the spirit. In a certain sense baptism is another symbolically experienced form of death and resurrection, as is any other religious example of ritualistic ablution in which the previous life is washed away to enable a new life and a new start. The cosmological activity of the Sun and Planet Venus inevitably symbolise and embody such cycles of 'descent to death' and 'resurrection to new life' to any soul who witnesses their heavenly rising and setting movements, and so again there is no 'patented property' when it comes to the cosmological activity that human souls witness, regardless of the era or culture from which it is viewed. But more importantly, the same could also be said of the inward state of illumination that such cosmological occurrences outwardly reflect, which thus encourage the soul to remember its True Identity through what the philosopher Plato describes as 'anamnesis'. Within a Christian-Platonist understanding such self-knowledge is looked upon as having been lost as a result of the Fall.

But the storyline of Inanna does contain various striking likenesses to the paschal storyline, and so it seems quite reasonable to suggest that the perceived significance of this perennial storyline had some influence on the perceived significance of the paschal story of Christ. This doesn't mean that the paschal storyline is a fabrication that never actually took place, but rather that it runs in accord with a perennial storyline of death-and-descent-followed-by-resurrection over a three-day period. Cosmologically speaking, this is rather like the three-day period of darkness during which the Moon disappears when she goes through her own experience of death – descent into darkness – and resurrection while she changes over from her waning to her waxing periods (i.e. at the new moon).

Returning to Inanna, the interesting correlation between the story of her descent into the underworld and the paschal storyline presents itself in the Gospel of Matthew via the Book of Jonah. It relates to the period of time that Inanna, Jonah and Christ all spend in the depths, or '... deep in the realm of the dead ...' as

6. See *Inanna and Sukaletuda: A Sumerian Astral Myth* by Jeffrey Cooley, 2008.

the Book of Jonah describes the interior of the whale (Jonah, 2:2). This deathly realm is known as 'Sheol' in the Hebrew tradition, and it is the same underworld that Christ descends into with his Harrowing of Hell.

In Matthew's Gospel Christ associates his death, descent into Sheol and Resurrection with the period of time that Jonah spent in the whale.

'For as Jonah was three days and three nights in the belly of a huge fish, so the Son of Man will be three days and three nights in the heart of the earth.'

12:40

The interesting thing about such an allegorical comparison between Christ and Jonah is that if one were to actually calculate the amount of time between Christ's death on the afternoon of Good Friday and his Resurrection on the morning of Easter Sunday, it adds up to a duration shorter than two days and only covers two nights. Having said this, there is no difficulty with talking about the number 3 in relation to the duration of Christ's Harrowing of Hell. If Good Friday can be looked on as 'day-one', Holy Saturday is then day-two and Easter Sunday becomes the 'third day'. But strictly speaking, this period of time can't be described as three days and three nights. Later in Matthew's Gospel Christ again refers to his death and Resurrection in relation to three days, although this time he says,

'The Son of Man is going to be delivered into the hands of men. They will kill him, and on the third day he will be raised to life.'

17:22–23

So the allegorical connection that Christ makes between his own story and that of Jonah's involves a certain stretching of number symbolism, although in spirit it has a clear numero-symbolic basis in the sense of them both moving downwards into the deathly realm of Sheol for a temporary period of time associated with three days.[7] But Jonah's story doesn't involve the cosmological symbolism of the planet Venus – i.e. the Morning Star and its rising in the east – whereas the stories of both Christ and Inanna do. Also Jonah is described as being in a whale whereas Inanna is in the underworld, which is more overtly similar to the description of Christ in the Exsultet, or indeed in Matthew's Gospel where Christ describes himself as being in 'the heart of the earth'. So in a certain sense Christ and Inanna's storylines appear to resemble one another more so. But on the other hand it is Jonah and Inanna who are in a deathly state for a period of three days and three nights. However, in all three cases this deep deathly realm involves a situation in which there is a judgement of guilt that results in some kind of tribulation. Inanna is given a death sentence as a result of her hubris, whereas Jonah has descended into his particular predicament specifically as a result of his evading God's request to preach to the people of Ninevah. Similarly the underworld that Christ descends into is a place containing souls that have been condemned to a deathly entrapment that has resulted from the fall of humanity. It is the prison of Adam and Eve, whose erring from God's law is pretty much the opening theme of the whole Judeo-Christian tradition. They are subsequently released as a result of Christ's journey downwards, along with various Old Testament figures who preceded Christ's time on Earth. St Paul addresses this in chapter 4 of Ephesians through a meditation on Psalm 68:

'But to each one of us grace has been given as Christ apportioned it. This is why it says:
"When he ascended on high, he took many captives and gave gifts to his people."
(What does "he ascended" mean except that he also descended to the lower, earthly regions? He who descended is the very one who ascended higher than all the heavens, in order to fill the whole universe.)'

---

7. The use of numerical symbolism in mythology is primarily to do with the quality of the number itself rather than a literal interpretation of precise and realistic numerical objects and/or durations of time. In this particular instance it is the association of the number 3 with what could be described as 'underworldly initiatic death and rebirth' which is the numerical quality that is being focused upon whether it be via '3 days and 3 nights' or a first, second and third day.

Musician Angels and the Harrowing of Hell. Anonymous - Flemish. 1290.

In all three storylines a judgement of guilt has brought about a deathly state in a place deep down below the surface of the Earth. But after a three-day period the deathly state comes to an end, which leads to a liberation in the form of a return back upwards and out of the depths. Inanna rises out from the underworld into the eastern sky in the form of the Morning Star, whereas Jonah is vomited out from the whale. In paschal terms Christ rises on the third day and brings Adam and Eve out from the underworld. In doing so he 'shed[s] his peaceful light on humanity' as the Bright Morning Star rising in the east. With all of this in mind we can then return to our focus on the Lady chapel at Wells, and it is inevitably of interest that the chapel's crowning image at the centre of the eightfold starburst dome overhead is one of the Risen and Ascended Christ. Indeed the five wounds that this image of Christ displays are also symbolically represented on the paschal candle in the form of five grains of incense that are inserted into the candle itself.

What are we to make of this recurring storyline of descent and resurrection over a three-day period? It is a story that Dante Alighieri very clearly uses in his *Divine Comedy*. Much like Christ – or rather in apparent emulation of Christ – Dante descends into the Inferno from the city of Jerusalem on the evening of Good Friday, and he travels down through the nine rings of hell quite literally into the 'heart of the earth'. he passes beyond the centre of the Earth, and subsequently rises back up to the Earth's surface on the opposite side. He then ascends the Mountain of Purgatory, which has the Garden of Eden at its summit.

The final stage of the journey is then his ascent up through the planetary spheres and beyond the stars to a final meeting with God in the Empyrean. All of this speaks of the initiatic journey of the soul, which has to begin with a 'descending' stage of some sort – a descent into the underworld to meet the minotaur – or in other words, the untamed animal of our being. This raw unsublimated state of soul needs to be vanquished, 'brought to order' or 'mastered'[8] before the soul is then ready to attempt the climb back up to its heavenly origin. Dante makes this climb, and just before his final union with God he uses the symbol of the Morning Star illuminated by the Sun as a description of St Bernard of Clairvaux – his final guide – illuminated by the solarity of the Virgin Mary. This can be understood to be the 'Marian' woman described in the Book of Revelation who is 'clothed in the Sun'.[9]

As just mentioned, the initiatic journey of the soul needs to begin with a challenging stage of some sort, which symbolically consists of a descent. This is a preparatory stage where the ground is prepared for the sowing of the seed. The seed itself needs to descend into the earth before there can be an ascent of the plant's greenness that grows forth irresistibly from the seed in an upward direction towards the heavenly illumination of the Sun. The fact that the preparation of the soil is necessary prior to this speaks of a harrowing of the soul and Christ's Harrowing of Hell, which is the necessary stage of descent that Christ goes through prior to his re-ascent. The harrow is an item of farming equipment that prepares the soil for the sowing of the seed, which it does by effectively refining the ground so it is

---

8. A particular interpretation here that accords with medieval Christian perceptions is that the Minotaur was itself conceived as a result of a lustful act on the part of King Minos' wife, Pasiphae, with a white bull (for example see Canto 26 of Dante's *Purgatorio*). Minos was supposed to have sacrificed this white bull for Poseidon, the deity from whom he had received it in the first place, but he actively avoided doing what Poseidon had requested and this subsequently led to Pasiphae's conception of the Minotaur. So again, with the underworld in mind as the place of confrontation of the soul with its lower tendencies, the Minotaur was conceived as a result of a human being (Minos) erring from a divine request, followed by another human being (Pasiphae) submitting to her unbridled 'animalistic' lust. From a Christian perspective the Minotaur could thus appear to be an embodiment, or a resulting outcome, of 1) the disobedience of King Minos (i.e. hubris) ... and 2) the untamed passions of Pasiphae (i.e. unbridled physical appetites). In other words, 'Whatsoever a man soweth, that shall he also reap.' (Galatians, 6:7) ... and so as a result of Minos' and Pasiphae's ignoble conduct the Minotaur was born and had to be locked up in the labyrinthine underworld for the sake of everyone's safety. Theseus is then the initiate who makes the descent into the labyrinth to confront and subdue/vanquish the Minotaur that is hiding, as it were, within the dark recesses and passageways of his soul.
9. *Paradiso*, Canto 32, 106–108.

ready to receive the seed and bring forth a good harvest.[10] However, this refining process is a rather 'harrowing' experience for the ground, because the harrow is quite literally dragged across it so as to break up the large clods of earth. The first stage of any spiritual path requires the breaking up of the large clods of ego and pride that form impassable obstacles to the soul's progress in the return to its True Self.

A harrow in Les très riches heures du Duc de Berry, *1412–16*

Such agrarian symbolism is used on various occasions within the bible particularly in the parable of the sower which focuses upon the essential need that the seed has for good soil if it is to grow well. Boethius also uses similar symbolism in one of his poems in his *Consolation of Philosophy*:[11]

'Whoever wants to sow in virgin soil
First frees the fields of undergrowth and bush,

Cuts back thick ferns and brambles with the scythe
And clears the way for crops of swelling wheat.'

Book 3, Chapter 1

Such 'virgin soil' symbolises the emptiness or 'kenosis' required before there can be any receipt of illumination.

Returning to Inanna, Jonah and Christ, there is a three-day period in all three of their stories, and indeed the number 3 is closely associated with initiation into the mysteries. The Greek Eleusinian Mysteries, for instance, consisted of three stages that can be described as Descent, Search and Re-ascent. To this day Freemasonry still has three degrees of initiation, and of course there is also Dante's threefold journey through the Inferno, Purgatorio and Paradiso. In the words of René Guénon,

'The division of initiation into three grades is moreover the most frequent and, we might say, the most funda-mental ... all the others [i.e. where there are more/less than three grades] only represent ... subdivisions of more or less complicated elaboration.' [12]

From a directly Christian perspective the number 3 also relates to the Trinity – the Father, the Son and their unity in the Holy Spirit. More widely speaking, the unifying quality of the third of three things is intimately connected to what could be described as a non-dual path of unity – or in other words, a middle way. Finding the mean between extremes is a 'centrally' important aspect of the spiritual path because it involves finding a unifying third way that unites all apparent polarities.[13] In this sense the third way is that which re-asserts the unity that is lost when the one original path divides into two separate paths. As will become clear, this perception of a middle path is absolutely key to the overall design symbolism of Wells Cathedral.

10. See John 12:24.
11. Also see Dante, *Purgatorio*, Canto 14, verses 88–105.
12. René Guénon, *Symbols of Sacred Science*, Sophia Perennis, 2004, chapter 10, page 75.
13. The story that immediately follows the Minotaur in the maze is that of Icarus and his attempts to fly with wings that had been made by his father, Daedalus. The young and inexperienced Icarus disregards the advice of his father (i.e. the experienced elder) to take the 'middle path' between the moisture of the sea and the heat of the Sun, as both of these extremes - essentially fire and water - will damage his wings. He subsequently flies too close to the heat of the Sun, which results in him crashing down into the moisture of the sea.

5.6 JERUSALEM – 'ESTABLISHED BY PLANET VENUS'

THERE IS AN INTERESTING etymological theory in relation to the name of the holy city of Jerusalem. Some scholars suggest that the name originates from *Yeru Shalim*, which is understood to mean 'established by Shalim'.

Shalim was the name of Planet Venus in the Canaanite tradition. However, Shalim was specifically the planet Venus in the form of the Evening Star rather than the Morning Star. The equivalent deity Shahar was the Morning Star, and he and Shalim were understood to be twin brothers.

Bearing in mind the cosmological association of the setting of the Evening Star in the west with a descent into the underworld, herein lies another interesting correlation with Christ, whose descent into Sheol also began from Jerusalem. This correlation takes on another dimension of interest in relation to the fact that the Holy Sepulchre – the church marking the place where Christ's body was interred after his death – was built over the site of a Roman temple dedicated to Aphrodite/Venus. There are differing opinions as to whether this temple preceded the site's association with Christ's Passion or vice versa, and this will probably forever remain unknowable. But the very fact that there is any association at all between these different characters who are associated with the Morning/Evening Star leaves us with an interesting coinciding of different figures from various traditions who symbolise a similar cosmic archetype.

There is also a geometric dimension to Jerusalem's apparent association with the planet Venus. This can be seen in the fact that the pentagram star was a symbol of the city in ancient times. Many examples have been found, of a stamp in ceramic, which display a pentagram star. The five consonants of Jerusalem's name (Y – R – Sh – L – M) are then written within the star with one consonant in each of the star's five stellations. This in itself appears to emphasise the 'fiveness' of the city's identity. Words and numbers are of central significance in Jewish beliefs.

In the final chapter of this book (sec 21.2) another apparently 'Venusian' aspect of Jerusalem will be expanded upon. The latitude of Jerusalem, and its association with the numbers five and eight, may suggest the reason why this city of *Death and Resurrection* is looked upon as having been 'established by Venus'.

CHAPTER 6.

The Virgin Mary as the Rose and the Stella Matutina

6.1 THE VIRGIN MARY AND THE
FIVE-FOLD ROSE OF EDEN

As well as being associated with the number seven the Virgin Mary is also associated with the number five, and this accords with what was written in the previous chapter about her title Stella Matutina and the five-fold movement of Planet Venus – the Morning Star. However, such a numerical association has only ever been present in Roman Catholicism, and not the Orthodox tradition. Its origins appear to lie in the 12th century, as this is when traces of it begin to become apparent. By the 14th century it was very much established, and a good example of a particular focus on such numerical symbolism is in a chivalric Arthurian romance called *Sir Gawain and the Green Knight*. The poem goes into great detail about the golden pentagram on Gawain's red shield and the five 'fivenesses' that it symbolises, which involve Christ, the Virgin Mary and Gawain's own physical body and moral character. The five fivenesses are his five senses, the five fingers on his hand,[1] the five wounds of Christ, the five joys of Mary, and five virtuous chivalric characteristics – generosity, fellowship, purity, continence and piety.

The golden pentagram is on the front of Gawain's shield, whereas an image of the Virgin Mary is on the back, or the 'inner' side – close to Gawain's heart and within his immediate view. The writer also associates the pentagram with King Solomon, an association seemingly first made in writing within the *Testament of Solomon* (c. 1st–5th century AD) in relation to the seal upon Solomon's ring.[2]

Another Marian fiveness that features prominently within medieval symbolism is the rose – which is five-

The wild rose with its five petals

fold in form. More generally it symbolises a 'heavenly' female – although, from an overtly Christian perspective, it is effectively the Virgin Mary who herself came to be known as Rosa Sine Spina (Thornless Rose) and Rosa Mystica (Mystical Rose). The wild or dog rose is the type of rose depicted in medieval iconography, and the flower has five petals and five sepals. The medieval depiction of the rose is usually symbolically understood to be a rose with no thorns, which is essentially a symbol of the Edenic soul. Going back to early Christianity, both St Basil and St Ambrose use this symbol within their written works about the six days of Creation (the Hexameron). The rose is said to have grown in the Garden of Eden, albeit without any thorns. The thorns are the passions or the suffering of the earthly world, as reflected by Christ's crown of thorns. The Old Testament understanding of this symbolism of thorns comes straight from the Book of Genesis in God's words to Adam and Eve once they had eaten of the tree of knowledge.

---

1. See the later section entitled 'The hand of Fatimah and the number five'.
2. Gervase of Tilbury mentions this Solomonic association with magic rings in his *Otia Iperialia* (c. 1209–1214).

'cursed is the ground for thy sake; in sorrow shalt thou eat of it all the days of thy life; Thorns also and thistles shall it bring forth to thee; and thou shalt eat the herb of the field'

Genesis 3:17–18

So these 'thorns and thistles' are identified with the rose thorns that are described as having eventually afflicted the rose after the fall of humanity. In his Hexameron, St Ambrose writes:

'... without thorns, the rose, most beautiful of all flowers, displayed its beauty without guile; afterwards, the thorn fenced around this charming flower, presenting, as it were, an image of human life in which what is pleasing in our activities is often accompanied with the stings of anxieties which everywhere surround us.'

Hexameron, Chapter 11

In this sense the Virgin Mary as 'the rose with no thorns' is a personification of the soul that has returned to the Garden of Eden, and this is again related to her role as Intercessor, because the Edenic soul could be described as being in a perpetual face-to-face relationship with God. Along with the five-fold rose, this floral symbolism also includes the six-fold lily, as described by St Bernard of Clairvaux in one of his sermons for the feast of the Virgin's nativity:

'Dearest Brethren, let us take care to have our souls adorned with lilies; let us hasten to root out the "thorns and thistles" and to plant lilies in their place; perchance then the Beloved will sometime show Himself so condescending as to come to feed even in us. Needless to say, He was wont to feed in Mary, and that the more abundantly in proportion to the multitude of lilies He found in her ...'

St Bernard is here also referring to the opening words of chapter 2 in the Song of Solomon:

'I am the flower of the field, and the lily of the valleys. As the lily among thorns, so is my love among the daughters.'

This floral symbolism of the Virgin Mary in the Garden of Eden would seem also to be connected to her association with the so-called Hortus Conclusus (enclosed garden) which, like the Marian lily, is mentioned in the Song of Solomon:

'A garden enclosed is my sister, my spouse; a spring shut up, a fountain sealed.'

4:12

This 'enclosed garden' is understood to be a sacred precinct or sanctuary due to it being walled off and thus inviolable. Such an inviolable inner place is in one sense a symbol of Mary's womb and her sexual virginity. But more importantly her virginity can itself be looked upon as a symbol of the soul's inward state, in which it is completely untouched, pure and empty (kenosis), which makes it possible to conceive the divine Logos, via the Holy Spirit.[3] Again there is the symbolism that the Virgin Mary personifies the Edenic state towards which the soul aspires through prayer and remembrance of God – the Divine Being in the image of which the soul was created.

The Garden of Eden brings us back yet again to the symbolism of an east end Lady chapel. In medieval world maps the Garden of Eden was depicted as being at the easternmost point of the map, rather like the Lady chapel at the easternmost point of a cathedral. The Wells Lady chapel is then also filled with thornless stone roses – a whole garland of them stretching around the walls. These are all symbols of the 'eternal spring' characteristic of Eden. In terms of orientational symbolism such a vernal and verdant state is symbolised by the eastern point of the compass. The east is also the region of the sky in which the Morning Star rises at dawn, heralding the return of the daylight in a similar way to springtime heralding the return of the light

---

3. An Islamic equivalent to this is Mohammed's illiteracy (whereby he is empty of worldly learning), which accordingly allows him to be open to the receipt of the divine learning of the Koran. Plato also speaks of a similar state in *Timaeus* 50e and 51a in relation to a liquid vehicle of a perfume needing to be devoid of any other scents if it is to truly embody the scent of the perfume.

Pentagram extending into a five petalled rose - Ermita de San Bartolomé

View of the window from the inside - a rose of light

within the annual cycle. This eternal spring symbolises the capacity of the eternally fecund, yet virginal, soul to conceive Christ at the spring equinox. But the symbolism also applies to the Resurrection of Christ at Easter, here described by the medievalist and musicologist David J. Rothenberg.

'In the liturgy of Easter ... spring blossoms were an earthly sign of the salvation made possible by Christ's Resurrection. The earthly vibrancy of the vernal season did more than provide a vocabulary of images common to both secular springtime song and sacred Paschal devotion; it symbolised a profound theological connection between the two. When an earthly beloved was venerated as a sweet rose or a fair lily, she was elevated through likeness to Mary. When Mary was praised with the same imagery, she was humanised, her mercy made more accessible and immediate. And when either Mary or an earthly maiden was aligned with the wonders of the spring season, she absorbed the salvific potential of the Resurrection.'

So in this sense the thornless flowers of Eden, the equinoctial conception of Christ, the Resurrection, the rising of the Sun and Morning Star are all associated with the east and the Edenic state of 'eternal spring'. As will

become clear later in the book, this idea of an eternal equinoctial spring is actually geocosmically expressed within the design of Wells Cathedral, and similarly also in John Milton's 17th-century poem *Paradise Lost.*[4]

Returning to the symbolism of the rose there is a distinction, as in medieval alchemy, between the red rose and the white rose. The white rose often symbolises the Virgin Mary and the red rose Christ. However the following words, again from St Bernard of Clairvaux, describe both types of rose in relation to the Virgin Mary, who unites their complementary qualities. He begins with a similar symbolism to St Basil and St Ambrose in relation to the fall and the rose's thorns, and describes Eve and the Virgin Mary analogously, whereby they are effectively the two opposite directions of movement on the same 'vertical' path that leads to and from Eden: Eve descends whereas the Virgin re-ascends.

'To commend His grace to us, and to destroy human wisdom, God was pleased to take flesh of a woman who was a virgin, and so to restore like by like, to cure a contrary by a contrary, to draw out the poisonous thorn, and most effectively to blot out the decree of sin. Eve was a thorn; Mary is a rose. Eve was a thorn in her wounding; Mary a rose

4. The association of 'eternal spring' with an ideal 'Edenic' state, tragically lost, is described by Ovid in Book 5 of his *Metamorphoses* in relation to Pluto's abduction of Proserpine. This event then causes the instigation of the seasonal fluctuation between solstitial light and dark after having originally been in an eternal 'equinoctial' spring, within which day and night-time hours were forever in an ideal and equal balance. The association of Eden with the rising of the Sun in the east is reflected in Dante's *Commedia* in that he enters Eden at sunrise and soon after associates Matilda with Proserpine. (see Purg 28 :49-51)

in the sweetening of the affections of all. Eve was a thorn fastening death upon all; Mary is a rose giving the heritage of salvation back to all. Mary was a white rose by reason of her virginity, a red rose by reason of her charity; white in her body, red in her soul; white in cultivating virtue, red in treading down vice; white in purifying affection, red in mortifying the flesh; white in loving God, red in having compassion on her neighbour.'

The Roman Breviary –
the Feast of Our Lady of the Rosary

A few traces of this rose symbolism remain in the Dowry of Mary itself. As mentioned earlier, England was known in the medieval era as the Dowry of Mary because of the great devotion that the English had to the Virgin. So it is perhaps of little surprise that the national symbol of England is a rose. The origins of this national symbol are ultimately in the white rose of York, which was a Marian symbol of the first Duke of York. The usual story is then that, at a later date, the red rose became associated with the Lancastrians and eventually the red and white roses were united in the form of the Tudor rose. However, the Tudor rose appears to be far more alchemical in its symbolism than is generally suggested by modern historians. The marrying of the white (feminine, i.e. Elizabeth of York) and the red (masculine, i.e. Henry VII) is a symbolism that appears to come straight out of the medieval Christian understanding of alchemy, which was at its height in the late medieval and Tudor eras.5

The other English association with the rose is the English Rose 'herself' – an epithet for a beautiful English woman of light complexion. This kind of symbolism, in which there is an idealisation of the female, would appear to have its origins in the medieval culture of courtly love and chivalry, which brings us back to the Virgin Mary and the rose as an image

of a 'heavenly' and 'thornless' female. The troubadours expressed this culture of courtly love in the form of poetry and music, and so the final word shall go to one such 13th-century troubadour/cleric called Peire de Corbiac. In the words of his 'Hymn to the Virgin' he addresses the Virgin Mary with the following invocation. Note the symbolic pairing of the thornless rose and the Morning Star in the first verse. This 'star' is the 'mother of the sun' because she immediately precedes the Sun in the same way that the Mother of God preceded her Son. She is therefore also the 'nurse' of her 'own father'.

'Lady, rose without thorn,
sweet above all flowers,
dry rod bearing fruit,
earth bringing forth fruit without toil,
star, mother of the sun,
nurse of thine own Father,6
in the world no woman is like to thee,
neither far nor near.

Lady, virgin pure and fair
before the birth was
and afterwards the same,
received human flesh in thee
Jesus Christ our Saviour,
just as without causing flaw,
the fair ray enters when the sun shines
through the window-pane.

Lady, star of the sea,
brighter than the other stars,
the sea and the wind buffet us;
show thou us the right way:
for if thou wilt bring us to a fair haven,
ship nor helmsman fears
not tempest nor tide
lest it trouble us'

---

5. This is sometimes depicted in Alchemy as the chemical marriage between the Red King and the White Queen.
6. This epithet is very similar to an epithet of Prophet Mohammed's daughter Fatimah Zahra, who is known to Shia Muslims as 'Mother of her father'. See the later section entitled 'The cosmological resemblance of the Virgin Mary and Fatimah Zahra'.

6.2 THE ROSE IN FAIRY TALES
AND THE RETURN TO EDEN

THERE ARE VARIOUS examples of fairy tales and ancient myths in which the symbols of a rose and a female play an essential part in the transformation of someone back into their 'True' or original state. This reflects the idea of the soul returning back to its Edenic state, which could be described as the soul's True Self because it was originally created in God's image. It was through the fall of humanity that the soul lapsed into its state of forgetfulness of its True Self and so accordingly it is through remembrance or 'anamnesis' that the soul is afforded a return to its original Edenic state. The storylines express this remembrance, and return of the soul via some sort of interaction with a female and a rose and often with the experience of love – because it is ultimately the forgetfulness of Divine Love that keeps the soul divorced or in exile from God.

One such fairy tale that follows this pattern is 'Beauty and the Beast', in which an expression of love by a woman who symbolises a rose brings about a transformation of a beast back to his original self, a royal prince.

Another fairy tale with a similar pattern is 'Snow White and Rose Red'. In this storyline there are two girls, who symbolise a red and a white rose, and whose kind and helpful behaviour help a bear to return to his true self, which is again a prince.

A much older storyline with a similar principle is Apuleius' 'Metamorphoses', which is also known as 'The Golden Ass'. This story is from the late 2nd century AD, although it is essentially pre-Christian because it didn't emanate from overtly Christian culture as such, and is far more associated with the culture of the ancient world. Interestingly, the story's association of the rose with Isis and their joint involvement in helping Lucius return to his original human state, after having unwittingly turned himself into an ass, resembles the eventual Christian use of the Virgin Mary and the thornless rose as symbols of the soul's return to Eden. St Basil and St Ambrose wrote about the thornless rose in the Garden of Eden just a couple of centuries after Apuleius' story was written.

Tudor Rose by Lily Corbett

For an overtly Christian example of this female rose we need look no further than the culmination of Dante's *Divine Comedy*, in which, after all of his journeying downwards and back upwards, he finally reaches a giant white rose in which the petals themselves are the souls of all the faithful. The Virgin Mary is at the centre of this rose, and it is through her intercession that Dante's final guide – St Bernard of Clairvaux – makes Dante's meeting with God possible. Dante at first geometrically describes the Trinitarian God as three circles. However, the moment of union itself comes in a flash and is beyond words or description. Dante had already used the geometric symbolism of the mathematical impossibility of the 'squaring of the circle' to express the incapacity of humanly understood words, ideas and material forms alone in allowing the soul to inwardly know a union between heaven and earth. But through a sudden moment of grace Dante's soul becomes aligned and as one with the Divine Love that pervades the whole universe.

'In the profound and shining-clear Existence
Of the deep Light appeared to me three circles
Of one dimension and three different colours.

One seemed to be reflected by the other,
Rainbow by rainbow, while the third seemed fire
Breathed equally from one and from the other.

O how pale now is language and how paltry
For my conception! And for what I saw
My words are not enough to call them meagre.

O everlasting Light, you dwell alone
In yourself, know yourself alone, and known
And knowing, love and smile upon yourself!

That middle circle which appeared in you
To be conceived as a reflected light,
After my eyes had studied it a while,

Within itself and in its colouring
Seemed to be painted with our human likeness
So that my eyes were wholly focused on it.

As the geometer who sets himself
To square the circle and who cannot find,
For all his thought, the principle he needs,

Just so was I on seeing this new vision
I wanted to see how our image fuses
Into the circle and finds its place in it,

Yet my wings were not meant for such a flight –
Except that then my mind was struck by lightning
Through which my longing was at last fulfilled.

Here powers failed my high imagination:
But by now my desire and will were turned,
Like a balanced wheel rotated evenly,

By the Love that moves the sun and the other stars.

Paradiso, Canto XXXIII 115–145

The final example of a story involving a woman and a rose is 'Sleeping Beauty'. This particular story has developed and been much added to since its written form was first produced by Charles Perrault, and this developed version is focused upon in the following description, because it follows the themes looked at in this section so closely.

The story is very much in keeping with the symbolism of the Morning Star – a slightly earlier written version of the story is called 'Sun, Moon and Talia', which itself contains traces of the ancient mythology of the Morning Star, such as the rape of Talia in her sleep, which reflects the ancient Sumerian storyline of the rape of Inanna in her sleep by a gardener called Sukaletuda. 'Sleeping Beauty' involves the idea of awakening in the morning light and in this sense it follows the theme of the soul's return via its reawakening to an illuminated state in the light of day. Aurora was the Roman Goddess of the Dawn, and mythologically she is a female to whom the soul becomes awake in the morning. The rose is very much associated with her, and she is also the mother of the Morning Star. Aurora is actually the name of the Sleeping Beauty herself.7

The story of Sleeping Beauty begins in a happy state within the walls of a royal palace or castle, in which she

7. This name was first used in Tchaikovsky's ballet, written in 1889, although in the German Grimm's version she is called Little Briar Rose.

is a princess who has been born to a king and queen after much longing on their part for a child. This is itself reminiscent of the story in the Protoevangelium of James of Joachim and Anne, the parents of the Virgin Mary, who struggled to conceive Mary. The castle walls are also symbolically reminiscent of the enclosed Edenic garden of the Hortus Conclusus. But at this princess's christening she receives a curse that she will prick her finger on a spindle and die. The curse is then transmuted into a lesser one in which Aurora will only fall asleep for 100 years rather than die.[8]

Sleeping Beauty by John Collier

All attempts are made by the King to stop this fate from befalling his daughter, but in the sense that it is impossible to stop a child from growing up into an adult, so the King is unable to keep his daughter from her slumberous fate. So, tragically, the spiritual wakefulness of the child falls asleep with the onset of adulthood, and in the story this is associated with the pricking of the finger on the spindle resulting in Aurora's bleeding, which in turn symbolises the onset of menstruation and puberty. The leaving of the Garden of Eden is symbolically associated with the onset of adulthood and sexuality, because it is when the human becomes 'ashamed to be seen naked'.[9] Everyone else in the castle falls asleep along with

Aurora, and a huge prickly briar slowly begins to grow around the castle, making it impregnable. So it is the 'passional' thorns that bar the soul from returning back to its inward Edenic state of spiritual wakefulness.

At this point in the story the focus moves beyond the castle walls into the 'outer world' that lies, as it were, beyond the Garden of Eden, and to a particular soul who is often portrayed as a prince. He is looking to find his way back into the world of inward wakefulness symbolised by the rosy illuminating aurora of dawn. He is aware that there is a beautiful princess who lies asleep within the castle walls, and his intention is to find her and (re)awaken her. But how can he make his way through the prickly briar rose thorns that have now grown up around the castle? Many who have attempted this journey previously, and tried to enter the castle, have become caught up in the rose thorns of earthly passion and perished. However, when the prince eventually approaches the briar it opens up of its own accord, creating a passageway through. This particular prince is pure of heart and is thus ready to enter within, because he has risen above the 'thorns and thistles' of earthly suffering. He walks through the sleeping castle until he finds Aurora in her slumber and awakens her with a kiss, which is sometimes described as being to her brow. In doing so he reawakens that which had fallen asleep 'within him' at the onset of adulthood. Henceforth the exile from Eden comes to an end, and the inner and outer worlds are united in matrimony.

Much like the artisan apprentice – the unconscious innocent – who is thrown out of the 'Edenic' workshop by the master to wander the outer world as a journeyman, the third and final stage of this artisan is to then return to the inner world of the workshop, but this time as a master who has perfected his craft. The apprentice and the master both reside within the same Edenic workshop, although they are in a radically different state of 'wakeful' knowledge compared to one another.

8. One hundred years of sleep prior to an awakening reflects Dante's final 'wakeful' meeting with God at the end of the one-hundredth canto of *The Divine Comedy*. See also the later section concerning '99 + 1', entitled 'The Tasbih of Fatimah and the ninety-nine beads'.

9. 'At that moment their eyes were opened, and they suddenly felt shame at their nakedness. So they sewed fig leaves together to cover themselves', Genesis 3:7.

6.3 THE ASSOCIATION OF THE ROSE WITH PLANET VENUS

WITH THE ASSOCIATIONS already mentioned in relation to the Morning Star, the Virgin Mary, the rose and the number five, we find ourselves going back into ancient history, because the rose is also one of the main symbols of various pre-Christian female deities who are associated with the Planet Venus and love.

Venus, the Roman Goddess of love, is strongly associated with the rose, as is her Greek equivalent Aphrodite. So the association of the Virgin Mary with the rose and the Morning Star appears to be a Christian version of this ancient archetype of love. It is the embracing and incorporating of perennial archetypes such as these that could be said to feed a religion in much the same way that oxygen enlivens the blood, which in turn facilitates the sending of the breath or 'spirit' around the body. Part of the historical fantasy of Puritanism is that there was once a pure and untouched version of Christianity that eventually became infiltrated and polluted by a pre-Christian paganism. But such pre-Christian influences have always been present in Christianity. As mentioned in section 1.1, St Augustine even wrote metaphorically about the 'Gold and Silver' that had been mined by previous traditions, and how it was of value to Christians as well. More generally, it could be said that nothing in this world appears randomly from nowhere without being influenced by anything else that preceded it. Religions perform an essential role in acting as vehicles for the transmission of perennial archetypal principles that the human soul requires for its survival, much like the body requiring water to stay alive. The blocking-off of such a water source is potentially catastrophic, and indeed if one considers the decline of Christianity in the modern Western world it is the eras of Puritanism and the Enlightenment in the 17th and 18th centuries that together helped to strip Christianity of its contemplative heart, thus leaving a 'bleached' religion that few seem to want to participate in any more.

Returning to the association of love with the Virgin Mary, it is important to make a Platonist distinction in relation to the aspect of Aphrodite and love that is associated with her. In Plato's *Symposium* the distinction is made between Aphrodite Pandemos and Aphrodite Urania, which in short relates to a distinction between worldly, lustful love and heavenly or divine love. These two types of love are at opposite ends of a ladder of ascent that leads from Pandemos up to Urania. The Virgin Mary is clearly an image of the Divine Love of Aphrodite Urania, which again accords with the idea that a Lady chapel would be at the eastern end of a cathedral as a place towards which someone 'climbs' when progressing 'anagogically' eastwards through a cathedral. With the east in mind, it would also make symbolic sense to associate Urania with the rising of the Morning Star in the east and then up into heaven. Pandemos would then be reflected by the descent of the Evening Star as it sets in the west and symbolically falls down into the Earth.

However, having mentioned this distinction between Pandemos and Urania, it is also important not to get caught up within a common misperception of Platonism, in which it is assumed that Plato is suggesting that heaven is 'good' and earth is 'bad'. It is earthliness *for its own sake* that is understood to be the problem, as opposed to earthliness that acts as a vehicle for orientating the soul's vision towards Heaven. Any ladder of ascent requires a solid earthly grounding, giving a stability that ultimately affords a safe and effective ascent. The only reason why the higher floors of a building are in a position to have such a lofty view, whereby they can see beyond the earthbound horizon, is because the lower floors of the building are in good repair and are thus supporting the higher floors towards which the soul climbs. That which is most *superior* in its vision is very much dependent upon being grounded in that which is most *fundamental*.[10]

10. These two words, 'superior' and 'fundamental', are used here specifically in their etymologically correct sense of 1) 'above, over or beyond' and 2) 'bottom'.

6.4 THE ROSARY BEADS AS A TALISMAN OF THE MORNING STAR

ANOTHER EXAMPLE of the 'Venusian' connections made in the previous section is the set of Christian prayer beads known as the Rosary. The very name 'Rosary' speaks of the rose, and indeed the word Rosary is generally understood to relate symbolically to both an Edenic rose garden about which the soul wanders contemplatively, as well as a garland of roses – in the sense of the beads resembling a garland of roses, or a collection of bead-like rosehips, which are the fruit of the rose. But it is the geometric arrangement of the beads that is of particular interest, because they are five-fold. There are five so-called 'mystery beads' that divide the circle of beads equally into five distinct sections, and then in each one of those sections there are the so-called 'decades' that are collections of ten beads. So the multiples within the bead arrangements correspond to the numbers associated with the five-foldness of the

rose and the movement of the Planet Venus. But perhaps the most overtly Venusian aspect of their design is that the very shape of the bead chain is the same as the alchemical planetary glyph for Venus. The symbol of Venus is well known in the modern era, because it is used as the symbol of the female gender. Its circle with a cross underneath resembles the Rosary beads – themselves a circle of fifty-five beads,[11] with a small string that leads off the circle containing five extra beads plus a crucifix. The idea that the numerical design of the Rosary beads is influenced by astrological talismanic symbolism may sound puzzling in the modern era, although it is a simple fact that the learned men and women of medieval Christendom had a close interest in astrology, alchemy and some also in talismanic magic.[12] It was specifically the fortune-telling element of astrology that the medieval church frowned upon.

The Rosary beads   Five-fold symmetry of rose and Rosary   Planetary glyph for Venus

---

11. An intriguing numerical fact about the poem *Sir Gawain and the Green Knight* is that a total of forty-six of its written lines are devoted specifically to describing the detail of the pentagram on Gawain's shield and its five-fold symbolism. The total number of written lines in the whole poem is 2,530 so therefore these forty-six lines that describe the pentagram make up precisely one-fifty-fifth of the whole poem. It is unclear whether this is a random coincidence or an intentional use of a Rosary number, which itself also happens to be the tenth Fibonacci number.

12. A good source on this subject is a book by Charles Burnett called *Magic and Divination in the Middle Ages*.

Hugh of St Victor mentions this in his *Didascalicon*:

'It is astronomy, then, which treats the law of the stars and the revolution of the heaven, and which investigates the regions, orbits, courses, risings, and settings of stars, and why each bears the name assigned it; it is astrology, however, which considers the stars in their bearing upon birth, death, and all other events, and is only partly natural, and for the rest, superstitious; natural as it concerns the temper or "complexion" of physical things, like health, illness, storm, calm, productivity, and unproductivity, which vary with the mutual alignments of the astral bodies; but superstitious as it concerns chance happenings or things subject to free choice.'

Book 2, Chapter 10

In his *Policraticus*, John of Salisbury expresses a similar outlook:

'Because it is plausible that there is some potency in the phenomena of the heavens, since on earth also it is believed that nothing is done which does not bestow from the hand of the Creator some beneficial result, inquisitive minds investigate the powers of celestial phenomena and endeavor to explain by the rules of their type of astronomy everything which comes to pass on this world below. Now astronomy is a noble and glorious science if it confine its disciples within the bounds of moderation, but if it be presumptuous enough to transgress these it is rather a deception of impiety than a phase of philosophy.'

Book 2, Chapter 19

Dante also gives his own poetic description of this in Canto 16 of *Purgatorio*:

*'You men on earth attribute everything
to the spheres' influence alone, as if
with some predestined plan they moved all things.*

*If this were true, then our Free Will would be
annihilated: it would not be just
to render bliss for good or pain for evil.*

*The spheres initiate your tendencies:
not all of them – but even if they did,
you have the light that shows you right from wrong,*

*and your Free Will, which, though it may grow faint
in its first struggles with the heavens, can still
surmount all obstacles if nurtured well.*

*You are free subjects of a greater power,
a nobler nature that creates your mind,
and over this the spheres have no control.*

*So, if the world today has gone astray,
The cause lies in yourselves and only there!*

(67–83)

The distinction that is made between astronomy and astrology is not one that throws out all aspects of astrology. There was a belief among the learned 12th-century churchmen and women that the cosmological movements of the heavens had an influence on what went on down here in the sublunary world as long as it was understood not to deny the human capacity for free will. With this in mind it becomes possible to have some understanding of a perception that recognises numerical talismanic significance in using cosmological numbers within prayer cycles. Such rhythmic and repetitive cycles of prayer could be said to bring the human microcosm into a numerical correspondence with the cyclical rhythmic movements of the wider macrocosm, of which the microcosm is a smaller image. Henceforth the whole of Creation accords numerically with the harmonious rhythms that are perpetually known in the Divine Mind. This reflects the words of the Pater Noster prayer '... Thy will be done on earth as it is in heaven'.

It is this mode of understanding that lay at the heart of the Hermetic tradition of Hermes Trismegistus, and this is one of the ancient traditions that had a degree of influence on the learned churchmen and women of the medieval world due to its partial concordance with Christian ideas. The central principle of the Hermetic tradition was that the macrocosm (the whole universe) is an image of God and that the microcosm (the human being) is an image of the macrocosm and therefore a second image of God. So to prayerfully count in fives and multiples thereof is to harmonise or even synchronise the soul with the numerical movements of both the planet and the flower associated with Divine Love.

6.5 ROSARY SYMBOLISM IN WELLS LADY CHAPEL

THERE IS A PARTICULAR feature of the Wells Lady chapel that accords with Rosary symbolism, and that is the numerical arrangement of its windows.

First of all there are five walls upon which there are windows, and each of these walls contains five tall windows (known as 'lights') standing in a row. So again, the number five is numerically prominent. But it is the tracery windows, one above each of these sets of five lights, that are of particular interest, because they are the same shape as the Pythagorean tetraktys, which is associated with the number ten.

Looking upwards at five tall 'lights' crowned by a tetraktys-shaped tracery

The tetraktys was described in section 1.2 of chapter 1. It is a triangular arrangement of ten dots that symbolically embody four levels – hence the prefix 'tetra' in its name. There is much that could be said about the

symbolism of the tetraktys, along with the fact that it was known about in the medieval church. For now it just needs to be said that for the Pythagoreans it was symbolically understood to be a geometric embodiment of the number ten, because the first ten numbers – the decad – were the primary focus in their number symbolism. So bearing in mind that the Wells Lady chapel has five of these tetraktys-shaped tracery windows, it becomes possible to suggest that they together embody a Pythagoreanesque Christian symbolism relating to 'five sets of ten'. This then accords with the five decades of the Rosary beads. Indeed the numerical symbolism is so evident in material terms that it is actually possible to use the five tetraktys windows to keep track of the ten Ave Marias (Hail Marys) that are contained within each decade of a Rosary prayer cycle.

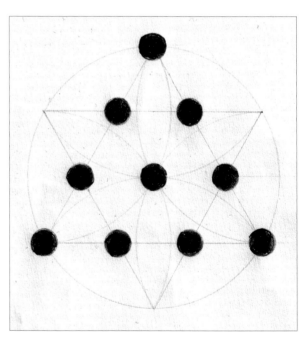

The Pythagorean Tetraktys

The oldest currently known depiction of the five-fold Rosary beads dates back to 1300, which is just a decade or two before the Wells Lady chapel began to be constructed.

One of the five tetraktys-shaped tracery windows in the Wells Lady chapel. Nine angels looking up to the One

The English image on the right, however, dates from between 1480 and 1490. It depicts a 'double rose', i.e. consisting of an outer rose and an inner rose. The five sepals of the outer rose point directly at small gold circles that represent the Rosary's five mystery beads. Then in between each of these mystery beads there are ten small white circles, which together represent the five decades. Even the outer green circle contains Rosary numerics, in the sense of it having five gold flowers that embody five-fold symmetry – which could be seen as mystery beads in that they line up with the five sepals of the inner rose. Then in between these five flowers there are ten small gold circles each in two sets of five. At the centre of the rose is an image of the Virgin Mary nursing the Christ Child.

6.6 THE OCTAETERIS, THE VENUS PENTAGRAM AND THE NINETY-NINE MOONS

THE VENUS PENTAGRAM/octagram cycle takes place over a period of eight years. The fact that an Earthly year is the period of time that it takes for Earth to orbit the Sun means that this Venus cycle could be described as involving the Sun as well as Earth and Venus. Eight years is the same as 2922 days because 365.25 days × 8 = 2922.

However the Moon also participates in this great cosmic dance, because it also has an eight-year cycle for both its sidereal and synodic periods. The sidereal cycle (27.32 days) is quite simply the amount of time it takes for the Moon to orbit the Earth once. Whereas the synodic cycle (29.53 days) is the amount of time between one full moon and the next. The phases of the Moon involve the impressions of light that the Sun makes on the Moon's surface as we see them from a geocentric perspective. From such a geocentric perspective the more obvious one of the two lunar cycles that we can see is the synodic cycle, because it involves the phases of the Moon. So this is the cycle we shall begin with. The simple calculation of 29.53 × 99 = 2923.47 days demonstrates how ninety-nine synodic cycles is very close indeed to eight years (2922 days).

It is this cycle of ninety-nine moons that governed the occurrence of the Olympic Games in ancient Greece. The Greeks referred to this eight-year period of time as the 'Octaeteris', and they would divide it up into two approximate periods of four years – this would govern the period of time between each Olympic Games. However, because ninety-nine is not an even number, the division was made on the basis of a forty-nine-moon gap of 'nearly' four years followed by a fifty-moon gap of just over four years. The eight-year cycle itself is connected to the longer calendrical cycle used by the ancients known as the Metonic cycle. This particular cycle is based on the fact that nineteen Earth years (6939.75 days) are virtually identical to 235 synodic lunar cycles (6939.55 days). Both the Octaeteris and the Metonic cycle were used within the design of the so-called Antikythera mechanism which was found in a shipwreck in the Aegean sea in the early 1900s. This very sophisticated calendrical device has now been dated to around 70–60 BC, and it has helped to show the sophistication of astronomical knowledge that existed in the ancient world.

Returning to the lunar aspect of the Octaeteris, if there are virtually ninety-nine synodic cycles in eight years then there are virtually 107 sidereal cycles in the same period of time. This can be seen in the calculation 27.32 days × 107 = 2923.24 days. Here we see the number eight yet again within the eight-year cycle, because there are eight more sidereal cycles than synodic cycles in a period of eight years.

So one of the main cosmological cycles that this book concentrates upon is now complete in its description. The cycle is eight years in length and involves the Sun, Moon, Earth and Venus. This eight-year cosmic relationship witnesses the generation of Venusian pentagram and octagram stars over a lunar period of ninety-nine synodic moons. This cycle is a primary focus of this book because it appears to be a primary cosmological focus in the design of Wells Cathedral. As will become clear, the Sun, Moon, Earth and Venus all directly feature in the cathedral's design. But before we look further into the design of Wells Cathedral, we shall briefly digress to look at a few examples of this cosmological symbolism in the Islamic world.

6.7 THE CRESCENT MOON AND THE STAR

ONE REMNANT OF ancient cosmology that appears to have passed into more recent times is the symbol of the crescent moon and the star. In the current era it is directly associated with Islam and appears on the flags of many Islamic countries. The star is generally a pentagram, although the pre-Islamic use of the symbol generally used an octagram star. The symbol came into Islam through its use by the Ottomans of Turkey, who seem to have inherited it from the flag of Byzantium in which the star was an octagram. The use of the pentagram and octagram in this symbol brings us back to the cosmic geometry of Venus and the Moon. This appears to be confirmed through the generally accepted idea that the crescent moon and star symbol is Babylonian/Sumerian in origin and represents Ishtar – the Babylonian Venus and the Babylonian Moon God Sin. Ishtar is the Goddess of Love, whereas Sin was known as the Lord of Wisdom. In Babylonian iconography the symbols of Planet Venus (Ishtar), Moon (Sin) and Sun (Shamash) were often depicted together, which again appears to reflect the connection between these heavenly bodies that accord with one another over the course of an eight-year cycle.

Turkish national flag with crescent moon and pentagram star

Byzantine Coin with crescent moon and octagram star

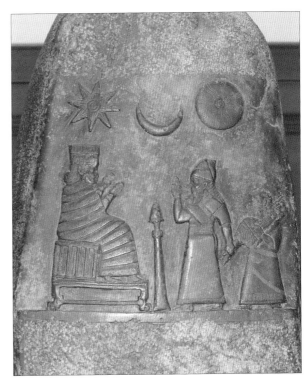

Ishtar (Venus), Sin (Moon) and Shamash (Sun) depicted as an octagram star, a crescent and an eight rayed roundel on the Stele of King Melishipak I.

97

6.8 THE COSMOLOGICAL RESEMBLANCE OF THE VIRGIN MARY AND FATIMAH ZAHRA

THE TASBIH OF FATIMAH AND THE NINETY-NINE BEADS

HAVING DESCRIBED THE lunar connection within the eight-year Venus cycle, a correlation can be pointed out in relation to the Islamic prayer beads which are generally known as a Tasbih or a Misbaha. This string of beads is used in a similar way to the Christian Rosary in terms of it acting as a counting mechanism for repetitive and rhythmic prayer cycles. The interesting numerical fact is that the bead-chain is formed of ninety-nine beads. Having said this, many of these bead-chains consist of thirty-three beads, although these are effectively an edited form of ninety-nine, whereby the thirty-three beads are counted three times over to complete the focal number of ninety-nine.

A common Islamic association with the number ninety-nine can be seen in the 'ninety-nine names of God', which are effectively the multiplicitous attributes of the one God. In some examples of this there is also a 'one-hundredth name', which is understood to be an 'unknowable name' in the sense of the ineffable unknowable essence of God.[13] Some prayer cycles will also include 100 repetitions of some kind which bears a numerical resemblance to the Biblical story of the shepherd who leaves his ninety-nine sheep to go in search of the one lost sheep. But rather than being associated with the ninety-nine names of God the beads are more commonly associated with three devotional proclamations – the 'Tasbih', 'Tahmeed' and 'Takbeer' – each of which is repeated thirty-three times. This set of prayers is known as the Tasbih of Fatimah (Tasbih Hadhrat Zahra) due to various stories surrounding the origin of the prayer cycle. So the fact that the 'five-fold' Christian Rosary beads appear to embody Venusian

numerical symbolism means that it is of interest that the Muslim prayer beads appear to contain an equivalent lunar numerical symbolism that applies to the same eight-year cosmological cycle of Venus. If both circles of beads can be see as symbolising an eight-year cycle, they accord with the Venusian/Lunar numeric in the sense that an eight-year cycle consists of five Venusian synodic cycles (like the five sections of the Rosary beads) but also ninety-nine moons (like the Misbaha). After all, both Christians and Muslims look up at the same heavenly vault with all of its cosmic numerical cycles.

However, this apparent connection deepens via the fact that the Islamic beads are specifically associated with Prophet Mohammed's daughter Fatimah Zahra, who herself bears a notable symbolic resemblance to the medieval Christian perception of the Virgin Mary. Both women are much revered for their piety, purity and motherhood, and have an immense number of titles that describe their spiritual qualities. However the most intriguing connection, which suggests a direct association with the cosmological symbolism of Planet Venus and the Moon, is that Fatimah's title/epithet 'Zahra' is understood to mean both 'flower' and 'princess', as well as being connected to the Arabic name for Planet Venus, 'Al-Zuhrah'. So Fatimah Zahra, who is associated with the 'lunar' Misbaha, appears also to have Venusian attributes. But then the Virgin Mary, who is associated with the 'Venusian' Rosary, is also associated with the lunar number ninety-nine insofar as there being various churches in different parts of the Christian world that contain symbolism relating to '99+1', all of which are dedicated to the Virgin Mary.[14]

---

13. Ninety-nine plus an ineffable one resembles Dante's *Commedia* in that the transition from Canto 99 to Canto 100 sees Dante go beyond the celestial rose that is centred on the Virgin Mary and approach his final meeting with the ineffable God, who is ultimately beyond any description that Dante feels able to give.

14. Such as St Mary the Virgin in Painswick, UK, Panagia Ekatontapiliani in Paros, Greece, and Santa María de Eunate in Navarre, Spain.

Misbaha with 33 beads

Misbaha with 99 beads (plus 10 extra small beads for counting multiples)

THE HAND OF FATIMAH AND THE NUMBER FIVE

ANOTHER SUBJECT OF INTEREST is the so-called 'Hand of Fatimah', which is a Middle Eastern talisman that assumes the form of an open hand with its five digits. Its name is Islamic, and is again a reference to Prophet Mohammed's daughter, although the talisman itself is seemingly of ancient Mesopotamian origin and associated with Inanna and Ishtar – the Sumerian and Babylonian equivalents of Venus. In the Middle East this talisman is also called a *khamsa*, which is the Arabic word for the number five. This five-fold association is with the five digits of the hand, which is itself reminiscent of one of the five 'fivenesses' symbolised by the golden pentagram on Gawain's red shield. So we are led back yet again to the number of the Planet Venus and the symmetry of the rose and the Rosary.

Jews in the Middle East call this talisman the Hand of Miriam, after Moses' sister, and Arab Christians call it the Hand of Maryam, after the Virgin Mary. It is associated with giving protection from the Evil Eye, which is another ancient belief from the eastern Mediterranean region. Such protection could also be said to be afforded to Gawain in the form of his protective shield with its golden pentagram on the front, and an image of the Virgin Mary on its inner side. With 'spiritual protection' in mind the earliest association of the Virgin Mary in Christianity is with being the 'Protectress'. The earliest written form of this description is in a 3rd-century hymn written in Coptic Greek:

'Beneath your compassion,
We take refuge, O Theotokos:
do not despise our petitions
in time of trouble:
but rescue us from dangers,
only pure, only blessed one.'

Bearing in mind that the Roman Catholic association of the Virgin Mary with the number five only appeared to develop from the early 12th century onwards, it appears possibly to be another example of symbolism that was brought back to Western Europe from the Holy Land in the era of the Crusades.

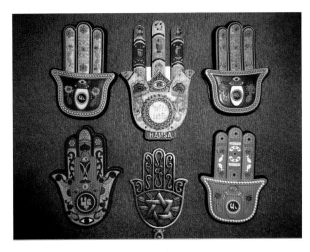

A collections of Khamsa's

6.9 ASCENT TO THE ROSE OF DIVINE LOVE

RETURNING TO THE cosmological design of Wells Cathedral and to the symbolism of the Virgin Mary as the Morning Star and the heavenly rose, it can now be pointed out how such symbolism appears to be present in the design of the cathedral, and how this symbolism can be described as an 'Ascent to the Rose of Divine Love'.

As will become clearer in the next chapter, there is a symbolism of ascent seemingly present within the design of Wells Cathedral. In one sense it could be looked upon as a Christian equivalent of the ladder of ascent to Aphrodite Urania. As mentioned earlier, the Virgin Mary is a Christian figure who appears to symbolise the Divine Love that is also associated with Aphrodite Urania, and so the eastward movement through the cathedral forms an ascent that culminates in the Lady chapel – an architectural image of Eden and the Morning Star. So as the Stella Matutina rises in the east, she reflects the light of the sun down to those who fix their gaze upon her as the Mediatrix of Divine Light.

From an overtly Christian perspective this ascent is also a return to the Edenic state where the rose is forever thornless, because this place (or inward state of being) is an enclosed garden that is only open to the light of the sun that shines over the garden's walls from above. Sometimes the Annunciation is depicted in a walled garden or sometimes an enclosed room into which only the sun rays of the Holy Spirit can enter. However, this eastern Edenic state of soul is a necessary prerequisite to the Logos being inwardly conceived within the soul, and so to climb to the 'eastern summit' of the cathedral is to embody such a return to the Garden of Eden at the summit of the human soul.

There is a famous and beautiful medieval illumination that appears to express symbolism such as this. It is perhaps not a surprise that the illumination in question is from the culture of chivalry and courtly love. It is from the Manesse Codex – a manuscript that was produced in the region of Europe that is now Germany. The codex contains images and poems relating to various famous troubadours – or *Minnesängers*, as they were called in this region.

In the image the *Minnesänger* is ascending the ladder towards the Heavenly Lady, who is waiting for him to reach her so that she can crown him with roses. There is no crown of thorns in the Garden of Eden and so a crown of thornless roses is what the Lady is holding out. It contains seven red roses and seven white roses. The *Minnesänger* is looking up to the Lady, who is effectively the summit of his soul, although she is not looking down towards him. She awaits his arrival with her crown of roses, but her gaze is forever fixed on her own True Image – the 'One above' ... who she is

Kraft von Toggenburg depicted in the Manesse Codex

looking up to and forever contemplating.[15] The *Minnesänger* has not yet reached the Lady because he is still seeing through a glass darkly, whereas she is forever face to face. The *Minnesänger* only knows in part, whereas the Lady knows even as she is also known.[16]

With the Manesse Codex in mind, another of its images is of interest in relation to Venusian numerical symbolism. Tannhäuser was a renowned *Minnesänger* of the 13th century. But his name has lived on partly because the German composer Richard Wagner wrote an opera about him in the 19th century, which included the legend in which Tannhäuser descends into the subterranean mountain of Venus where he worships her for a period of time amounting to years. The general storyline of this legend appears to have a much older origin which doesn't involve Tannhäuser or Venus, so the fact that both characters have been incorporated into this ancient myth suggests a pre-existing association between them. Such an association would presumably have been something to do with Tannhäuser's involvement in the culture of courtly love.

In the image on the right Tannhäuser is dressed as a Teutonic knight. Bearing in mind that green is the colour of Venus as well as of springtime, it is notable that there are Venusian numerics in the green foliage that surrounds him. These collections of vine and oak leaves are arranged in such a way that the vine leaves are singular, whereas the oak leaves are in sets of three.

As we look at Tannhäuser there are five of these collections of leaves on the left of the image, and eight on the right. So accordingly, the numbers of Planet Venus are present within these green leaves which characterise the eternal spring and the rising of the Bright Morning Star in the east.

Tannhäuser depicted in the Manesse Codex

15. In the second Canto of *Paradiso* Dante and Beatrice ascend to the sphere of the Moon and line 22 reads as "My gaze on Beatrice, hers on Heaven"
16. See 1 Corinthians 13:12

From 'The Etymologies'

*A 7th century encyclopedia written
by Archbishop St Isidore of Seville*

The inventors of geometry, and its name
(De inventoribus geometriae et vocabulo eius)

1. It is said that the discipline of geometry was
first discovered by the Egyptians, because,
when the Nile River flooded and everyone's
possessions were covered with mud, the
onset of dividing the earth by means of
lines and measures gave a name to the skill.
And thereupon, when it was greatly perfected
by the acumen of wise men, the expanses
of the sea, sky, and air were measured.

2. Stimulated by their zeal, these sages began,
after they had measured the land, to inquire
about the region of the sky, as to how far
the moon is from the earth, and even the sun
from the moon; and how great a distance there
is to the pinnacle of the heavens. And so, using
reasoning capable of being tested and proved,
they determined the distances of the vault of
heaven and the perimeter of the earth
in terms of the number of stadia.

3. But because the discipline began with
measuring the earth, it retained its name
from its origin, for geometry (geometria)
takes its name from 'earth' and 'measure.'

Book 3, Chapter 10

CHAPTER 7.

Pyramid Geometry and the Size of the Earth

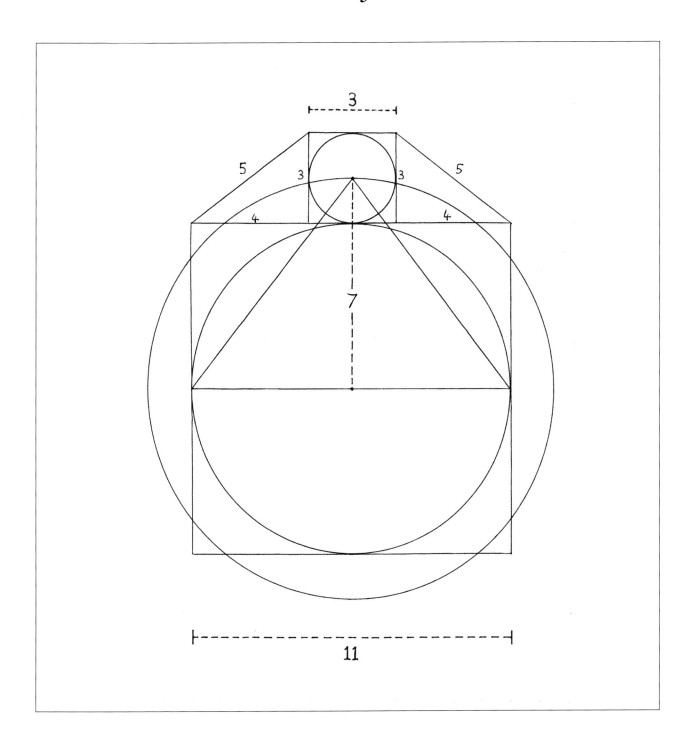

7.1 THE GREAT PYRAMID'S COSMIC MYTHOS

IN THE CURRENT TIME the subject of the Great Pyramid of Giza in Egypt includes several out-of-the-ordinary associations that didn't exist until more recent centuries. This is not the place to list them all, but the reader may be aware that theories about the Great Pyramid and its origins have become increasingly ungrounded, to the point where there are some who now believe that it was built or inspired by aliens.

The ancient Egyptians were famously religious. In his *Account of Egypt*, the Greek historian Herodotus of Halicarnassus (c.484 BC - c.425 BC) stated that:

'They are religious excessively beyond all other men'

II-37

Along with this the Egyptians were also famously interested in geometry and cosmology, which is continuously mentioned in the writings of the ancient world. Pythagoras, for example, was told to go to Egypt by his teacher Thales to learn about geometry and cosmology. But perhaps, most importantly, these Egyptian emphases on religious observance and quadrivial knowledge were interconnected, as they also were for the Pythagoreans, who flourished after Pythagoras returned from his travels in Egypt and Babylon. Herodotus even compared the Pythagoreans to the Egyptians, or at least said that they had similar practices.[1]

This perception of the ancient Egyptians followed through into medieval European Christian culture. Charles Burnett observes that *'... it was the priority of the Egyptians in geometry and astronomy (with the accompanying arts of astrology and magic) that is most frequently mentioned in the Middle Ages'.*[2]

The learned churchmen and women of medieval Europe even looked upon ancient Egypt as the birthplace of quadrivial knowledge itself. In his guide to the arts, for example, the 12th-century Platonist monk Hugh of St Victor wrote:

'Egypt is the mother of the arts and thence they came to Greece and thence to Italy.'

This was in keeping with the general high regard that learned 12th-century Christians had for the knowledge of the ancient world. Such a sentiment was expressed in John of Salisbury's words, which have subsequently become formulated into the famous saying:

'We are like dwarfs standing on the shoulders of giants.'

John of Salisbury was quoting his Platonist teacher Bernard of Chartres. Bernard was expressing the indebtedness that 12th-century Christian scholars felt they had in relation to the knowledge of the ancient world. John of Salisbury wrote about this in his *Metalogicon*:

'Our own generation enjoys the legacy bequeathed to it by that which preceded it. We frequently know more, not because we have moved ahead by our own natural ability, but because we are supported by the [mental] strength of others and possess riches that we have inherited from our forefathers. Bernard of Chartres used to compare us to dwarfs perched on the shoulders of giants. He pointed out that we see more and farther than our predecessors, not because we have keener vision or greater height, but because we are lifted up and borne aloft on their gigantic stature.'

Bk 3, Ch 4

So even though the 12th-century Christians felt that their vision superseded that of the ancient world, there was still a recognition that such lofty vision was only possible due to the knowledge of the ancient world that had come before them.

---

1. See Herodotus' *Account of Egypt*. Online Gutenberg version https://www.gutenberg.org/files/2131/2131-h/2131-h.htm then wordsearch 'Pythagoreans'
2. C Burnett, 'Images of Ancient Egypt in the Latin Middle Ages' in *The Wisdom of Egypt: Changing Visions Through the Ages,* UCL Press, 2003, page 75.

Pyramids, Camels and Backpackers

The opening sentences of Adelard of Bath's book *On the Same and the Different* express a similar feeling of indebtedness and 'smallness' in relation the ancients:

'When I examine the famous writings of the ancients – not all of them, but most – and I compare their talents with the knowledge of the moderns, I judge the ancients eloquent and the moderns dumb. Granted, the ancients did not know everything, nor are the moderns wholly ignorant. So, just as the ancients did not say it all, the moderns should not keep silent about all. Therefore, I believe that something should be written – modest though it may be – lest the moderns in their fear of contagion of envy, should incur the accusation of ignorance.'

So the idea that medieval Christians might have taken an interest in the Great Pyramid and its geometry and dimensions is not controversial or odd, as long as there is a recognition that the more ungrounded ideas of pyramidology are comparatively recent, and in no way existed in the medieval European world.

Despite all of this, some scholars would still seem uncomfortable approaching any notion of cosmically spiritual and mathematical significance in relation to the Great Pyramid. This is regardless of the fact that it would appear a reasonable association to make, bearing in mind the pyramid's unmistakably geometric shape and its very precise cosmological orientation, along with the renowned religiosity of the Egyptians.

The origins of the ungrounded modern myths about the Great Pyramid look possible to trace back to medieval Islamic alchemical writings concerning Idris, who is the Islamic equivalent of the Judeo-Christian character Enoch. Both of these figures are also associated with the Greek god Hermes. However, these stories are part of a more profound Hermetic wisdom tradition that found its way into medieval Europe around the 12th century. Considering the interest that Adelard of Bath had in the quadrivium as well as Harranian talismanic magic, he was inevitably aware of this Hermetic mythos, which was seemingly characteristic of the culture of Harran.

Harran was a small medieval outpost of ancient quadrivial and astrological knowledge in the eastern Mediterranean, located just by the modern-day border between Turkey and Syria. The Harranians believed for instance that Hermes was interred in one of the larger pyramids at Giza, and they actually went on pilgrimages to the Giza pyramids in recognition of this. Indeed Hermes is even said to have built the pyramids himself. Medieval Arab thought was significantly influenced by the ancient Hermetic knowledge of Harran, because various Harranians were taken to Baghdad to be involved in a medieval Islamic university called the House of Wisdom (Bayt al-Hikmah).

In his *Book of Thousands* (Kitab al-Uluf), the Islamic astrologer Abu Ma'shar describes Hermes as being the first to ponder celestial events such as the movement of the stars and the hours of the day and night. He is described as being the first to build temples and pyramids and to study medicine, as well as to write poems about things celestial and terrestrial. He is also said to have predicted a great flood and celestial cataclysm that would befall the Earth, that would consist of the opposite extremes of fire and water. As a result of this he built temples such as the 'mountainous' Temple of Akhmim, in which he carved information about the arts and sciences so that they would not be lost in the flood.

This story of a great flood appears to be where some of the earliest pyramidology ideas come from; it associated Noah and the Hebrews more generally with the building of the Great Pyramid. The Jewish-Roman writer Josephus (AD 37–100) even describes the Jews as being forced to build pyramids when enslaved in Egypt, and so there appeared to be an ancient source for this. The Jewish connection was suggested in a book written in the 1850s by a publisher called John Taylor. This was expanded on by the Astronomer Royal of Scotland Charles Piazzi Smyth, who believed in British Israelism, which suggests that the British are a lost tribe of Israel. A few decades later saw the development of so-called 'pyramid prophecies', in which certain numerical measurements of the Great Pyramid were seen as predicting significant future events on dates that contained the same numerics as

the pyramid's measurements. However, there were also similar suggestions to this as early as the 18th century, as have recently come to light in the research of Isaac Newton. He associated the cubit measurements of the Great Pyramid with the Temple of Solomon, as well as seeing them as containing some kind of numerical indication concerning the Apocalypse. As will soon become clear, he appears to have been engaging with a symbolic mythos that is also present in the design of the first English Gothic cathedral.

Returning to the Islamic–Hermetic mythos, it was suggested that there were three different related characters called Hermes, who were Grandfather, Father and Son. The Hermes described above was the first one, whereas the second was in Babylon after the flood and was the teacher of Pythagoras. The third Hermes – 'Trismegistus' (thrice great) – was the one who appears in the Hermetic writings such as the Asclepius dialogue, which was read by the medieval Christian culture that built the Gothic cathedrals.

In some modern educational settings such symbolic mythological storylines will be misunderstood as poor attempts to recount historical facts, and are accordingly relegated to the realm of 'superstition'. But as Martin Lings points out in his book *Ancient Beliefs and Modern Superstitions*:

'... a superstition is something which is "left over" from the past and which continues to prevail without being understood.'

So in this sense the accusation of 'superstition' that is often made of pre-modern cultures is a kind of projection. A superstitious perception, as Lings suggests, is rooted in a materialistic mindset that attempts to understand things purely through looking at their immediate outward appearances, rather than attempting to perceive their deeper spiritual meaning that exists 'below the surface' as it were.

However, the idea that aliens (or some kind of alien intelligence) are behind the building or design of the Great Pyramid seems to be a confused attempt to

reconcile the spiritual imagination with a post-Enlightenment insistence on empirical scientific 'facts'. So in this sense the association of the eternal forms of number with the Divine Intelligence – that transcends this world – becomes relegated to being seen as an alien intelligence that physically exists in the cosmos, albeit beyond Planet Earth. The 'descent' of numerical revelation from the Divine Mind into the human mind that contemplates it then becomes the literal descent of ancient aliens in spaceships, back in the distant past when humans were far too 'primitive' and un-enlightened to be able to do anything as brilliant as build the Great Pyramid. This denigration of the ancient world, and indeed of humanity itself, can perhaps be seen for the projection that it is in the rather telling characterisation by which the Divine Intelligence comes to be looked upon as 'alien'. It could in fact be suggested that the modern mind has become alienated from itself as a direct consequence of having become alienated from its divine origin – so much so that the modern mind now regularly dismisses Divinity as mere superstition.

In this sense, the ungrounded alien fantasies and the overly grounded materialism of atheists appear to be opposite aspects of the same blurred vision, with the former floating 'up in the clouds' and the latter refusing to accept that the sky even exists! The essential connection between the Above and the Below becomes lost, because Lady Philosophy's ladder of ascent is no longer bridging the chasm between Heaven and Earth.

Another confused association that has developed in relation to the Great Pyramid is that of conspiracy theories. It could be said that conspiracy theories generally say more about what is going on in the soul of the theorist rather than the alleged conspirator. No doubt there are always many people in the world who are conspiring to do all sorts of nefarious things, but the mythologically ideal way that conspiracy theories seem to play out would appear to make them more a part of the human imagination. But this book certainly does not use words like 'myth' and 'imagination' as pejorative terms, because mythology and the imagination are vehicles by which the soul can engage in a deeper understanding of things. Words like these are currently understood as pejoratives because we live in times of shallow materialism – in which, as already mentioned, it is wrongly assumed that myths are merely poor attempts at recounting historical events correctly rather than stories by which the soul can engage in a deeper understanding of itself and the world around us. So conspiracy theories do actually appear to address the age-old battle between light and dark, as well as the notion that we are having some ideal and final realisation of truth intentionally withheld from us. However, the problem with these theories is that they also appear to be outward projections of a struggle that is actually going on within the human soul. Worse still they appear to be self-imposed obstacles within the soul's journey back to its True Self. This is because the one conspiracy that is certainly very real is the conspiracy of the ego to distract the soul from remembering the True nature of its identity – i.e. that it originates in the Divine Image. This is not because the ego is evil, but rather that it wants to be centre stage with all of its vitality and expansive energy. However, whereas such expansive energy is very useful when channelled in the right direction, it must never be the navigator of the soul's journey. So accordingly, it could be suggested that the foremost conspiracy actually takes place within the soul, and that it is a misdirected and unchannelled ego that 'keeps us from the truth' in terms of a remembrance of who we actually are.

Returning to the subject of the Great Pyramid, there is one cosmically profound association it appears to have – albeit one that still sounds fantastical to the modern mind. This association is with the ancient knowledge of the size of the Earth. The subject of such cosmological knowledge is actually mentioned in various places within the ancient and medieval worlds. The word 'geometry' itself relates to it, in the sense that it means 'Earth measure', *geo-me-tria*. So for example, in his 7th-century encyclopedia under the heading of

'The Inventors of Geometry and its name', Archbishop St Isidore of Seville describes the ancient Egyptians in the following way:

'And so using reasoning capable of being tested and proved they determined the distances of the vault of heaven and the perimeter of the earth in terms of the number of stadia.'

Julius Caesar, in his written work The Gallic Wars, describes the Druidic culture of Britain as follows:

'... they have many discussions [about] the stars and their movement, the size of the universe and of the earth, the order of nature, the strength and powers of the immortal gods, and hand down their lore to the young men'

This sounds fantastical to our modern minds because there remains a prevailing post-Enlightenment view of human knowledge which leads us to believe that we are cleverer now than we were in the past. So how could the people of the distant past possibly have had such seemingly advanced knowledge without the technology of the modern age? The answer to this would appear to lie in the knowledge and intelligent use of the quadrivial arts, as well as a spiritually focused recognition that pattern and harmonious measure is inherent to the cosmos itself, from the very smallest cosmic element to the very largest.

Such ancient knowledge apparently re-surfaced in medieval Europe, and this chapter looks at a few aspects of it that could be called 'pyramid geometry', and how it relates to the size of the Earth, and indeed how the measurements of the Great Pyramid itself are a foremost embodiment of this knowledge. The reason for focusing on this ancient and medieval knowledge of Earth-measure is because it appears that it was used in the design of Wells Cathedral, as well as the designs of some other English Gothic cathedrals.

7.2 THE PYRAMID TRIANGLES

CENTRAL TO THIS RESEARCH are two distinct pyramid triangles – so-called because they embody the cross-section of a certain type of square-based pyramid. Having said this, because the two triangles are distinct from one another they are different, and therefore so are the two square-based pyramids from which they derive. However, the two triangles are so similar that they are virtually interchangeable if used at large scale within an architectural design. The reason for suggesting this design potential is because it is seemingly what happens in the design of Wells Cathedral, in which both of the triangles are used as if they are the same triangle. To put it another way, there is a multi-layering of geometric grids, whereby both triangles are used according to their particular measurements but nonetheless they are placed, as it were, on top of one another. Because of their immense similarity, they can be seen from a design perspective as two variations of the same triangle.

The similarity of these two triangles is such that in modern mathematical terminology they would be described as a *mathematical coincidence*. However, if we are going to attempt to look at this geometric analysis from the perspective of a highly educated medieval Christian artisan – who would have been steeped in an overtly spiritual understanding of symbolism – then it would seem more useful to describe the mathematical likeness of these triangles as *'significantly similar'* rather than *mathematically coincidental*.

There are various other interesting relationships between the two triangles, such as the fact that one of them is based on an approximation of pi whereas the other one is based on phi (i.e. the golden ratio). Also, one of them consists of rational (commensurable) measurements, whereas the other is based on irrational (incommensurable) measurements. Another relationship is that they have both been suggested as the possible basis of measurement for the design of the Great Pyramid in Egypt.

In the diagram below, the whereabouts of this triangular cross-section within the pyramidal form is shown by the red dotted line.

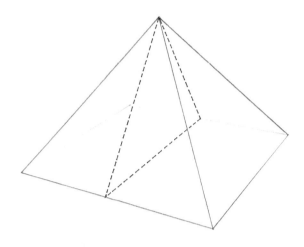

A pyramid triangle as the cross-section of the pyramidal form

We begin by looking at the triangle that embodies the golden ratio, here called the Golden Pyramid Triangle.

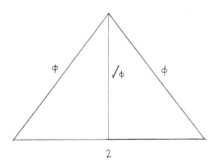

As the diagram demonstrates, when the Pyramid Triangle is in its golden ratio form it is has a base of 2 and sloping edges of 1.618033... – i.e., the golden number or phi (written as Φ). The height of the triangle is also numerically significant, because it measures the square-root of phi, which is 1.272019 (written as $\sqrt{\Phi}$). This is the number which, if multiplied by itself, produces the golden number.

i.e. 1.272019 × 1.272019 = 1.618033

Another way of looking at this is to say that the Golden Pyramid Triangle is formed of two right-angled triangles – one left-handed and the other right-handed. These triangles each have a short edge of 1, a long edge of 1.272019 ($\sqrt{\Phi}$) and a hypotenuse of 1.618033 (Φ). This type of right-angled triangle is known as a Kepler triangle, and it is the only right-angled triangle that runs in geometric progression (i.e. $1 - \sqrt{\Phi} - \Phi$). This is similar to the first of the Pythagorean triangles, which has edge-lengths that run in arithmetic progression (i.e. $3 - 4 - 5$).

A network of lines can be drawn within the Golden Pyramid Triangle that demonstrate the many golden section relationships that it contains. The following sequence of diagrams gradually include more and more of these lines, indicating how they produce golden section relationships within the triangle. Each example is first shown on the left (labelled '1') with red dotted lines that actually create the golden sections. Then next to it the triangle is repeated (labelled '2') albeit with added purple and green lines that denote the 'Lesser' (L) and 'Greater' (G) golden section relationships.

1

2

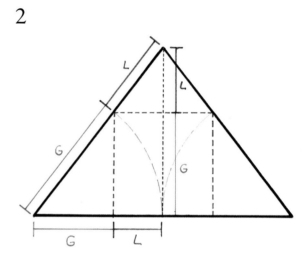

The dotted-line arcs are drawn by placing the point of the compasses onto the triangle's two bottom corners and using half of the baseline as the radial measurement. These arcs mark the positions, on the triangle's sloping sides, from where the vertical and horizontal red dotted lines are drawn.

The purple and green stretches of line that are labelled with 'L' and 'G' denote 'Lesser and Greater' relationships that embody the golden section.

1

2

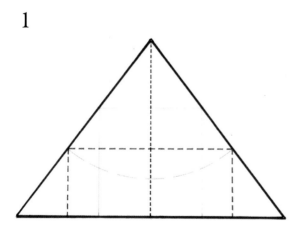

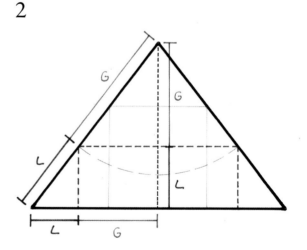

The dotted-line arc in this image is drawn by placing the point of the compasses on the triangle's apex and using the same radial measurement as was used in the previous diagrams. This produces the new positions from where to draw the new red dotted lines. The lines that were dotted red in the previous diagrams are included in this diagram albeit as a faint grey line.

These new purple and green lines invert the three 'Lesser and Greater' relationships that were highlighted in the image above.

1

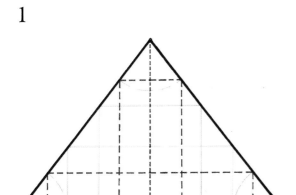

The dotted-line arcs are again drawn from the two bottom corners of the triangle. The faint grey line, that was dotted red in the previous image, is here used to obtain the radial measurement. This particular radius is also used to draw the dotted-line arc nearer the top of the triangle. These three arcs produce the points from which to draw the new red dotted lines.

2

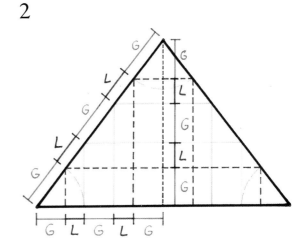

These new red dotted lines are presented here in relationship with the faint grey lines (that derive from the previous stages). They together produce a whole sequence of 'Lessers' and 'Greaters'.

1

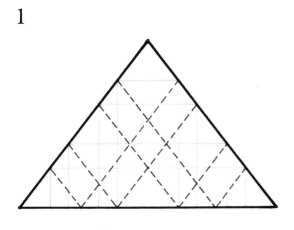

The final example shown here brings in a diagonal grid that derives from the vertical and horizontal red-dotted lines used in the previous stages. The irregular distances between the various sets of parallel lines accord with the 'Lesser and Greater' of the golden section. But as the image to the right shows there are several horizontal divisions too.

2

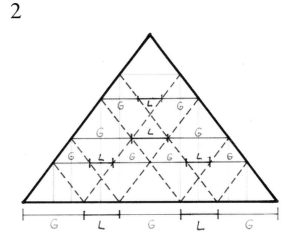

There are also various vertical golden sections that could be marked into this diagram and indeed more golden sections elsewhere within the triangle that have not been shown in this analysis. But it is hoped that this sequence of diagrams adequately demonstrates the golden ratio identity of this particular version of the Pyramid Triangle.

Having looked at this golden ratio version of the pyramid triangle, we shall now look at the other one, which will be called the Pi Pyramid Triangle. The reason for this name will become clear in the next section of this chapter.

As the image to the right demonstrates, this particular version of the pyramid triangle has a base of 11 and a height of 7. Which is 'very slightly' taller than the

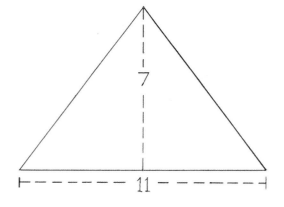

Golden Pyramid Triangle shown above. If this relationship of numbers is directly compared to the Golden Pyramid Triangle – whereby the baseline of the Pi Pyramid Triangle was seen as measuring 2 rather than 11 – its height would then be 1.272727.

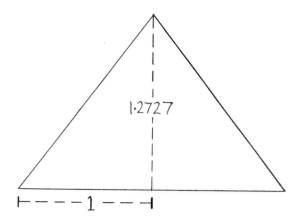

In this comparison it becomes clear how very similar the two triangles are, because whereas the height of the Pi Pyramid Triangle is 1.2727, the height of the Golden Pyramid Triangle is 1.2720 (i.e. √Φ).

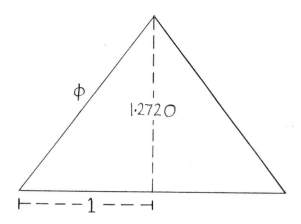

If both of these triangles were scaled up so that they had a baseline the same length as the equivalent triangle in the Great Pyramid in Egypt, the two triangles would be just a little over 3 inches different from one another in height. Anyone who has stood next to the Great Pyramid will be aware of its vast size, and how a difference of around 3 inches is therefore a proportionally tiny difference at that scale. The size of these two

pyramid triangles – as they are used in their singular form in the design of Wells Cathedral – is such that they only differ in height from one another by around two-thirds of an inch. With this in mind, it becomes clear that they could have been used by the designer as if they were effectively the same triangle.

Having said this, the two triangles are used in different ways in relation to the measurement numbers that they contain. The Golden Pyramid Triangle is used to obtain polygonal geometric shapes, as well as the golden section lines shown above, whereas the Pi Pyramid Triangle is used to express unit measurements of cubits and feet. This is due to the different type of numerical measures that the triangles contain. The golden ratio measurements of the Golden Pyramid Triangle generate golden ratio geometric forms such as pentagons and decagons, along with their equivalent polygon stars. The golden number itself is what is known as an *incommensurable number*, which in practice means that it cannot be expressed in rational bounded numbers. When expressed in decimal numbers it begins 1.61803398... but these decimal places then carry on indefinitely and randomly, without ever resolving into a repeating number pattern (i.e. such as a rational 'repeating' decimal like 1.6181818). So using a number such as this to express rational units of measure is not possible. However, such incommensurable numerics can generate geometric polygons from a circle.

The Pi Pyramid Triangle, on the other hand, consists of rational measurements. Its base measures 11 and its height 7, so it is possible to reflect such rational numbers in units of measure.

Returning to the Golden Pyramid Triangle, there is a way of rationalising its irrational measurements, and that is to express the golden ratio measurements in approximate form – i.e. through something like Fibonacci numbers. When this happens, something very interesting occurs in the relationship between the golden ratio version of the triangle and the pi version: they appear to show similar measurements if particular Fibonacci numbers are used.

If the Golden Pyramid Triangle is divided into its two right-angled triangles, it could be said that the short edge measures 55 (i.e. the tenth Fibonacci number). The hypotenuse would then be said to measure approximately 89 (i.e. the eleventh Fibonacci number), and this relationship of 89/55 is a Fibonacci approximation of the golden ratio, because it closely approximates the relationship of 1.618033... to 1:

i.e. 89 ÷ 55 = 1.618181

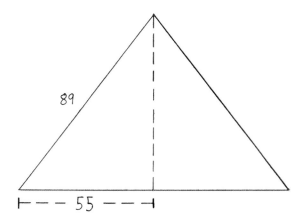

Fibonacci approximation of the Golden Pyramid Triangle using 55 and 89

The connection that this all has to the Pi Pyramid Triangle can be seen in the fact that it has a baseline of 11. So if this triangle were divided into its two right-angled triangles, the short edge of these triangles would measure 5.5. The number 5.5 is ten times smaller than the short edge of the Fibonacci right-angled triangle, which is 55.

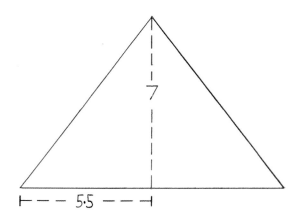

Pi Pyramid Triangle - baseline measure of 5.5 (i.e. ten times less than 55)

So with all this in mind, it is possible to see how the Pi Pyramid Triangle and the 'Fibonacci-ised' Golden Pyramid Triangle virtually 'cross paths' and become alike in terms of their measurements.

GOLDEN RATIO POLYGON GEOMETRY IN THE GOLDEN PYRAMID TRIANGLE

IT IS ACTUALLY POSSIBLE to derive golden ratio polygon geometry from the Golden Pyramid Triangle.

In the example depicted below, the point of the compasses is first placed onto the apex of the triangle. The radial measurement of the compasses needs to then be set to the height of the pyramid triangle, and a circle drawn.

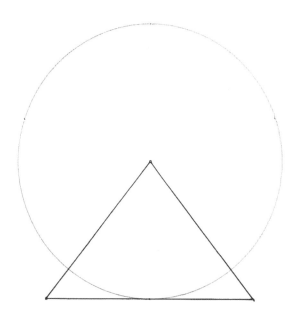

Next, the point of the compasses needs to be located at the midpoint of the triangle's baseline.

The radial measurement for this second circle is such that its circumference needs to tangent the sloping sides of the triangle. (see the image on following page)

The difference in size of these two circles embodies the golden ratio, and this then generates five-fold symmetry

The two intersection points of the two circles mark off precisely 1/5 of the circumference of the larger circle.

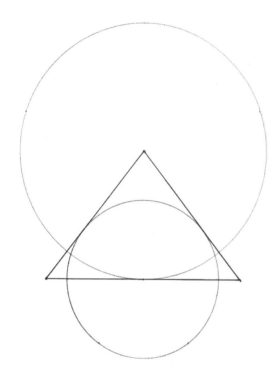

This makes it possible to draw a five-fold shape within that circle – in this particular instance, a pentagram star.

As well as marking off 1/5 of the larger circle, the two intersection points also mark off 2/5 of the smaller circle and so it becomes possible to also draw a five-fold form in the smaller circle too. Again, in this instance it is another pentagram star, albeit smaller by a scale of 1.618 to 1.

As will become clear, the inner pentagon of the larger pentagram star is used to form the pentagonal east end of Wells Cathedral.

If we now convert the pyramid triangle into a pyramid rhomb, and repeat the drawing of the larger circle from the bottom point of the rhomb, (see diagram 1 on next page) the intersections of this new larger circle with the smaller circle allow the upside-down pentagram to be added to the diagram, which turns the smaller pentagram star (diagram 2) into a stellated decagram star. (diagram 3).

An interesting characteristic of the decagon and decagram star is that a rectangle can be derived from either of them, which is very close to being a 1 × 3 rectangle (diagram 4). The rectangle actually measures 1 × 3.078.

1

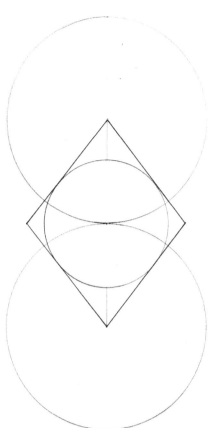

2

3

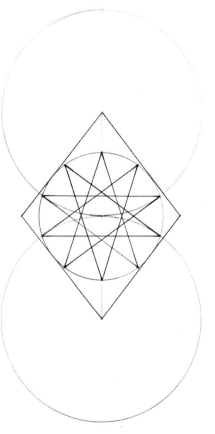

4

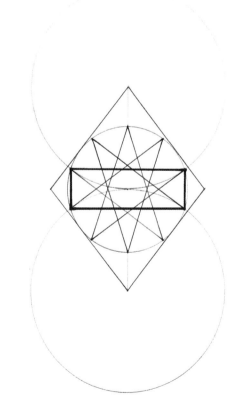

115

This rectangular measurement, as well as the pyramid rhomb diagram from which it can be derived, is used in relation to the size of the quire at Wells Cathedral via the fact that it approximates the 1 × 3 rectangular ground plan of the Temple of Solomon.

The way in which the Golden Pyramid Triangle generates pentagram geometry is reflective of the description of the Kepler triangle, which Johannes Kepler described in a letter to his teacher, Michael Maestlin. There are earlier decriptions of this triangle by other mathematicians although it is this particular written description that has caused the triangle to be given its name. Kepler described the triangle as follows:[3]

'If on a line which is divided in extreme and mean ratio [i.e. the golden ratio] *one constructs a right angled triangle, such that the right angle is on the perpendicular put at the section point, then the smaller leg will equal the larger segment of the divided line.* [i.e. Φ]'

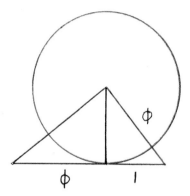

Circle centred on the right angle using Kepler's 'perpendicular' as a radius

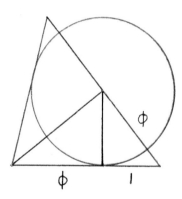

Add on another Kepler triangle so that they meet at their longer edges

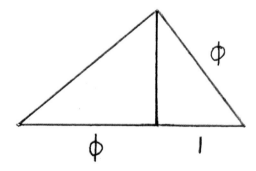

A diagram of Kepler's Description of the 'Kepler Triangle'

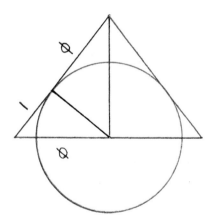

Rotate the diagram clockwise by just over 128° and you get the Golden Pyramid Triangle as shown on the previous pages with its tangenting circle

The diagrams on the right show how the pyramid geometry on the two previous pages relates directly to Kepler's description. The smaller circle that is inside the pyramid triangle or rhomb is generated through using Kepler's 'perpendicular' as its radius. The circle is accordingly centred on the triangle's right-angle.

3. See Mario Livio, *The Golden Ratio,* Broadway Books, 2003, page 149.

The Golden Pediment Triangle

THERE IS ANOTHER golden ratio isosceles triangle that will feature in the geometric analysis in this section – the Golden Pediment Triangle. The reason for this name will become apparent with the triangle's shape.

But first we will look at a sequence of isosceles triangles that leads to this pediment triangle. In all of the following isosceles triangles, the two sloping sides are of equal length and they both measure the golden number – 1.618...

The sequence shows the gradual lengthening of the triangle's baseline by one unit at a time until such lengthening can no longer continue.

The first triangle has a baseline of 1 and sloping sides of 1.618... (i.e. Φ).

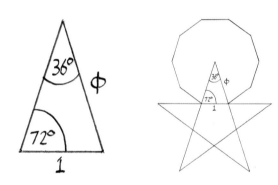

It is a significant isosceles triangle in that the size of its smaller angle is precisely half that of its two larger angles (36° and 72°). It is also significant within polygon geometry, because it is effectively the stellated point of a pentagram star as well as being one sector of a decagon.

The second isosceles triangle is one that has been shown above – namely the Golden Pyramid Triangle. The difference between this triangle and the one just described is that the baseline has increased from 1 to 2. But again, the sloping sides measure 1.618. The significance of this triangle has already been detailed above.

The final triangle in the sequence is produced by lengthening the baseline from 2 to 3, and thus the Golden Pediment Triangle becomes formed with its base of 3 and sloping sides of 1.618...

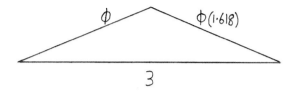

It should be noted that this is the final triangle in the sequence. If the baseline were lengthened to 4, the two sloping sides of 1.618... wouldn't be long enough to meet one another at an apex.

The Golden Pediment Triangle has a similar quality to the Golden Pyramid Triangle in that it can be transmuted into a significant triangle with rational measurements through being 'Fibonacci-ised'. This happens in the following way.

First of all, the triangle needs to be divided into its two right-angled triangles – right-handed and left-handed. These two triangles inevitably contain the same measurements – a long edge of 1.5, a hypotenuse of 1.618... and a short edge with an obscure irrational measurement of 0.6066...

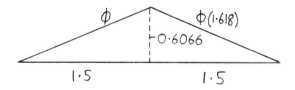

A transmutation into a very significant triangle then occurs if the hypotenuse of 1.618... is 'Fibonacci-ised' into 1.625. This is the Fibonacci approximation of the golden number that arises from 13/8, which was mentioned earlier in relation to the Venus Pentagram.

For the hypotenuse to lengthen from 1.618... to 1.625 it is required to lift up a little, which also involves the short edge of 0.6066 becoming a little longer/taller.

The point at which the hypotenuse takes on a length of 1.625 also involves the rationalising of the short edge, which increases from 0.6066... to 0.625.

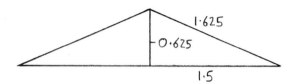

So this newly rationalised right angle triangle has a short edge of 0.625, a long edge of 1.5 and a hypotenuse of 1.625. To finish off this sequence all that is required is for each of these measurements to be multiplied by 8, and then the triangle presents itself in its most renowned form – namely the Pythagorean triangle, which has edges of 5, 12 and 13.

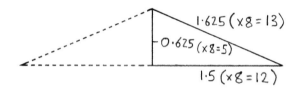

The 5, 12, 13 triangle is very significant in terms of lunar cosmology, and this is expanded on later in this section.

Finally, within the geometric design of Wells Cathedral there are two separate examples of where the pyramid and pediment triangles are used together in such a way that they are overlaid, and with the same length of baseline. (see next diagram)

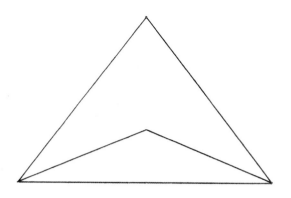

Another point of interest in relation to the overlaying of the two triangles is their comparative relationship of height. 1 to 3.1451 – a close approximation of 1 to π.

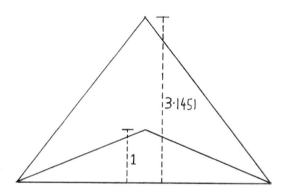

As will become apparent in section 21.3 it is this particular geometric arrangement of pediment and pyramid triangles that appears to hint that the use of pyramid geometry in the design of Wells Cathedral isn't entirely separate and different to its use within the design of the Great Pyramid itself. Indeed, it also suggests that the Great Pyramid does intentionally contain rationalised golden ratio approximations.

THE FIBONACCI PYRAMID TRIANGLE

THE FINAL TRIANGLE THAT needs to be described is actually yet another type of pyramid triangle that is formed of Fibonacci numbers. But unlike the one described earlier, with measurements that closely resemble those of a Pi Pyramid Triangle, this particular triangle has a baseline of 8 and a height of 5. This happens to embody an interesting relationship in comparison to the Pi Pyramid Triangle with its baseline of 11 and height of 7. This can be demonstrated by actually showing how the measurements are used within the design of Wells Cathedral.

If the Pi Pyramid Triangle's baseline of 11 is multiplied by 8, and inversely the Fibonacci Pyramid Triangle's baseline of 8 is multiplied by 11, the answer in both cases is 88. However, if the heights of the two pyramid triangles are now inversely multiplied in a similar way – i.e. using the numbers 11 and 8 again – there is a significant difference that becomes apparent.

If the Pi Pyramid Triangle has its height of 7 multiplied by 8, it becomes 56. However, when the Fibonacci Pyramid Triangle's height of 5 is multiplied by 11 it becomes 55.

So the difference in height between the Pi Pyramid Triangle and this particular Fibonacci Pyramid Triangle is 56 to 55. However, they both share the same baseline of 88. These are the cubit measurements of one of the main geometric master diagrams used in the design of Wells Cathedral. Again, it involves a multi-layering of grids, whereby a pyramid triangle is used by the designer as if it is both a Pi Pyramid Triangle with a baseline of 88 cubits and a height of 56 cubits, but also a Fibonacci Pyramid Triangle with a baseline of 88 cubits and a height of 55 cubits. This will all be developed in Part Three of the book. But for now we will look at a quite remarkable and very significant piece of research by a unique geometer called John Michell. It concerns the geometry, arithmetic and cosmology of a Pi Pyramid Triangle.

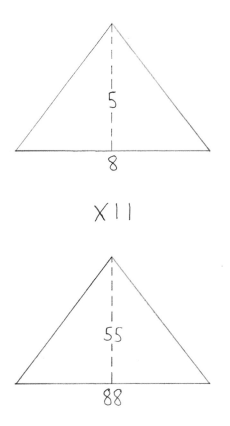

The measurements of a Pi Pyramid Triangle, with a base of 11 and a height of 7, increase to 88 and 56 when multiplied by 8

The measurements of a Fibonacci Pyramid Triangle, with a base of 8 and a height of 5, increase to 88 and 55 when multiplied by 11

7.3 JOHN MICHELL AND THE EARTH-MOON PYRAMID DIAGRAM

John Michell in 1992 having just been made an honorary Archdruid

IN THE EARLY 1970S a maverick writer, researcher and artist called John Michell made an immensely significant discovery concerning the cosmological geometry and metrology of the Earth and the Moon. But for some reason the significance of this discovery hasn't been that widely recognised. It has not yet gained the wider recognition within academia, for instance, that it deserves. This might be because Michell was renowned for researching unconventional subject matter. For example he believed in the deeper significance of ley lines and crop circles, which did not endear him to the average academic institution.

However, a particular feature of his Earth-Moon discovery is that it is all mathematically provable as well as empirically verifiable. It is also very significant in terms of what it suggests in relation to the intelligent design of the cosmos, and it is possibly this aspect of it that does not sit comfortably within the generally atheistic outlooks that pervade mainstream academia. Michell's suggestion that there is intelligent design in relation to the cosmos is by no means a new idea, and Michell would have been the first to insist on this. The understanding that the cosmos works according to numerical patterns is ancient, as indeed can be understood from the use of the word 'cosmos' itself, from the Ancient Greek for 'order'. But Michell's research also points in the direction of imperial measures as being a naturally existing system of cosmic measurement units, as opposed to a system of measure consciously invented by humans – as with the invention of the metric system.

The smaller units of imperial measure such as the inch, the foot and the cubit have associations with parts of the human body. The word 'foot' for instance speaks for itself, as to some degree does the word 'cubit', which derives from the Latin word for the elbow (*cubitum*). The cubit is the measurement associated with the distance from the elbow to the tip of the outstretched fingers.

This association of measurement units with body parts would naturally lead one to assume that such measures were actually derived from the human body for use in the practice of measure, and that they eventually became formalised into systems of measure. But if this is the case, whose body were such measures taken from in the first place? The English foot, for example, has a very particular size and there are specifically 5280 of them in an English mile. If we were to imagine that such measures were derived from a particular person's body, whose body would it have been? Someone significant such as a king, perhaps? But if so, which king? And from which culture did he come? And why the foot measurement of this particular king, and not his father or son who were king before and after him? The whole argument that the defined units of imperial measure are derived from a particular person's body begins to look rather tenuous to say the least. Indeed, the very notion that a unit of measurement is derived from the body of a king reflects more the mythical idea of a king as an archetypal embodiment or representative of the whole human microcosm.

So if it were to be suggested that there is a naturally existing cosmic system of measurement units, it could also be suggested that the size of everything in the cosmos approximately reflects such units. The size of the average human foot could then be understood to roughly resemble the existing cosmic unit that we have subsequently come to call a foot due to its resemblance to the size of the average human foot. Continuing this line of reasoning, it could also be said that the very nature of this resemblance between the human foot and the foot-unit of measure is itself because the human foot reflects one of these many cosmic units because we are cosmic beings. We humans are born of the cosmos as much as a planet or a solar system, and all that is being suggested is that everything is proportionally related in terms of its measures regardless of its magnitude.

So with this particular way of looking at measurement units, the association that imperial units have with the human body remains in place. However, the rationale of *what is derived from what* gets turned around into something that appears more reasonable. The fluctuating and impermanent world of organic forms, of which the human body is a good example, can then be looked upon as an imperfect reflection or copy of an unchanging system of cosmic measures that are forever known in the Divine Mind. As mentioned earlier, the basis of the Hermetic tradition is that the whole cosmos (macrocosm) is an image of God and the human being (microcosm) an image of the macrocosm, and therefore also an image of God. In the words of the mythical sage, Hermes Trismegistus:

'... *For there are two images of God; the Kosmos is one, and man is another, inasmuch as he, like the Kosmos, is a single whole built up of diverse parts.*'

From Hermetica – Walter Scott

Bearing in mind that a larger measurement such as a mile is made up of a certain number of feet, it can then also be suggested that larger cosmic forms such as planets and stars (like our Sun) accord with such a naturally existing measurement system.

An interesting example of such numerical interconnections between the foot and mile can be observed through comparing the number of feet in a mile (5280) with the number of miles in the mean diameter of the Earth (7920) which together express the very simple ratio of 2:3.

There is no particular objection to the idea that mathematics governs the world of plants and flower growth here on Earth. Molecular structures, the growth patterns in shells, spiral phyllotaxis in flowers and many other things here on Earth are recognised as having outward forms that are governed by geometry and number. So it can be asked why such mathematical order would suddenly stop occurring once we leave the surface of Planet Earth. The cosmos beyond our planet appears to consist of an indefinite number of spheres that are moving in circular motions around larger spheres, which in turn are forming into beautiful spiral-shaped galaxies. The cosmos that we live in, and are a part of, is seemingly a rather geometrically ordered place – although at the same time dynamic and ever-changing, but not disordered or chaotic.

With such a thought in mind, let us approach John Michell's Earth-Moon Pyramid diagram.

The diagram begins with two circles, one larger and one smaller. They embody the relationship of size between the Earth and the Moon. Numerically this is a relationship of 11 to 3.

In the second diagram various straight lines have been added. Both circles are now contained within squares, and the squares reflect the size of the circles. The larger square has an edge-length of 11 and the smaller one has an edge-length of 3. The other straight-line shape that has been added is a pyramid triangle. This is the Pi Pyramid Triangle, because it has a base of 11 and a height of 7.

In the third diagram a new circle has been added. The radius of this circle is the same as the height of the pyramid triangle, i.e. 7 units.

So if the radius is 7, the diameter of this new circle is 14.

By multiplying 14 by pi (π) it will become clear what the circumference measurement of the circle is.

$$14 \times \pi = 43.982297...$$

The result is an incommensurable number that is very close to 44. However, if the 22/7 – rational approximation of pi – is used, then the result becomes rationalised. This approximation of π accords with the diagram because the radius of the circle is 7. It is also known that the ancients used the relationship of 22/7 as an approximation of π.

$$\pi = 3.14159265...$$
$$22/7 = 3.142857$$

If 22/7 is used in the calculation of the circle in the diagram, there is a slightly different result.

$$14 \times (22/7) = 44$$

So in this sense it can be said that a circle with a radius of 7 has an approximate circumference of 44. The reason why this is significant within the diagram is because 44 is also the peripheral measurement of the Earth-square. The fact that the Earth-square has an edge of 11 means

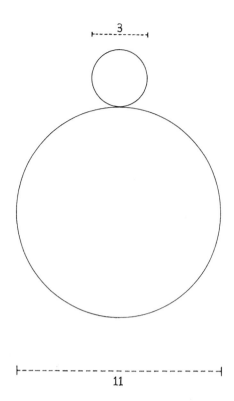

Larger and smaller circles with diameters of 11 and 3 which is the size of Earth in relation to the Moon

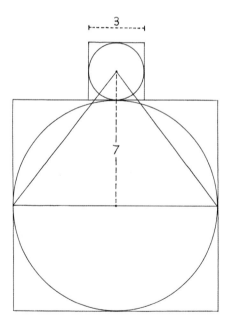

Squares are placed around the circles and the Pi Pyramid Triangle is added

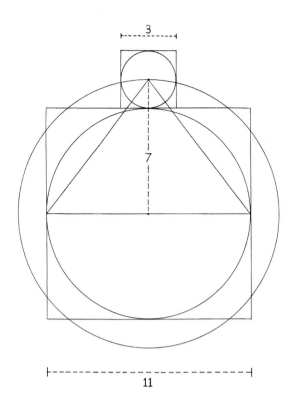

parts of the circumference, marking off the 44 units of the circumference. This all happens by virtue of the fact that a circle with a radius of 7 has an approximate circumference of 44.

Bell rope hole in Wells Cathedral with circumference of 44 foliate forms

that its four edges together measure 44. So with the help of 22/7 it can be said that the larger circle and the Earth-square have the same peripheral measurement. This coinciding of measurements produces a cosmic example of the symbolic process mentioned in section 2.2 known as the 'squaring of the circle'.

Interestingly, a circle with a circumference of 44 is present within the carved stone of Wells Cathedral itself. There is a circular hole in the vault of the south-west tower through which the bell ropes would have originally hung. If you have the patience to count the carved foliate forms that line the edge of the circle it becomes apparent that there are 44 of them. This is by no means a standard compasses-and-ruler division of the circle; there are much simpler divisions of the circle that could yield a similar numbers of sectors with a lot less work. A division into 48 or 40, for instance, would be much simpler. Having said this, a simple way of dividing a circle into 44 is to take on the techniques of the so-called 'rope stretchers of Egypt'. By dividing a length of string into seven equal parts and then using this length of string as a radius to draw a circle, it would then be possible to wrap it around various

As mentioned in section 2.2, there is a symbolic relationship between the circle and the square that reflects something of the relationship between Heaven and Earth. Indeed, within the diagram it is the circle that is centred on the Earth (i.e. the earthly form) but with a circumference passing through the centre of the Moon (i.e. the heavenly form) that actually allows this numerical concordance between a heavenly circle and an earthly square to become apparent. A circle is associated with Heaven, and one symbolic example of this is the fact that it is based on the incommensurable number pi, whereas the earthly square is as rational as can be because it simply measures 1 × 1. This relationship between rational and irrational numbers is itself interesting in symbolic terms: it is ultimately not possible for the human mind to fully know an irrational number because it cannot be expressed within a ratio (hence the term *ir-ratio-nal*). In his medieval encyclopedia Isidore of Seville is quite direct about this:

'Rational magnitudes are those whose measurement we can know; irrational magnitudes are those whose measurement is not known.'

Book 3, Chapter 11

The incapacity of the human mind to know the absolute reality of God reflects itself in such a mathematical fact. For the circle and the square to become reconciled in the diagram, the pi measurement of the circle had to take on a rational form, i.e. 22/7, and only then could the circle and square outwardly reflect a unified likeness to one another. This is why the expression 'squaring of the circle' is associated with the apparent un-resolvability of a problem. How can we bring this ideal theory into a working practice? How can a square peg fit a circular hole? How can the human soul come to know the heavenly circle if it only contemplates the earthly square? Having said this, it was shown in section 2.2 that the square can be recognised as a circle that has been turned inside out. In this sense the contemplation of the earthly square can remind the soul of the perfect circle, albeit in inverse form. The contemplation of outward forms as a way of engaging with the inner world is what lies at the root of any practice of sacred art. The geometer 'gives birth' to the eternal forms of number by drawing them geometrically. It is through the workings of this external geometry – a geometry that is perceived by the senses – that the soul can begin to contemplate aspects of its own inner being. The Islamic brethren known as the Ikhwan al-Safa address this in their writings on geometry:

'Know oh brother … that the study of sensible geometry leads to skill in all practical arts while the study of intelligible geometry leads to skill in the intellectual arts because this science is one of the gates through which we move to the knowledge of the essence of the soul, and that is the root of knowledge.'

Rasa'il, Book 1

It is a similar interaction within the soul that Hermes Trismegistus refers to when he says:

'Man, and man alone of all beings that have soul, is of twofold nature. Of the two parts of which he is composed,

the one is single and undivided; this part is incorporeal and eternal, and we call it "that which is formed in the likeness of God". The other part of man is fourfold, and material; and within it is enclosed that part of him which I just now called divine, to the end that, sheltered therein, the divine mind, together with the thoughts of pure mind, which are cognate to it, secluded from all else, may dwell at rest, fenced in by the body, as it were by a wall.'

Asclepius, Book 1, W. Scott 4

From a Christian perspective these two aspects of the soul inevitably resemble the dual nature of Christ. Whereas Christ is ultimately divine and thus eternal, he also experienced the suffering of the material world on the four-fold cross. Something similar is also symbolised in the depiction of Christ's five wounds as the four extremities of the body around a centrally located and pierced heart. There is also the tradition of Christ's clothes being divided up into four equal parts, except for a seamless undividable coat over which lots had to be drawn. All of these descriptions speak of a quincuncial arrangement in which there is a 'quintessential' centre that transcends four corners.

A geometric way of depicting such a relationship in which the undividable One transcends the four-fold materiality is with a square-based pyramid with its four earthly corners that are crowned by its fifth corner in the form of its singular apex above.5 From an overhead view this again presents a quincuncial arrangement. Interestingly, the pyramidal form that we are considering via John Michell's Earth-Moon diagram has a height of 7 units, and so within this particular pyramid it can be symbolically understood that there are seven steps of ascent between the two regions of the soul described above (i.e. the four-fold square base and the singular apex). Such numerics are again reminiscent of the ancient storyline of the soul's ascent through seven levels from Earth upwards through the heavens.

4. *Hermetica*, Solos Press, 1993.
5. This could be looked upon as Christ in the form of the cornerstone, 'the head of the corner', i.e. the apex of a pyramid.

Returning to the relationship of 11 to 3 that exists between the sizes of the Earth and the Moon, there are similar numbers associated with the actual mean distance between the Earth and the Moon. One way of looking at the relationship of size between Earth and Moon is to say that three Earths lined up in a row are equivalent to eleven Moons.

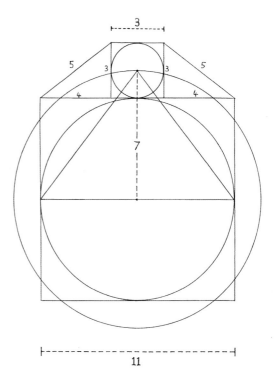

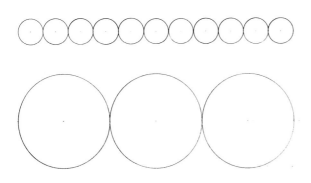

11 Moons in a row form the same distance as 3 Earth's in a row

Pythagorean 3 - 4 - 5 triangles added to the diagram

If this distance - of 23,760 miles - is then multiplied by 10, we get the actual mean orbital distance of the Earth from the Moon - 237,600 miles. Put another way, there are 30 Earths or 110 Moons between the Earth and the Moon when at their mean distance from one another.

Returning to the Earth-Moon diagram, the final part of it, shown in the diagram on the right, involves highlighting the two Pythagorean 3 – 4 – 5 triangles that the diagram contains. These triangles complete the drawing of the diagram, although the numerical concordances now move on to an altogether different level.

As mentioned earlier, a central aspect of John Michell's research was the notion that imperial measurement units are a naturally existing system of measure, as opposed to one that was humanly invented. The way in which the mileage measurements work in the Earth-Moon diagram is a good example of this, as will soon become apparent. The mile in question is the English mile, which as mentioned earlier consists of 5280 English feet.

The number of miles in the mean radius of Earth can be reasonably rounded up to 3960,[6] whereas the number of miles in the mean radius of the Moon is 1080.[7] When combined, these two numbers add up to 5040. As can be seen in the following diagram, the 7-unit height of the pyramid triangle corresponds to this combined distance of the radii of Earth and Moon.

6. The precise mean measurement of Earth's radius is 3958.8, which is 99.97% of 3960.
7. The precise mean measurement of the Moon's radius is 1079.6, which is 99.96% of 1080.

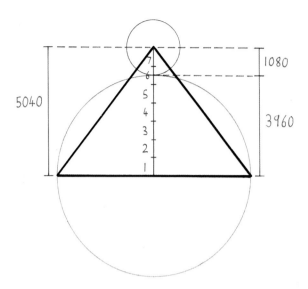

The number 5040 is significant in the philosophy of Plato. In his final dialogue – *The Laws* – this number is put forth as the ideal number by which to order a society. Michell also pointed out a remarkable fact about the relationship between the numbers 7 and 5040. This relationship works within the parameters of the decad, i.e. the first 10 numbers which happen also to have been the focal interest of the Pythagoreans. Michell demonstrated that, in using factorial counting, the numbers from 1 to 7 produce 5040 – but so also do the numbers from 7 to 10. In this sense 7 is a mediating or mean number within the decad in relation to a factorial total of 5040.

$$1 \times 2 \times 3 \times 4 \times 5 \times 6 \times 7 = 5040$$

$$7 \times 8 \times 9 \times 10 = 5040$$

If a similar process is applied to any other number in the decad, the likeness of result doesn't occur. For instance, if 6 or 8 is the stopping and re-starting point within the calculation the following uneven results occur:

$$1 \times 2 \times 3 \times 4 \times 5 \times 6 = 720$$

$$6 \times 7 \times 8 \times 9 \times 10 = 30,240$$

$$1 \times 2 \times 3 \times 4 \times 5 \times 6 \times 7 \times 8 = 40,320$$

$$8 \times 9 \times 10 = 720$$

For the numbers lower than 7 (such as 6) the first result is smaller (720) and the second result bigger (30,240) Whereas for numbers larger than 7 the inverse occurs.

However, the repetition of the number 720 in these two sequences is itself of significance here, in that it is the mileage number of one unit in Michell's diagram. If the Earth-square with its edge of 11 can be understood to be a grid of 11 × 11 squares, each one of these squares could be described as having an edge-length of 720 miles. This can be seen clearly in the fact that the 7 units of height of the pyramid triangle also represent 5040 miles.

$$7 \times 720 = 5040$$

The number 720 then gives rise to various other remarkable concordances within this whole schema. Another beautiful number relationship that Michell pointed out involves the first 11 numbers. As will become clear, the reason for involving the first 11 numbers in this particular relationship is because they encompass the two pyramid triangle numbers of 7 and 11. First let us refresh our memory of the two multiplication sequences that led to the number 720. They were $1 \times 2 \times 3 \times 4 \times 5 \times 6$ and $8 \times 9 \times 10$. As can be seen, the two numbers missing here are 7 and 11. This then leads to the remarkable concordance in which the mileage numbers of the pyramid triangle become apparent through consecutive multiplications from within the first 11 numbers.

$$1 \times 2 \times 3 \times 4 \times 5 \times 6 = 720 \ldots$$

If the 7 is then multiplied on it becomes 5040

$$1 \times 2 \times 3 \times 4 \times 5 \times 6 \times 7 = 5040$$

If this sequence of counting then proceeds beyond the number 7…

$$8 \times 9 \times 10 = 720 \ldots \text{ but with the 11 multiplied on}$$

$$8 \times 9 \times 10 \times 11 = 7920$$

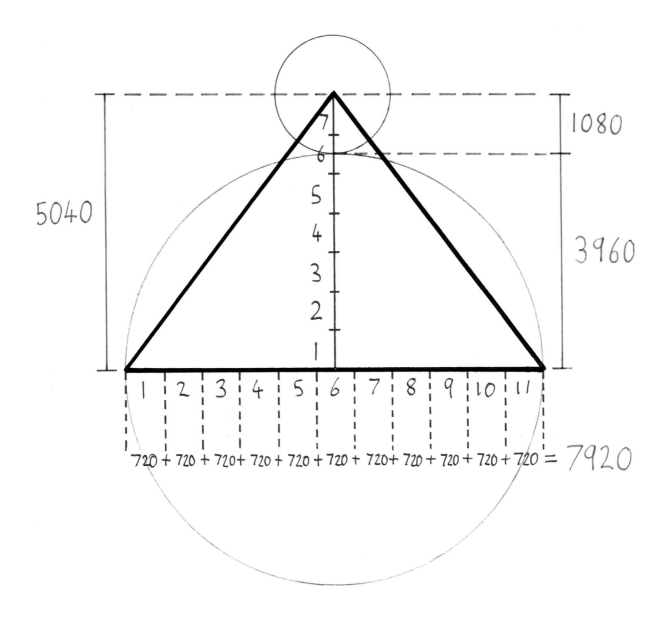

The number 7920 is the number of miles in the base-line of the pyramid triangle, which represents the mean diameter of Earth – or the edge-length of the 11 × 11 Earth-square.

11 × 720 miles = 7920 miles.

So the mean diameter of Earth (i.e. the baseline of the pyramid triangle) is 7920 miles, whereas the joint radii of Earth and Moon (i.e. the height of the pyramid triangle) is 5040 miles. But as just shown, these two numbers also occur within the consecutive multiplications contained within the first 11 numbers.

What is to be stressed here is that all of these remarkable numerical concordances, relating to measurable distances, can only be described as occurring within Michell's Earth-Moon diagram if it is the English mile that is used as the geographical unit of measurement.

At the beginning of chapter 17 (sec 17.1) another set of numerical concordances will be shown, which make a very direct connection between Michell's diagram and the Great Pyramid in relation to the size of the Earth. It involves the number 55,440, which is produced by the consecutive multiplication between the pyramid's two numbers 7 and 11.

So much time has been spent here on the Earth-Moon diagram because it appears that is was also known by medieval cathedral designers – or at least the person or people who designed the cathedrals at Wells, York and Southwell. Its use in the design of Wells even indicates the designer's knowledge of the diagram's mileage measurements of 7920 and 5040. This will all be demonstrated as the book proceeds. The use of the diagram in the design of Wells also seems to include a system of musical ratios that reflects a theory by the late musicologist Ernest McClain. He suggested that this particular system of ratios underlies the description of Magnesia in Plato's *Laws* dialogue. This is the written work mentioned earlier that includes the description of the number 5040.

But before all of this can be addressed, there is still more to show in relation to this particular system of measure.

The next stage of the numerical story requires us to look at some numbers identified by an American geometer called Randall Carlson.

Carlson pointed out that the four Platonic solids that Plato assigned to the four earthly elements together contain a significant number of degrees within their various polygonal faces. The three 60° angles of an equilateral triangle together add up to 180°, and so it can be said that an equilateral triangle contains 180°. If a similar calculation is made in relation to the four 90° corners of a square, it can be said that a square contains 360°. The four Platonic solids that Plato assigned to the four earthly elements of fire, air, water and earth were the tetrahedron, octahedron, icosahedron and cube.

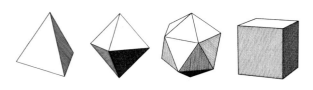

As can be seen, these four solids are made up either of equilateral triangles or squares. So it becomes possible to calculate the number of degrees in each solid.

For example, the tetrahedron is composed of four triangular faces, each of which contains 180°. So henceforth it can be calculated that 4 × 180° = 720°, and this is the number of degrees in a tetrahedron.

Carlson pointed out that if all the degrees in all the polygonal faces of these four 'earthly' solids were added together they come to a total of 7920° – the same number of miles in the mean diameter of Earth.

There is a correlation between Michell's and Carlson's research that can now be demonstrated. It shows a concordance between their particular findings, and again it is the numbers of the Fibonacci sequence that take centre stage within the correlation.

The tenth Fibonacci number is 55 and the twelfth one is 144. Interestingly 55 is also the tenth triangular number while 144 is the twelfth square number. But it is the multiplication of these two numbers which produces a rather startling result:

$$55 \times 144 = 7920$$

So the number of miles in the mean diameter of Earth shows itself in very simple form via the two Fibonacci numbers that sit on either side of the eleventh Fibonacci number (i.e. 89), and of course the Earth-square is itself 11 x 11 squares. Interestingly there is a number pattern within this Fibonacci example of 7920 which actually roots out of the eleventh Fibonacci number, 89.

$$89 \times 89 = 7921$$

This calculation multiplies the eleventh Fibonacci number by itself, whereas, as was just shown, with the two Fibonacci numbers – one before and one after 89 – the calculation produces 7920. If we continue this movement upwards and downwards through the Fibonacci numbers starting from 89 we see another Fibonacci-esque number pattern appear, which is shown in the following table. With 7921 as a starting point, each new result in the first column differs from 7921 by increasing sequential squared Fibonacci numbers.

Fibonacci number multiplication (beginning from 89^2)	Difference in relation to 7921	Square root of the difference as a Fibonacci number
$89 \times 89 = 7921$	$7921 - \mathbf{7921} = 0$	$\sqrt{0} = 0$
$55 \times 144 = 7920$	$\mathbf{7921} - 7920 = 1$	$\sqrt{1} = 1$
$34 \times 233 = 7922$	$7922 - \mathbf{7921} = 1$	$\sqrt{1} = 1$
$21 \times 377 = 7917$	$\mathbf{7921} - 7917 = 4$	$\sqrt{4} = 2$
$13 \times 610 = 7930$	$7930 - \mathbf{7921} = 9$	$\sqrt{9} = 3$
$8 \times 987 = 7896$	$\mathbf{7921} - 7896 = 25$	$\sqrt{25} = 5$
$5 \times 1597 = 7985$	$7985 - \mathbf{7921} = 64$	$\sqrt{64} = 8$
$3 \times 2584 = 7752$	$\mathbf{7921} - 7752 = 169$	$\sqrt{169} = 13$
$2 \times 4181 = 8362$	$8362 - \mathbf{7921} = 441$	$\sqrt{441} = 21$
$1 \times 6765 = 6765$	$\mathbf{7921} - 6765 = 1156$	$\sqrt{1156} = 34$
$1 \times 10,946 = 10,946$	$10,946 - \mathbf{7921} = 3025$	$\sqrt{3025} = 55$
$0 \times 17,711 = 0$	$\mathbf{7921} - 0 = 7921$	$\sqrt{7921} = 89$

Similar patterns of squared Fibonacci numbers occur from a beginning point of any squared Fibonacci number. So whereas this pattern started with the square of 89, a similar but different one would generate from the square of 55, or of 144, and so on.

Returning to the concordance between Michell's diagram, the Platonic solid angles and the multiplying of the Fibonacci numbers 55 by 144 giving 7920, this Fibonacci relationship accords with the Earth-Moon diagram because the number 55 can be divided by the Earth-square's edge of 11.

$$55 \div 11 = 5$$

What can thus be suggested is that each of the 11 small square units that bound the Earth-square have an edge-length of 5 × 144 miles. This calculation of 5 × 144 yields a result of 720 miles, as inevitably it should because this is the number of miles that each of these small square units represents.

If this result of 720 is then multiplied by 11 it produces 7920. So in other words, if the 5 × 144 calculation is repeated 11 times in a row their cumulative results add up to 7920.

At this point it then becomes possible to show how the Platonic solid angles accord with Michell's Earth-Moon diagram.

As mentioned above, the total number of degrees contained in a tetrahedron is 720. This is also the number of miles in one small square unit of the 11 × 11 Earth-square. So it can be said that one of these small squares represents the tetrahedron. Moving on to the next solid, it can be pointed out that the octahedron contains a total of 1440°, and this number is a doubling of 720. So the octahedron can be said to represent two

of the small square units. The cube contains 2160°, which is a trebling of 720, so the cube represents three small square units. Then finally the icosahedron contains 3600°, which is the result of 5 × 720.

So these numerical totals that all relate to 720 bring forth the numbers 1, 2, 3 and 5:

1 × 720 = 720° (tetrahedron)

2 × 720 = 1440° (octahedron)

3 × 720 = 2160° (cube)

5 × 720 = 3600° (icosahedron)

The numbers 1, 2, 3 and 5 are the second, third, fourth and fifth Fibonacci numbers, and together they add up to 11; the numbers 720, 1440, 2160 and 3600 together add up to 7920; and this is how Michell's Earth-Moon diagram and the Platonic solids correlate via the numbers of the Fibonacci sequence.

Again, it should be stressed that all of these numerical concordances only occur if the unit of measurement in question is the mile that consists of 5280 English feet. The final words can go to John Michell himself.

'Confronted with facts such as these, it is scarcely possible to avoid the conclusion, orthodox in every age but the present, that the cosmic canon, inherent in the solar system as in every other department of nature, was revealed to men, not invented by them.'

City of Revelation

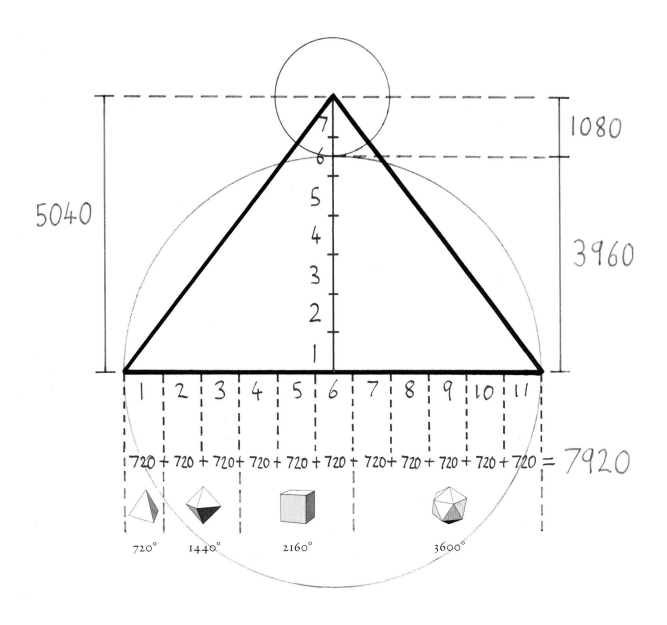

The Earth-Moon diagram with mileage numbers that accord with the total number of degrees in the four 'earthly' Platonic Solids

7.4 THE LUNAR COSMOLOGY
OF THE 5-12-13 TRIANGLE

ANOTHER TYPE OF LUNAR measure used in the design of Wells Cathedral can be found in a 5 – 12 – 13 right-angled triangle. This is the Pythagorean triangle that was shown earlier as being a rationalised form of the Golden Pediment Triangle.

The word 'month' derives from the word 'Moon' because a month approximates the duration of a single lunar cycle. So it can be suggested that there are 12 lunar cycles in a year because there are 12 months. But having said this, if four 7-day weeks can be said to form a single month, we are drawn towards the number 13 because 4 weeks consist of 28 days and 28 × 13 = 364. So in this sense it could be said that there are 13 months   plus 1 extra day – in a year. In cosmological actuality there are 12.369 synodic lunar cycles of 29.53 days within the duration of a single year.

365.25 days ÷ 29.53 days = 12.369 synodic cycles.

So it could also be said that the actual number of synodic lunar months in one year is neither 12 nor 13 but rather in between these two numbers. There is a remarkable geometric expression of this cosmic mathematics in the right-angle triangle with edges that measure 5, 12 and 13.

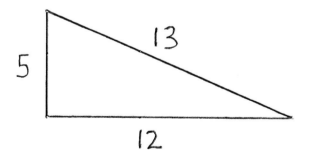

The 5 – 12 – 13 right-angled triangle is one of the Pythagorean 'triple' triangles. These are the right-angled triangles in which all three of the edges have whole-number measurements. The two longer edges of this triangle measure 12 and 13, so it would follow that somewhere between these two edges there is another line that measures the same as the annual lunar measure of 12.369. Remarkably, this particular line cuts the triangle's short edge of 5 *precisely* at its division into 2 and 3.[8]

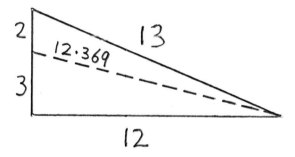

Another significant aspect of this cosmic geometry is that the numbers 2, 3, 5 and 13 are all Fibonacci numbers – and nearly all consecutive Fibonacci numbers, too. But having said this, where is the number 8? This is the Fibonacci number that falls between the numbers 5 and 13. Interestingly it was the number 8 that turned the 'Fibonacci-ised' Golden Pediment Triangle into a 5 - 12 - 13 triangle a little earlier on in this chapter (see p 118).

There is actually another lunar measure that can now be pointed out within this 5 – 12 – 13 triangle, and it occurs specifically as a result of including the number 8 into the whole schema. This is done by dividing the

8. See Robin Heath, *Sun, Moon & Earth*, Wooden Books, 2012, page 51.

hypotenuse of 13 into its constituent Fibonacci numbers of 5 and 8. If the measurement of 5 is swung across from the triangle's short vertical edge of 5 onto the hypotenuse of 13, it divides the hypotenuse into a longer segment of 8 and a shorter segment of 5.

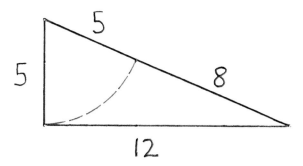

These are the two constituent Fibonacci numbers that together add up to 13. This bears some resemblance to the earlier description, in which the triangle's shorter edge-length that measures 5 became divided into its two constituent Fibonacci numbers of 2 and 3. Another similarity is that dividing the hypotenuse in this way presents another very accurate synodic lunar measure. The measure in question could be described as the Moon's synodic week, because it is very accurately one-quarter of 29.53 days.

As the next diagram demonstrates, when a vertical line is dropped from the hypotenuse's Fibonacci division, the triangle's baseline of 12 shortens into a length of 7.384

This is virtually identical to one-quarter of the number of days in a synodic lunar cycle.

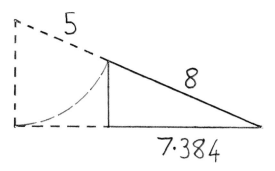

$$7.384 \times 4 = 29.53$$

Another way of looking at this is via the Fibonacci approximation of the golden number that is calculated by dividing the number 13 by the number 8:

$$13 \div 8 = 1.625$$

If the number 13 is divided by 1.625, the resulting calculation is 8. But if the number 12 is divided by 1.625, the resulting calculation ends up giving the number for a synodic week.

$$12 \div 1.625 = 7.384$$

As will become clear in Part 3, this particular lunar measure is used within a fascinating 'golden section doorway' that leads into the cathedral's sacristy.

7.5 THE PYRAMID ANGLE AS THE LATITUDE OF WOODSTOCK, OXFORD, CRESSING TEMPLE AND TEMPLE COWLEY

AT THIS POINT WE WILL take a diversion into an area of cosmological geometry that this research is calling 'latitude geometry'. There have been a few examples of these geographical geometries pointed out in the recent past by John Michell amongst others, and there will now be a few more pointed out by this research – although a whole book needs to be written on the subject, and perhaps it will be once this book has been finished. The few examples that will be shown here are appropriate to this book's specific subject matter.

Latitude geometry could simply be described as the intentional and conscious locating of a human built form at a very precisely calculated and measured latitude. Such latitudes are in some way geometrically/metrologically significant in relation to the sphere of Planet Earth upon its polar axis.

This practice appears to go all the way back to at least Neolithic times, as can be seen in an example pointed out by John Michell in which the line of latitude that runs through the middle of the Avebury stone circle is very precisely 1/7 of Earth's circumference north of the equator. Michell actually describes the latitude as being 4/7 of the distance between the equator and the north pole, which is another way of defining it. The accuracy of this measurement is exceedingly precise, whereby there either has to be the usual insistence that it is all a very large random coincidence or else an acceptance that Neolithic cultures could actually define latitude with very great precision indeed. But the practice of latitude geometry also appears to have been used in the medieval era as well, and we need not even leave Avebury to observe this. One of the findings in this research is that the medieval church building imme-diately outside of the Avebury circle, on its western side, is also very precisely at this same latitude. So also is the medieval well, which the Red Lion pub has been built around in more recent centuries. The well is currently below a glass-topped table in the pub, and it is possible to peer down into the watery womb of the Earth while enjoying a pub lunch.

To make this fact geometrically clear, the diagram below shows a simple example of a circle which represents a profile view of Planet Earth. It is divided into seven equal parts in such a way that the horizontal radial line on the right side of the circle could be said to coincide with 0° latitude on Earth's equator. The line immediately above it is therefore at 51.428571°, which is simply 1/7 of 360°. This is then the latitude of the middle east–west axis of the Avebury circle, which also passes precisely through the Avebury Church of St James and the Red Lion's well-table.

$$360 \div 7 = 51.428571 \text{ (or } 51^{3/7}°)$$

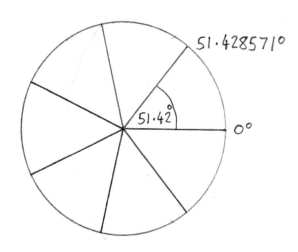

Profile view of planet Earth divided into seven equal parts. The latitude of Avebury is precisely 51.428571° north of the equator which is at 0°.

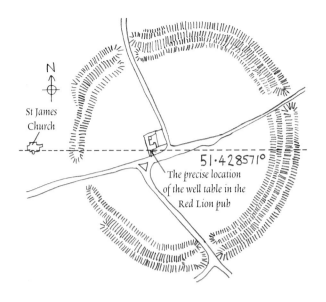

Road map of the Avebury circle with the latitude 51.428571° marked on

Moving beyond Avebury, the particular example of latitude geometry that will be considered in more detail within this section involves angles of latitude that are also the angles of elevation found in both the pi and golden ratio Pyramid Triangles. These particular latitudes are just a little to the north of the latitude of Avebury. Interestingly, the places in question are the first two English manors of land that were granted to the Knights Templar. The first manor of land is called Cressing Temple, which is in the county of Essex. It was granted to the Templars by Matilda of Boulogne, wife of King Stephen of England, in the year 1136. As mentioned in chapter 3 (sec 3.3), Matilda of Boulogne was familially connected to the Kingdom of Jerusalem via two of her uncles, who were the first two rulers of the Crusader Kingdom – Godfrey de Bouillon (1099–1100) and his brother King Baldwin I of Jerusalem (1100–1118). However, it was a few decades later, during the reign of King Fulk of Jerusalem (1131–1143), that the manor of land in Essex was granted to the Templars. Fulk was a renowned crusader and a close associate of the Templars from very early in their existence as a religious order in the Crusader Kingdom. Fulk was also the grandfather of Henry II, who ascended to the English throne immediately after King Stephen.

Before looking more closely at this particular example of latitude geometry, we need to look at an apparent written description of it by the famous medieval writer, poet and scholar Geoffrey Chaucer. In his treatise on the astrolabe Chaucer actually mentions the angle of the pyramid triangle – which is 51°50' – as being the latitude of Oxford. He doesn't mention 'the pyramid triangle' as such, although the only significant mathematically definable form that has this very specific angle in it is the pyramid triangle. When the measurement is defined in 'degrees, minutes and seconds' the Pi Pyramid Triangle has an angle of 51°50'34" whereas the Golden Pyramid Triangle has an angle of 51°49'38".

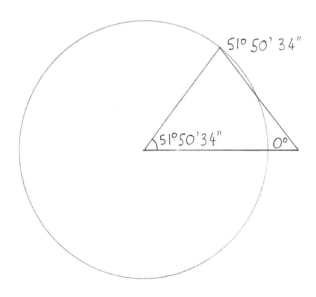

Pi Pyramid Triangle on profile view of planet Earth - Latitude of 51° 50' 34"

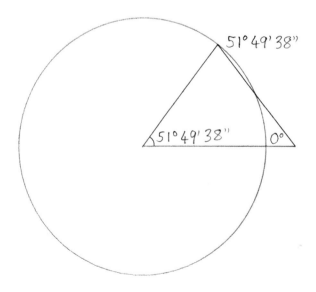

Golden Pyramid triangle on planet Earth defining a latitude of 51° 49' 38"

135

It can of course be suggested that Chaucer happened to mention this angle purely because it is the latitude of Oxford, and in no way because it happens also to define the angular elevation of a pyramid triangle. But in actual fact 51°50' is not the latitude of Oxford, and Chaucer was even seemingly aware of this! There is an interesting quandary in relation Chaucer's description of this angle, which has brought about questions among translators of his treatise because, having mentioned the angle as defining the latitude of Oxford, he then later corrects himself and says that it is not precisely this angle but rather that the correct latitude is a few minutes less – which is absolutely correct. The latitude of the university Church of St Mary the Virgin in Oxford is actually 51°45'10" whereas the Pi Pyramid latitude angle – seemingly described by Chaucer – is actually the latitude of Woodstock, a few miles to the north. Indeed this line of latitude passes within a few hundred feet of the site of the old royal palace at Woodstock which is now in the grounds of Blenheim Palace. The latitude actually goes right through the northeast wing of the Blenheim Palace building.

So if Chaucer knew that 51°50' is not the latitude of Oxford, we are left with the question of why he initially defined it as being so only to then correct himself a little later on. Woodstock and Oxford are not the same place! Could it possibly be that Chaucer was of the opinion that there is something significant about this angle beyond it just being the latitude (or rather the 'non-latitude') of Oxford? If it was a matter of rounding his numbers up or down to the nearest useful total, it would seem to make more sense to go with the actual latitude of Oxford, which can effectively be defined with the much simpler measure of 51¾° (i.e. 51°45'00"). This particular latitude is actually a very small amount further to the south of the Church of St Mary the Virgin – which is the original centre of Oxford University. But having said this, 51¾° happens also to be the precise latitude of Christchurch Cathedral, which was built on the site of St Frideswide's 7th-century convent, which is an older focal point of Oxford. The site of St Frideswide's shrine itself – on the cathedral's north side – is then 1" north of 51¾°.

There is more that could be said about all of this, including the significant fact that the actual distance between Woodstock's Pi Pyramid angle of latitude and the Church of St Mary the Virgin in Oxford is 'precisely' one-thousandth of the distance between the equator and the north pole, which is 324" of latitude. This would appear to be a potential reason why Chaucer mentions the Woodstock pyramid latitude in relation to Oxford. Interestingly, this particular geographical unit of measurement will become apparent again a little later on in relation to the latitude of St Andrews Cathedral in the town of St Andrews in Scotland. It will also be explained how this somehow all manages to relate to St Andrew's Cathedral in Wells, which is of course the main study of this book.

Meanwhile, Cressing Temple presents a very interesting example of pyramid geometry. Within New Age lore there is sometimes a tenuous link made between the Templars and knowledge of the Great Pyramid of Giza. The sceptical blogger Jason Colavito points out on his website that there was a speech given at an anarchist congress in Chicago in the 1870s in which it was suggested that the development of trade union culture was influenced by the Templars, along with their knowledge of ancient Egyptian wisdom such as the dimensions of the Great Pyramid. On the surface this suggestion seems random, if not rather wacky. But what this research is increasingly considering is that these sorts of apparently ungrounded connections are a kind of embroidered remnant of a medieval Christian interest in the quadrivial knowledge of the ancient world. It can be suggested that such traces of initiatic culture may have passed through into the early modern era via Rosicrucianism and Freemasonry. Such ideas have subsequently become increasingly fantastical as the post-Enlightenment era has proceeded. But such is the post-Enlightenment malaise, in which occultism and New Ageism progressively disappear off up into the clouds, while scientific rationalism and materialism come crashing down to Earth.

As is presumably clear, there are no suggestions in this book that Elvis Presley was a secret Templar who crash-landed a Nazi UFO on the back of the Loch Ness Monster while covertly making his way to take part in the First Zionist Congress. All that is being pointed out is that the first manor of land given to the Templars by Queen Matilda of England in AD 1136 is at the latitude of 51°50' and that this could appear to be an intentional example of 12th-century latitude geometry involving a knowledgeable use of the Pi Pyramid Triangle.

To be precise, the site of Cressing Temple is actually between the latitudes of the Pi Pyramid Triangle (51°50'34") and the Golden Pyramid Triangle (51°49'38"). There is around a mile of distance between these two very similar latitudes, and the modern-day site of Cressing Temple actually falls within this mile or so of north–south distance at Chaucer's 51°50' latitude between 11" and 20". However, within this short range of 9" (just under one-fifth of mile) we shall focus on a precise latitude of 51°50'16". The reason for settling on this specific latitude is because it passes through what was the site of a Templar chapel dedicated to the Virgin Mary that had its own graveyard. Cressing Temple is particularly famous for its medieval barns, and many daytrippers visit the site in the current time to look at these old and very impressive timber buildings. But if there were going to be a building placed at a significant latitude, one might assume that it would be a religiously important building such as a chapel with a graveyard, rather than storage barns.

In short, the latitude in question returns us to the geographical unit mentioned earlier in relation to St Mary's Church in Oxford, and St Andrews Cathedral in Scotland. This geographical unit is 324" of latitude. If the 324" is divided by 18 it produces a shorter geographical unit of 18", because 324 is quite simply the square of 18.

$$18 \times 18 = 324$$

This measurement of 18" is then the distance between the Pi Pyramid latitude and the site of the Templar chapel dedicated to the Virgin Mary. This measurement is also 1/200 of a degree of latitude.

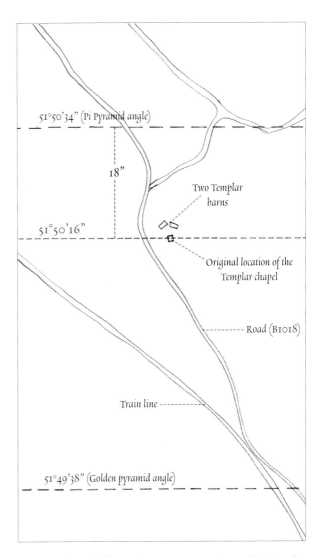

The latitude angle of the Templar preceptory at Cressing Temple is situated between the angles of elevation found in the pi and phi pyramid triangles. A Templar chapel was located precisely 18" south of the pi latitude.

It is also pretty much exactly 1/3 of the distance between the two pyramid triangle latitudes.

Whether this system of latitude geometry was used for the locating of Cressing Temple is unclear, as it is impossible to know all of the buildings that the site once contained. However, the simple fact that the site is so precisely located between the two pyramid latitude angles is intriguing to say the least. Considering that there are around 6222 miles between the equator and the north pole, a single mile within this range is a very small distance indeed, and so it makes for a rather large coincidence that the first Templar manor in England is located within it.

But Cressing Temple is not the only piece of early Templar land situated around these pyramid angles of latitude. In AD 1139, a few years after the granting of Cressing Temple, Queen Matilda gave the Templars more land, although this time at what came to be known as Temple Cowley. This brings us back to Oxford, where Temple Cowley is a suburb. Yet again it is the geographical unit of 324" (0.09°) of latitude that appears to be used although, rather than being related to Woodstock's Pi Pyramid Triangle latitude, it works specifically in relation to the angle found in the Golden Pyramid Triangle. As mentioned a little earlier, this is 51°49'38" (51.827292°). The Temple Cowley latitude of 51°44'14" (51.737292°) is 324" to the south of the Golden Pyramid Triangle latitude. The line of latitude passes directly through a small school playing field – an area of grassland that is enclosed on its northern and eastern sides by 'Temple Road'. The name of this road is pretty much the only remaining trace of the Templar preceptory itself. Again, its latitudinal distance south of the angle found in a Golden Pyramid Triangle is precisely one-thousandth of the distance between the equator and the north pole. As mentioned earlier, the centre of Oxford University, which began to develop only a few decades after the establishment of the Templar manors, is precisely the same latitude distance to the south of the Pi Pyramid Triangle latitude in Woodstock as Temple Cowley is from the Golden Pyramid Triangle latitude.

Finally, we are left with the question of how such precise latitude measures could be defined without modern technology, and an answer is admittedly not so easy to offer. A simple geocosmic fact is that the altitude of the Celestial North Pole (i.e. its angle of elevation upwards from the true horizon) is the same as the angle of latitude of the person who is viewing it. So in short, if someone were to stand at a latitude of 51°50'16" the Celestial North Pole would be that many degrees, minutes and seconds above the true horizon. But to calculate this measurement very accurately without modern technology is not so easy. Another way of defining latitude is to measure the shadow caused by the Sun at midday on the equinox in relation to the gnomon that is casting the shadow.

But again, to gain a very accurate measurement from this is not easy.

In his book *On the Same and the Different* Adelard of Bath describes a simple and clever way to measure the height of a very tall object by using a 45° angle of observation. Bearing in mind that 45° is produced by the diagonal line of a square, along with the fact that the vertical and horizontal edges of a square are the same length as one another, these simple geometric facts can be used to measure the height of something much taller than a human. By looking at the top of a tall object in such a way that the viewer's vision is angled upwards at 45°, it can be said that the height of the object is the same as the distance of the viewer from the bottom of the object, in much the same way that the height of the square is the same as the length of its horizontal baseline. The horizontal distance is thus measurable by someone of human height even if the vertical measurement is not. This is all done by applying a simple geometric fact in an intelligent way.

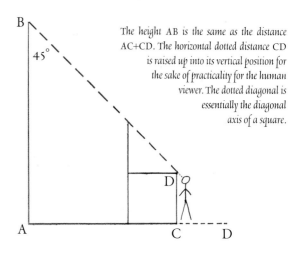

The height AB is the same as the distance AC+CD. The horizontal dotted distance CD is raised up into its vertical position for the sake of practicality for the human viewer. The dotted diagonal is essentially the diagonal axis of a square.

The very precise calculating and defining of latitude was presumably done with a simple and clever use of geometric techniques – in a similar vein to the one described above by Adelard. But up to now this research is unable to say exactly how this was done.

Later in the book the latitude geometry of Jerusalem, Hermopolis, Haran, the Great Pyramid and St Andrews in Scotland will all be considered, along with a suggestion as to why such practices appeared to take place in the ancient and medieval world.

CHAPTER 8.

The Use of Pyramid Geometry in Gothic Cathedral Design

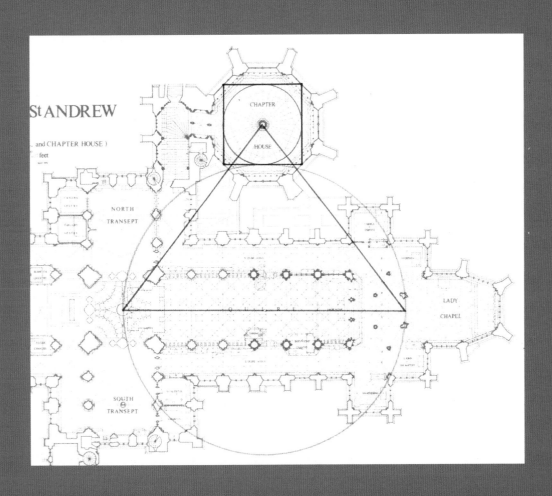

8.1 PYRAMID GEOMETRY IN THE DESIGN OF WELLS CATHEDRAL

THIS CHAPTER WILL now demonstrate how the pyramid geometry shown in the previous chapter appears to have been used in the design of Wells Cathedral. The following images and descriptions are a more general marking-out of the geometries as they appear to be used in the various designs. The whole of Part 3 is then devoted to close arithmetical detail of how these geometries show themselves within the very precise measures of the building itself. So the following images, in which geometries are overlaid on the ground plan, are not the primary proofs of the design theory but rather an initial indication of what will be presented in more detail in Part 3.

THE LADY CHAPEL AND THE RETROQUIRE

THE LADY CHAPEL and retroquire at Wells were the final areas of the cathedral church to be added. They were built in the early part of the 1300s. This places them chronologically over 100 years after the initial building of the cathedral, which started around 1175.

The architectural style of these two areas is clearly from a later period. They also replaced an older Lady chapel that was at the original east end of the earlier building, which only reached as far as the beginning of the current retroquire. So with these facts in mind it has understandably been concluded that the current Lady chapel and retroquire were designed at a later date, and were therefore not part of the original design.

This research will gradually demonstrate that from a perspective of mathematically provable and empirically verifiable design rationale it appears as though the ground plans of these two areas were always part of the original design. However, the parts of the fabric that were then built in a 'vertical' direction upwards from the ground plans of the Lady chapel and retroquire would have been subject to the changes in technology and architectural style that occurred prior to the final building of their walls and vault in the early 1300s. The reasons for suggesting this will become clear as this story develops.

The geometric master diagram of the retroquire and Lady chapel is centred around a Golden Pyramid Triangle. (see diagram 2 on the next page)

A Golden Pediment Triangle is also added to this pyramid triangle, and its apex defines the centre of the square arrangement of pillars. (see diagram 3)

The two circles can now be added. The larger circle uses the apex of the pediment triangle to define its radius. (see diagram 4)

As shown in the previous chapter, the intersections of these two circles allow the drawing of a pentagram star.

What then becomes clear is that the inner pentagon of this star defines the pentagonal east-end of the Lady chapel. (see diagram 5 after the next page)

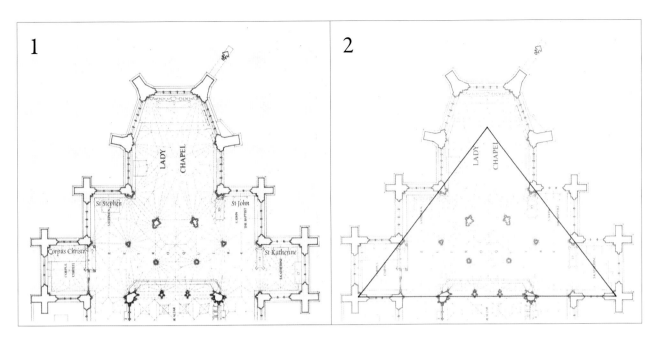

1

The Lady chapel and retroquire lie immediately beyond the cathedral's rectanglar quire. The retroquire contains four chapels two of which are dedicated to 'solstitial' saints - John the Baptist and Stephen. The other two chapels are dedicated to St Katherine of Alexandria and the Corpus Christi visions of St Juliana of Liège. Along with the Lady chapel itself these three chapels are the only ones in the whole cathedral dedicated to, or associated with, females. There is a possibility that the Corpus Christi chapel was originally intended to be dedicated to St Mary Magdalene. The Virgin Mary, St Katherine and St Mary Magdalene are the only three females whose feasts were kept as part of the Templar rule.

2

This part of the cathedral is governed by a Golden Pyramid Triangle. Note the sloping sides of the triangle passing diagonally through the four chapels of the retroquire. The three corners of the pyramid triangle are situated in the three chapels that are dedicated to females.

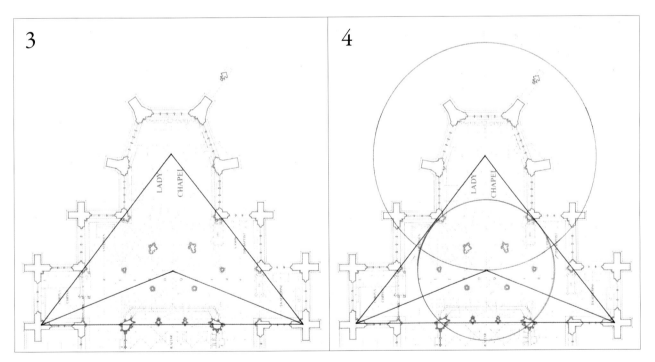

3

The Golden Pediment Triangle is added into the pyramid triangle. The apex of the pediment triangle lies at the centre of a square arrangement of pillars as well as equidistantly between the two pillars that mark the corners of the St John and St Stephen chapels.

4

The two circles are added into the diagram. They are centred upon the apexes of the two triangles. The circle's two mutual intersection points mark off 1/5 of the larger circle and 2/5 of the smaller circle.

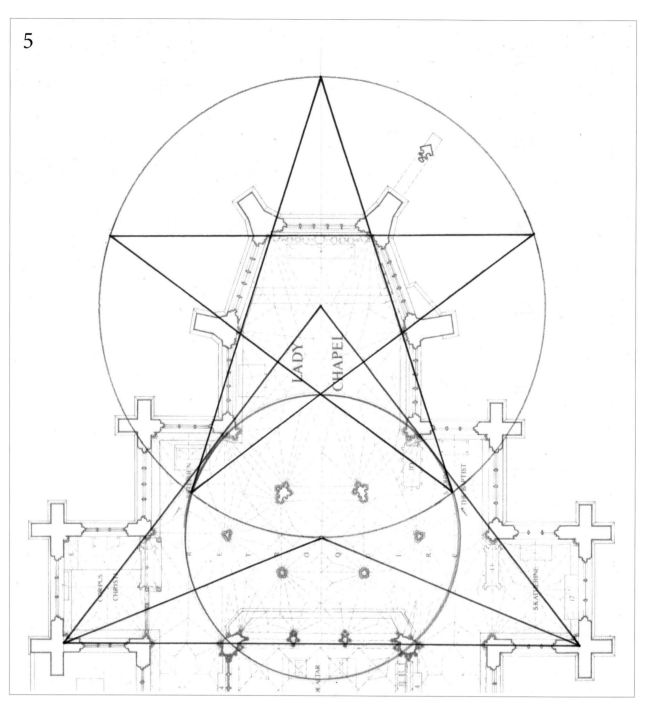

The pentagram star is added into the diagram. Its inner pentagon forms the pentagonal east-end of the Lady chapel and thus the east-end of the whole cathedral.

This pyramid triangle is the geometric origin of the pentagram shown first in chapter 5 (sec 5.4), and so it can also be added that this golden ratio pyramid triangle is cosmologically associated with the golden ratio activities of the Planet Venus – the Bright Morning Star rising in the east at the cathedral's eastern end.

It was also shown in chapter 5.4 (p.73) how the octagonal western end of the Lady chapel was derived from an octagram star. (see diagram on following page). This star is generated from a circle that is centred on the bottom corner of the pentagon i.e. which itself derives from the centre of the pentagram star. As is clear from the diagram on the previous page, the smaller circle also passes through this particular intersection of red lines.

These master diagrams show the basic geometry that governs the layout. However, there is another more sophisticated layer of measurements arising from this diagram in the form of units of measure – specifically three different feet and a cubit that all share a common micro-unit. There are actually two very slightly different measurement variations of the pyramid triangle that are effectively present in the design here, and the interactions of these slightly different measurements begin to show the way in which musical ratios and metrology also underlie the design. This will all be developed in Part 3 – 'The Arithmetical and Musical Design Elements of the First English Gothic Cathedral'.

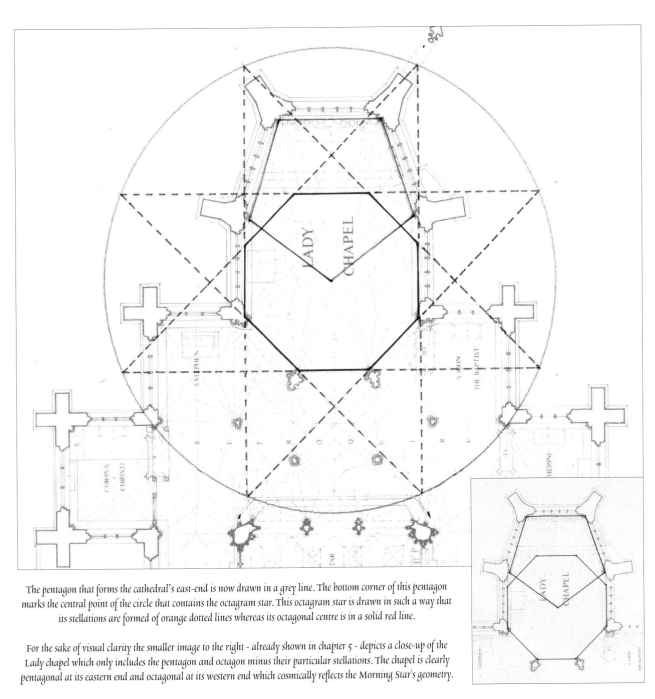

The pentagon that forms the cathedral's east-end is now drawn in a grey line. The bottom corner of this pentagon marks the central point of the circle that contains the octagram star. This octagram star is drawn in such a way that its stellations are formed of orange dotted lines whereas its octagonal centre is in a solid red line.

For the sake of visual clarity the smaller image to the right - already shown in chapter 5 - depicts a close-up of the Lady chapel which only includes the pentagon and octagon minus their particular stellations. The chapel is clearly pentagonal at its eastern end and octagonal at its western end which cosmically reflects the Morning Star's geometry.

THE QUIRE AND chapter house area of Wells Cathedral is where the building work started in the 1170s. The process of cathedral building was such that work would generally begin at the eastern end and then move westwards. The most important area to complete was the quire, which was the centre of liturgical activity. The original east end of the quire at Wells was around the middle of the current quire, and there was an older Lady chapel covering the area that is now the eastern half of the current quire/presbytery.

The use of pyramid geometry in this area of the cathedral corresponds to both the earlier ground plan/layout as well as the current one. The pyramid triangle that is used in this area stretches beyond the original eastern end of the cathedral. This is the first indication that the original east end was looked upon as a temporary final design that was always intended to eventually be adapted into its current form.

The building of a cathedral took place over a very long period of time. But within this long period of time there would inevitably have been a desire on the part of the church to start practising the liturgy in the building at the earliest possible date. So the need to build in temporary smaller stages that could eventually be adapted and extended appears to be why there was an earlier east end prior to the current one. From an art history perspective it makes sense to suggest that the current east end was a later design that replaced an earlier and original east end design. But from the perspective of a geometric design rationale, the idea that the original east end of the ground plan was a temporary design later to be extended into the current east end makes more sense.

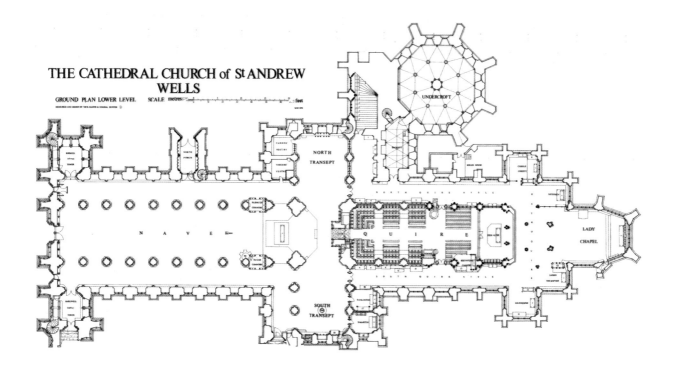

The ground plan of Wells Cathedral in its final form - (minus the cloister). The findings of this research suggest that this ground plan was always the intended final design even though the retroquire and Lady chapel area, up at the east-end, were not completed until the early 1300's. Before the cathedral was extended eastwards the area that eventually became the eastern 'presbytery' half of the recatangular quire was where an earlier square-ended Lady chapel once stood. At that time the rectangular quire took up the area between the three westerly bays of the current quire as well as the crossing and the most easterly bay of the nave. (see second diagram on the following page).

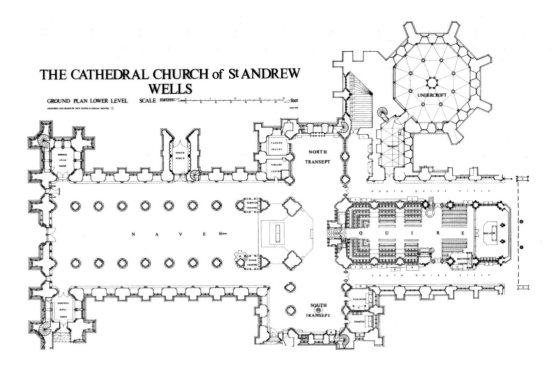

The red dotted line marks the original eastern end of the foundations and therefore the eastern limits of the original building. The two small black rectangles that lie beyond this red line are the tombs of Dean John Godelee (1305-1333) and Bishop John Drokensford (1309-1329) - the Dean and the Bishop who were in office when the east-end extension was begun. Their monuments mark the movement beyond this original eastern limit of the foundations.

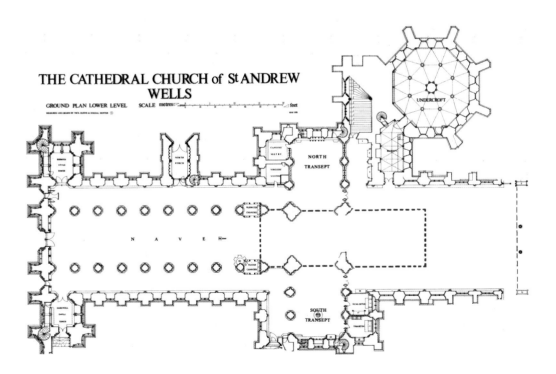

The new thicker red dotted line shows the area that contained the original rectangular quire. Beyond this quire - to the east - there was a Lady chapel as well as altars dedicated to other saints - Mary Magdalene is known to have been one of them. Could it be that John the Baptist, Stephen and Katherine were the other dedications and that, when these four dedications were transferred to the new east-end extension, Mary Magdalene's dedication was changed to Corpus Christi?

The pyramid triangle in the retroquire and Lady chapel area points eastwards. This could be described as the orientation of the liturgy. The baseline of this triangle passes through the quire's high altar, which is effectively the focal point of this eastward moving liturgy. But the pyramid triangle covering the quire and chapter house area points northwards. Its baseline runs through the east–west length of the quire, and its apex falls in the middle of an octagonal area which consists of two octagonal halls – one located above the other. As can be seen below, the two bottom corners of this pyramid triangle are located with one in the centre of the cathedral's crossing, and the other at the threshold of the Lady chapel. This particular image shows the ground plan of the octagonal chapter house, as opposed to the octagonal treasury/undercroft that is one floor below it.

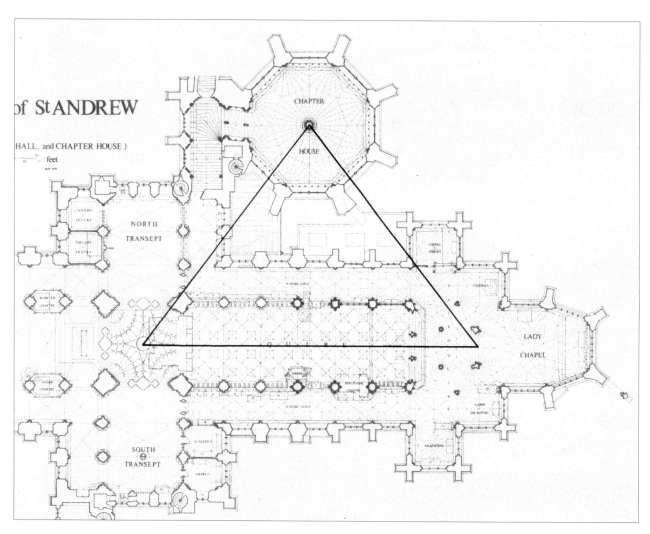

The 'northward-pointing' pyramid triangle that governs the quire and chapter house area with its three corners located at the cathedral's crossing, the centre of the chapter house and threshold of the Lady chapel.

There are various different uses of this pyramid triangle, from which particular parts of the design are derived. In relation to the design of the treasury/undercroft, i.e. below the chapter house, the pyramid triangle has the pediment triangle contained within it, and more generally it is the same version of the pyramid diagram as the one used in the retroquire/Lady chapel area. This particular use of the pyramid triangle only governs the size of the undercroft, however, which as mentioned above is the lower of the two octagonal rooms. Bearing in mind that the Golden Pyramid Triangle can naturally produce five-fold geometric forms

(such as a pentagram star) we are left with the question of why there is an octagonal shape in the ground plan of the building. The answer lies in the fact that the designer appears to have intentionally substituted a pentagram star for an octagram star. (see diagram on following page)

One of the reasons for this will become clear in Part 3, in which the metrology is examined – suffice to say that the transmutation of pentagram into octagram causes the design's theoretical wall-to-wall measurement of the octagonal undercroft to become *precisely* 51 feet.

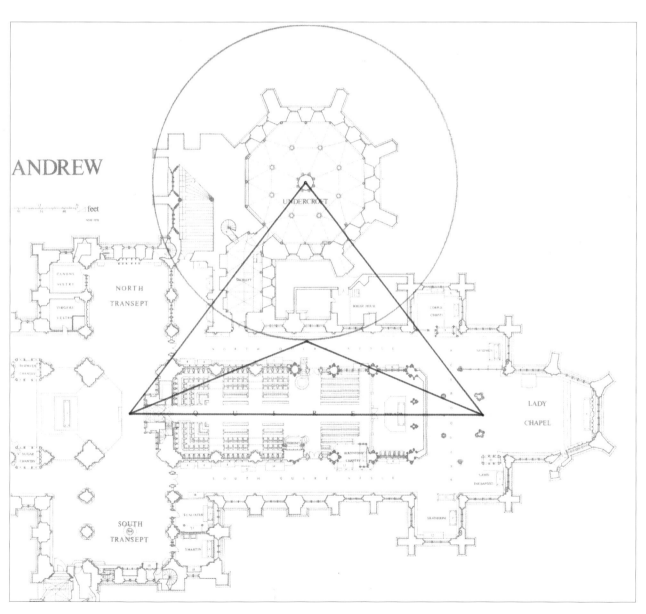

The use of the pyramid triangle in the design of the octagonal undercroft includes a pediment triangle which produces a particular size of a container circle

As mentioned in section 5.4, there is a close geometrical and mathematical concordance between pentagram and octagram stars, whereby the circle that contains the pentagram's inner pentagon is virtually identical in size to the circle that is contained by the octagram's inner octagon.

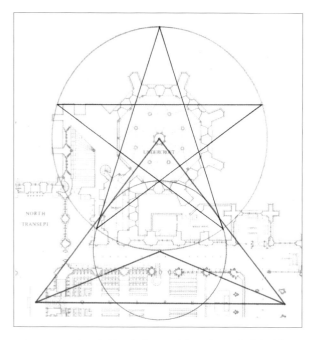

The pentagram is an 'arithmetically correct' shape that can be derived from a Golden Pyramid Triangle. But the Undercroft is octagonal in shape so the pentagon at the centre of the pentagram star is clearly not the shape that has been used to produce the octagonal form of the undercroft.

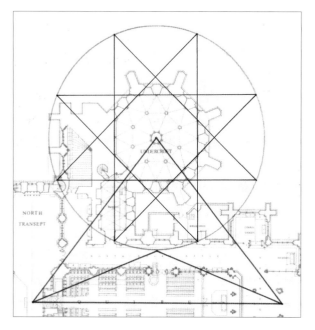

If the Pentagram star is replaced by an Octagram star its inner octagon clearly aligns with the octagonal shape and size of the undercroft. The edges of the octagon accurately mark the inner wall of the undercroft.

The next use of this pyramid triangle occurs in relation to the upper octagonal hall, which is the chapter house. In this particular case the triangle is used as if it is a Pi Pyramid Triangle rather than a Golden Pyramid Triangle. As mentioned earlier, the difference in height between the Pi Pyramid Triangle and the Golden Pyramid Triangle, in the scale at which they used in the design of Wells, is around two-thirds of an inch. So this is a minor discrepancy that does not in any way stand out to the human eye. In purely practical terms it is most likely that the pi triangle was the actual one that was marked out by the builders. But it was then theoretically understood and indeed used as if it were both a pi and a phi triangle at the same time.

The geometric diagram used in this particular instance is none other than the Earth-Moon diagram that John Michell *re*-discovered in the early 1970s. As will become clear, the remarkable fact about the use of this diagram in the design of Wells Cathedral is that it even incorporates the numbers 7920 and 5040 for the baseline and height of the pyramid triangle, indicating that the designer was aware of this particular cosmological aspect of the diagram. To be explicit, such a knowledge on the part of the designer would involve the dimensions of the Earth and the Moon in imperial miles. This sort of knowledge is not generally associated with 12th-century Western European master masons, and so this design theory opens up a debate as to whether there was more knowledge among these people than is generally assumed.

The two cosmic numbers from the Earth-Moon diagram (7920 and 5040) are present in the form of the micro-unit that is common to all the foot and cubit units used within the cathedral's design. This will be developed further in Part 3.

The other point to make here is that the design suggests that the chapter house in some way symbolises the Moon, whereas the Temple of Solomon-shaped quire and more generally the chancel area symbolise Earth. This lunar aspect of the chapter house will be developed in the next chapter.

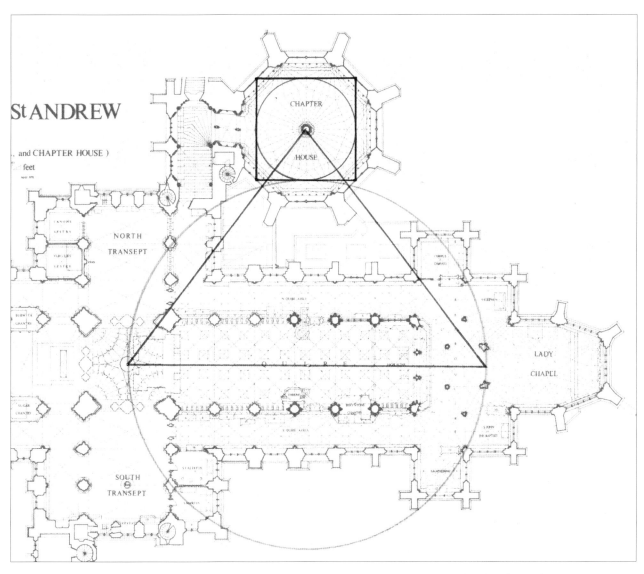

St ANDREW

, and CHAPTER HOUSE)

feet

The earth-moon pyramid triangle diagram is used in such a way that the chapter house is the Moon and the chancel area is the Earth

There is also a golden ratio use of the pyramid triangle, on this particular level where the chapter house is located, and it relates to the various golden section divisions within the pyramid triangle that were shown in the previous chapter (sec 7.2). As the image on the next page demonstrates, the golden section lines that are produced on either side of the pyramid triangle accord with various measures of the chapter house as well as the staircase that leads up to it, and also the eastern end of the quire along with the cathedral church's northern wall. The measurement units of this design schema will be shown in chapter 16 (sec 16.1.)

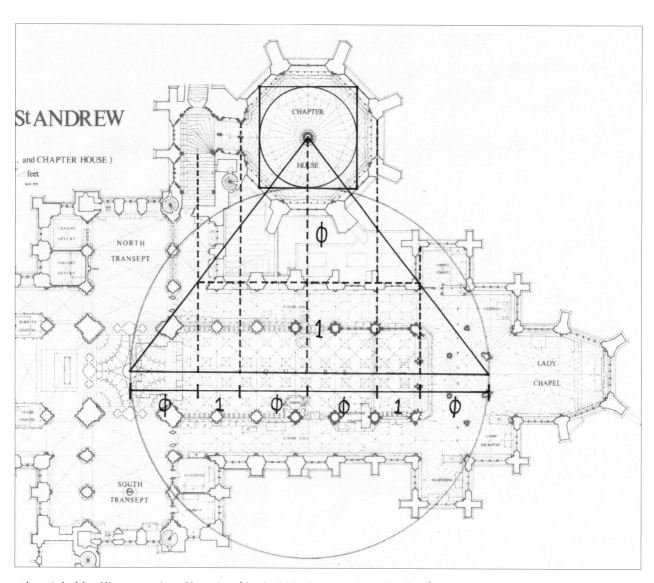

The vertical red dotted lines create various golden sections of the triangle's baseline. These relationships of 1 to ϕ are also written in red. Note the various relationships they reflect within the architectural design - mainly in the chapter house area - such as the opposite edges of the octagonal chapter house as well as the middle axis of the chapter house staircase. Also the axis of the high altar arches, which divides the quire from the retroquire. This appears to be the only relationship that is produced by these golden section lines within the quire area of the design. The horizontal red dotted line runs along the north wall and also creates a Golden Section division of the triangle's central vertical axis. Here the 1 - ϕ relationship is written in blue because its numerical values are different to the 1 - ϕ relationships that are written in red. Later in the book it will be demonstrated that these golden sections are all actually Fibonacci divisions.

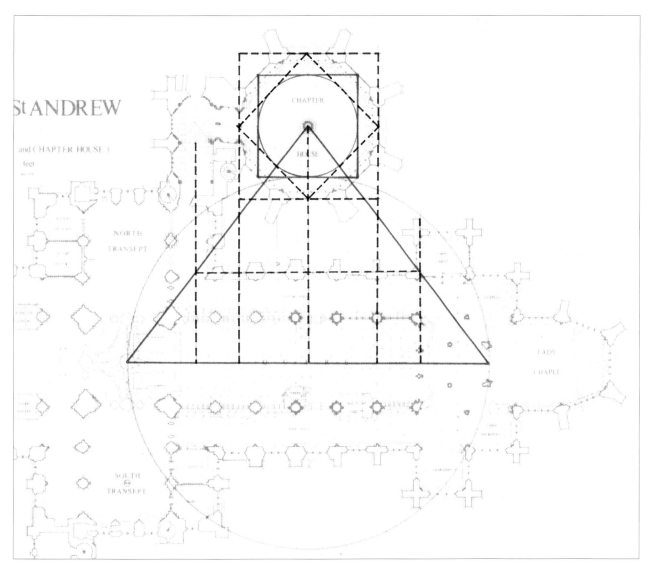

In this image the two vertical red dotted lines that mark the opposite edges of the octagonal chapter house have been used to create a complete red dotted square around the chapter house. The blue dotted square is the same size as the smaller red Moon-square but it is turned into a diagonal orientation. This accordingly demonstrates that the Moon-square's diagonal measurement interacts with this new larger red dotted square. But whereas the red dotted square derives from the golden section lines of a Golden Pyramid Triangle, the Moon-square derives from the pyramid triangle in its pi form - i.e. with a base of 11 and a height of 7. This interaction of different pyramid measures deriving from different pyramid triangles will be looked at in more detail in part 3.

The final use of the pyramid triangle in this quire/chapter house area is related to the dimensions of the quire itself. In the pyramid rhomb diagram, in section 7.2, it was shown how it is possible to generate a decagram star consisting of two opposed pentagrams, and how this geometry naturally brings forth a rectangle that is a close approximation of a 1 × 3 rectangle.

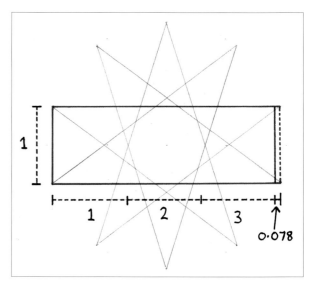

Rectangle measuring 1 x 3.078 deriving from a decagram star

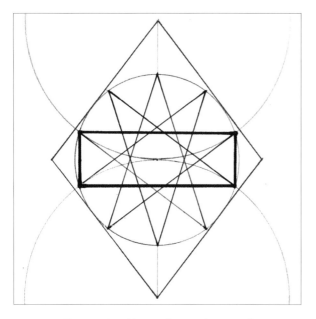

Decagram star with rectangle measuring 1 x 3.078

The rectangle is actually 1 × 3.078... The larger number here is an irrational number – although the designer of the quire appears to have truncated the rectangle at its eastern end, transmuting it into a rational 1 × 3 rectangle. This truncation of the rectangle is marked by the existence of the feretory wall that is located immediately behind the high altar. As for the non-truncated eastern end of this rectangle, it precisely marks the original eastern end of the whole cathedral building. (see diagram on next page). So both the original east end as well as the later one, that still remains to this day, correspond to this particular aspect of the diagram. Such a fact begins to bring into focus the suggestion in this research that the older east-end was a temporary architectural termination, beyond which the design was always intended to move further to the east. As the following diagrams show, there is a whole section of the pyramid triangle that goes beyond the original eastern end of the building all the way up to the entrance of the current Lady chapel. If the final intended design only went as far as the eastern end of the decagram star, why would the designer not have utilised the bottom right-hand corner of the pyramid triangle?

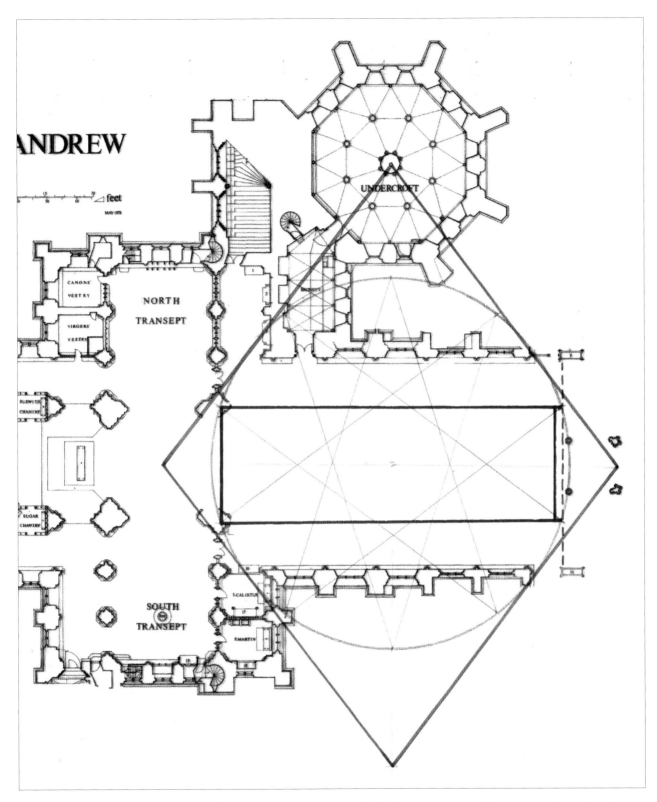

ANDREW

The red dotted line marks the original eastern end of the foundations. However, the pyramid triangle-rhomb goes beyond this line thus suggesting that the earlier east-end was always only a temporary eastern termination of the building. The pyramid rhomb, with its decagram star, naturally produces the line that governs the old eastern termination of the building. But it also produces the 1 x 3 rectangle used in the quire as it is now stands - and has done since the early 1300's.

153

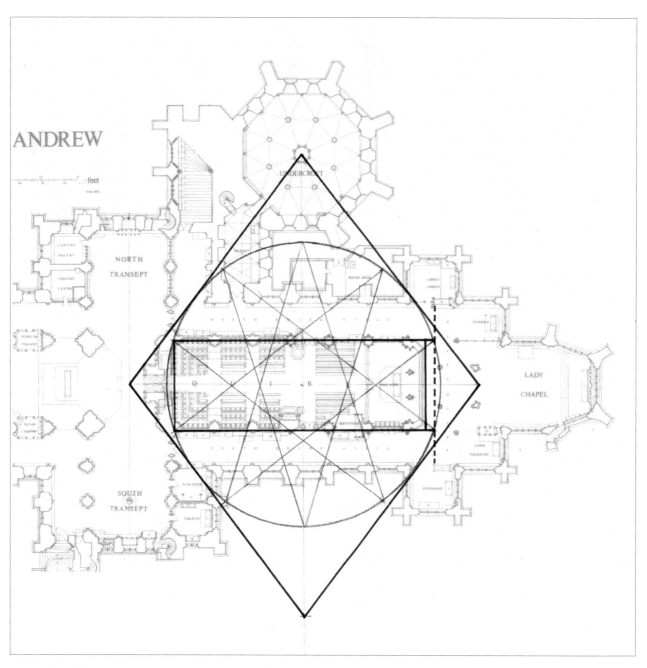

When the decagram star is applied to the full ground plan of the current quire it becomes clear as to how accurate this geometric analysis appears to be. The truncation of the 1 x 3.078 rectangle into a 1 x 3 rectangle neatly fits the quire in its final form. But the extra 0.078 determines the original east-end.

Another interesting geometric detail is in relation to this use of pentagrams to form the rectangle that emulates the ground plan of Solomon's Temple. In the *Testament of Solomon* there is a description of a ring worn by Solomon on which there was a pentagram. This pentagram ring was then used as a way of trapping demons, who were subsequently put to work on the building of his temple. This storyline will be described in more detail in chapter 20 in the section entitled *The pentagram of Solomon and Gawain*. Another fascinating possibility is that this double pentagram geometry, derived from a pyramid rhomb diagram, could actually be the original geometry used for the Tabernacle and thus by extension also the Temple of Solomon itself. The measurement details of this will be shown in chapter 15 in section 15.2.

THE WEST FRONT AND THE NAVE

FOR VARIOUS REASONS, mainly relating to a desire to obtain very accurate measurements, this whole study is concentrated mainly on the design of the cathedral's ground plan. A few vertical measurements are also included, but they are more general overarching diagrams rather than the very detailed mathematical diagrams and descriptions that will be shown in Part 3 in relation to the ground plans.

One vertical measurement that can be pointed out here is a pyramid triangle used in the design of the west front, which also swings down, as it were, on to the ground plan, where it forms an eastward-pointing pyramid triangle on the ground plan of the nave. The detail of the measurements of this pyramid triangle will

follow in Part 3, but suffice to say for now that the triangle can be understood both through Fibonacci approximations of the golden ratio as well as the 11 – 7 version of the pyramid triangle that is used in John Michell's Earth-Moon diagram. The Fibonacci measurements that are used correspond to some of the golden section divisions of a pyramid triangle shown in chapter 7 (see p.110).

The following diagrams show the pyramid triangle projected on to the image of the west front. This overlaying of the triangle on to an image of the west front is not the evidence used to create the following geometric theory. The theory has been confirmed by in-situ laser measurements, and so what is shown in the following images illustrates these confirmed measurements that have been made on the fabric of the west front.

The west front of Wells Cathedral

The pyramid triangle projected onto the west front of Wells Cathedral

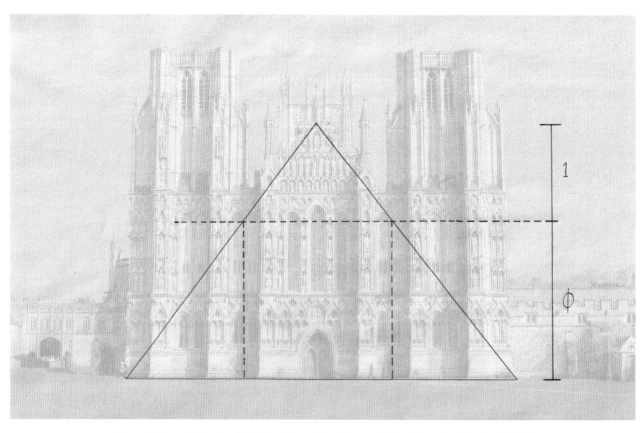

Golden section lines added into the triangle. The horizontal dotted line marks the golden section of the triangle's height.

The apex of the triangle reaches the top of the gable just above the head of the modern statue of Christ. The two bottom corners of the pyramid triangle coincide with the width of the west front on the ground level.

The second image again shows the pyramid triangle, but with a 'square-ish' rectangle added on, in dotted line which marks various golden section lines.

The upper horizontal edge of this rectangle marks the golden section of the triangle's height. This line – along with its dotted line extensions – coincides with the springing line of all of the higher arches on the west front. This includes the arches at the top of the three tall lights (i.e. stained-glass windows).

The statuary depiction immediately above this golden section line is of people rising out of their graves, which reflects the eschatological idea of Universal Resurrection at the end of time. This in turn resonates with the idea of the Heavenly Jerusalem's appearance at the end of time. It also reflects Ezekiel's recounting of God's words.

'I am going to open your graves and bring you up from them; I will bring you back to the land of Israel.'

Ezekiel 37:12

This only serves to re-emphasise the association that the cathedral has with Jerusalem, and the fact that the cathedral was designed and built in an era during which many Europeans had 'returned' to the Holy Land with the setting up of the Kingdom of Jerusalem. Such a return was of course a spiritual return, to the 'holy origin' as it were, rather than a return to a native land, which for the Crusaders was of course Western Europe.

This raising of people from their graves is also associated with Christ's death and Resurrection in Matthew's Gospel, where saints were resurrected from their graves and entered Jerusalem.

'And the graves were opened; and many bodies of the saints which slept arose,
And came out of the graves after his resurrection, and went into the holy city, and appeared unto many.'

Matthew 27:52-53

Returning to the measurements of the west front and the square-ish rectangle in the image on the previous page, the two sides of the rectangle mark the golden sections of each of the two 'half-baselines' that together make up the triangle's complete baseline. These two vertical lines coincide with the two side doors that lead into the cathedral's two side aisles. So in this sense there is a direct association between the resurrection from the grave, and a return to Jerusalem, with an entry into the cathedral itself.

In mathematical terms this geometry means that the three doors on the west front together express a formula for the golden ratio. This particular formula is $(\sqrt{5} + 1) \div 2 = 1.618...$

A simpler way of expressing this using only the number 1.618... is to point out the simple fact that $\sqrt{5}$ is actually the same as 1.618...+ 0.618...

So to add 1 to $\sqrt{5}$ is to add 1 to 1.618... + 0.618...

In other words it is quite simply 1.618...+ 1.618... and this becomes clear in the following diagram of the three doors on the west front of the cathedral.

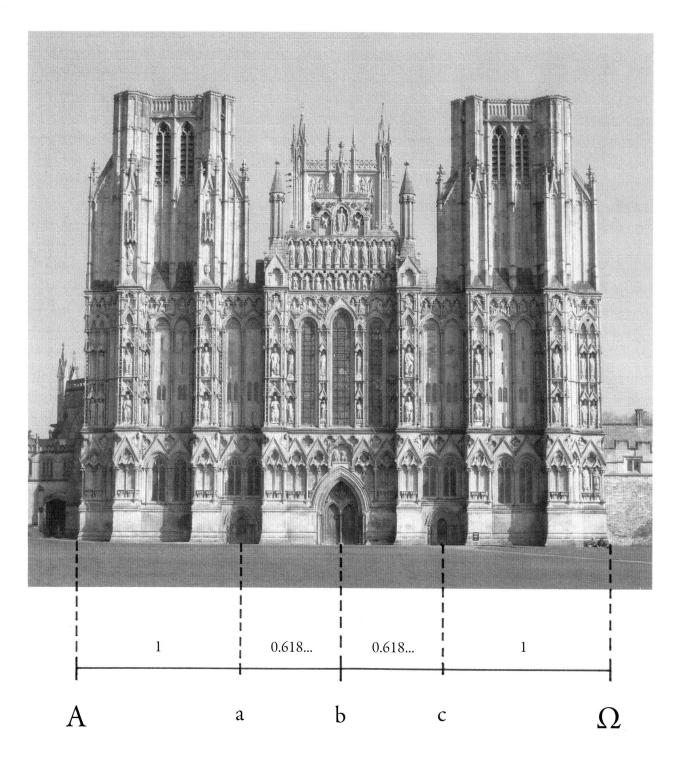

If the distance from A to c is $\sqrt{5}$ (2.236) then the distance from c to Ω is 1.

The main west door at b then divides this distance into two equal halves, i.e. $(2.236 + 1) \div 2$.

The result is thus 1.618... in the sense that the distances from A to b and from b to Ω both measure 1.618...

Both of these distances are divided into lesser and greater parts, which accordingly measure 1 and 0.618... and the division line in each case is marked by one of the smaller side-west doors. So with these various golden sections there appears to be an association made between the golden section and some kind of passage, movement or transition from one 'state' to another. In one sense this is expressed as a movement through a doorway from the 'outer world through to the inner world', but in relation to the stone images of people resurrecting there is a suggestion of an ascent to a higher level in spiritual terms – a raising of the soul beyond a significant threshold by which mortality transmutes to immortality. The Universal Resurrection at the 'end of time'.

The other significant doorways that are positioned at the golden section of their surroundings are the front and back doors of the cathedral's sacristy. They will be shown later on, suffice to say that they also appear to symbolise a 'passage between different states'.

There is a great deal more going on within the west front, and this will form a future study once some very accurate measurements can be taken.

Returning to the pyramid triangle on the west front, if this triangle is laid down horizontally so that it is pointing eastwards, it corresponds to the design of the nave as shown in the image below. The apex of the triangle falls precisely into the midpoint of the sixth bay, which is the bay that the Canon's door enters into on the nave's northern side. There are various overlaid measurement grids then used in the design of the nave, some of which derive from this pyramid triangle. These will be described in detail in Part 3.

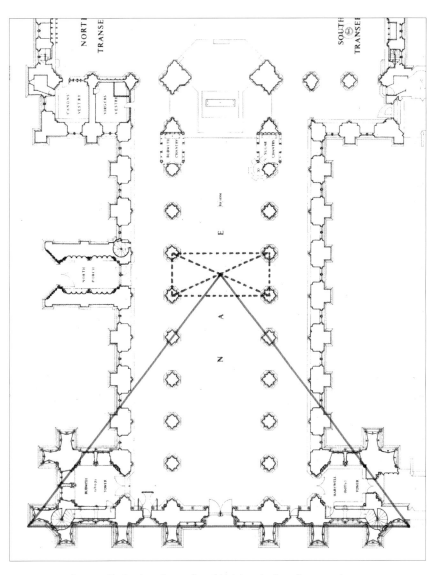

The pyramid triangle on the west front folded down horizontally to cover the nave.
The apex of the triangle coincides precisely with the centre of the sixth bay.

DANTE AND BEATRICE ASCEND TO THE SPHERE OF THE MOON

By that innate and never-ending thirst
for God's own realm we sped up just as fast
as human eyes can rise to meet the skies.

My gaze on Beatrice, hers on Heaven,
in less time than an arrow strikes the mark,
flies through the air, loosed from its catch, I found

myself in some place where a wonderous thing
absorbed all of my mind, and then my lady,
from whom I could not keep my thirst to know,

turned toward me as joyful as her beauty:
"Direct your mind and gratitude," she said,
"to God, who raised us up to His first star."

We seemed to be enveloped in a cloud
as brilliant, hard, and polished as a diamond
struck by a ray of sunlight. That eternal,

celestial pearl took us into itself,
receiving us as water takes in light,
its indivisibility intact.

Dante, *Paradiso*, Canto II, 19 - 36

160

CHAPTER 9.

The Octagonal Chapter House as an Image of the Moon, the Eighth Heaven and Wisdom

9.1 THE EARTH-MOON DIAGRAM AT WELLS, YORK AND SOUTHWELL

THE EARTH-MOON DIAGRAM appears to have been used in the designs of the cathedrals at York and Southwell in a similar way to how it is used at Wells.

The following three images show the diagram first in the design of Wells, then York and finally Southwell.

The main feature to point out in relation to the use of the diagram in Wells is the Moon-square, and how it is nested within the octagonal area of the chapter house.

But in the design of York Minster the Moon-square neatly contains the octagon within it, rather than being contained within the octagon as is the case at Wells. As the diagram makes clear, the chapter house at York also contains a skew in its orientation

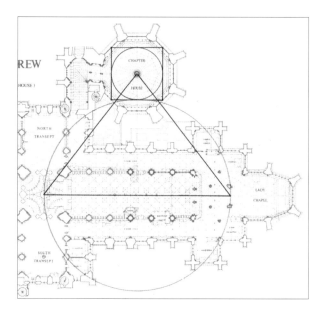

The Earth-Moon diagram used in the design of Wells Cathedral

The Earth-Moon diagram at York appears to use the Earth-square within the design of the transepts. The left-hand-side vertical edge of the Earth-square is off-centre within the transepts in the sense that it divides the 'Five Sisters' windows in the north transept into 2 + 3. The south transept door is also fully included within the bottom left-hand corner of the Earth-square rather than cut in half as it would be if the left-hand edge of the square was centrally located within the transepts.

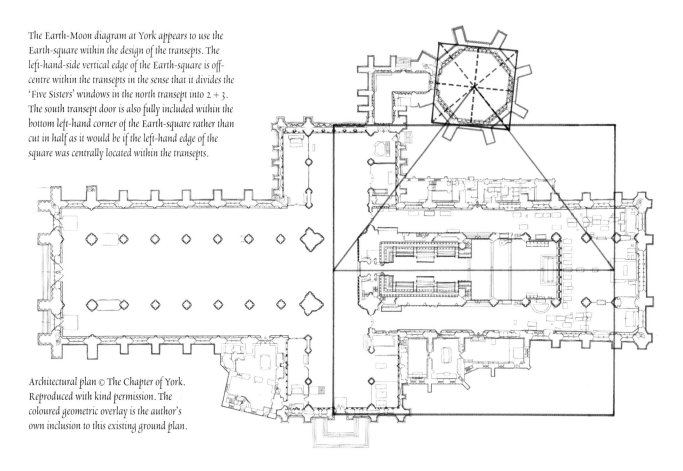

Architectural plan © The Chapter of York. Reproduced with kind permission. The coloured geometric overlay is the author's own inclusion to this existing ground plan.

in relation to the cathedral church. As will be shown a little later, this appears to accord with the idea that the chapter house is a symbolic representation of the Moon, because the degree of the skew is the same as a lunar cosmological angle. At Southwell the diagram works in a similar way as it does at York (see below), in the sense that the Moon-square contains the octagonal form of the building. This particular area of the minster, which accords with the Earth-Moon diagram, is a later Gothic addition to a Romanesque building. The bottom left-hand corner of the pyramid triangle is very precisely located at the westernmost extreme of the Gothic work, which consists of three arches leading off the crossing and onwards into the quire. The off-centre position of the doorway that leads into this chapter house embodies the same angle as the skew in orientation of the York chapter house (see sec 9.3).

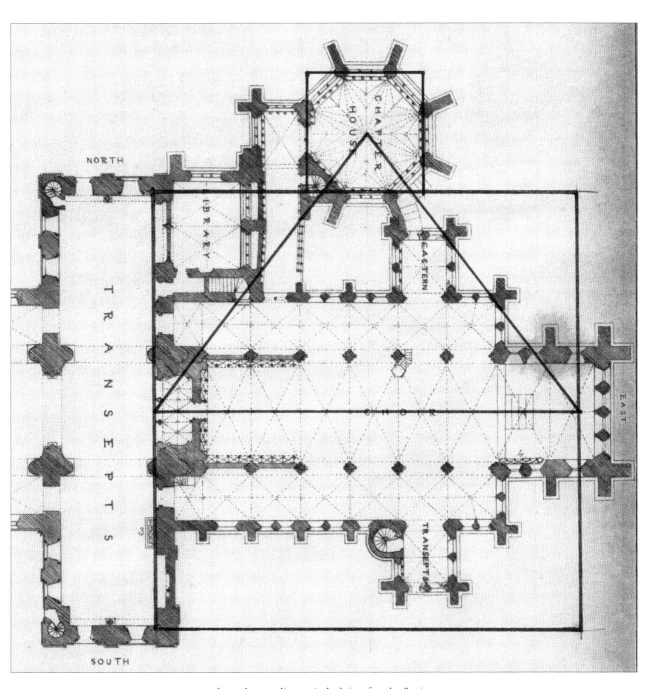

The Earth-Moon diagram in the design of Southwell Minster

In all three examples the octagonal chapter house clearly appears to geometrically interact with the Moon-square, although as outlined above the Moon-square is contained within the octagonal form of the Wells chapter house, whereas inversely the Moon-square contains the octagons at York and Southwell. This leads to the chapter houses at York and Southwell being relatively smaller in comparison to the size of their quire and cathedral church than at Wells. The chapter houses at Wells and York for instance are quite similar in size, although the cathedral church at Wells is significantly smaller than at York. Similarly, the cathedral church at Southwell is only a little smaller than at Wells, but its chapter house is significantly smaller than the Wells chapter house. So in this sense the Earth-Moon diagram is actually the common denominator that explains the relative size differences between the cathedral church and chapter house at Wells in comparison to York and Southwell.

York and Southwell minsters were connected via the Bishopric of York. York and the Gothic part of Southwell both started to be built in the early to mid-1230s, which suggests that a similar knowledge was used in relation to both of their designs. Whether this means that the same designer was involved in both buildings is hard to know for sure, but it seems quite likely.

In these examples, with the exception of Southwell, the bottom right-hand corner of the pyramid triangle falls within, or at the entrance of, a Lady chapel. The lack of a Lady chapel at Southwell results from the fact that the whole church is dedicated to St Mary the Virgin. But the designs take on another layer of interest when the sizes of these pyramid triangles are measured, because they all embody simple fractional relationships with the size of the equivalent triangle in the Great Pyramid. In short, the baseline of the Wells pyramid triangle is effectively 1/5 the length of the baseline of the Great Pyramid, whereas the Southwell triangle is 1/6. The York Minster triangle is reduced in size from the Great Pyramid by $\sqrt{5} + 1$, which as mentioned before, is part of the formula for the golden ratio. The details of the Wells triangle will be expanded on in detail in Part 3.

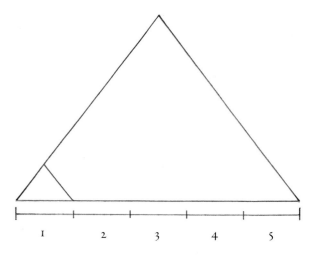

The baseline of the pyramid triangle at Wells is 1/5 of the Great Pyramid

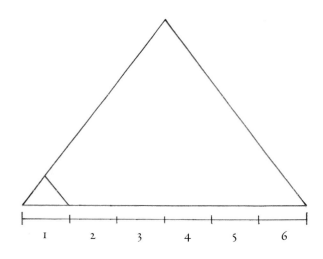

At Southwell it is 1/6 of the Great Pyramid

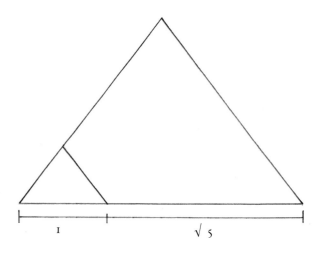

At York it is 1 to $\sqrt{5}+1$ of the Great Pyramid

9.2 THE MOON AND THE MAGIC SQUARE IN THE CHAPTER HOUSE STAIRCASE AT WELLS

THERE IS A BEAUTIFUL staircase in Wells Cathedral that leads from the north transept up to the chapter house. Just before reaching the chapter house the staircase begins to bifurcate into two separate routes, one of which then carries on beyond the chapter house and up to a bridge called the chain gate. There is a famous photo of this staircase taken in 1903 by Frederic H. Evans entitled 'A Sea of Steps' – a title which beautifully describes the water-like flow of the curve in the staircase. This curve, as viewed from the bottom of the staircase, is the gradual forking of the staircase rightwards in the direction of the chapter house. If the stair-climber takes the left fork they effectively carry straight on up the staircase,

passing the chapter house on the right and eventually reaching the chain gate. On closer inspection, the stair-count of this staircase (its number of countable steps) appears to embody numbers that accord with the apparent lunar symbolism of the chapter house. When the stair-climber ascends the staircase and takes the curving right fork into the chapter house there appear to be both twenty-nine-*and-a-half* steps but also twenty-seven-*and-a-third* steps. Both of these numbers relate to lunar cycles. However, if the stair-climber takes the left fork, thus climbing beyond the chapter house all the way to the top of the staircase, the stair-count then appears to embody significant number combinations from a particular

The chapter house staircase in Wells Cathedral

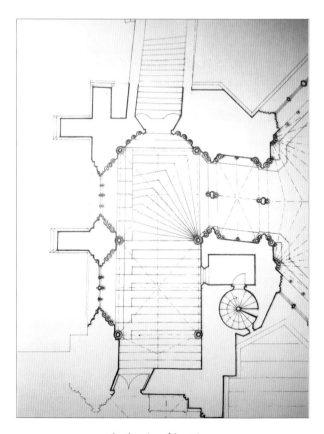

The plan view of the staircase

magic square, which in Europe is sometimes called the Freemason's Magic Square.

So in relation to these two different stair-counts, the staircase can be seen as consisting of two different routes – one that leads up to the chapter house, and another that leads up to the chain gate. However, the two routes effectively share the same staircase prior to the fork, which results in them slowly dividing into their distinct and separate routes. This perception of the staircase as being 'two routes in one staircase' becomes more apparent if we observe the *lunar-count* of steps, which leads up to the chapter house, as opposed to the *magic square-count* of steps, which leads up to the chain gate. These two stair-counts are thus the two different routes that partly use the same staircase.

We shall begin with the lunar-count of steps which itself contains two different lunar numbers.

It was mentioned in section 6.6 that the two primary cosmological cycles associated with the Moon are its sidereal and synodic cycles. The sidereal cycle of the Moon takes 27.32 days to complete – which, in simple terms, is the amount of time that it takes for the Moon to orbit the Earth. So the sidereal cycle expresses a relationship that exists between the Earth and the Moon. The synodic cycle expresses a relationship that exists between the Earth, the Moon and also the Sun. This cycle takes 29.53 days to complete, which is 2.21 days longer than the sidereal cycle. During this extra couple of days, the relationship between the Earth and the Moon recalibrates its relationship with the Sun. This recalibration occurs necessarily as a result of the fact that the Earth and Moon have together been orbiting the Sun during the time in which the Moon has been orbiting the Earth. So in this sense, the lunar journey can be expressed in round numbers as one cycle that consists of 27 + 2 days (or more precisely 27.32 + 2.21 days), and this then expresses the sidereal and synodic cycles as one numerically definable process.

Returning to the staircase in the cathedral, the first step within the staircase is narrower in comparison to the

steps that follow on beyond it. This occurs as a result of it being located within the doorway that leads on to the staircase. To a very close accuracy (around 1/5 inch) this narrower step is 5/12 the width of the next few steps beyond it. The significance of this 5/12 ratio will become apparent shortly – suffice to say that 5/12 is the arithmetic mean between 1/2 and 1/3.

The first step has a narrower width than the steps beyond it

Beyond this initial narrower step there are twenty-seven more steps, which lead up to a right-angular L-shaped step. This twenty-seventh step is the final one that is situated within both staircase routes. From here onwards the two staircase routes separate from one another. So the right-angular step can be seen to embody the number 27, which thus relates it to the sidereal cycle of the Moon. There are then two more steps beyond the twenty seventh, which finally deliver the stair-climber into the chapter house vestibule. So in this sense there are 27 + 2 steps up to the chapter house, and so as well as the sidereal number 27 the synodic number 29 is also present. However, the sidereal and synodic cycles are actually 27.32 days and 29.53 days – and this is where the narrower step at the bottom of the staircase becomes significant.

The number 27.32 is easily rounded up to 27 + 1/3 (i.e. 27.333...) and the number 29.53 is easily rounded down to 29 + 1/2.

But as mentioned earlier, the narrower step is actually 5/12 of the width of the steps beyond it.

The fraction 5/12 is the arithmetic mean between ½ and 1/3. This can be explained easily enough through looking at the fractions 6/12 and 4/12. The fraction 6/12 is the same as ½, whereas 4/12 is the same as 1/3. So the halfway point between 4/12 and 6/12 is 5/12, and thus 5/12 is the arithmetic mean between 1/2 and 1/3.

With this simple arithmetic in mind, the narrower step at the bottom of the staircase can be looked upon as embodying both 1/2 of a step as well as 1/3 of a step at the same time, because its actual physical size refers to both of these measurements by materially embodying their mean. As Iamblichus wrote in his *Theology of Arithmetic*:

'... the means between extremes are in a sense more authoritative than the extremes themselves, because the terms on either side incline towards the means.'

So it can be suggested that the staircase embodies both 27 + 1/3 steps but also 29 + 1/2 steps at the same time.

Another interesting feature of this narrower step at the bottom of the staircase is its parallelogram shape. The long edges of the step, as already mentioned, are 5/12 of the width of the steps that follow on from it. But the angle at which the step's shorter and longer edges are set in relation to one another is very similar to the axial tilt of Earth – around 23.5° – a cosmological fact that was certainly known in 12th-century Europe.

Having returned to the bottom of the steps, we now need to look at the staircase as leading up to the chain gate rather than the chapter house. This is the route that contains the *magic square-count*. As mentioned earlier, this magic square is sometimes referred to in Europe as the Freemason's Magic Square, and this appears to be to do with the significance in Freemasonry of the number sequence 3 – 5 – 7, which can be seen in the middle line of the magic square. However, it has quite a diverse history in various different regions of the world. The oldest known use of it is in China, where it is known as the Lo Shu, and it is central to the ancient Chinese

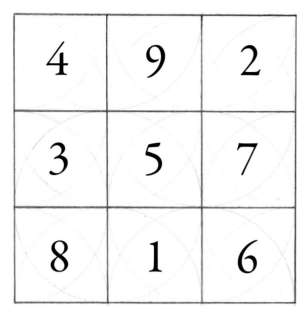

The 3 x 3 Freemason's magic square - known in China as the 'Lo Shu'

system of cosmology. In India there is a variation of it called the Kubera Kolam. It was also significant in medieval Islamic alchemy, and it seems probable that this is the route of its transmission into medieval Europe. There are descriptions of it that were written by Islamic and Jewish scholars in Toledo in the 11th and 12th centuries.

Returning to the staircase, the number of steps, from the bottom all the way up to the top, totals forty five – which is the sum of all the numbers in this Magic Square.

Within the Arabic alchemical tradition – particularly associated with Jabir ibn Hayyan (or 'Geber', as he was known in medieval Europe) – this magic square was divided up in such a way that four of the nine numbers – 1, 3, 5 and 8 (all of which are Fibonacci numbers) – were grouped together and added to create the sum of 17 (see diagram on next page). The number 17 was central to Hayyan's alchemical system, and this square arrangement of numbers was known as 'the seed'. The remaining numbers – 2, 4, 6, 7 and 9 – were then added together, giving a total of 28. This collection of numbers within the magic square was called the 'gnomon' because of the right-angular shape that their arrange-

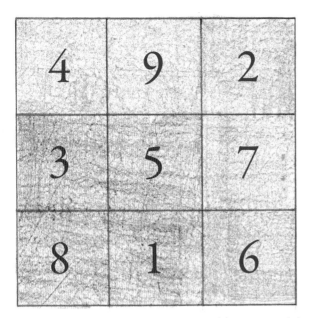

The 3 x 3 magic square with Jabir ibn Hayyan's 'seed' (17) and 'gnomon' (28)

result will always yield the number 15. So for example the addition of the horizontal arrangement of three numbers 3, 5 and 7 adds up to 15. But so does the vertical row of the numbers of 9, 5 and 1, as well as the diagonal arrangement of 4, 5 and 6.

Finally, the number 5 is significant within the square because of its central position. There are eight different ways in which the numbers can be arranged within the square whereby the magic constant will be 15. But within all eight of these configurations the number 5 is always at the centre. This is ultimately due to the fact that 5 is the arithmetic mean between the numbers 1 and 9, and the square itself contains all of the numbers from 1 to 9.

So for these reasons the significant numbers within this magic square are 5, 15, and 45 along with the specifically 'Jabirian' numbers of 17 and 28. If these five numbers are then applied to the staircase that leads up to the chain gate, they are all present within various stair-counts that are formed by significant architectural zones within the staircase.

First of all, due to there being no halves or thirds within the numbers of the magic square, the first narrower step within the staircase should just be looked upon as 'one step', or more simply 'the first step'. This then leads towards the first example of a magic square number – the number 5. The first five steps fall within a demarcated architectural zone, or 'bay', that leads up to the first window. The ribbed vault overhead changes at this point, and indeed the stairs change in their form and width on the left-hand side of the staircase.

Another feature at this point in the staircase is that on either side of the stair-climber, there are corbels on which there are left-handed dragon-slayers[2] – one of

ment produced within the square (as shown in the diagram shaded in green). A gnomon is the angular stick that produces the shadow on a sundial. But a right-angular gnomon also has a symbolic association with the set-square tool with which the geometer obtains a measured right-angle. Such Masonic set-square symbolism is also significant in relation to the so-called 'Pythagorean gnomon', in terms of how it occurs within the square of four – a geometric form that the Pythagoreans swore an oath over.[1]

Along with 17, 28 and the square's sum of 45, the other significant numbers in this magic square are 15 and 5.

The number 15 is what is known as the *magic constant* of the square. This is the sum of all the numbers that are situated in any row, column or diagonal of the square. It is this particularity of the square that gives it such a perceived significance. Whichever row, column or diagonal of three numbers are added together, the

---

1. This gnomonic symbolism within the square of four produces the Masonic number sequence of 3 – 5 – 7. Beginning with a single square, a gnomon consisting of three squares is first added. The next gnomon consists of five squares and the final one seven squares.

2. These left-handed figures that are situated on the left (i.e. north) side of the cathedral could be described as 'Sofianic' via Sophia's association with the left side, where whereby she is the 'Aristera' – i.e. 'the left handed'. See the section in Part 4 entitled *'Where is the north? One striking difference from a modern-day Freemason lodge room'*

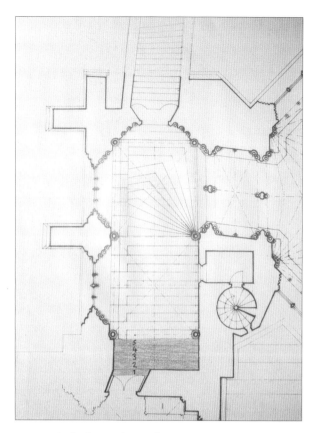

The first five steps form the first architectural zone or 'bay'

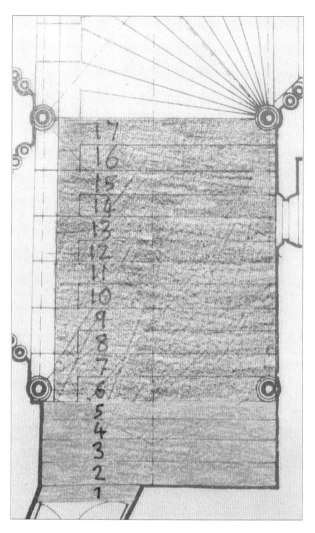

The next distinct 'bay' consists of 12 steps which brings the total to 17

whom looks more monastic and the other more courtly. The stair-climber passes between these two dragon slayers as a result of moving beyond the fifth step – and so the stair-count continues.

By walking another twelve steps beyond the first five steps, the walker reaches the seventeenth step. The number 17 is the sum of the so-called *seed* of the magic square, and this number appears in the stair-count as the final rectangular-shaped step prior to the curving fork in the staircase. Beyond this seventeenth step the subsequent steps become wedge-shaped or L-shaped. The seventeenth step is also the final one within a definable rectangular zone or bay with its own arrangement of cross-ribbed vaulting overhead. This particular rectangular bay area started back at the fifth step.

Beyond the seventeenth step, the walker ascends eleven more steps up to the right-angular L-shaped step, which is as significant within this magic square-count of the staircase as it is within the lunar-count.

However, within the magic square-count this particular step brings the total stair-count to twenty-eight rather than twenty-seven. In the lunar-count the right-angular step was the twenty-seventh due to the first step at the bottom of the staircase being counted as ½ and 1/3. But in the magic square-count the first step is just a normal single step, so the right-angular step is the twenty-eighth step.

The number 28 is the next significant one from the magic square due to the numbers contained within the gnomon adding up to 28. The fact that this twenty-eighth step is the one with which the curving form of the staircase finally achieves a right-angle is of interest, considering that the right-angular gnomonic arrangement of numbers within the magic square also

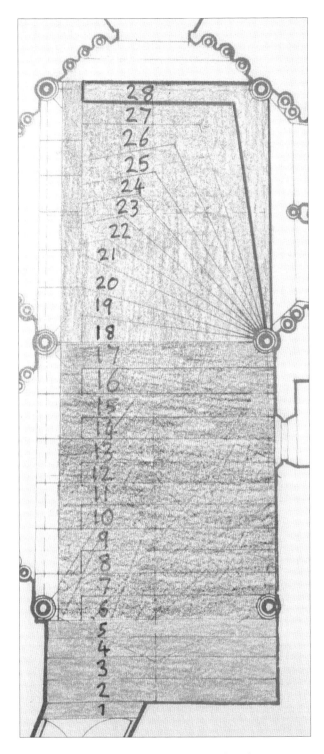

The next 11 steps bring the total to 28 and the 28th step

adds up to 28. The shape of the step itself even resembles the appearance of a medieval set-square, with a tapered narrowing arm.

'Geometria' holding a set-square with a tapered narrowing arm

Again, this significant numerical stage within the stair-count reaches the limits of an architectural zone because the twenty-eighth step defines the limits of the bay which started at the seventeenth step. Beyond this right-angular 'gnomonic' twenty-eighth step there are seventeen more steps that proceed up to the Chain Gate. However, the first two of these seventeen steps lead up to a doorway on the staircase, which passes through into a different architectural zone. These two steps are beyond the architectural zone that finished with the twenty-eighth step, but they are still distinct from the new architectural zone beyond the doorway. The staircase then continues with the final fifteen steps, which accordingly emphasise the number 15 – the magic constant of the square. Once these stages of ascension have been completed the stair-walker will have climbed a total of forty-five steps.

There is a possible connecting symbolism between the Moon and the 3 × 3 magic square, which would thus connect the two counts of the staircase described above. Having said this, the 3 × 3 magic square is more commonly associated, in astrological terms, with the

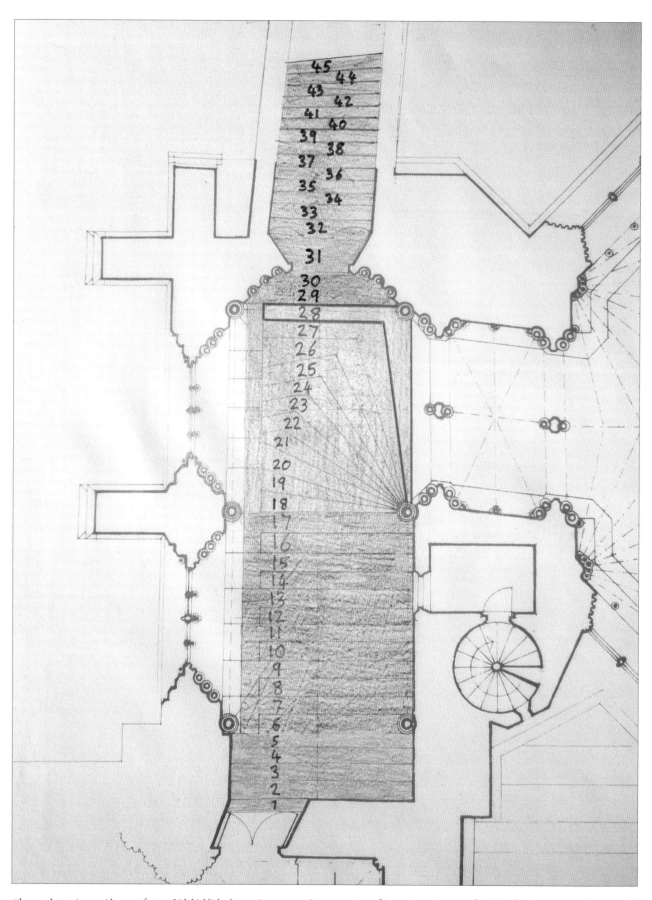

The complete staircase with zones of steps which highlight the magic square numbers 5, 17, 28, 15 (shown in purple as 31-45) and 45 (i.e. the sum total of all the steps)

planet Saturn, although it is sometimes also associated with the Moon.[3] The association with Saturn seems to be a specifically Arabic/Islamic aspect of the square's symbolism. The letters in the Arabic name for Saturn, Zuhal, have a gematria total of 45, thus connecting the word with the sum of the magic square's numbers. But the Chinese and Indian use of the square makes no such Saturnine connection. Indeed, the Indian use of the square – the Kubera Kolam – suggests a lunar numerical symbolism.[4]

The various number combinations within the magic square are also more lunar – such as the number 15, which is associated with the day of the full Moon, and also the number 28, which in astrology is associated with a whole lunar cycle. As will become clear a little later, the number 17 is also significant within the so-called 'Lunation Triangle', and more generally the relationship that it has with the numbers 51 and 153, which are used in the measurements of this part of the cathedral. It is also associated with the day on which the Moon begins to visibly wane,[5] which is symbolically associated with the death of Osiris on the seventeenth day of the month. When looked at in full the numeric of Plutarch's description of Osiris' death is of particular interest here because he describes it as occurring on the seventeenth day of the third month during Osiris' twenty-eighth year of his age or of his reign. The numbers 3, 17 and 28 all speak in very clear terms of Jabir ibn Hayyan's numerical interpretation of the magic

square with its 3 × 3 form and its seed of 17 and gnomon of 28. Osiris' death and resurrection, and its association with the Moon, is also a very appropriate symbolism within this whole numerical schema. But perhaps the most visually clear similarity and apparent connection is the fact that the lunar geometry of the chapter house is specifically based on a 3 × 3 square. In the Earth-Moon diagram the Earth-square is 11 × 11 and the Moon-square is 3 × 3, so a 3 × 3 square has a natural connection to the Moon, as indeed does the number 3 itself.

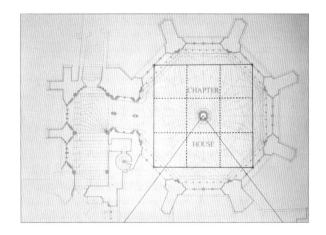

The 3 x 3 Moon-square contained within the chapter house design

There is yet another lunar feature within the chapter house staircase, and it uses the numbers from the Lunation Triangle. However, as this involves the metrological and musical units of measure it will be explored in Part 3.

---

3. Such as in the writings of the Ikhwan al-Safa (Brethren of Purity), Jabir ibn Hayyan and the Italian Renaissance polymath Gerolamo Cardano.
4. The numbers in the Kubera Kolam would be the same as they are in the Freemason's Magic Square except for having had 19 added to each one of them. For example the middle horizontal line of 3 – 5 – 7 becomes 22 – 24 – 26. So the magic constant of the Kubera Kolam is 72, which means that the sum of all the numbers in the square is 216, and this is 1/10 of the miles in the diameter of the Moon. But if this 3 × 3 magic square were to have a sum of 2160, which is the actual number of miles in the Moon's diameter, the magic constant would need to be 720. This would require adding 235 on to each of the numbers within the Freemason's Magic Square. So in that particular instance the middle horizontal line of 3 – 5 – 7 would become 238 – 240 – 242. Rather amazingly, the numbers 19 and 235 together express the metonic cycle, which is the amount of time that it takes for the Sun and Moon to return to the same position in relation to one another. So in other words, 19 solar years are virtually the same period of time as 235 synodic lunar cycles.
5. See ch.5 p.151 of *The Moon - symbol of transformation* by Jules Cashford. The Greystones Press 2016

9.3 THE LUNAR INCLINATION ANGLE IN THE YORK AND SOUTHWELL CHAPTER HOUSES

THERE IS A SKEW in the orientation of the chapter house at York Minster. This apparent 'mis-alignment' occurs in relation to the orientation of the cathedral church that it stands beside, but also in relation to the 'set-square shaped' vestibule passageway that leads into it. This appears to be another example of lunar symbolism in terms of it embodying a lunar cosmological angle. This corresponds with the apparent use of the Earth-Moon diagram in the design of the cathedral, in which the chapter house geometrically accords with the Moon-square.

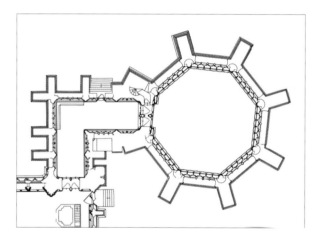

The York chapter house - skewed in its oriantation by around 5°

Various theories have been put forth as to why this clearly intentional skew in orientation is present. The notion that it might be a mistake or the result of bad workmanship is very unlikely. The fact that the builders of York Minster could build a ribbed vault with such a wide span that was around 90 feet above the ground suggests that they were very skilled indeed. The idea that they would make the relatively simple mistake of unintentionally misaligning a ground plan does not stand up to artistic scrutiny. As any practitioner of the arts knows, if something is marked out inaccurately the first time around, it will just be repeated again and again until it is correct. But having said this, the mark-

ing out of a correctly orientated octagon down on the ground is by no means difficult in comparison to other procedures that took place during the construction of York Minster.

Of the other theories that have been suggested, one is that the building was skewed southwards so as to avoid a parish boundary line that runs very close to it. But it seems unlikely that one of the two most important cathedrals in England would need to take account of such a boundary.

The angle of the skew is a little over 5°, which also happens to be the angle of the Moon's inclination. The inclination of the Moon is the angular difference between the orbital plane of the Moon around the Earth in relation to the orbital plane of the Earth around the Sun. This cosmological fact is known to have been worked out by the Greek astronomer Hipparchus back in the second century BC. So it is not unrealistic to suggest that a medieval master mason, who might have been on a Grand Tour of the eastern Mediterranean and Holy Land, would have encountered such cosmological knowledge. Alternatively, it could be part of an orally transmitted indigenous knowledge that goes back to the ancient world of the British Isles. It has already been pointed out that Julius Caesar wrote in his *Gallic Wars* that the Druids of the British Isles knew things such as the size of the Earth. Recent findings are also suggesting that Neolithic Orkney was the centre of a culture with a significant knowledge of cosmology. The main cluster of Neolithic sites on Orkney for instance are located in very close proximity to the 59° line of latitude with one of the sites just to the north of it and the rest just to the south.

The chapter house at Southwell Minster appears to contain the angle of the Moon's inclination as a result of the off-centre position of its entrance. The way into

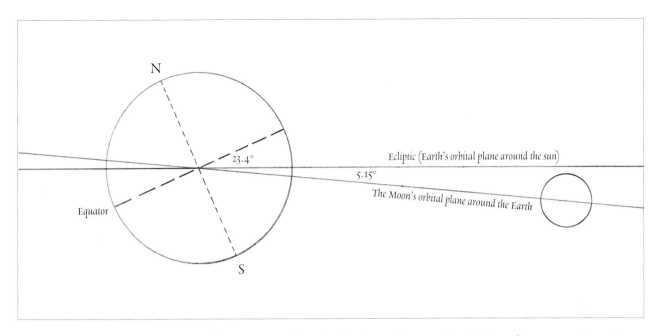

The inclination of the Moon is the angular difference between the orbital plane of Earth around the Sun and the orbital plane of the Moon around the Earth

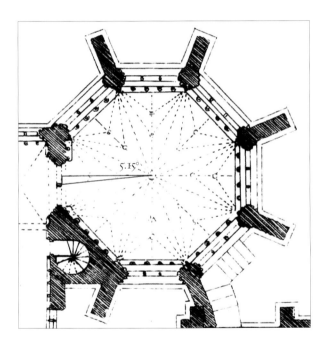

The lunar angle as produced by the off-centre position of the doorway leading into the chapter house at Southwell Minster

the chapter house consists of two doorways that are separated by a slim stone pillar and it is the vertical position of this pillar which then creates the angle of the Moon's inclination. Interestingly the position of the pillar also marks the golden section of the wall's horizontal width or rather the Fibonacci division of 13/8. The angle of 5.15° then falls within the pillar around an inch away from its central vertical axis.

The doorway into the Southwell chapter house. Its central pillar is at the 13/8 division of the wall. This off-centre position also marks the lunar angle.

9.4 THE LUNAR INCLINATION ANGLE AT THE DOORWAY THAT LEADS INWARDS

THERE ARE FIVE EXAMPLES of doorways that appear to architecturally relate in symbolic terms to the lunar inclination angle of 5.15°. Two of these doorways are in Wells Cathedral, two are in York Minster and the other one is in Southwell. In all five cases this angle of just over 5° results in some way from the geometric design of the octagonal 'lunar' chapter houses at these cathedrals.

It was shown in the previous section how the whole chapter house at York appears to contain this angle in the skew of its orientation. However, the angle is also present at Wells specifically within the orientation of the vestibule that leads from the chapter house staircase into the chapter house itself (see image below).

An apparent misalignment such as this is again not something that can be simply put down to bad workmanship, especially when one looks at all the very well-aligned work that surrounds it in all directions. Such a 'mistake' would have been easily put right at the early stage of marking out. But the fact that it happens

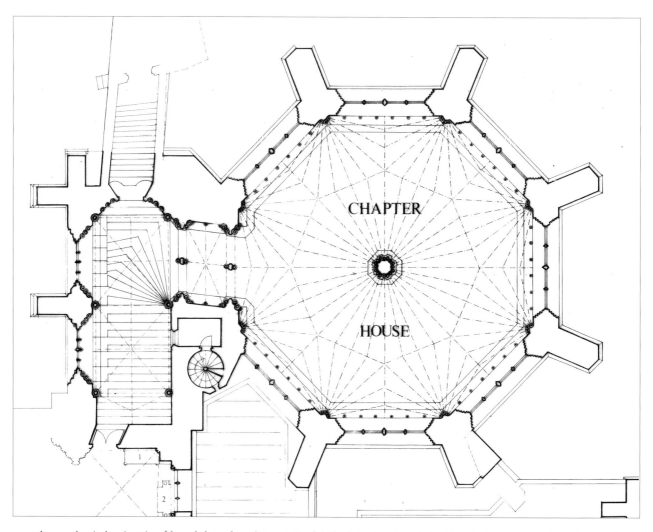

The 5.15° skew in the orientation of the York chapter house is present at Wells in the chapter house's vestibule between the staircase and the chapter house itself

specifically at the doorway of the chapter house is perhaps of most interest, because this is also where the skew in alignment of the York chapter house takes place. At Southwell it is the off-centre position of the doorway on the wall that brings about the angle.

Doorways are symbolically significant places. In spiritual terms they are associated with inward transitions from one state or level to another, and in this sense the door outwardly reflects the movement from one 'world' to another. So by physically walking through a doorway there can be an outward enactment of what is essentially an inner process of transition – an earthly embodying of a movement taking place within the heavens. This could be said to occur every time a religious adherent walks through the doorway of their place of worship, whereby they physically enact a transitional movement from the 'outer world' through to the 'inner world' of prayer, ritual, meditation and anamnesis. In Christian symbolism 'the doorway' is associated with Christ himself in that he is the mediating relationship between the divine and the human natures[6] – the One who brings Heaven and Earth together into relationship.

In the Roman tradition Janus was the god of the doorway. An example of this association that still features in our daily routines is the fact that the word 'janitor' derives from the name Janus because the janitor is 'the one who opens the door'. But a more profound dimension of this association can be seen in the fact that Janus was the god of initiation into the mysteries, which relates to the idea of passing through a doorway that leads 'inwards' towards the inner spiritual world. He was also the patron deity of the Roman craft guilds, and they would keep the solstices as feasts in recognition of his two faces, which symbolise the solstices along with various other polar opposites such as past and future. He was also the doorway into the new year and so the month of January, which commences soon after the winter solstice, is named after him too.

Initiation into the mysteries is commonly associated with the practice of sacred art in various traditions, and this is perhaps because the practice of sacred art involves a physical engagement in a process of both inner and outer transformation. They both involve processes in which some raw unrefined material is fashioned into a form that in one sense reflects, but in another sense also embodies, a divine reality. The bringing forth of such eternal forms, albeit via transient material bodies, helps to bring the soul into a conscious awareness of the eternal realm that it perpetually inhabits but has become blind to as a result of the forgetfulness of True Identity, i.e. that the soul is created in God's Image.

The linking of initiation with the practice of the arts can be seen to some degree in Freemasonry, in that it involves the use of symbols, metaphors and allegories related to the architectural arts. The building of Solomon's Temple is used as a symbolic focus for the building of the temple 'within the soul', and the various processes of building equate with stages of inward development and transformation on the part of the initiate. Even though modern Freemasonry is to some degree a remnant or a relic, in the sense that it is not an actual practising guild of architects and builders, it does appear to carry some sort of lineage involving a language of symbols that goes back at least to the medieval craft guilds who built the great Gothic cathedrals – possibly even earlier. This association between Gothic cathedral design and modern Freemasonic symbolism will become clearer later in the book. It appears to be central to the overarching design symbolism of the whole of Wells Cathedral.

Returning to the five doors that were mentioned earlier, and to the fact that the chapter house vestibule at Wells is one of them, there is an intriguing suggestion that has been made about a set of four carved stone faces that are in the vestibule's vault up above. The skew in alignment of the vestibule can be seen clearly in its vault, within the orientation of the stone rib that

6. John 10:9

The skewed alignment in the vault of the chapter house's vestibule at Wells

links the apexes of the two arched doorways that lead in and out of the vestibule (see image above). At the central crossing of all the ribs, there are four faces of old bearded men. It is not entirely clear who they are – and more generally, the chapter house, which is an unconsecrated area, does not contain so much overtly biblical imagery as such.

Four faces at the centre of the vestibule vault - a four-fold image of Janus?

One suggestion that has been made is that the four faces are an image of Janus, who was sometimes depicted with four faces rather than two. Such an association would fit with what has been written above concerning Janus and his association with the Roman craft guilds. But as ever we are left with more questions than answers, such as why a Roman god would be depicted in a Christian cathedral, albeit in an unconsecrated area. However, the openness to the ancient world that was present in the 12th and 13th century church does not make such a suggestion completely out of hand. The underlying archetypal 'polar' symbolism of Janus is in keeping with much of the design of Wells Cathedral, and as will be shown later there is an apparently quite overt Janic symbolism within the chapter houses at York and Salisbury in relation to a stone-carved head of multiple faces that will feature in the next section.

Returning to York Minster, it was mentioned earlier that the doorway into the York chapter house is where the skew in alignment of the whole building actually occurs. There is a wedge-shaped flagstone in the floor, within which this change of alignment can be seen. At Southwell it is the off-centre position of the door on the wall that causes the inclination angle to be present. The slim pillar dividing the two doors creates the cosmological angle in relation to the chapter house's east–west axis. As has already been pointed out, this also occurs as a result of the slim pillar being positioned around the golden section of the wall.

So three of the five doors that relate to the lunar inclination angle are specifically the doorways into the chapter houses at Wells, York and Southwell. The other two doors – one at Wells and one at York – are specifically doorways that lead into private areas of their respective cathedrals. The door at York is of particular interest, because it is specifically related to the chapter house doorway; it is right next to it. The York chapter house has two noticeably out-of-the-ordinary features. The first one is its skew in alignment, and the other is a very oddly placed door that leads to the mason's loft. This first-floor loft is another set-square-shaped room that is situated immediately above the set-square-shaped vestibule passageway that leads to the chapter house itself. The doorway to the mason's loft is rather awkwardly placed in that it is directly on the left after the chapter house entrance. What this means in practical terms is that when the large wooden chapter house doors are opened, the doorway to the mason's loft becomes covered and obscured.

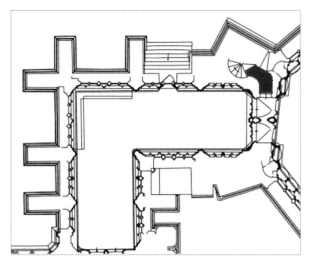

The set-square shaped vestibule leading to the chapter house doorway. Immediately beyond this doorway, to the left, is the door leading to the mason's loft. The passage between this door and the spiral staircase is shaded red.

The doorway to the mason's loft. When the large chapter house door is fully open it covers and obscures this doorway.

This doorway actually opens up to a short passageway which then leads to a spiral staircase leading up to the loft itself. But despite the spiral staircase actually being closer to the wall of the vestibule passageway, the designer appears to have wanted the doorway to the mason's loft to be situated specifically in the chapter house. However, even rudimentary design know-how would preclude placing one door behind another, as this is awkward in practical terms.

All of this suggests that some intentional doorway symbolism has been used by the designer. But what makes this possibility all the more compelling is the fact that the doorway to the mason's loft very specifically interacts with the skew in alignment of the chapter house. The fact that the chapter house is 'mis-aligned' southwards, as it were, means that the two walls on either side immediately beyond the chapter house entrance are of different lengths. As one walks into the chapter house the wall immediately to the left (i.e. on the north side) is a little longer, whereas the wall to the right is a little shorter. The doorway to the mason's loft happens to be situated on the longer length of wall on the left, and so from a perspective of symbolism it looks as though the mis-aligning of the chapter house in a southerly direction 'lengthens' the northern wall and in doing so it symbolically 'opens the way' to the mason's loft.

Such doorway symbolism shouldn't be misconstrued according to what might be described as 'Da-Vinci-Codism'. Spiritually meaningful symbolism was very much the language of religious art forms in the Middle Ages, and if a symbolically 'hidden doorway' leads to a 'hidden room' it would be more useful to view this through the doorway symbolism that was expressed a few paragraphs ago rather than as some sort of adventure that leads to the cracking of a code which in turn results in all mysteries being sorted out and resolved.

A true spiritual path leads the soul into ever greater mystery, because the Absolute Reality towards which it is orientated is beyond anything the human mind has the capacity to know. In the post-Enlightenment world of empirical observation and rationalism there is a hostility towards the unknowable mystery of the Spirit, and it is this kind of desire to resolve and thus eradicate all mystery that ultimately lies at the root of the fast-food Codism of airport novels. Sacred geometry is more profound than just a code waiting to be cracked!

The fact that the mason's loft doorway is located in such an impractical position also symbolically suggests that when the chapter house is open the mason's loft is closed or inaccessible. Meanwhile, when the chapter house is closed (i.e. in private session) the mason's loft becomes accessible. This may suggest that the mason's loft, and what goes on inside it, is symbolically associated with Wisdom that is hidden. Such an association with Wisdom accords with the depiction of a master mason with the compasses or dividers, much like the medieval depiction of God the Creator – or in Freemasonic terminology, 'the Great Architect of the Universe'. It has already been pointed out that the mason's loft itself is even the shape of the mason's set-square. This accords with the apparent use of set-square symbolism in the chapter house staircase at Wells.

Privacy or secrecy is also associated with the symbolism of the rose, in what is generally referred to as 'Sub Rosa'. A tradition dating back to at least the Middle Ages involves a condition of secrecy in relation to the proceedings of any meeting that takes place underneath an image of a rose. This symbolism appears possibly to be included in a Latin inscription located directly next to the doorway that leads to the mason's loft. The inscription, which covers seven lines of writing, reads as follows.

'Ut rosa flos florum, sic est domus ista domorum.'

(As the rose is the flower of flowers,
so this is the house of houses).

Inscription in the York chapter house about the rose

Whether there is any connection between all of these things is impossible to say. But one thing that can be said is that the use of symbolism was prevalent within the medieval religious traditions of the arts and philosophy/theology. To suggest that medieval Christian places of worship were built with only mundane practicality in mind is to project a modern aspiritual perception on to a deeply religious medieval past. Indeed, there is very little in the way of mundane practicality in putting one doorway immediately behind another.

As to what went on in the mason's loft itself, it was clearly a place of practical artworks, because in its north–south leg there is a tracing floor, which was probably used for marking out life-size images of forms that were to be carved in stone for the on-site building work. But with modern Masonic symbolism and ritual also in mind, it can't be ignored that the loft has an east–west rectangular leg, which resembles the traditional description of a Freemasons' lodge room as being a long rectangle with an east–west orientation. Such a layout is partly in emulation of the Temple of Solomon, although the eastern orientation of a lodge room also symbolically faces the rising of the Sun and the Bright Morning Star, which could be said to emphasise the symbolic solarity of the morning as a time of 'awakenings' and illumination. But if it were suggested that this loft was purely a place of practical work with no higher symbolism associated with it, we can then ask the question of why its doorway leads downstairs into a very grand chapter house that is associated with the rose, no less, and described as the 'House of Houses'.

When one considers the deep religiosity of the medieval Christian world along with the contemplative and imaginal inclination of artists, it seems unlikely that any medieval version of Freemasonry, whatever form it might have taken, would have had no dimension of symbolism to it. The idea that so-called 'speculative' (i.e. philosophical) Freemasonry just popped up out of nowhere at the beginning of the modern era seems to be yet another myth of the Enlightenment. Deeper meaning as expressed via symbolism was central to what the 20th-century monk and medievalist Marie-Dominique Chenu described as the 12th century's 'symbolist mentality'. Chenu quotes the female character *Natura* in relation to this from a poem by the 12th-century Platonist monk Alanus de Insulis.

'Poetry's lyre rings with vibrant falsehood on the outward literal shell of a poem, but interiorly it communicates a hidden and profound meaning to those who listen. The man who reads with penetration, having cast away the outer shell of falsehood, finds the savoury kernel of truth wrapped within.' [7]

Returning to the five doors mentioned above, the fifth and final doorway is in Wells Cathedral. It possesses the particularly interesting characteristic of having its central vertical axis positioned at the off-centre golden section of the bay in which it is situated. There is no purely practical reason why this should be so. If the doorway were centrally located in the bay it would still open up into the sacristy into which the door leads.

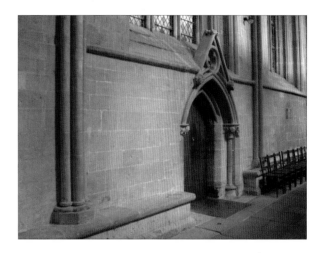

Doorway to the sacristy - positioned at the golden section of its bay

This clearly intentional measured positioning of the doorway also brings it into an interesting relationship with some of the geometry that was shown in the previous chapter. The undercroft is the octagonal hall that is situated immediately underneath the chapter house, and as was shown earlier its octagonal shape appears to arise from the use of an octagram star that replaces a pentagram star within a pyramid triangle diagram.

On closer inspection there is a very interesting geometric feature possessed by the octagram's lower-left stellation. Its vertical axis passes along the eastern wall of this golden ratio doorway. The apparent reason for this is again to do with the lunar inclination angle, which the designer quadrivially incorporates in the most ingenious way.

7. M.D. Chenu, *Nature, Man and Society in the Twelfth Century*, University of Toronto Press, 2013 – see the very beginning of chapter 3.

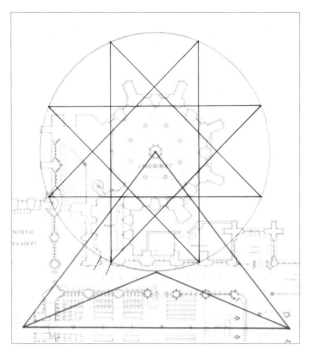

The octagram star that defines the octagonal shape of the undercroft with black dotted lines added at the sacristy doorway (detail in next the image)

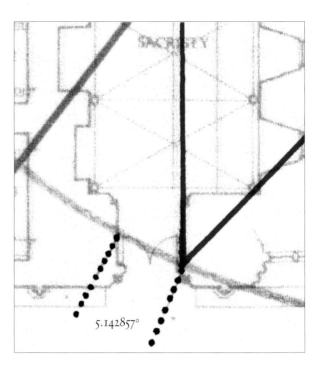

The lower-left stellation of the octagram star defines the right-hand wall of the sacristy's doorway which itself takes up 5.142857° of the star's circle

The image on the right demonstrates that the red line of the star's stellation runs along the right-hand wall on the inside of the sacristy's doorway. The grey circle that contains the octagram then arcs diagonally through the width of the doorway. Let it now be imagined that the octagram star is turned clockwise through 1/70 of the circumference of its container circle. The number of degrees that it would have turned through would accordingly be 5.142857. This is quite simply because 360 ÷ 70 = 5.142857 (i.e. 5 1/7). By turning through this 1/70 of the circle's degrees the octagram would then become skewed by the same number of degrees as the York chapter house and the Wells chapter house vestibule because 5.142857° is effectively the number of degrees in the Moon's inclination. But the main significance of this is that the stellated point of the octagram star would then effectively move from the right-hand side of the sacristy's doorway over to the left-hand side thereby symbolically suggesting an 'unlocking' of a 'through-way' into the Sacristy.

Much like the doorway to the mason's loft at York, there is a geometric symbolism here that is suggestive of the opening or revealing of a doorway as a result of the lunar inclination angle. The fact that this is effected at Wells through the symbolic turning of a 'lunar' star by 1/70 of its 360° circumference is inevitably reminiscent of Plutarch's description of Thoth gaining 1/70 of the Moon's light so as to add 5 extra days to the 360 day year. So it can be symbolically understood that the circle contains its 360° albeit with the 1/70 extra producing '5.14' extra 'days' (i.e. degrees).

Another point of interest here is that if the 1/70 of the circle was looked upon as actually bringing about one edge of a 70-sided polygon then this edge can be arithmetically demonstrated to measure precisely six English feet. These kinds of measurement units are approached in much detail in Part 3.

As to what lies beyond the sacristy doorway, there is of course the sacristy itself, which will be described in more detail in chapter 19. At the back of the sacristy there are two more doors. The door on the right leads into the octagonal undercroft, and interestingly, much like the sacristy's front door, this back door is also positioned at the golden section of the wall upon which it is located - i.e. on the undercroft's wall. But as the

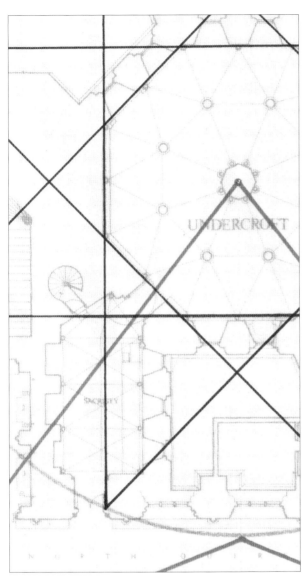

The green golden ratio line of the pyramid triangle passes directly through the sacristy's 'golden ratio' back door into the octagonal Undercroft

image here also shows, the left-hand slanting edge of the green pyramid triangle actually passes directly through this doorway. If the pyramid triangle was understood, in this instance, to be a Golden Pyramid Triangle, it would effectively mean that this slanting edge of the triangle is actually the golden ratio line of the triangle and it is passing directly through the Sacristy's golden ratio back door. (see image to the left). More details relating to this will be shown in Part 3 (sec 15.4).

The left-hand doorway at the back of the sacristy leads up a staircase to a couple of rooms, about which nothing is known. The first room, halfway up the staircase, is a very small, vaulted cell-like room. Its only light source is from a small grille that looks on to the chapter house staircase. The second room is yet another octagonal room, which is actually directly above the chapter house. But this room is in an unfinished state. Beyond this final room the staircase leads out on to the chapter house roof. The final point of interest here is that these two doorways at the back of the sacristy both lead to octagonal rooms – one that is below the chapter house and the other one above. But, the chapter house itself is only reached through the much grander public entrance via the chapter house staircase. With the existence of these three different levels, there appears to be a symbolic emphasis within this part of the cathedral on the number 3. This will be expanded upon in Part 3 in the section entitled The Prevalence of the number 3 on the north side of Wells Cathedral.

9.5 THE EYE OF PROVIDENCE AND THE THREE SEATS WITH AN ALL-SEEING VIEW

Iｎ the octagonal chapter houses at both Salisbury and York, there is a small carved-stone head high up on the side of the bishop's seat. The head at Salisbury depicts a male, whereas the equivalent head at York is female. The striking characteristic of these two heads is that they are each comprised of three faces.

This is reminiscent of one of the images of Wisdom, or 'Philo-Sophia', surrounded by the Seven Liberal Arts that was shown in section 1.3. The image from the *Hortus Deliciarum* depicts Philo-Sophia enthroned at the centre of the image, and she has three faces on top of her head that together look down in the direction of all that lies below them.

These three faces are sometimes associated with the three subjects that formed the discipline of Philosophy – namely Ethics, Logic and Physics/Metaphysics. In his *Convivio*, Dante symbolically associates Philosophy with that which lies beyond the seven planetary spheres, whereas the planetary spheres themselves he associates with the Seven Liberal Arts. So in this sense, Philosophy enables the soul's capacity for seeing and understanding to be raised aloft, beyond the usual earthbound human vision, and indeed beyond the seven planetary spheres. This would appear to be why the three faces are located above the head of the anthropomorphic image of Philo-Sophia, suggesting an engagement with knowledge that goes above and beyond the normal human view. But in another sense, her anthropomorphic form also suggests that the human body itself microcosmically 'incarnates' the seven steps of ascent so that the eighth sphere of Philosophy is then above the crown of her head in the form of the three faces that represent the three subjects of Philosophy. An image was shown in section 1.4 from one of the various medieval illuminated manuscripts of *The Consolation of Philosophy*, in which the depiction of Lady Philosophy's ladder consists of seven steps that actually have the names of the Seven Liberal Arts written on them, and this ladder is generally projected onto her body.

As to the three-faced heads at Salisbury and York, they too are high up on the side of the bishop's seat, affording vision that rises above and beyond that of a human, who would be standing next to them. This confers a certain capacity for Wisdom on to the Bishop, above whose seat these heads are located. Indeed, in the image from the *Hortus Deliciarum,* Philo-Sophia is holding a banner, upon which is written 'All Wisdom comes from God; only the wise can achieve what they desire'.[8] The inner circle that contains Philo-Sophia, and the two philosophers Socrates and Plato, has text written around it that translates as 'I, Godlike Philosophy, con-trol all things with Wisdom; I lay out seven arts which are subordinate to me.' [9]

The Seven Liberal Arts were symbolically associated with the seven planetary spheres, (see sec 1.4) and in this sense, they form a seven-step cosmic ladder up to Philosophy, in the eighth heaven of the fixed stars and beyond. The seven planetary spheres were also symbolically associated with the Seven Gifts of the Holy Spirit, and sure enough the *Hortus Deliciarum* image also mentions that the Seven Liberal Arts are inspired by the Holy Spirit.[10]

But it is the resemblance of these various examples of three-faced heads to the Roman god Janus that appears to present another layer of symbolism suggestive of the Eye of Providence. Janus, the Roman god of the doorway, has two 'polar' faces, one of which looks into the past and the other into the future. However, as he is the god of the doorway – i.e. the threshold between two places – it could be suggested that he also has a third invisible face that looks directly on the eternal present. The eternal present is accordingly the threshold or doorway between the past and the future. In the words of René Guénon:

'the true face of Janus, that which looks at the present, is neither one nor the other of those that we can see. This third face is, in fact, invisible because the present in its temporal manifestation is but an ungraspable instant ...'

Symbols of Sacred Science, Chapter 37 [11]

In *The Consolation of Philosophy,* Lady Philosophy instructs Boethius in relation to providence and fate. She suggests that whereas Fate characterises the human experience of the gradual unfolding of things over the course of time, Providence is the heavenly view by which God sees all things at one and the same time.

8. See www.plosin.com/work/HortusDetails.html.
9. Ibid.
10. Ibid.
11. *Sophia Perennis*, 2004, page 235.

'What is, what was, what is to be,
In one swift glance His mind can see.
All things by Him alone are seen,
And Him the true sun we should deem.'

A clock face (or 'dial') is an ideal visual symbol by which to contemplate such a relationship. The hub of a clock is stationary yet also turning. In this sense it embodies a description of God as the Unmoved Mover. Through being at the unmoving centre of the circular clock, the hub is outside the cycle of time and therefore rooted in the timeless and the unchanging. However, the hub is also turning, and as a result of this it causes the hands of the clock to externally express that which is 'inwardly' known by the hub through sequentially pointing to each new minute and hour of the night and day with the continuing passage of time. But each new moment is nothing more than yet another one of the countless moments that are forever known by the clock's hub in the simultaneity of the timeless. Henceforth the saying associated with Plato that 'Time is a moving image of eternity'.

This is the vision witnessed by the Eye of Providence, which is also known as the all-seeing eye. The depiction of this eye usually takes the form of a human eye inside a triangle, which expresses a three-fold symbolism that would appear in one sense to relate to Boethius' description of the past, the present and the future, although in overtly Christian terms it also came to be associated with the Trinity.

In relation to all of this some of the polygonal chapter houses, such as those at Wells and Salisbury, have a central pillar that appears to embody a symbolism expressive of a three-fold vision that sees everything at once. This all-seeing vision again occurs in relation to the view from the bishop's seat, along with the seats of the dean and the precentor, who sit on either side of the bishop.[12] Their three seats are the only three in the whole chapter house that have a complete and uninterrupted view of every other seat in the whole room. The reason for this is to do with the pillar that stands at the centre of the chapter house. When viewed from any of the seats in the whole room, the pillar obscures the view of the seats that are directly opposite. Or rather, it obscures the view from all seats except for those of the bishop, the dean and the precentor. This is because their three seats are directly opposite the doorway that leads into the chapter house,[13] and so this is what the central pillar obscures from their view. But there is not a single seat that is obscured from their view, and this reflects the threefold nature of the all-seeing eye. Such three-fold 'all-seeing' symbolism would also appear to relate to the three-faced heads above the bishop's seat in the chapter houses at Salisbury and York, albeit without the third face being invisible. This inclusion of a third face might have been to visually distinguish it from Janus, so as not to resemble a Pagan god too closely. The Janic principle itself of *past–present–future* is as Christian as Boethius and his *Consolation*, although to go as far as depicting a recognisable Pagan god in a Christian building – even if within an unconsecrated chapter house – may have been a step too far. But the three-fold symbolism of the faces appears to possibly also relate to various other threenesses, which would necessitate a third face anyway. As mentioned earlier, the Trinity is one such threeness that became associated with the Eye of Providence.

Another more biblical symbolism that has been suggested in relation to the English polygonal chapter houses is that they are a depiction of Pentecost,[14] which as mentioned in Section 1.2 is very much a part of the 'seven-fold' Wisdom tradition. The iconographical depiction of Pentecost has the Virgin Mary seated at the

12. The dean and the precentor are the head and deputy head of the cathedral.
13. This doorway leads into the chapter house vestibule, which as mentioned earlier appears to have an image of a four-faced Janus up in its 'skewed' vault. So this brings about a direct architectural connection between the 'Janic' three seats in the chapter house and the 'double Janus' up in the vestibule vault.
14. Nigel Hiscock, *The Symbol at your Door,* Routledge, 2016, page 255.

The eastern wall of the chapter house contains seven seats. The middle one is the bishop's seat and then to his/her right (or on the left as this photo shows it) is the seat of the dean. The precentor's seat is then to the bishop's left. These are the only three seats from which there is an uninterrupted view of all the other seats in the chapter house.

The photo on the right shows the view from the Bishop's seat. The chapter house's central pillar is only obscuring the bishop's view of the middle part of the double doorway portal that leads into the chapter house.

The four photos on the following page then show the views first from the dean and precentor's seats. (top left and top right). They each have a view of one of the doorways contained within the doorway portal but not the the other doorway. The dean can see the doorway on the right and the precentor the doorway on the left. This matches their seated position in relation to the bishop.

The other two photos (bottom-left and bottom right) show the views from the seats that are the next ones along from the dean and the precentor's seats. Note that these are the first seats to have an obscured view of any of the other seats within the chapter house. The single seats that are situated on either side of the doorway are now obscured by the central pillar. From here onwards all of the other seats in the chapter house have a view of the other seats that is somewhere obscured by the central pillar. So it is only the three main Clerics who together have an uninterrupted view of all the seats as well as both of the doorways within the portal.

The Precentor's view

The Dean's view

The seat to the left of the Precentor - the seat on the right of the doorway is obscured

The seat to the right of the Dean - the seat on the left of the doorway is obscured

Pentecost in the Black Hours MS

189

centre of the twelve apostles who are encircled around her, and so in this sense the central pillar found in some of the chapter houses is an image of the Virgin herself. Indeed the very image of twelve-around-one also cosmologically resembles the twelve signs of the Zodiac circulating around the Celestial North Pole, which relates to the Virgin's 'polar' title, Stella Maris. This was a very commonly used title for the Virgin in the 12th and 13th centuries.

The fifty-one seats found in the chapter houses at Wells and Salisbury also appear to suggest Pentecostal numerics, because if the three seats with the all-seeing view are, in symbolic terms, a three-fold unity, then when they are added to the other forty-eight seats there could be said to be forty-nine altogether which reflects the '7 × 7 days' in the calculation of Pentecost. The actual Pentecostal 'fiftieth day' would then be the central pillar 'herself', Whose central position reflects the fact that on Pentecost they were all gathered 'with one accord in one place' (Acts 2:1), experiencing the 'unity' of the Holy Spirit in the form of Its seven gifts – the greatest of which is Wisdom. Along with all of this, the chapter house has seven walls that contain seven seats, and this again reflects Pentecostal numerics. The eighth wall has the doorway and two single seats, one on either side of the doorway.

Returning to the Eye of Providence, the final symbolism to point out here is the fact that within the underlying geometric design of Wells Cathedral the chapter house is centred on the apex of a pyramid triangle. The position of the Eye of Providence at the apex of a pyramid is famously associated with an image from the American one-dollar bill that some suggest is Freemasonic in origin. This is another profound spiritual symbol that has been dragged down into the realms of conspiracy theories and their egoic obsessions with worldly power. Such a misunderstanding of symbolism is one of the characteristics of a modern materialism that causes the soul to lose touch with its innate spiritual vision – indeed to lose touch with its very capacity to behold the world through the Eye of Providence itself. In visual symbolic terms, the Eye of Providence accords with the peak of a pyramid or the summit of a mountain, because this is the one position on the mountain from which all paths to the summit can be observed at the same time – and likewise where all four faces of a pyramid become visible. This all-seeing position is again the eye of God rather than that of any worldly human power. But in *The Consolation of Philosophy* Lady Philosophy is keen to remind all those who are prepared to raise their eyes to her that the all-seeing eye affords the true and original vision of the soul owing to the fact that humanity was created in the Divine Image.

If you desire to see and understand
In purity of mind the laws of God,
Your sight must on the highest point of heaven rest
Where through the lawful covenant of things
The wandering stars preserve their ancient peace.

So in this sense, as well as symbolising the Moon, the octagonal buildings at Wells would also appear to symbolise the eighth heaven that is centred on the Celestial North Pole. The eighth heaven symbolically corresponds both to the three-fold Eye of Providence and to the three subjects that form Philosophy.[15] As mentioned above, the Celestial North Pole is itself also associated with the Virgin Mary via her title Stella Maris (Star of the Sea, i.e. the Pole Star).

The apex of the pyramid triangle coincides in the ground plan with the position of the Marian 'Pentecostal pillar', located as it is at the centre of the chapter house. The triangle's apex is also seven units of height

---

15. Another threeness that is associated with the eighth heaven is found in Dante's *Commedia*. Faith, Hope and Love feature in Dante's eighth sphere of ascent. The association of Sophia with the eighth heaven, as well as Dante's mention of Faith, Hope and Love, recalls the early Christian martyr St Sophia and her three martyred daughters, who had the names Faith, Hope and Love.

above the triangle's baseline. This 'earthly' baseline then runs through the middle east-west axis of the 'Solomonic' quire – the temple at the centre of the world.

So, in symbolic terms, it could be suggested that the chapter house is associated with the eighth heaven through being its earthly Pentecostal reflection, in which the twelve 'Zodiacal' apostles encircle the Stella Maris. It is from this eighth clime that the Seven 'planetary' Gifts of the Holy Spirit descended on to those who were gathered in the Upper Room. But this descent of the Seven Gifts subsequently presents a ladder of seven steps, by which the soul can return to its heavenly origin

which ultimately lies beyond the 'Ogdoadic' eighth sphere of the fixed stars – which themselves circulate around the Celestial North Pole. So in turn this particular pyramid triangle in the design of Wells Cathedral could be said to contain seven steps of ascent northwards from the quire – itself an image of the temple of the 'wise' King Solomon – up to Philo-Sophia's Eye of Providence in the octagonal eighth heaven. This emphasises the importance of the descent of the Holy Spirit in the aftermath of the Ascension of Christ, the Holy Wisdom, Whose return to Heaven points the soul in the direction of the way that leads back up to its heavenly origin.

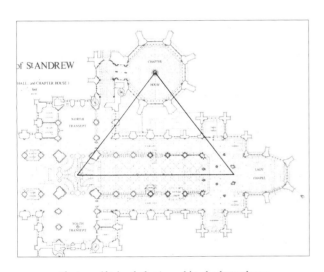

The pyramid triangle that 'ascends' to the chapter house

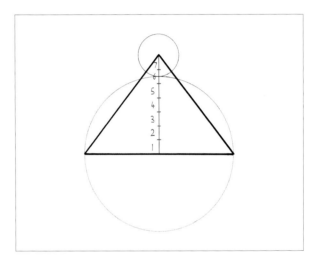

The Earth-Moon pyramid triangle with its seven units or 'steps' of ascent

9.6 HARRAN – CITY OF THE MOON AND THE MYSTERY TO THE NORTH

IN IAMBLICHUS' WRITINGS about Pythagoras, it is mentioned that Pythagoras went to both Egypt and Babylon, where he learnt from their Wisdom traditions and particularly about the four quadrivial arts.

'In Egypt he frequented all the temples with the greatest diligence, and most studious research, during which time he won the esteem and admiration of all the priests and prophets with whom he associated. Having most solicitously familiarized himself with every detail, he did not, nevertheless, neglect any contemporary celebrity, whether a sage renowned for wisdom, or a peculiarly performed mystery. He did not fail to visit any place where he thought he might discover something worthwhile. That is how he visited all of the Egyptian priests, acquiring all the wisdom each possessed. He thus passed twenty-two years in the sanctuaries of temples, studying astronomy and geometry, and being initiated in no casual or superficial manner in all the mysteries of the Gods. At length, however, he was taken captive by the soldiers of Cambyses, and carried off to Babylon. Here he was overjoyed to be associated with the Magi, who instructed him in their venerable knowledge, and in the most perfect worship of the Gods. Through their assistance, likewise, he studied and completed arithmetic, music and all the other sciences. After twelve years, about the fifty-sixth year of his age, he returned to Samos.'

Life of Pythagoras - Ch 4

With the current subject in mind, it is of interest that within both of these ancient civilisations Wisdom – the object of Pythagoras' travels – was associated with the god of the Moon.

In ancient Egypt Thoth was the god of the Moon as well as of Wisdom, and his three-fold lunar symbolism can be recognised in relation to his epithet 'Thrice Great'. This description went on to become a title of the mythical sage Hermes Trismegistus (i.e. 'thrice great' Hermes) who was a synthesis of Thoth and Hermes – the herald of Greek Gods. As mentioned in section 1.3, the learned churchmen and women of the 12th century took an open interest in a written dialogue attributed to Hermes Trismegistus called *Asclepius*, because parts of it bore close resemblance to various Christian beliefs as well as to the Platonist 'way of seeing' that was so concordant with an educated medieval Christian outlook.

In Babylon the god of the Moon was called Sin. He was known as 'the Lord of Wisdom', and such wisdom was directly associated with a knowledge of astronomy and astrology. There were two principal centres in which Sin was worshipped. The main one was Ur, and the other Harran. The second of these two places presents an interesting connection within the study of Wells Cathedral, because Harran was a kind of medieval outpost of ancient quadrivial knowledge all the way up until the 11th century. Indeed various Harranians – who were known as Sabians – were taken to Baghdad to be involved with the Bayt al-Hikma (House of Wisdom), which was a significant centre of learning in the early Islamic world between the 8th and the 13th centuries.

But what does this all have to do with the smallest city in England, along with the design of its cathedral? A potential answer to this lies in the fact that a local diocesan inhabitant – Adelard of Bath – was a significant European translator of Arabic texts into Latin. More to the point, he was centrally interested in the quadrivial knowledge of the ancient world as well as steeped in the philosophy of Plato, Aristotle and Boethius, whose style of writing he closely emulated in his book *De Eodem et Diverso (On the Same and the Different)*. Adelard is also known to have travelled extensively, seemingly in search of quadrivial knowledge – particularly that of astronomy and astrology. He was also the first person to translate Euclid's geometry books *(The Elements)* from Arabic into Latin. Adelard is known to have travelled in the Principality of Antioch – one of the Crusader states – and Antioch itself was one of the main centres of the 12th-century translation movement. The border of the next-door Crusader state – the county of Edessa – was actually just a few miles away from Harran itself.

One of the most significant Sabians of Harran who went to Baghdad was Thabbit ibn Qurra, and Adelard translated Thabbit's book on the use of astrological talismans. So the fact that the design of Wells Cathedral seems to place such an emphasis upon cosmology shines a spotlight on Adelard, as someone who may have had some involvement in the cathedral's design. Along with this, he is thought to have died only around twenty years before Wells Cathedral started to be built. Adelard was also the childhood teacher of Henry II, as well as seemingly being his astrologer.[16]

Returning to the northern emphasis within the design of Wells Cathedral, there appears to be a very interesting connection between both a lunar and a polar cosmology if one looks specifically from an ancient Harranian perspective.

Central to Harranian cosmological beliefs was the so-called 'Mystery to the North'. In his 10th-century encyclopedia *Al-Fihrist* Al-Nadim wrote about the Sabians of Harran and their planet-religion, which revolved around the significance of the seven planetary spheres as well as what lay beyond them. He mentions that they looked to Hermes and Plato as part of their focus on wisdom. But he also makes particular mention of the northern focus of their daily cycle of prayers:

'They have adopted one direction for prayer, which they have fixed towards the North Star in its course. The intelligent thus seek to inquire for wisdom' [17]

Also of interest is the description of the physical movements associated with these prayers, which involve the 'Venusian' Fibonacci numbers 3, 5 and 8.[18] The timings in the day of the prayers are interesting too, because they symbolically relate to the three primary points of a Freemasons' lodge room – sunrise in the east, midday at the zenith (i.e. towards the south) and sunset in the west.

'The prayers ordained for them each day are three. The first one of these is half an hour or less before the rising of the sun, finishing at sunrise. It is composed of eight inclinations [of the body], with three prostrations during each inclination. They end the second prayer at the time of [the beginning of] the descent of the sun [noon]. It is composed of five inclinations with three prostrations in the course of each inclination. The third is like the second, finishing at sunset. These three times [for prayer] are necessary because of the directions of the three fixed points, which are the fixed point of the east, the fixed point of the zenith, and the fixed point of the west.' [19]

Another group associated with the Sabians of Harran is the Mandeans. They are a Gnostic group with a religion that is seemingly Babylonian in origin and interestingly, with Christianity in mind, their central figure is John the Baptist. Adrian Snodgrass describes their northern focus of worship.

'The Mandeans worship the King of Light, who is represented by the Pole Star: "the King of Light sits in the far north in might and glory." The Mandeans accordingly direct their prayers northward to the Pole Star, which is the "Gate of the World of light" and the "Door of Abathur".' [20]

Another description of Harran of interest in relation to the lunar symbolism of English Gothic chapter houses involves Harran's Moon temple. The Islamic historian Al-Masudi described various temples in Harran that were dedicated to the seven planets, and according to

16. See J.D. North, 'Some Norman Horoscopes'.

17. Bayard Dodge, *The Fihrist of al-Nadim, a tenth-century survey of Islamic culture,* Columbia University Press, 1970, page 746.

18. These are also the Fibonacci numbers contained in the seed of the 3 × 3 magic square as understood by Jabir ibn Hayan.

19. Ibid, page 747.

20. A. Snodgrass, *Architecture, Time and Eternity* – Volume 1, Aditya Prakashan, 1994, page 118.

him the Moon Temple – much like the 'lunar' chapter houses at Wells, York and Southwell – was octagonal.

'The Harranian Sabians have temples according to the names of the intellectual substances and the Stars. To these temples belong: the temples of the first cause and of Intelligence, but I do not know whether it is the first or second intelligence; also, the temple of world order, Necessity. The temple of the soul is round, of Saturn, hexagonal; of Jupiter, triangular; of Mars, long (rectangular); the Sun square; that of Venus, a triangle in a quadrangle; that of Mercury, a triangle inside an elongated quadrangle, and that of the Moon, octagonal. The Sabians have in them symbols and mysteries which they keep hidden.' [21]

Perhaps the most intriguing potential within all of this is a geo-cosmological fact that appears to associate the latitude of Harran with both the Moon and the Celestial North Pole at the same time. This is another example of what this research is calling 'latitude geometry'. This apparent practice from the ancient and medieval world was mentioned at the end of chapter 7 (sec 7.5) in relation to the latitude of the first Templar manor, at Cressing Temple in Essex.

Just a few hundred feet to the north of the northern gate of Harran there is line of latitude with an angle that is identical to the smaller angle in the Pythagorean 3 – 4 – 5 triangle. To six decimal places this angle is 36.869897°, although it can be easily rounded up to 36.87°. This is relevant because if the Sabians looked towards the Pole Star when they prayed, they would effectively be looking upwards at an angle of 36.87° – the altitude of the Celestial North Pole is the same angle as the latitude of the person who is looking up to it. But if we also refer to John Michell's Earth-Moon diagram, it is clear that the 3 – 4 – 5 triangle appears within it and actually interacts with the Moon according to the angle in question.

The diagram below shows a detail of the Earth-Moon diagram – specifically the Moon-circle and one of the 3 – 4 – 5 triangles that sits next to the Moon-square.

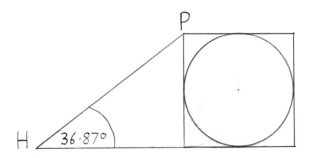

First let it be suggested that point H in the diagram is a person standing at the north gate of Harran looking northwards towards the Pole Star. Point P is then, figuratively speaking, the Celestial North Pole. The angle of elevation up to the pole coincides with the angle of the 3 – 4 – 5 triangle, but by looking at this angle the viewer is also 'encompassing' the view of the Moon-circle as it appears within the Earth-Moon diagram. This interpretation mixes measurable cosmological data with a perception of the Earth-Moon diagram as understood via the spiritual imagination. So it would not be acceptable to a modern-day cosmologist. But can the same thing be said of a medieval Sabian who was following a seemingly ancient planet-religion in one of the two most important ancient centres of the Babylonian Moon god, Sin?

Another hint that this Harranian latitude geometry is not just a random coincidence can be seen if we look at another significant lunar centre from the ancient world which is also at the same latitude. The site of Carthage is very precisely at the latitude of 36.87°, and the matron deity of Carthage was a Moon goddess called Tanit. But it is her resemblance to John Michell's Earth-Moon diagram that is particularly striking.

21. From Mas'udi, *Meadows of Gold* (Muruj al-Dahab), as quoted in Tamara M. Green, *The City of the Moon God*, pages 115–116.

Tanit was depicted in the form of a geometric symbol that looks as if it could have been derived from the Earth-Moon diagram. The pictures below show an image of Tanit from a Punic stele, followed by a highlighted image of Tanit derived from the Earth-Moon diagram.

The key point to emphasise here is that the association of Wisdom with a knowledge of the heavens was significant in the ancient world. To contemplate the cosmic order was to align the human mind with the Divine Mind. The central focus of this contemplation was quadrivial knowledge, because the central focus of the Quadrivium is the eternal and unchanging reality of number. It would appear to be an outlook of this kind that also lay at the heart of medieval cathedral design.

Punic Stele with the symbol of Tanit

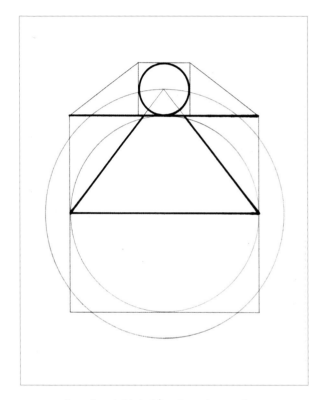

The Tanit symbol derived from the Earth-Moon diagram

Madonna of the Rose Bower by Stefan Lochner

9.7 THE VIRGIN AND THE ROSE IN THE EAST END ROSE WINDOW AT LAON

IN THE CHAPTER HOUSE at York, there is an inscription on the wall about the rose (see sec 9.4). Its Latin words form a rhyming verse:

'Ut rosa flos florum, sic est domus ista domorum'

(As the rose is the flower of flowers,
so this is the house of houses.)

The same inscription is also present in the octagonal chapter house at Westminster Abbey, and so such symbolism does seem to specifically relate to these 'rose-shaped' polygonal architectural forms.

This confers a high status onto the chapter house, particularly in relation to what was written in previous chapters about the symbolism of the rose as an Edenic state to which the soul 'ascends' in the form of a return to its True Self.

An interesting visual concordance can be pointed out here in relation to the ground plans of York, Wells and Southwell cathedrals and the central image from the east end rose window at Laon in France. The north rose window at Laon was described at the beginning of chapter 1, because it depicts Lady Philosophy surrounded by the Seven Liberal Arts and Medicine. Indeed, the cathedral school in Laon was one of the most important centres of education in the 12th century, and also 'a favoured place of study for the administrators of the English court',[22] Laon also had a significant Templar presence along with one of the only polygonal Templar churches in the whole of France. But a particular point of interest in relation to this study is that it was also one of the main universities that Adelard of Bath is known to have visited as a teacher.

The rose windows at Laon are all early in Gothic terms, and started to be constructed in the late 12th century, around the time Wells Cathedral began to be built. The image that will now be focused upon lies at the very centre of the rose window at the east end of the cathedral. So, therefore, in a symbolic sense it could be seen

The east-end rose window at Laon Cathedral

22. C. Burnett, *Adelard of Bath, Conversations with his Nephew,* Cambridge Univeristy Press, 2006, page xv.

as the most important stained-glass image in the whole of Laon Cathedral. The image is of the Virgin Mary seated on a throne with Christ on her lap, and so again this is an image of the Mother of God as the Sedes Sapientiae (Throne of Wisdom). But it is the eight-fold red rose she is holding in her right hand which seems to be of so much importance because Christ – the Holy Wisdom himself – is looking up to it. With this image in mind, we return to the ground plans of York, Wells and Southwell cathedrals – each of which has an octagonal chapter house on the north side – and it is possible to see the likeness between this particular image of the Sedes Sapientiae and the ground plans of the three cathedrals.[23]

The central image in the east-end rose window at Laon Cathedral

23. I am grateful to the painter Emma Alcock for pointing this resemblance out to me.

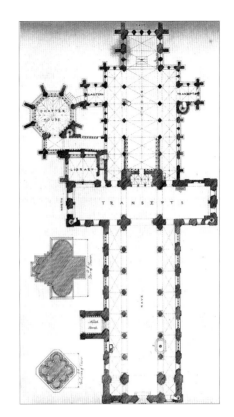

Southwell

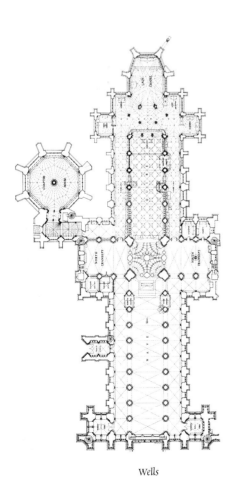

Wells

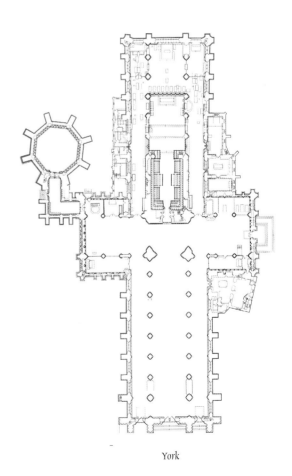

York

The inscription from the York chapter house in which it is associated with the rose appears to accord very well with all of this. But also, the fact that all three chapter houses embody the same octagonal geometric symmetry as the eight-fold rose that the Virgin is presenting to us, as if to remind us of our True Identity. It is clearly a very important object within the image because, as well as Christ, the angel on the left is also looking directly towards it rather than at the Mother of God - who is looking directly at us in the eternal present. The roses that grow in our gardens are always based on five-fold symmetry, which in modern day roses can still be seen in their number of sepals. So this rose at Laon would appear to have been made eight-fold intentionally rather than just being a copy of a rose that the artist saw growing somewhere. It is also interesting that two of these cathedrals are/were 'crowned' at their east ends by Lady chapels, which accords with the Laon image of a Coronated Virgin as the Throne of Wisdom. In this sense the cathedral building itself is the Throne of Wisdom, as well as housing the 'cathedra' – the throne of the bishop. It is after all the bishop who has the three-faced head of Wisdom above his/her seat in some of the chapter houses, and as mentioned earlier some of the octagonal chapter houses appear to symbolise the eighth heaven or 'Ogdoad' – the residing place of Mother Sophia. More will be said about this heavenly 'Celestial' rose 'in the north', and how it also features as part of the culmination of Dante's *Divine Comedy*.

CHAPTER 10.

The Wells Bishop's Palace

10.1 NORTHERN DEAN AND SOUTHERN BISHOP

AT THIS POINT WE will briefly leave the cathedral building to look at the Wells Bishop's Palace.

The Palace lies immediately to the south of the cathedral, which presents a similar symbolic north–south schema as the one used in the design of Lincoln Cathedral. This symbolic division exists in relation to the Dean and Chapter, as opposed to the Bishop. At both Wells and Lincoln, the chapter house and medieval deanery are situated to the north of the cathedral, whereas the Bishop's Palace is on the south side. Lincoln Cathedral even has a rose window in each transept, one known as the 'Bishop's Eye' (south transept) and the other the 'Dean's Eye' (north transept). There is then a north–south symbolism specifically at Lincoln concerning these two 'eyes' of the cathedral.

'For north represents the devil, and south the Holy Spirit
and it is in these directions that the two eyes look.
The bishop faces the south in order to invite in
and the dean the north in order to shun;
the one takes care to be saved, the other takes care not to perish.
With these Eyes the cathedral's face is on watch for the
candelabra of Heaven and the darkness of Lethe (forgetfulness).'

The Metrical Life of St Hugh, c.1220-1235

The north rose window at Lincoln Cathedral - 'The Dean's Eye'

The south rose window at Lincoln Cathedral - 'The Bishop's Eye'

However, this particular aspect of the north–south symbolism shows no sign of being present at Wells. It has in fact been suggested that there are no depictions or mentions of Hell anywhere in Wells Cathedral, and this accords with the symbolism of the Heavenly Jerusalem, in which everything and everywhere is blessed. But there does appear to be a symbolism of the infernal within the centre of the nave, and this will be shown later on – suffice to say here that it is a necessary darkness the soul needs to pass through on its way towards the light.

There were various close connections between Wells and Lincoln cathedrals while they were being built. Bishop St Hugh of Lincoln, for instance, was first brought to England from France by Bishop Reginald De-Bohun of Bath to run England's first Carthusian monastery – situated at Witham, not far from Wells. This was only a few years after Bishop Reginald had instigated the building work on Wells Cathedral. After seven years at Witham – and with the direct support of Reginald – Hugh was then elected Bishop of Lincoln in 1186, and it was under his short reign that a building campaign started at Lincoln in the aftermath of a devastating earthquake that had severely damaged the cathedral. Of particular interest in relation to this building work is that the new east end was pentagonal, i.e. much like the pentagonal east end that eventually came to be added to Wells Cathedral in the early 1300s. These are the only two examples of pentagonal east ends among all English cathedrals, and yet again it suggests that the pentagonal east end at Wells was always an originally intended final design dating back to the late 1100s, despite over a century elapsing before it was finally built. After the death and canonisation of St Hugh, the east end at Lincoln was extended into its current square east end.

A few decades later, in the early 13th century, a pair of brothers from Wells – Jocelin and Hugh Trotman – were concurrent Bishops of Bath and Lincoln. It was during their respective reigns that building work started on the Wells Bishop's Palace. Despite the land for this palace being granted in 1207 – over thirty years after the cathedral started to be built – there appears to be an orientational connection between the ground plans of the cathedral and the Bishop's Palace. But first we will concentrate on the most remarkable feature of the palace in relation to this research, and that is the pyramid triangle in the positioning of the moat walls that bound the whole palace complex.

10.2 THE MOAT WALLS AT WELLS AND THE GREAT PYRAMID IN EGYPT

THE PYRAMID GEOMETRY in the underlying design of the Wells Cathedral ground plan is not overtly present, because it is not possible to actually see pyramid triangles in any direct physical form within the building's fabric. But such geometries can be looked upon as present in the form of a hidden underlying ordering principle within the design of the ground plan. The underlying design theories that include these pyramid triangles do measure up in-situ with an accuracy that makes it difficult to suggest that pyramid geometry was not used in this design, and that the pyramid triangles fractionally relate to the size of Egypt's Great Pyramid

and therefore also to the size of the Earth. Having said all of this, there is actually one single physically existing example of pyramid geometry in medieval Wells in which a pyramid triangle can be seen with the human eye. However, the medieval human eye would have had no access to such a view, and so in this sense it could be said that this particular pyramid triangle was as hidden as all the theoretical pyramid geometry underlying the cathedral's design. With an aerial view afforded by aviation or satellite it is possible to see that there is a pyramid triangle formed by the two longest stretches of moat wall that bound the southern area of the Palace complex.

The moat that surrounds the Bishop's Palace in Wells and the two long stretches of moat wall that together form a pyramid triangle

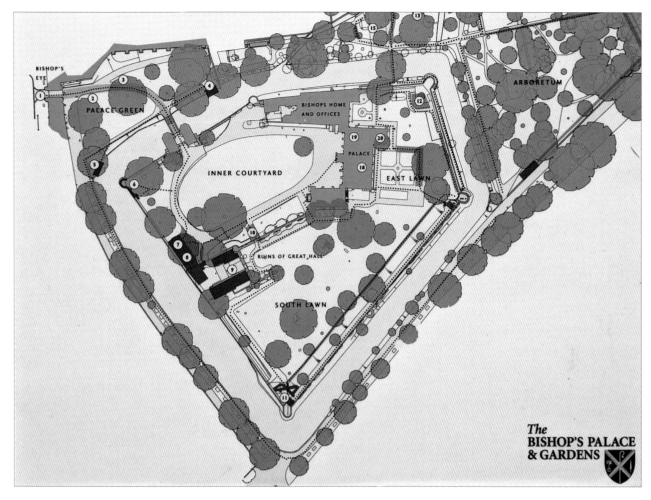

Ground plan of the Bishop's Palace - note the pyramid triangle formed by the moat walls which form a southward pointing pyramid triangle

Even more remarkable is that these two long and straight stretches of wall are also the same length as the height of the Great Pyramid in Egypt. This bears a kind of resemblance to the pyramid triangles used in the underlying design of the cathedral – which, as mentioned earlier, share simple fractional relationships with the size of the Great Pyramid.

This all appears to be part of the medieval interest in the quadrivial knowledge of the ancient world, and specifically with the ancient knowledge concerning the dimensions of the Earth. As mentioned earlier, many of the more recent speculations concerning the Great Pyramid need to be recognised as a purely modern phenomenon along with the fact that they have become increasingly ungrounded as time has gone on. Such speculations only date back to the 19th century, and thus have no bearing on a medieval Christian and

Islamic interest in the Great Pyramid and ancient metrology. But it inevitably appears that the more recent speculations originate from the medieval interest in such ancient knowledge – albeit in a degraded form. The prevailing mythos, moving into the modern era, suggests that the measurements of the Great Pyramid embody a profound cosmological wisdom. However, rather than space ships and ancient aliens this wisdom appears to be that of the Ancient's knowledge of both the Earth's dimensions and the derivation of the imperial measurement units from such a knowledge.

First, the geometric design used for the Palace will be looked at, before being applied to the bird's-eye view of the Palace complex.

The first diagram shows an upside-down pyramid triangle. The reason for this inverted orientation is to reflect the way that we shall view the Palace's ground plan shortly. The sloping sides of the triangle measure 280 Egyptian royal cubits, which is the same number of cubits as in the height of the Great Pyramid.

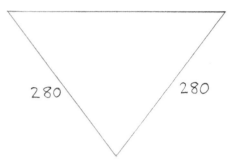

The next two diagrams bring this cubit measurement of 280 from the sloping sides around to the central axis of the triangle, thereby forming a new larger triangle that expresses the dimensions of the cross-section of the Great Pyramid itself, because the 280-cubit measurement now forms the height of this new larger triangle.

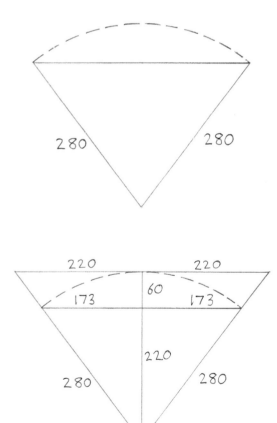

There are also cubit numbers that have been added to various parts of this triangle to show its various measurements. All these numbers are rounded up to their nearest cubit and this then seems to demonstrate the significance of the diagram. It appears to bring forth the dimensions of Solomon's Temple (60 × 20 cubits) via a relationship that also embodies the relative size of the Earth to the Moon (11:3).

First of all, the extra height of triangle which was added on in the last image - enlarging the triangle from the first image - measures 60 cubits. This measurement is the length of Solomon's Temple. As to the entire height of the whole pyramid triangle, it is 220 cubits + 60 cubits, and their sum of 280 cubits is then the height of the Great Pyramid. A measurement of 220 cubits is also present in each half-baseline of the whole triangle.

The greatest common divisor shared by 220 and 60 is 20, and so if this becomes a unit of measure it can be suggested that the pyramid triangle, as it is used here, has a baseline unit measurement of 22 of these units (22 × 20 cubits = 440 cubits) and a height of 14 of them (14 × 20 cubits = 280 cubits), and this again reflects the cubit measurements of the Great Pyramid. The other significant point about a 20-cubit measurement unit is that, along with 60 cubits, it defines the width and length measurement of Solomon's Temple. So like the cathedral's design the Palace design also incorporates the measurements of Solomon's Temple. But it also includes the Earth-Moon relationship within the same dimensions. This is because the measurement of 220 cubits can be divided up into 11 sets of 20 cubits, whereas 60 cubits is divided up into 3 sets of 20 cubits. So the relationship of 220 to 60 can be expressed as 11 to 3, which is also the size ratio of Earth to Moon.

This is geometrically demonstrated in the diagram on the next page. Indeed, the sizes of the two circles in the diagram that represent Earth and Moon are fractionally related to the actual size of the Earth and the Moon themselves by a ratio of 1 to 110,880. This very large number is a doubling of the number 55,440 which, as will become clear in section 17.1, is a significant number in relation to the Great Pyramid itself as well to John Michell's diagram of the Earth and the Moon.

These 500 cubits are thus demarcated in the following way:220 cubits + 60 cubits + 220 cubits = 500 cubits

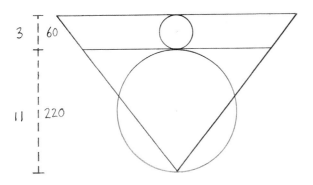

The size of Earth and Moon within the pyramid triangle diagram

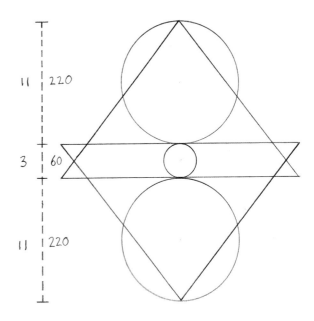

A symmetrical pyramid triangle is added which forms a kind of rhomb

In the following diagram another pyramid triangle has been added, which partially overlaps the original pyramid triangle. This new symmetrical inclusion helps to form a kind of pyramid triangle rhomb. The total height of this rhomb is 500 cubits as is shown, and it also presents the possibility of drawing in another Earth-circle.

So even before any correlation is made between these geometries and the measurements/layout of the Wells Bishop's Palace, it can be seen that this is an interesting geo-cosmic diagram in and of itself.

10.3 THE OVERALL LAYOUT IN RELATION TO WELLS CATHEDRAL

THE DIAGRAM DESCRIBED in the previous section will now be demonstrated in relation to the Palace layout. First, when the initial pyramid triangle is added to the plan of the Palace it can be seen that its three corners coincide with three bastions located in the moat wall.

The upside-down apex of the triangle is centrally located in its bastion. The corner to the east is off-centre within its bastion (the reason for this will be expanded upon in section 17.3). The position of the other corner (to the west) is only just about visible through the tree canopy (i.e. on Google Maps). Again it falls a little off-centre of its bastion.

The two edges of this triangle that follow the moat walls are the same length as the height of the Great Pyramid in Giza (280 cubits). This has been checked and verified with a theodolite in relation to the corner

to the east although the corner to the west is obscured by a hanging tree canopy. But the satellite measurement can be trusted to give an accurate reading because the satellite reading for the bastion to the east is the same as the theodolite reading that was made for that particular measurement.

The other key thing to focus upon at this stage is that the upturned baseline of the triangle runs along the southern edge of the actual Palace building.

In the third image the triangle is extended as was shown in the previous section, so that it becomes the same size as the cross-section of the Great Pyramid. What then becomes clear is that the extra measurement of 60 cubits appears to define the northern edge of the Palace building. So the diagram suggests that the north–south length of the palace building is 60 cubits.

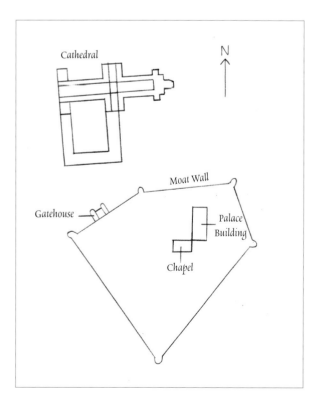

Diagram of Bishop's Palace moat walls with the cathedral to the north of it

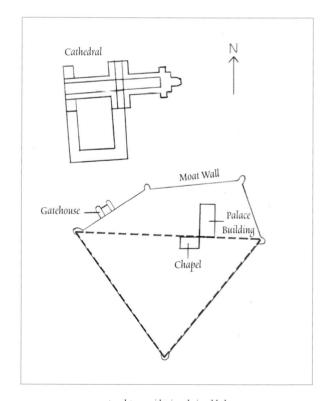

A red pyramid triangle is added

An overhead geographical diagram such as this can only ever suggest a possibility of measurement layouts, because it is far too inaccurate to form a reliable empirical demonstration of measurement. The thickness of the pen lines on the diagram would effectively be a few feet wide if they were projected down onto the ground in-situ, and with lines of such thickness there can be very little, if any, accuracy.

However, what diagrams such as these can do is suggest possible design layouts, which can then be checked in-situ with a much finer degree of accuracy. So as these diagrams suggest that a measurement of 60 cubits is present in the north–south length of the Palace building, it becomes possible to make an accurate measurement of this dimension within the building itself to see if the measurement theory holds true. In short ... does the north–south length of the Palace building measure 60 cubits? The two most obvious measurements to check are the external and internal wall-to-wall measurements.

Sure enough, it turns out that the internal wall-to-wall measurement of the palace is pretty much exactly 60

cubits in length. The measurement from the doorway entrance of the Great Hall on the southern wall of the Palace building up to the medieval stonework around a small window at the opposite end on the internal northern wall is around half an inch off a measurement of 60 cubits. This is an accuracy of around 99.96% of the in-situ measurement in relation to the theory suggested by this geographical diagram.

But things become even more interesting when the diagram is extended into the rhomb diagram that was shown in the previous section. The northern apex of this rhomb appears to be located at the centre of the octagon within the ground plan of the cathedral's Lady chapel. This octagon is one of the two polygons that appears to define the shape of the Lady chapel.

What these apparent relationships suggest is that the design of the 14th-century moat walls and Lady chapel are actually a part of a much earlier design schema. The Palace building – which sits so significantly within the pyramid triangle – was started in the early 1200s, and so it would appear that the moat walls were part of this same overall design. But the fact that they also seem to

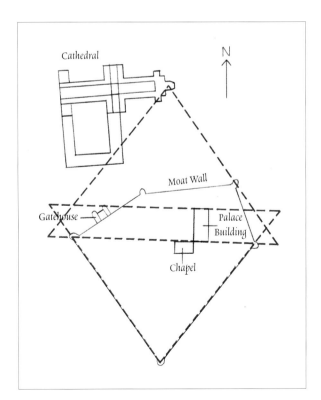

The triangle is extended - the extra 60 cubits define the palace building's length

The other pyramid triangle is added and it's apex reaches the Lady chapel

209

be aligned towards what would be an eventual Lady chapel suggests that the ground plan of this Lady chapel also goes back to the original design along with the marking-out of the cathedral in the 1170s.

So again, we are left with the clear and strong evidence that a master mason's knowledge included pyramid geometry which related to the size of the Great Pyramid and therefore also of the Earth. In this particular instance the pyramid triangle is physically present in the fabric of the building itself. So this reinforces the suggestion that the designer of Wells Cathedral used pyramid geometry in the underlying design of this architectural edifice as well as also in the cathedral.

The Bishop's Palace and Wells Cathedral as seen from a hot air balloon

CHAPTER 11.

The Cathedral Nave as an Image of Planet Earth

11.1 THE EQUATOR–ECLIPTIC ANGLE
AND THE SALTIRE OF ST ANDREW

AT SOME POINT IN the medieval era, St Andrew's martyring by crucifixion became associated with the diagonal Saltire cross. An earlier account of his crucifixion in the Acts of Andrew (c. 2nd century) describes him as being crucified, but not specifically on a Saltire cross.

St Andrew's Saltire is used on the Scottish national flag, and the use of the Saltire in an official Scottish context, such as on seals, appears to date back to the 1180s at the very earliest,[1] which is around the same time that St Andrews Cathedral in Wells started to be built (c.1175).

The Saltire of St Andrew as the Scottish national flag

The reason a Saltire came to be associated with St Andrew is not entirely clear, but it appears possibly to be more of a Western European development rather than an Eastern Orthodox one, where the cross that is associated with St Andrew has a long vertical column and two horizontal bars plus a lower diagonal bar. Indeed, of all the countries that have St Andrew as their patron saint, it is only Scotland that has a Saltire on its flag.

A Scottish myth that has developed over time describes a vision witnessed by Óengus mac Fergusa, a 9th-century king of the Picts, in which he saw a heavenly image of the Saltire up in the sky. This vision took place soon after St Andrew had spoken to Óengus in a dream, telling him to look upwards for this sign of Christ's cross. Óengus saw it just before a battle against the armies of the English King Athelstan, which he then went on to win as a result of this heavenly signification from St Andrew. The battle is said to have taken place at Athelstaneford, which is around 20 miles to the east of Edinburgh.

In 20th-century versions of the myth this heavenly Saltire has come to be understood as a cross of white clouds on the blue background of the sky, which resembles the Scottish flag. But the Scottish writer Michael T.R.B. Turnbull points out that this doesn't reflect the earliest descriptions of the myth, in which the heavenly sign is understood more as some kind of light emanating from the sky. Turnbull uses this to point out how much the story of King Óengus resembles the story of Constantine the Great[2] and his victorious battle at the Milvian Bridge in Rome, prior to which Constantine saw an image of the Chi-Rho symbol emanating from the Sun.[3] The Chi is effectively the shape of a Saltire.

With such a solar emphasis in mind, one suggestion is that the Saltire has a cosmological association with the equator–ecliptic cross. The ecliptic is, after all, the path that the Sun takes through the sky day after day. The reason such astrological/cosmological symbolism is being considered within the context of this study is

---

1. See National Records of Scotland website: https://www.nrscotland.gov.uk/research/image-gallery/hall-of-fame/saint-andrew
2. Constantine the Great was seen as a significant figure in Scotland at this time, and there were various Pictish and Scottish kings named after him in the 9th and 10th centuries – including Óengus's own brother, who preceded him as king.
3. Michael T.R.B. Turnbull, *Saint Andrew, Scotland's Myth and Identity*, Saint Andrew Press, 1997.

because the Cathedral Church of St Andrew in the City of Wells has a nave that is geometrically governed by the cosmological angle formed by the equator–ecliptic cross. This is the angular measure of Earth's equator in relation to the ecliptic. It is this cosmological relationship that causes the solstices and equinoxes to occur. In practical terms, what this means in relation to the design of Wells Cathedral is that its rectangular nave has diagonal axes that run at an angle of 23.4°. This particular angle is the axial tilt of Earth in relation to the circular plane on which it orbits the Sun. So Earth's equator is tilted away from this circular orbital plane by 23.4°.

Therefore, a Saltire consisting of two of these crossed diagonal lines could be said to govern the geometric shape of the nave in this cathedral church that is dedicated to St Andrew.

Another solstitial solar symbolism of the Saltire, and indeed one that also symbolically suggests St Andrew himself, relates to his reputed journey to the 'ends of the Earth'. This is a description of the journey taken by St Regulus from Patras in Greece – where Andrew was martyred – to the modern-day Scottish town of St Andrews. It was on this mythical journey that Regulus actually brought the remains of St Andrew to Scotland.

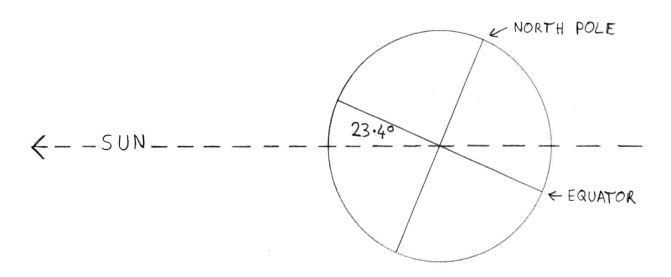

The axial tilt of Earth's equator in the relation to Earth's orbital plane around the Sun (i.e. the ecliptic)

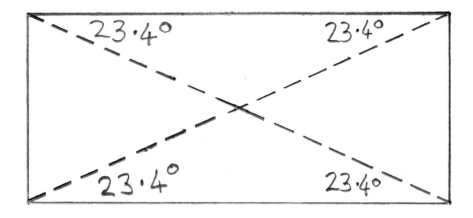

The type of rectangle used in the design of the Wells Cathedral nave

A Saltire geometrically embodies a movement from a single central point, outwards to the four corners of the quadrilateral frame that contains it. In terms of geometric symbolism, there is accordingly a movement from the centre to the four corners – or the extreme limits – of the 'square Earth'.

This symbolic squareness of Earth is both spatial and temporal at the same time if the sunrise and sunset points on the two solstices are used to produce the square – i.e. within the circular horizon.

On the equinoxes, the sun rises in the east and sets in the west.

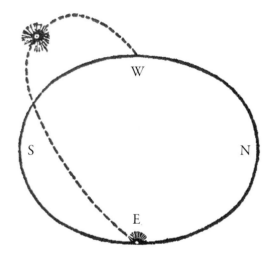

But beyond the spring equinox both the sunrise and sunset points slowly – day by day – move further northwards around the horizon until they reach their most extreme northerly points at the summer solstice.

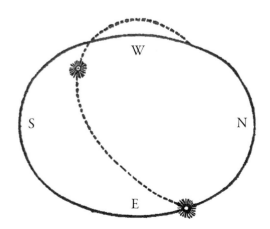

After this the sunrise and sunset points begin to move back towards the eastern and western points of the horizon once again, which they eventually reach at the autumn equinox.

An equivalent movement southwards then takes place around the horizon between the autumn equinox and the winter solstice.

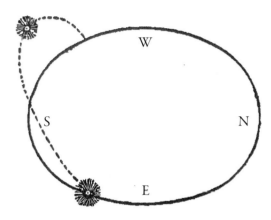

After this, the Sun moves back towards the east and the west again for the following spring equinox.

This annual movement northwards and southwards to the extreme sunrise and sunset points at the two solstices naturally creates four points on the circular horizon, and in turn these points create the coordinates for a quadrilateral within the horizon. If someone is standing on the equator these extreme solstitial points will be 23.4° to the north and the south of the east–west axis.

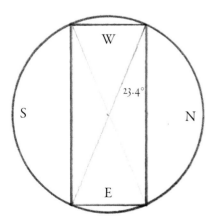

As will be shown in the following section this particular type of quadrilateral can be viewed as a rectangle with a short edge of 13 and a long edge of 30, because this type of rectangle has a diagonal of 23.4°.

But if one views this from within horizons that are further north or south of the equator, the extreme solstitial points will move further northwards and southwards around the horizon from which they are being viewed. The effect that this has on the quadrilateral shape within the circular horizon is to gradually make it less rectangular and more square the further north or south of the equator from which one views it. The point at which the rectangle becomes perfectly square is just around half a degree of latitude to the south of Athelstaneford and St Andrews in Scotland. The actual latitude of the square is where many Scottish border abbeys can be found, as well as Lindisfarne Priory, Balantrodoch – (the medieval headquarters of the Knights Templar in Scotland), Rosslyn Chapel, the oldest Freemasons' lodge, known as Mother

Kilwinning and also the old royal burgh of Irvine which contained the largest presence of the Templars in the whole of Scotland.

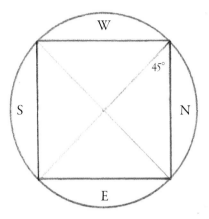

The solstitial sunrise and sunset points form a square in the horizon at the latitude that runs between Irvine (in the west) and Lindisfarne (in the east)

So, in this sense St Andrew did travel to the extreme ends of the square Earth via the diagonal Saltire cross.[4]

4. In his book *Symbols of Sacred Science* René Guénon describes Constantine's 'Chrismon' as an image of the six-armed three-dimensional cross. Whereas the rho (P) is seen as the vertical axis leading up to the Sun (represented by the loop at the top of the 'P'), the chi (X) is seen as an oblique representation of the horizontal four-armed cross of the four directions. So again, the chi relates to the 'fourness' of the Earth, albeit via the four directions of north, south, east and west rather than with the four solstitial points as described above.

11.2 SEVEN BY THREE & THIRTY BY THIRTEEN

I N HIS BOOK *Sun, Moon and Earth*, Robin Heath presents two examples of right-angled triangles with hypotenuses that embody an angular slant closely approximating the axial tilt of Earth.

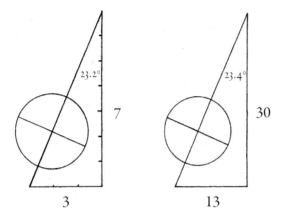

The hypotenuses of the triangles coinciding with Earth's polar axis

This angle varies over the course of 41,000 years between the larger and smaller angles of 24.5° and 22.1°. So for instance in the 12th century, when the design and building work for Wells Cathedral was instigated, the equator–ecliptic angle was 23.5° rather than the 23.4° angle that we currently have.

As the triangular diagrams above demonstrate, a right-angled triangle with a long edge of 7 and a short edge of 3 has a hypotenuse with an angular slant of 23.2°. The other triangle has edges of 30 × 13, embodying an angular slant of 23.4°.

Heath shows these triangles in relation to Planet Earth whereby the hypotenuse of each triangle follows the polar axis of Earth, and this is what is shown in the diagrams to the left. But for reasons that will become clear in the next chapter, the following diagrams present the triangles in such a way that their hypotenuses coincide with Earth's equator and their long edges with the ecliptic which, as mentioned above, is the circular plane upon which Earth orbits the Sun.

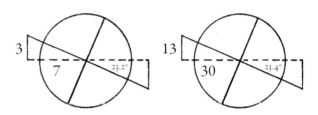

The hypotenuses of the triangles are now coinciding with Earth's equator

Both of these triangles are used within the design of the nave at Wells, albeit in a rectangular form, and this appears to be directly related to a cosmological association in which the nave symbolises Planet Earth. This is another indication of the ascent symbolism contained within the cathedral's design, whereby the western end of the cathedral is the 'earthly' beginning of an ascent that leads eastwards, towards the rising of the Bright Morning Star up at the cathedral's east end.

There's more detail on all these measures in chapter 13.

11.3 THE EXTREMITIES OF CANCER AND CAPRICORN, AND THE EQUINOCTIAL MIDDLE WAY

THERE IS AN INTERESTING cosmological symbolism in relation to the rectangular nave at Wells. As was just shown, the hypotenuse of a 30 x 13 right-angled triangle runs at an angle of 23.4°. A similar thing could also be said of the diagonal line within a rectangle that has edges of 30 and 13. The rectangle's diagonal lines produce the same angle as the 23.4° axial tilt of the Earth.

The way in which this appears to have been used by the designer at Wells is to express a seasonal symbolism that relates directly to the Christian feast of Easter, which as mentioned in chapter 6 is calendrically associated with the season of spring. This seasonal association was particularly prominent in the era during which Wells Cathedral was built, and was often expressed through the floral spring-time symbolism associated with courtly love.

The following circular diagrams show profile views of Planet Earth. The top and bottom of each circle are the geographic north and south poles. The horizontal dotted diameters are then the Earth's equator.

The second diagram also includes the tropics of Cancer and Capricorn. The third diagram then uses the tropics of Cancer and Capricorn to produce a rectangle within the circular profile of Earth. This rectangle has a diagonal axis running at an angle of 23.4°. So in short, this is the type of rectangle used for the design of the nave in Wells Cathedral. In this sense the north and south walls of the nave can be looked upon as symbolising the Tropics of Cancer and Capricorn, whereas the middle east–west axis of the whole building symbolises Earth's equator.

But what would such a cosmological symbolism suggest in relation to ascent symbolism within a medieval Christian building?

The Tropics of Cancer and Capricorn are so called because within the annual cycle they correspond to the first days of the zodiacal months of Cancer and Capricorn. What is meant by this is that Earth's axial tilt causes the Tropic of Cancer to be the part of the Earth that is closest to the Sun on the first day of the month of Cancer, which is also the northern hemisphere summer

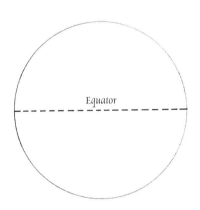

A profile view of planet Earth with its equator

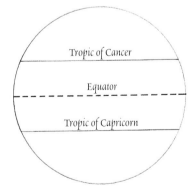

The tropics of Cancer and Capricorn are now added above and below the equator

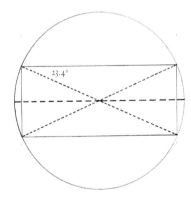

The tropic lines are now used to form the same type of rectangle as the one used for the design of the nave in Wells Cathedral

solstice. Inversely the Tropic of Capricorn is the part of Earth that is closest to the Sun on the first day of the month of Capricorn, which is also the northern hemisphere winter solstice. So with this in mind the north and south walls of the nave at Wells could also be described as symbolising the two solstices, i.e. the longest and shortest days of the year. The summer solstice is the day of most light, whereas the winter solstice is the day of most darkness.

But what of the equinox – the time when night and day are the same length as one another? The equator of Earth is halfway between the tropics, and indeed it is on the days of the equinoxes in March and September – halfway between the solstices – that the equator is the part of the Earth that is closest to the Sun.

Therefore it can be suggested that the equator of Planet Earth – shown in green dotted line – coincides with the central aisle or axis of the cathedral nave, and this cosmologically symbolises a kind of 'middle path' of balance between the solstitial extremes of light and dark.

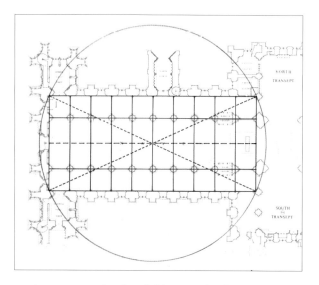

The 30 x 13 rectangle as the underlying geometric grid used within the design of the nave at Wells. The nave accordingly symbolises planet earth.

But again, what would such a cosmological symbolism suggest in relation to ascent symbolism within a Christian building?

The answer lies in the Paschal/Easter symbolism of Christ and the story of Holy Week, which begins with Palm Sunday and culminates with the Resurrection of Christ a week later on Easter Sunday. The calculation of Easter is such that it is the first Sunday after the first full Moon after the spring equinox, and so this associates the middle axis of Wells Cathedral with both an equinoctial and a paschal symbolism at the same time, because they are calendrically connected to one another. So the association, described in section 4.2, that the west front of the cathedral has with Palm Sunday, and the association, described in section 5.5, that the Lady chapel has with Christ's Resurrection on Easter Sunday suggests that the passage through the cathedral, from west to east, symbolically follows the eight days of Easter from Christ's entry into the Holy City to his Resurrection a week later. But because the north and south walls of the cathedral are associated with the two solstices, it also makes Christ's paschal journey a kind of equinoctial middle path of balance between the light and dark extremes of Cancer and Capricorn.[5]

The final section of the book will show how this particular solstitial and equinoctial symbolism is used in relation to the paschal story of Christ and Holy Week, and how the eastward movement through Wells Cathedral architecturally embodies a mythical cosmic journey in which the soul returns to its divine origin via the Death, Resurrection and Ascension of Christ. Having entered Jerusalem on Palm Sunday as the Messiah, Christ eventually descends into the centre of the Earth after his death on the cross. He then resurrects as the Bright Morning Star on Easter Sunday and finally ascends into Heaven forty days later.

5. Another Christian example of such 'equinoctial' symbolism, concerning the 'Middle Path', features within a prayer written by John Donne (1572-1631) called *Our Last Awakening*. "Bring us, O Lord God, at our last awakening into the house and gate of heaven, to enter into that gate and dwell in that house, where there shall be no darkness nor dazzling, but one equal light; no noise nor silence, but one equal music; no fears nor hopes, but one equal possession; no ends nor beginnings, but one equal eternity: in the habitations of thy majesty and glory, world without end. Amen." For more about the 'Middle Path' see chapters 18 and 19.

11.4 THE ORTHODOX CROSS OF ST ANDREW

THE EARLIEST DESCRIPTIONS of St Andrew's crucifixion don't specifically mention a Saltire cross. In the Orthodox church the cross that is often associated with St Andrew has horizontal and vertical bars as well as one small diagonal bar (see diagram below). The cross is effectively the same as a Latin cross, although it also has an extra horizontal bar that is shorter and even higher up than the usual horizontal bar. This extra bar is sometimes associated with the sign placed on Christ's cross, on which was written 'Jesus the Nazorean, the King of the Jews'. Lower down on the cross there is another small bar that is sometimes described as 'Christ's footrest'. But it also has an interesting polar symbolism associated with it, in which its slant – upward-to-the-right and downward-to-the-left (from Christ's perspective) – refers to the penitent and impenitent thieves – Dismas and Gestas – who were crucified, one on either side of Christ. The penitent thief on the right side of Christ was destined, as a result of his penitence, to rise upwards into Heaven, whereas the impenitent thief on the left was destined, as a result of his impenitence, to descend into hell. As will become clear in Part 4, these two directions of movement – first downwards and then upwards – are an essential counteraction within Christ's paschal journey. It is this journey, first downwards into hell and then upwards into Heaven, that is effectively mapped out within the eastward movement through Wells Cathedral. But such descent into darkness and ascent towards the light is also understood symbolically in relation to the annual seasonal cycle, within the fluctuation between winter and summer. In this sense there is a descending half of the year which is then followed by an ascending half, and this fluctuation between dark and light is again caused by the equator–ecliptic angular relationship between Earth and Sun.

Another interesting design feature of the cathedral's ground plan is that it has two pairs of north–south transepts. The usual transepts are present at the cathedral's crossing, but there are also smaller transept chapels further up the cathedral, just beyond the quire. If the cruciform shape of a cathedral can in one sense be associated with the cross of Christ, then these two pairs of transepts emulate the two horizontal upper bars of the Orthodox cross of St Andrew. The polar symbolism of heaven and hell is then situated further down the cross in its short diagonal bar, which symbolises the penitent and impenitent thieves. In relation to the design of Wells Cathedral it is further down the building, i.e. in the nave, that the descent/ascent symbolism of the seasonal cycle is present in which the solstices of Cancer and Capricorn symbolise the descending and ascending halves of the year. As will be shown in Part 4, this dual movement is also reflected within the cathedral's design in a very similar way to how Dante describes his descent into the centre of the Earth followed by his re-ascent to the Earth's surface on the other side, followed then by his ascent of the Mountain of Purgatory and finally through the heavens.

One final architectural feature of the nave that relates to all of this is the canon's entrance on the north side, which reflects the position of the small diagonal bar in the Orthodox cross of St Andrew. It will be shown in chapter 19 how in one sense this doorway can be understood to symbolise the upward-slanting right-hand-side of Christ's footrest.

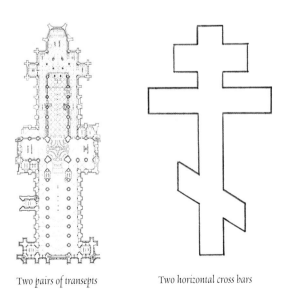

Two pairs of transepts *Two horizontal cross bars*

Part III

The Arithmetical

and Musical Design Elements

of the First English Gothic Cathedral

CHAPTER 12.

The Measurement Units

12.1 THE RECONCILIATION OF HEAVEN AND EARTH VIA THE 'INCARNATION' OF NUMBER

PHILOLAUS WAS A PYTHAGOREAN, and in the remaining fragments of his written work he describes the cosmos as being composed of a harmonious interplay between the unbounded (Apeiron) and the bounded (Peiron). This duality can also be understood to relate on the one hand to that which is unknowable, and on the other, to that which is knowable. Such a polarity brings to mind a quote on the subject of geometry from Isidore of Seville's medieval encyclopedia that was also used in chapter 7 (sec 7.3).

'Rational magnitudes are those whose measurement we can know; irrational magnitudes are those whose measurement is not known.'

Book 3, Chapter 11

Isidore is here talking about commensurable and incommensurable numbers within geometric forms. Both of these types of number are commonly found together in the polygonal geometries derived from the circle. The triangle, the square, the pentagon – indeed, any of the regular polygons arising from the circle – all contain a harmonious interplay between these two different types of number. However, in terms of numerical theory commensurable and incommensurable numbers are completely irreconcilable. Yet through the 'embodiment' of such numerical theory – i.e. through geometry – there becomes a harmonious interplay between them.

So every time we see a geometric symmetry of this sort contained in a beautiful flower we are witnessing this interplay of commensurable and incommensurable numbers as one small example that reflects Philolaus' description of the cosmos being formed of Apeiron and Peiron. If the edge of an equilateral triangle measures 2 then its height is the square root of 3 ($\sqrt{3}$). If the edge of a square is 1 its diagonal is $\sqrt{2}$. If the edge of a pentagon is 1 its diagonal is $(\sqrt{5} + 1) \div 2$. All of these square roots are 'irrational' (without ratio) which means that they

cannot be expressed through a fractional relationship between two rational numbers. So in this sense incommensurable numbers in some way reflect the unknowable nature of the unbounded, which is also suggested by the decimal expression of incommensurable numbers whereby they run on to an indefinite number of decimal places in no fixed or repeating pattern. So whereas the golden ratio, for example, is incommensurable and reads as 1 to 1.61803398875..., a relationship between the two commensurable numbers 55 and 89 brings about a very similar, albeit commensurable, relationship of 1 to 1.61818181818... The numbers 55 and 89 are so-called 'Fibonacci numbers', which means that they are part of a number sequence that begins from 1 which brings about increasingly accurate approximations of the golden ratio. But because Fibonacci numbers forever remain rational and 'bounded', as it were, they can never fully express the 'unboundedness' of an incommensurable number but rather only approximate it to an increasingly closer degree.

If one were to draw a symbolic analogy between Heaven and the unbounded then such an analogy would be completed by associating Earth with the bounded. This then leads to the geometric symbolism mentioned in chapter 2 (sec 2.2) concerning the 'squaring of the circle'. The circle symbolises Heaven, while the square is Earth. This is symbolically reflected in the fact that the periphery/circumference of the circle is based on an incommensurable number, i.e. pi (3.141592...) whereas the square has a commensurable peripheral measurement of 4 (i.e. 4 edges, each measuring 1).

In a similar sense the rational/irrational interrelations, embodied by geometric forms, hold a place that is, symbolically speaking, between Heaven and Earth. More specifically it is actually through the geometric embodiment of these eternal forms of number that Heaven and Earth are brought together into a harmonious relationship. That which is hidden – the eternal forms of number themselves – becomes geometrically revealed because the geometric forms reflect the eternal forms of number through embodying them. Such ideas concerning what could be described as the 'incarnation of number' form a numerical analogy with the Christian understanding of Christ as the Incarnation of the Word.

There are various ways of expressing the Christian Trinity geometrically, and one uses the circle. The centre of the circle is hidden because it is an indefinitely small non-dimensional point. But it is outwardly reflected, or indeed embodied, by the circle because every point on the circumference is equidistant from the hidden central point. So a circle is what the centre looks like when it expands outwards into the world of embodied forms. Such a relationship reflects that of God the Father to God the Son in the sense that the centre itself is beyond our worldly vision, but it becomes visible through taking on the embodied and bounded form of the circle.[1] The relationship of unity between centre and circumference is then brought about by the radius that runs between them – rather like a dove descending from the above to the below. Indeed, it is the Holy Spirit as a 'linear' ray of light, shining through the window of an enclosed room, by whom the Virgin Mother of God traditionally conceives the Word made Flesh. It is the extending forth of this 'radial' ray of light which reflects the opening of the compasses so as to begin the drawing of an embodied circumference that will 'encompass' both Heaven and Earth. The first mention of the Holy Spirit in the New Testament is actually in relation to the Annunciation, when this symbolic ray of light shines forth from God the Father to the Mother of God and the circle then begins to be drawn.

So if the geometry of the circle unites the incommensurable with the commensurable, what of purely commensurable number itself?

If taken on its own, and completely divorced from the incommensurable, it runs the risk of collapsing into a materialism that loses sight of its heavenly origin. This can occur as a result of the soul wanting to be able to rationally explain and resolve everything, rather than allowing itself to contemplate the Unknowable Mystery. But when these rational numbers are understood to be reflecting irrational numerics, the connection between the two worlds remains in place. However, the rational measures can be seen as the final fixation down here on Earth of the incommensurable numerical forms that have descended from the heavenly circle above. The incommensurable number pi becomes rationalised as 22/7; the golden ratio shows itself through various Fibonacci relationships such as 89/55; the square root of 2 becomes 99/70 ... and so on.

Even though geometric forms take on visible and fixed bodies, their magnitude is still changeable through being dependent on how widely one opens up the pair of compasses to draw their initial containing circle. So geometry with a pair of compasses has only become partly fixed in its finalised form, but there is still some flexibility present. However, with the rational measurement units of metrology – the foot, the cubit, the mile and so on – there is no flexibility or changeability. A unit is a unit and that is that. Every rational unit has a fixed rational relationship with every other rational unit. But some of these relationships are also rationally reflecting irrationals too, albeit through bounded approximations.

1. The Sanskrit word for the circle – *mandala* – is understood to mean 'the container of the essence', which can in turn be understood as 'the boundary of the unbounded'.

So if it could be said that there is a symbolic movement of three stages from the boundless to the bounded, it could be said to begin with the pure Apeiron, which is unknowable. Then there is the interplay of Apeiron with Peiron, which shows itself in the geometric relationships that exist between commensurable and incommensurable numbers. The final Peiron is then the fully rationalised, fixed unchanging units of measure and it is with this final fixation that the turning circle of heaven becomes fixed and finalised as the square of Earth. However, a concordance between different rational measurement units presents a harmonious earthly image of the One as expressed through a coherent arrangement of the Many. This accordingly reflects the Divine Unity that transcends all rational multiplicity here in this world of boundaries.

In practical building terms this final 'earthly' fixation of measurement units concerns the use of a measurement rod rather than a movable pair of compasses, opening and closing to a variety of different measurements. One such measuring rod is mentioned in the Book of Revelation within the description of the 'cubic' Heavenly Jerusalem.

'The angel who talked with me had a measuring rod of gold to measure the city, its gates and its walls. The city was laid out like a square, as long as it was wide. He measured the city with the rod and found it to be 12,000 stadia in length, and as wide and high as it is long. The angel measured the wall using human measurement, and it was 144 cubits thick.'

Revelation 21:15–17

As mentioned above, this final rationalisation of measures that is associated with a measurement rod is analogous to the final Peiron that brings the necessary boundedness to the unbounded Apeiron.

However, the essential point that must be forever remembered is that an over-concentration of Peiron on its own – which reflects the rational materialism of our modern age – is a potentially catastrophic departure from the middle path between the unbounded and the bounded. If anything, it is the Apeiron that is primary and ultimate. But the Peiron is a necessary ordering principle to allow the Apeiron to become known in this world of boundaries. In a similar way the primary reason to practise the sacred art of geometry is to be able to contemplate the boundless through the bounded. Geometry on its own and for its own sake can act as a materialistic entrapment for the soul, whereas when it is used as a contemplative process it can act as a vehicle that aids the soul's liberation.[2]

The design of Wells Cathedral is actually based entirely on rational units of measurement, albeit ones that reflect geometric polygons, cosmological cycles, musical ratios and beautiful arithmetic relationships. The design is a masterclass in the Platonist quadrivial art of Remembrance, and so it is ideal as a design for a religious building such as a cathedral.

This part of the book goes into great detail concerning these measurements. To fully understand such numerical detail through the written word can potentially be quite taxing, so it is recommended that the reader also consults the appropriate slide-show presentations that go together with this chapter. They can be found on the website **www.tombreegeometry.com**

---

2. See Hermes Trismegistus' description of this in Asclepius 12–14 (B. Copenhaver, *Hermetica*, Cambridge University Press, 1996, page 74).

12.2 THREE FOOT-UNITS, ONE CUBIT AND THEIR COMMON MICRO-UNIT

THERE ARE FOUR different measurement units used in the design of the Wells Cathedral ground plan. Three of them could be described as feet, whereas the fourth one is a cubit. The reason for using three different sizes of foot appears to be to do with the design's arithmetic inclusion of musical ratios as well as cosmological numbers and ratios. But it is also centrally to do with a system of metrology known as the Cosmic Canon, which is related to the size of the Earth. The details of this will become more apparent as the chapter develops.

As for the units themselves, they all contain a common micro-unit that is just over 1/5 inch in size. To be precise the micro-unit is 8/35 inch. The details of this will gradually unfold in the following paragraphs.

The three foot-units are all very similar in length. Their small differences are governed by their common micro-unit in the sense that they all contain different quantities of this micro-unit, and so are related to one another via this micro-unit.

The medium-sized foot is the so-called *English foot* from the imperial measurement system that is still used by some in the UK and as standard in the USA. In the following pages this foot will be referred to as the English foot, although it must be stressed that the word

'English' is not being used in the sense of it being the invention of the English. For historical reasons relating to legal definitions of measure it has come to be known as the English foot, although it is viewed here as a cosmic unit of measure that has not been invented but rather discovered because it is a naturally existing unit of measure.

Within the design of Wells Cathedral the number of micro-units in the English foot is 52½. A question that arises at this point is why the foot is not divided into 12 units – i.e. inches. The answer would appear to be that the sophisticated nature of the system of musical ratios used in the design would not be possible if the unit were restricted to 12 divisions. However, these micro-units do fractionally relate to an inch whereby there are 4 3/8 of them in a single inch.

The other two foot-units will be referred to in the following paragraphs as the *greater foot* and the *lesser foot*, owing to the fact that one is a little bigger than the English foot and the other one a little smaller. The diagram on the following page shows three long rectangles that are intended to resemble measuring rods embodying the relative size relationships between the three different foot-units – the greater foot, the English foot and the lesser foot.

The greater foot - 56 micro-units

The English foot - 52½ micro-units

The lesser foot - 50 micro-units

The greater foot consists of 56 micro-units. So its relationship to the English foot can be expressed as 56 to 52½. However, by dividing both of these micro-unit numbers by 3½ they can be reduced to the simpler ratio of 16:15. Much like the previous image, the diagram

below shows the three foot-units in the form of measuring rods. the dotted lines also demonstrate the 16:15 relationship of the greater foot to the English foot. This relationship of 16:15 is the first example of a musical ratio – namely a semitone. It will be described in more

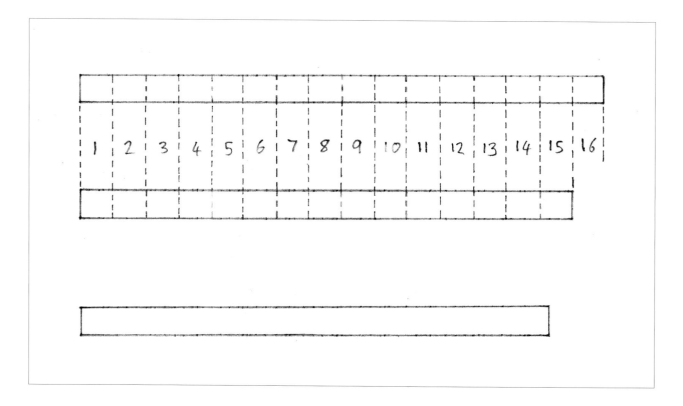

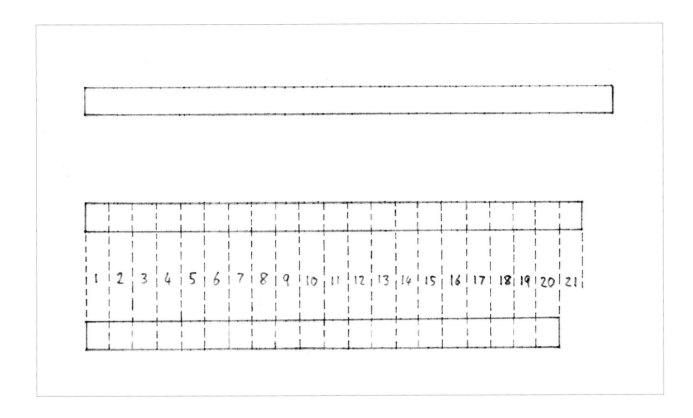

detail in the next section. The lesser foot consists of 50 micro-units. So the relationship of the English foot to the lesser foot can be expressed as 52½ to 50. But this time, by dividing both micro-unit numbers by 2½ the

ratio can be reduced to 21:20, which in musical terms is another type of semitone. By visually comparing the three foot-units via these two ratios of 16:15 and 21:20 it becomes possible to see the common micro-unit shared

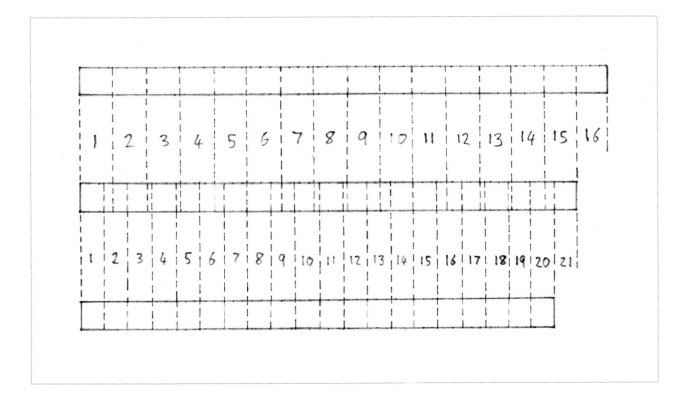

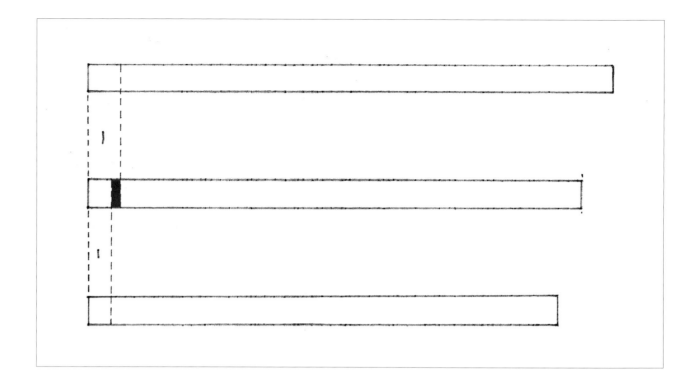

by all the units in the Wells design. The second diagram on the previous page shows both of the ratios on the three measuring rods. The diagram above then edits the previous one to highlight the difference between a single unit from each ratio. The difference in size is marked in red. This is the micro-unit that is common to the three feet and the one cubit. The diagram below then shows the division of the three feet into this common micro-unit. The greater foot contains 56, the English foot 52½ and the lesser foot 50.

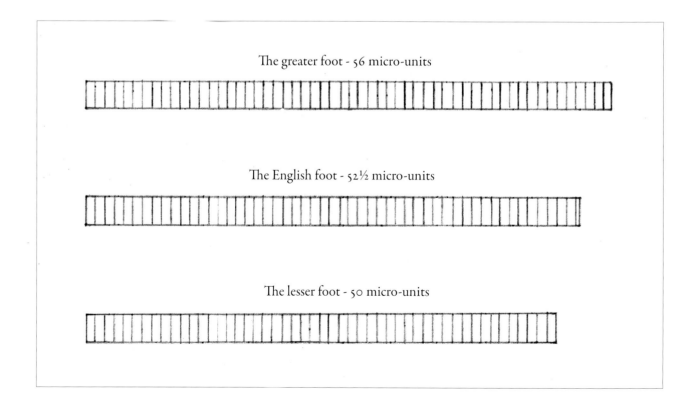

The greater foot - 56 micro-units

The English foot - 52½ micro-units

The lesser foot - 50 micro-units

The English foot - 52½ micro-units

| | 1 | 2 | 3 | 4 | 5 | 6 | 7 | 8 | 9 | 10 | 11 | 12 | |

The cubit - 90 micro-units

Finally, the cubit consists of 90 micro-units. This particular size of cubit presents a significant relationship when compared to the English foot. If they are both divided by 7½ their relationship of 90 to 52½ reduces to 12:7, which is a significant numerical relationship in quadrivial terms and thus also within the knowledge and beliefs of various parts of the ancient world. The Muslim writer Al-Sarakhsi said of the Harranians for instance that for them the 'guiding forces are seven and twelve'.[5]

In arithmetic terms the numbers 7 and 12 arise from various interactions between the numbers 3 and 4 – the numbers of 'soul' and 'matter'.[6] The numbers 3 and 4 are the first odd and even numbers that are associated with 'embodiment', because in geometric terms three points together make a two-dimensional plane (i.e. a triangle), whereas four points make a three-dimensional solid (i.e. a tetrahedron). With embodiment in mind the relationship that 3 and 4 has with 7 and 12 occurs through the generative processes of addition and multiplication. By adding 3 and 4 together the resulting sum is 7, whereas by multiplying them they produce 12.

A geometric instance of 7 and 12 can be seen in the packing of circles. First of all, 6 circles fit perfectly around a seventh central circle, which they all touch.

The first 'orbit' around this inter-related cluster of 7 circles consists of a total of 12. The 12 circles can then either be placed in a hexagonal or dodecagonal arrangement around the pack of 7.

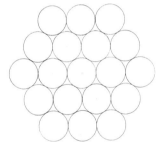

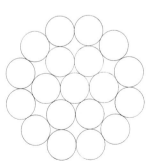

5. *The City of the Moon God*, Tamara M Green, E.J. Brill, 1992, page 183.
6. A relationship of 3 to 4 is present in the synodic periods of Venus (584 Earth-days) and Mars (780 Earth-days). The discrepancy of this 3 to 4 relationship is 1 Earth-day – i.e. if 780 is 4 then 3 would be 585 rather than 584. After all, these synodic periods are occurring in relation to the Earth who can be symbolically understood as the intermediary between soul (i.e. Venus) and worldly energetic life-force (i.e. Mars)

Cosmologically the numbers 7 and 12 are associated with the seven planetary spheres followed then by the 12 heavenly mansions (i.e. zodiacal signs) in the eighth heaven of the fixed stars.

Musically the numbers 7 and 12 are fundamental to Pythagorean tuning. This is because 12 musical fifths are virtually identical to 7 musical octaves – bar the so-called *Pythagorean comma*, which is the small discrepancy by which the 12 fifths and 7 octaves are not quite the same.

Another musical instance of 7 and 12 presents itself in the fact that the 8 notes of the diatonic scale are divided from one another by 7 musical intervals. These are the 7 distances between the 8 notes of the octave scale. Most of these 7 intervals are tones, although two of them are semitones (half a tone). But if all of the tone intervals

were divided into the two semitones of which each is composed, the number of notes in the scale would then increase to 13, and this is known as the chromatic scale. The octave scale contains 7 intervals, whereas the chromatic scale contains 12 intervals. Herein lies another significant musical example of 7 and 12.

The basic scale diagrams below visually demonstrate these notes and intervals. The short vertical lines with numbers above them represent the actual notes of the scales. The numbered gaps between these lines then represent the intervals between the notes. The larger gaps are tones, and the smaller gaps are semitones. In the octave of 8 notes there are 7 intervals. Of these 7 intervals 5 of them are tones (1, 2, 4, 5 & 6) and 2 of them are semitones (3 & 7). In the chromatic scale of 13 notes there are 12 intervals, all of which are semitones.

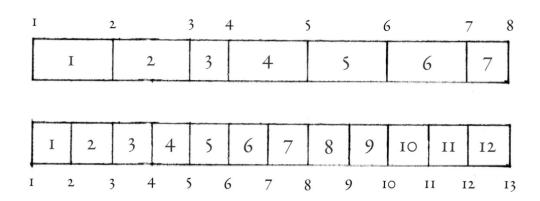

12.3 THE MUSICAL RELATIONSHIPS
OF THE THREE FOOT-UNITS

IN THIS RESEARCH process the units and their common micro-unit, described above, were slowly worked out as a result of various measurement analyses. Musical relationships were not one of the contributing factors in the discovery of the units. However, when the

research had reached an advanced stage the rationale of musical ratios was applied to these measurement units and it turned out that they happened to embody a very interesting musicality. So it is important to note that the following musical connections were not made consciously, but were rather found to be present within measurements that had already become part of a geometric and metrological design theory.

It was shown in the last section that the relationship of the greater foot to the English foot is 16:15, which in tuning theory is known as the *Just diatonic semitone*. As the name suggests, it is the main semitone used in so-called 'Just intonation'.

The relationship between the English foot and the lesser foot is 21:20, which is known as the *minor semitone* or the *septimal chromatic semitone*. The mathematician Ptolemy described it as a 'soft' semitone.[7] As its modern name suggests, it is a semitone that is used in what is known as 'septimal' or 'seven-limit' tuning. Both Just intonation and septimal tuning are known to have been used and written about in the ancient world by 'quadrivialists' such as Archytas and Ptolemy.

The fact that the two 'musical' intervals between the three different foot-units are both semitones means that the difference in size between the greater foot and the lesser foot is a certain type of tone, because as any musician knows, two semitones make a tone. This relationship between the greater and lesser foot is 56:50, which reduces to 28:25. This particular tone is not a commonly used one,[8] but again it appears that the designer of Wells Cathedral uses it because it creates another interesting musical division between two other significant musical tones, both of which are used in Just intonation.

The two different tones used in Just intonation are 9:8 and 10:9. The historical development of musical tuning systems saw a movement from what is described as Pythagorean 'three-limit' tuning to 'just' 'five-limit' tuning. Pythagorean tuning only uses the 9:8 tone, whereas the development of Just intonation involved the inclusion of the 10:9 tone along with the 9:8. This development from Pythagorean to Just tuning became possible

through the use of a small musical interval known as the *syntonic comma*, which has a value of 81:80, and this is the numerical difference between 10:9 and 9:8.

A few decimal calculations can help to make all of this easier to comprehend. First of all, these ratios can be read in decimal form if their first number is divided by the second one. So $10 \div 9 = 1.1111...$, whereas $9 \div 8 = 1.125$. Accordingly, 1.1111 is the decimal form of 10:9 and 1.125 that of 9:8.

The 1.125 can now be divided by 1.11111 and the result is 1.0125, and this is the decimal form of the syntonic comma because $81 \div 80 = 1.0125$.

Returning now to the 28:25 tone, the reason for mentioning the syntonic comma that divides the 10:9 tone from the 9:8 tone is that the 28:25 tone falls within it.

In this sense the 28:25 tone is a little higher in pitch than the 10:9 tone, but a little bit lower than the 9:8 tone. This reflects a movement into seven-limit tuning, which is the form of tuning used within the musical ratios of the Wells design. It is this seven-limit tuning system that appears to reflect a musical system proposed by the musicologist Ernest McClain as being alluded to by Plato within the numerical storyline of the mythical city of Magnesia which he describes in his *Laws* dialogue.

The 28:25 tone divides the syntonic comma up into two smaller ratios. These are 225:224, which is known in musical terms as the *marvel comma*, and 126:125, which is known as a *septimal semicomma*. The marvel comma features in Ernest McClain's theory of the musical measures of Plato's *Magnesia*, whereas the ratio 126:125 is central to the metrology research of John Neal – a close friend and associate of John Michell.

All of this will be briefly considered a little later.

7. J. Murray Barbour, *Tuning and Temperament: A Historical Survey,* Dover, 2004, chapter 2.
8. If this tone is used with a semitone of 16:15 it makes quite a reasonable diatonic scale.

The use of means,
multi-layered grids
and micro-variations
throughout the ground plan

An absolutely vital aspect of the use of measurement units within the design of Wells Cathedral is that there is never just one single measurement grid used in any particular area of the ground plan. There is a multi-layering of various different grids, which presents itself in such a way that the various built forms in the fabric of the building will generally contain measures that apply to more than one grid at the same time. So in this sense some of the actual built forms in the building don't even directly embody the measurement grids as such, but rather materially reflect relationships existing between the multiple grids. All of these various grids could then be described as being 'theoretically' present, within the intended design, even if not actually present through being directly expressed by the presence of a built form. So for example the central axis of a pillar may correspond directly to a line on one particular grid, or alternatively it may be located at a measured mean between a line on one grid and another line on another grid.

In the use of such mean measurements there is effectively an inclusion of both grids within the design, even if neither is directly marked by any built form. However, these different grids should not be seen as random and unrelated because their very relationships will often present something that is of interest in quadrivial terms, and this would seem to explain why multiple grids have been included. In this sense there is a great deal going on within the design on a theoretical level that is of significance and interest – and all of this mathematically provable and, as it were, 'theorial' beauty is brought down into earthly embodiment within built forms that refer to the numerical relationships existing between these various different grids.

Another numerical aspect of the design is the use of micro-variations. This is where a particular measurement is adapted very slightly by a very small ratio so as to bring about a mathematically harmonious resolution. These micro-variations are often musical in nature, and resemble the use of small musical commas within musical tuning systems. They are also sometimes used to round a measurement up to a whole number of micro-units, or alternatively to allow a number to conform with a cosmologically significant number which it comes very close to but just slightly misses.

The average human being who interacts with sacred architecture containing sophisticated measurement systems such as those described above will not be consciously aware of all the mathematical complexity contained within the building's design. A similar kind of 'invisibility' is often pointed out in relation to the presence of tiny and detailed exquisite carvings, so high up in a cathedral's vault that no human eye could ever possibly see them from down below. So it can understandably be asked what practical purpose all this mathematical complexity may have if it is not obviously visible to the person who walks within it. The answer would appear to relate to the eternal forms of number that are forever contemplated in the Divine Mind. To architecturally manifest such numerical relationships is to bring these eternal forms and divine thoughts down to Earth so that we can actually physically reside within them – as they do in us. So on the one hand this beauty of material form can be witnessed through the physical eyes of humanity. But the numerical coherence that underlies the material form is forever beheld and known within the theorial eyes of God.

So a design's mathematical coherence is as important – if not more so – than its outward material form. Although it is through such cosmic outward appearances that the eternal numerical thoughts of the Divine Mind can become known as a result of the architect's conscious inclusion of them within an architectural design.

This use of multiple grids and mathematical means will now be demonstrated, beginning with the measurements of the nave. As shown in chapter 11, this part of the cathedral appears to cosmologically symbolise the tropical zone of Planet Earth.

CHAPTER 13.

The Nave and the Musical Numbers of Planet Earth

13.1 THE TWO MEASUREMENT GRIDS AND THE 'EARTHLY' RATIO 365:364

THE DESIGN OF THE nave's ground plan consists of two different measurement grids that each use a different foot-unit. One of the grids is made up of greater feet, while the other one consists of lesser feet. In the following diagrams the greater feet will be presented via the red measurement grids and the lesser feet via the blue grids.

As mentioned earlier, the key feature of this area in the cathedral's design is the cosmology of Planet Earth, and in this sense the nave is an image of the Earth. This is symbolically concordant with the idea that the journey of 'ascent' through the cathedral from the west door 'up' to the east end Lady chapel is one that begins from the Earth. However, as will become apparent in Part 4, the journey 'through' the Earth itself is also part of this symbolism of ascent in that there is first a descent 'downwards' into the Earth, followed by an ascent upwards out of the Earth and then upwards again from the Earth's surface.

The characteristic geometric form within the design of the nave is a particular type of rectangle. The diagonal of this rectangle produces an angle that closely approximates the equator–ecliptic angle. It was shown in chapter 11 that the ecliptic is the orbital plane on which Earth orbits the Sun. The equator of Earth is tilted by around 23.4° in relation to this orbital plane, and it is this equator–ecliptic angle that is embodied by the diagonal of the rectangle.

More specifically, there are actually two rectangles of this sort that are used within the nave's design. One has a long edge of 7 and a short edge of 3, whereas the other one has a long edge of 30 and a short edge of 13. So in effect these rectangles are simply two right-angled triangles, such as the ones shown in chapter 11 (sec 11.2), placed together to form a rectangle. Their joint hypotenuses then form the rectangle's diagonal line.

The 7 × 3 rectangle has a diagonal that runs at 23.2°. Over the course of 41,000,000 years Earth's axial tilt variates between two extremes of 24.5° and 22.1°. The arithmetic mean between these two angular measurements is 23.3°, which closely approximates the 23.2° angle in the diagonal of a 7 × 3 rectangle.

Meanwhile the 30 × 13 rectangle has a diagonal with an angle of 23.4°, which is the current angle of Earth's axial tilt.

The way in which these two rectangles show themselves within the design of the nave is as follows.

The first diagram below is of a 7 × 3 rectangle. The second diagram then shows this rectangle with two 3 × 3 squares added one on either side.

The second diagram also demonstrates the fact that the entire length of the conjoined trio of quadrilaterals is equal to 13 with a height of 3. These two numbers move us in the direction of the rectangle that measures 13 × 30.

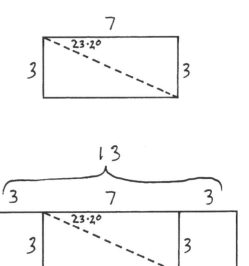

By producing a stack of ten of these quadrilateral trios, we end up with a rectangle of 13 × 30. The first diagram below shows this grid of quadrilaterals, which brings together the two equator–ecliptic rectangles of 7 × 3 and 30 × 13. The 23.4° angle of the rectangle's diagonal line is also marked in. The reason for showing this grid of quadrilaterals is because it is effectively one of the two grids that underlies the design of the nave in Wells Cathedral. This is shown in the second diagram below. This is the grid mentioned earlier that is formed of greater feet. The meeting points of the corners of the rectangles and squares could be said to coincide with the central points of the bay pillars – although a more precise description of this will follow shortly. To work out how many greater feet the grid contains, the numbers in the grid below just need to be multiplied by 5. So the 7 × 3 rectangle – which is essentially one of the

nave's rectangular bays – numerically increases to 35 × 15 feet. The whole nave rectangle – which is 30 × 13 – becomes 150 × 65 feet.

Even though this grid is formed of greater feet, there is also the possibility of seeing an English foot measurement in it. The shorter edge of the bay rectangle having become 15 greater feet can also be defined as 16 English feet, and this expresses the 16:15 semitone relationship between these two different foot-units. The entire length of the nave also reflects this musical relationship because it is 150 greater feet, which is the same as 160 English feet.

The concordance between these various measurements that use different foot-units can be seen more clearly if the feet are read in terms of their common micro-unit.

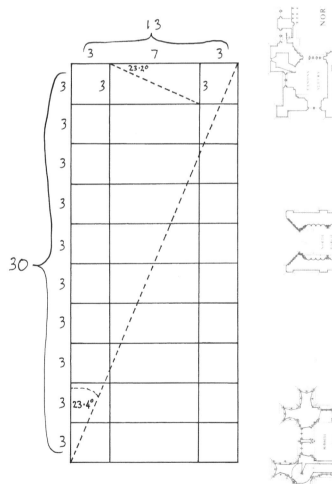

The 7 × 3 and 30 × 13 equator-ecliptic rectangles incorporated into one measurement grid in the nave.....

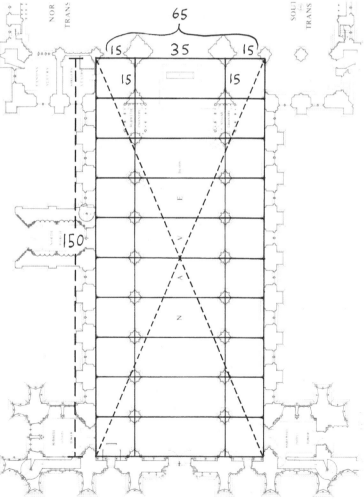

.....and then multiplied by 5 to obtain the number of greater feet

Fifteen greater feet are made up of 840 micro-units because 15 feet × 56 micro-units = 840.

But 16 English feet are also made up of 840 micro-units because 16 feet × 52.5 micro-units = 840.

As to the length of the nave, 150 greater feet are made up of 8400 micro-units, as are 160 English feet.

Indeed, when there is a focus on the detail of micro-unit measurements there are various numerical points of interest arising. This will be returned to shortly once we have looked at the second measurement grid.

The second measurement grid in the design of the nave is formed of lesser feet. The width of the whole grid is 73 lesser feet, and its length is 168 lesser feet.

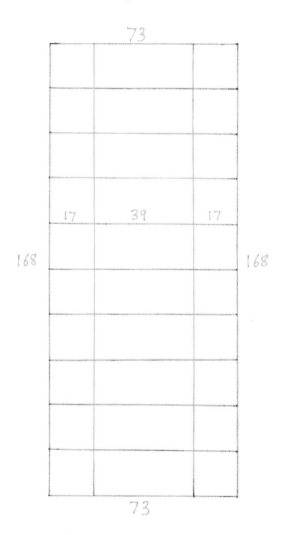

Returning to the micro-unit measurements, it can be seen that 168 lesser feet is the same as 150 greater feet and 160 English feet because 168 feet × 50 micro-units = 8400.

However, when the calculation is made of the number of micro-units in the 73 lesser feet that form the width of the nave, there is an interesting feature that begins to become apparent.

The red grid had a width of 65 greater feet so therefore the following micro-unit calculation applies:

65 feet × 56 micro-units = 3640 micro-units.

However, the 73 lesser foot width of the blue grid yields a slightly different result:

73 feet × 50 micro-units = 3650 micro-units.

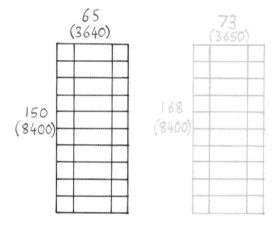

So the two grids are slightly different to one another in their width, and that difference can be defined by the ratio 3650:3640. This ratio reduces to 365:364, and herein lies a significant ratio relating to the cosmology of Planet Earth. The two grids differ in their width by 1/365, and the two numbers in this fraction are associated with the relationship of the ecliptic to the equator. In the period of time that it takes for Planet Earth to orbit the Sun on the ecliptic on 1 occasion the equator of Earth will have circulated about its axis approximately 365 times. In simpler terms, all that is being said here is that there are approximately 365 days in 1 year. But more to the point, this is specifically as a result of the numerical interaction between Planet Earth's equator and the ecliptic, which is the very cosmological relationship embodied by the 7 × 3 and 30 × 13 rectangles that make up the nave's geometric design.

A question that needs to be asked at this point is how this difference in width between the two grids shows itself within the actual built fabric, and indeed how accurate all these theoretical measurements actually are when tested in-situ. It is all well and good having a beautiful and concordant theoretical design, but if it does not measure up accurately in-situ the heavenly numerical thoughts of the Divine Mind cannot be said to have come down to Earth and become 'cosmically incarnate' within the measurable 'body' of the cathedral building.

When measured in-situ, the actual width of the nave between its north wall and south wall very accurately reflects the 73 lesser foot width of the blue grid. This is the measurement that translates into 3650 micro-units. The distance between the north wall and south wall generally veers off this measurement by only around a quarter of an inch along their complete lengths. But the question still remains as to whether there is anything materially present to suggest that the red grid was actually used within the design. This is the grid with a width of 3640 micro-units or 65 greater feet. The answer to this lies in the positioning of the bay pillars.

As mentioned earlier, the size of the bay rectangle in the red grid is 35 × 15 greater feet. 35 greater feet translates into 1960 micro-units because 35 × 56 = 1960.

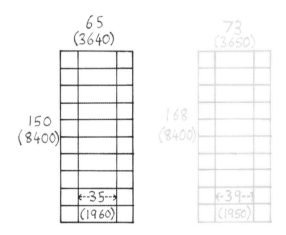

But looking at the measurement of the bay rectangle in the blue grid, we see a difference in size. The bay rec-

tangle in the blue grid is 39 lesser feet, which translates into 1950 micro-units.

$$39 \times 50 = 1950.$$

So the theoretical sizes of the bay rectangles are different within the two different grids. This requires analysis of the actual in-situ measurement of the bay, which again turns out to be very accurate in its consistency for the whole length of the nave. The central points of the bay pillars are actually 1955 micro-units away from one another, which means that the in-situ bay measurement embodies the arithmetic mean between theoretical measures of 1950 and 1960. This mean measurement that falls within a 10 micro-unit difference between different grids has already shown itself in the difference of widths between the red and blue grids. The width difference between 3650 and 3640 is also 10 micro-units, although the two grids are centred on one another so that there is a five micro-unit difference between the red and blue grids on the north side and another five on the south side. A similar thing applies with the bays, whereby the difference between the two bay measurements shows itself as 5 micro-units on either side.

The two images on the following page show horizontal cross-sections of the bay pillars – i.e. as if looking down from above. The image on the left depicts a northern bay pillar (i.e. to the left as viewed from the middle of the bay while facing east), and the image on the right represents a southern bay pillar. As the pictures make clear, the red lines that mark the larger bay measurement (i.e. 35 greater feet) are a little too wide to fit the actual in-situ bay measurement, while the blue lines of the smaller bay measurement (i.e. 39 lesser feet) are too narrow. The middle axes of the pillars fall halfway between each pair of red and blue lines, which are themselves 5 micro-units apart from one another. These 5 micro-units to the north and 5 to the south together account for the difference between the theoretical bay measurements of 1960 and 1950 micro-units that occur within the two different grids.

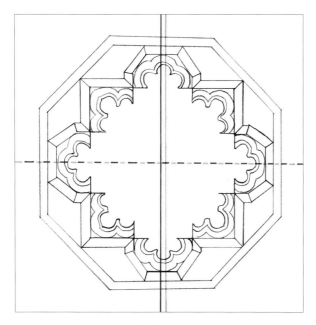

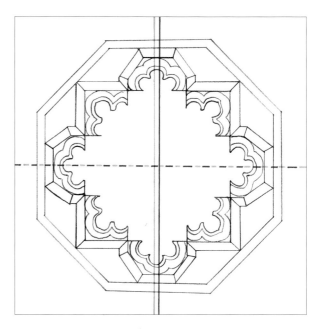

Cross section of north-side nave bay pillar.
The red line from the grid of greater feet is beyond the pillar's
central axis whereas the blue line from the grid of lesser feet falls
short of it. There are 5 micro-units of distance between them.

Cross section of south-side nave bay pillar.
The equivalent thing happens in this image but the other way around.
The vertical red lines in the two images are 1960 micro-units
apart whereas the vertical blue lines are 1950 micro-units apart.

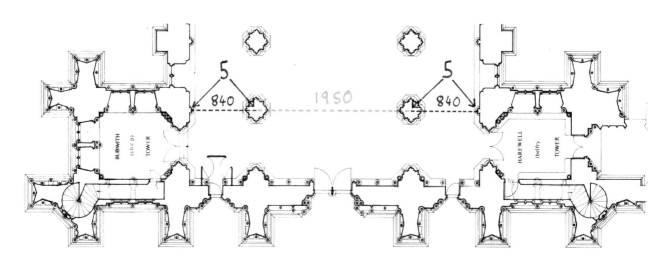

Western end of the cathedral's ground plan showing the micro-unit breakdown of the nave's width as 5 + 840 + 5 + 1950 + 5 + 840 + 5 = 3650

In the end the interaction between the two grids causes the 3650 micro-unit measurement of the nave's width to be seen as made up of the following collections of micro-units: 5 + 840 + 5 + 1950 + 5 + 840 + 5 = 3650. The 840 measurement can be looked upon as deriving from the red grid of greater feet because there are 840 micro-units in 15 greater feet. The 1950 measurement then reflects the bay in the blue grid of lesser feet because there are 1950 micro-units in 39 lesser feet. So it is the locating of the pillars at this mean measurement

between a line from each grid which materially demonstrates that both grids are theoretically present within the design. The 65 greater foot width of the red grid is not directly or indirectly marked by anything at all, because the wall-to-wall width of the nave is 73 lesser feet, which is the wider of the two grids. But the fact that the pillars are located where they are demonstrates that the red grid is also theoretically present. This then demonstrates the fact that there is a cosmic ratio of Planet Earth in 'theoretical' use – that of 365:364.

13.2 THE LUNAR YEAR
OF TWELVE SYNODIC MOONS

ANOTHER cosmological measure appears to be included in the design of the nave, and this time it numerically reflects Planet Earth's interaction with the Moon. It is the shorter width measurement of the nave that stretches between the stone benches that run east–west along the north and south walls of the nave.

south-side stone bench - coloured in red on the ground plan

The width measurement described in the previous section relates to the wall-to-wall width of the nave, but there are stone benches at the bottom of these north and south walls, and they reduce the nave's width measurement by a small amount because they extend out a foot or so from the walls.

The fact that these benches begin from the wall means that they are effectively aligned with the blue grid with its width measurement of 73 lesser feet. However, the actual depth of the bench is 1 greater foot on each side. This presents us with the interesting question of why a greater foot is being used on a grid of lesser feet.

The answer would again appear to be cosmological, and as mentioned above related to Planet Earth's interaction with the Moon.

There are roughly 12.369... synodic lunar cycles in one year. So the nearest whole number of synodic cycles is obviously 12, and this could be seen as a certain type of lunar year. Indeed 12 synodic cycles are used to define the Islamic year, which is around 11 days shorter than the solar year.

The calculation of 12 synodic cycles is as follows:

$$29.53 \text{ days} \times 12 = 354.36 \text{ days}.$$

If this number is now compared to Earth's annual cycle of 365.25, it can be seen that the lunar year is just under 11 days shorter:

$$365.25 - 354.36 = 10.89.$$

In the width measurement of the nave the micro-unit number that represents Earth's annual cycle is 3650. This number is effectively the number of days in a year rounded down to the nearest whole day with a zero added on to the end of it. So the actual annual cycle of 365.25 days first becomes 365 and then finally 3650.

If one were to follow the same rationale with the number of days in the lunar year, the number would first change from 354.36 to 354 and then with a zero added on it would become 3540. This number 3540 is virtually the reduced width measurement of the nave when the measurement takes the stone benches into

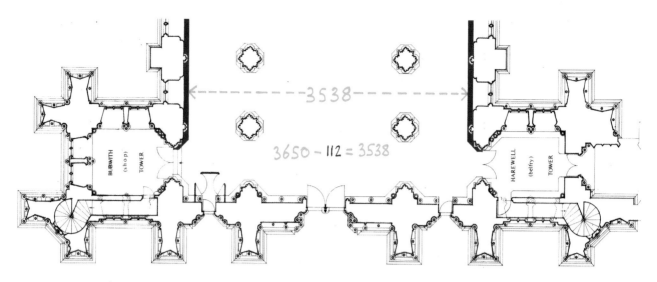

Western end of the cathedral's ground plan showing the micro-unit width of the nave minus the north and southside stones benches (shaded in red)

account. The fact that each stone bench is 1 greater foot means that the total reduction of the nave's width measurement is 112 micro-units, because this is equal to 2 greater feet. So if 112 is subtracted from 3650:

$$3650 - 112 = 3538$$

This number 3538 is only two micro-units short of 3540, which is the number that would ideally represent the lunar year. For the number 3540 to actually work out within the design the size of foot required would need to be 55 micro-units, making a total of 110, which when subtracted from 3650 would result in 3540. But there is no foot-unit used in the design which consists of 55 micro-units, so it appears as though the greater foot of 56 micro-units is the nearest the designer can get to the correct calculation. In practice this discrepancy is only about half an inch in size. There is also an 'unknown' factor here in the sense that radiators were placed on the walls of these stone benches in the 20th century. So although the walls look as though they are in their correct positions, they may have been taken out and replaced, and this could have affected their measured positions.[1]

THE NUMBER 33 AND THE COSMIC CHRIST

FINALLY, LET US RETURN to the length of the nave, which was mentioned above as measuring 150 greater feet or 160 English feet (or 168 lesser feet). This distance is also precisely 1/33 mile.

1 mile (5280 English feet) ÷ 33 = 160 English feet

The fact that this particular fraction of 1/33 occurs within an architectural design that is embodying temporal measures relating to Earth's annual cycle would seem appropriate from a perspective of Christological cosmology. This is because the 365 days of an annual cycle happen also to be 1/33 the amount of time associated with Christ's time spent on the Earth.

Christ's cosmic 'solarity' is also present in the fact that the Sun rises from the same point of the horizon once every 33 years. But this solar 33-ness of Christ also dances with the Moon, because a period of 33 solar years is virtually the same as 34 of the lunar years mentioned above, consisting of 354.36 days.

1. If this is the case it could be suggested that the measurable distance was originally 3540 micro-units and that the 56 micro-units of the greater foot were micro-varied by 56:55 to create a foot of 55 micro-units which would then bring about the required measurement. For more about the repeated use of the 56:55 ratio in the design of Wells Cathedral see the next chapter and specifically the sub-section on page 245 entitled "The use of the ratio 56:55"

INFORMATION ON THE CHAPTERS 14 TO 17

THE CHAPTERS 14, 15, 16 AND 17 are available as a free downloadable pdf from a website with the address **www.tombreegeometry.com.** This has become a necessary compromise in the production of this book as a result of the currently very high cost of printing and shipping. However, the following eight pages after this one contain a selection of images and diagrams, taken from these four chapters. These are designed to give a brief idea of the areas that the chapters cover. There is a two-page spread for each chapter.

It has already been pointed out that Part 3 of this book contains the very detailed numerical analysis of the design theory and in-situ measurements. So in one sense it is the primary and most authoritative proof of the whole design theory described in this research. So therefore, taking a look at chapters 14 – 17 is very much recommended so as to gain a deeper understanding of the designer's immense skill. The pdf containing the four chapters is accompanied, on the website, by various films of illustrated talks. They are designed to make these more numerical chapters easier to understand and digest.

Beyond the following eight pages the book proceeds again from the beginning of Part 4 which commences on page 316. The numbering of the book's pages, and the listing of these pages within the contents, index and image credits, proceed as if all four parts of the book follow the one sequence of page numbering. So in other words all the page numbers from 241 to 315 (i.e. chapters 14 – 17) are still included in the contents at the front of the book as well as in the index and image listings at the back of the book.

A SELECTION OF DIAGRAMS FROM CHAPTER 14

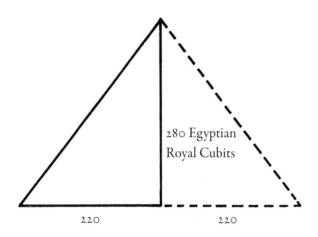

280 Egyptian
Royal Cubits

220   220

Pyramid triangle with Egyptian Royal cubit measurements
that reflect the dimensions of the Great Pyramid in Egypt

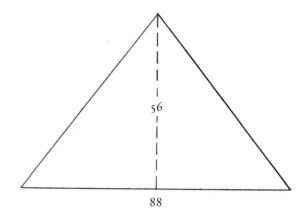

56

88

The Pi Pyramid Triangle master diagram at Wells uses the
Egyptian Royal cubit with a base of 88 cubits and a height of 56

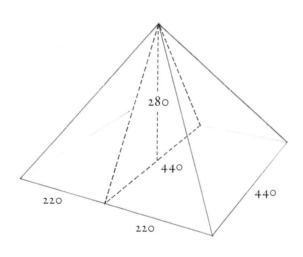

280

440

220   440

220

The pyramid triangle shown within the three-dimensional Pyramidal form

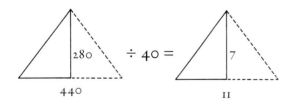

280   ÷ 40 =   7

440   11

The cubit measurements of the Great Pyramid are 40 times greater than the
simplest measurements of a pi pyramid triangle i.e. base of 11 and height of 7

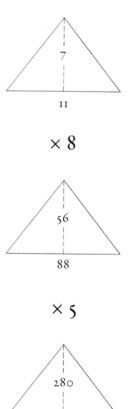

7

11

× 8

56

88

× 5

280

440

The cubit measurements of the Wells pi pyramid triangle are
8 times larger than the 11 - 7 pyramid triangle and 5 times
smaller than the cubit measurement of the Great Pyramid

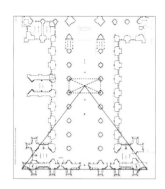

The image on the left shows the pyramid triangle as it is used in the design of the nave whereby its apex coincides with the centre of the sixth bay (in red dotted line). The image on the right shows the cruciform core of the nave pillars and how this core is 205 micro-units in width. This measurement is the arithmetic mean between 4 lesser feet (200) and 4 English feet (210). The central point of the pillar marks the corners of the bay rectangles and this accordingly means that half of the 205 measurement (i.e. 102.5) falls within the bay rectangle whereas the other half does not. However if the extra 102.5, beyond either end of the bay rectangle, is added onto the bay's measurement it increases the bay measurement of 1955 to 2160 (i.e. 1955 + 102.5 + 102.5 = 2160 - see diagram below). This is the number of miles in the Moon's diameter. In the diagram below the nave's micro-unit measurements are shown in detail along with the way that the Moon circle geometrically interacts with the size of the bay rectangle. This suggests that every bay is centred on a Moon. See 20.1 'The initiatic descent of the Moon into the Earth'.

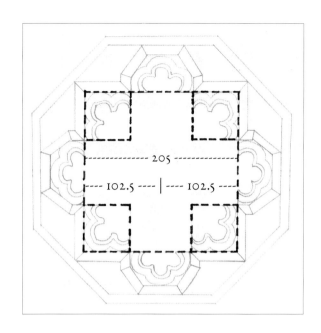

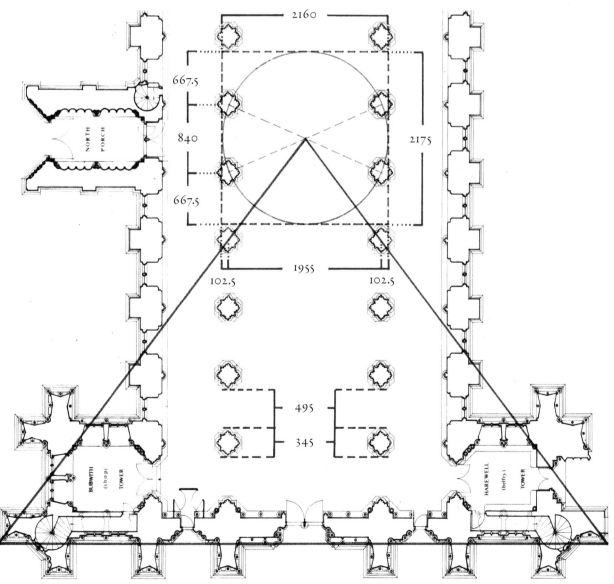

A SELECTION OF DIAGRAMS FROM CHAPTER 15

The front door of the sacristy is at the golden section of its bay. The image on the right shows a plan view of this doorway area. The red dotted lines and numbers demonstrate this golden section of the doorway. The green dotted line is a golden section division of the Pyramid triangle (see image below).

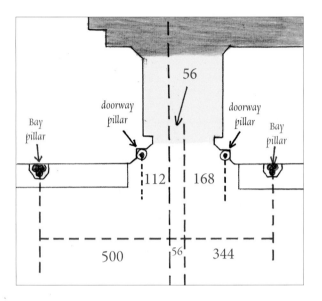

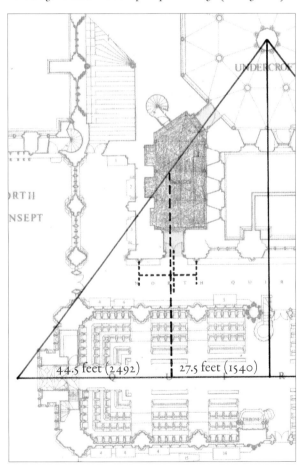

The left-hand half of the pyramid triangle's baseline is divided at the golden section - or rather at the 144/89 division which divides the line into 44.5 greater-feet (2492 micro-units) and 27.5 greater-feet (1540)

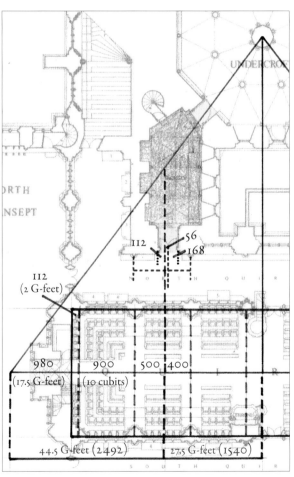

The metrological measurements of the quire and sacristy area. 980 + 112 + 900 + 500 = 2492 and this leads up to the green golden section line. Another 56 more marks the red golden section of the bay.

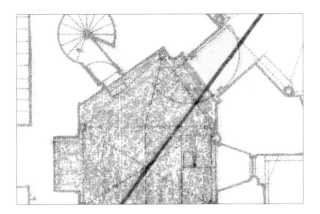

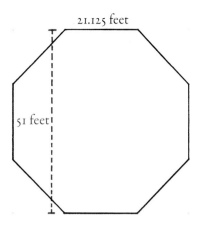

The back door of the sacristy is at the golden section of one of the walls in the octagonal undercroft (see diagram below). The left-hand 'golden ratio' slanting edge of the pyramid triangle (green line) also passes directly through this doorway into the undercroft towards the undercroft's central pillar.

The octagon with an edge of 21.125 has an approximate height of 51. The octagonal Undercroft has a wall-to-wall measurement of 51 feet.

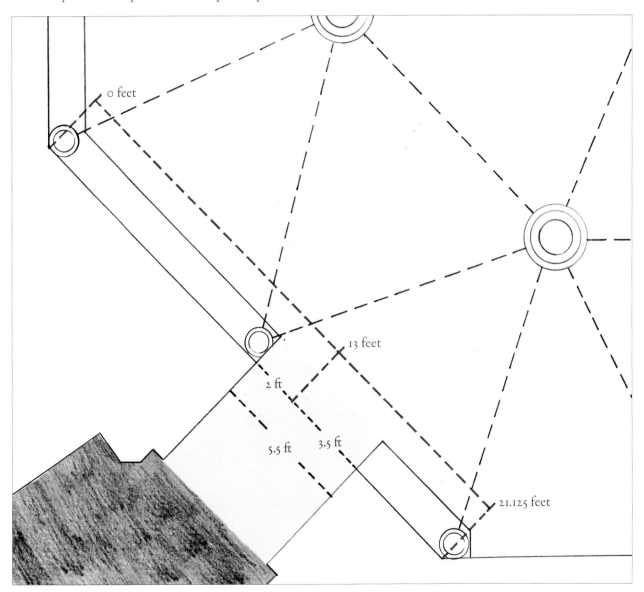

The measurements of the undercroft wall and the position of the sacristy's back door. The golden section of the undercroft wall coincides with the door's 11/7 division.

A SELECTION OF DIAGRAMS FROM CHAPTER 16

The two diagrams below show a pyramid and pediment triangle together bringing about a circle with a radius of 3500. This circle then contains an octagram star with an octagon at its centre containing an edge-to-edge measurement of 2677.5 (51 English feet). This is the wall-to-wall measurement of the undercroft. The calculation occurs via the ratio 153/200 in the sense that when the numbers of this ratio are increased by 17.5 they become 2677.5/3500. This ratio produces a close rational approximation of the side-circumradius measurement for an octagon. The rest of the diagrams on this page, and the following one, show various relationships within the octagonal chapter house.

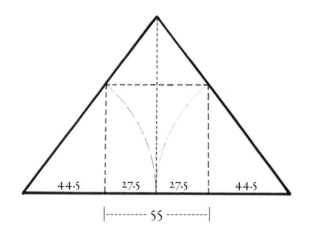

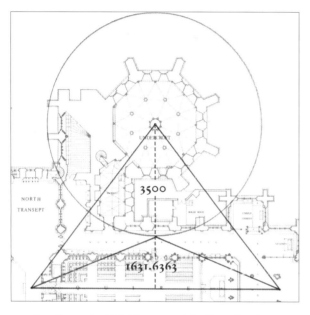

The pediment triangle's height creates a circle with a radius of 3500

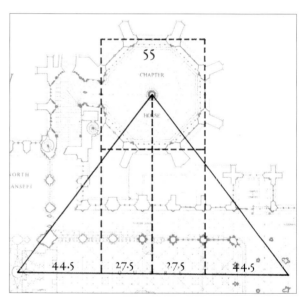

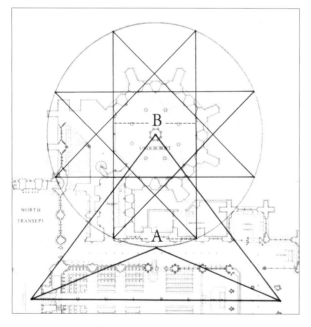

The distances marked 'A' & 'B' measure 2677.5 micro-units or 51 English feet

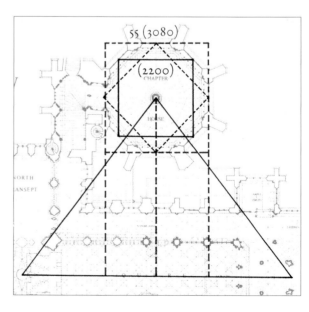

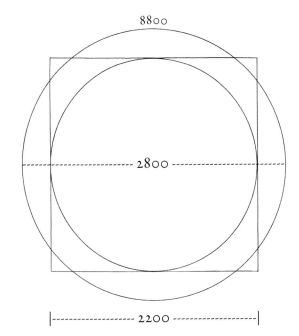

8800

2800

|------------------ 2200 ------------------|

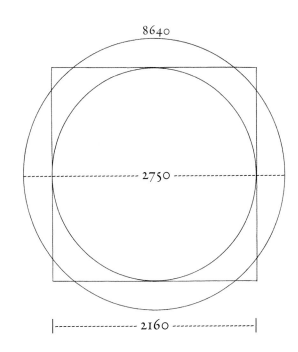

8640

2750

|------------------ 2160 ------------------|

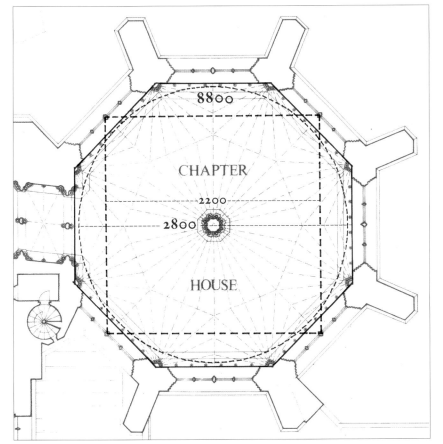

8800

CHAPTER

2200

2800

HOUSE

The Moon-square is marked in green dotted line. The edge-length of the square is 2200 micro-units. Its peripheral measurement is therefore 8800.

The circle that is marked in red dotted line has the same 8800 measurement in its circumference which accordingly means that its diameter measures 2800.

This diameter measurement falls just slightly short of the chapter house's inside walls which are between 2850 and 2856 micro-units apart from one another - i.e. and therefore 1 lesser foot (50) and 1 greater foot (56) more than 2800.

So this circle - which is seemingly not materially marked by anything - can be looked upon as existing 'theoretically' as a kind of symbolic 'round table' that passes through the body of everyone who is present - sitting in-the-round - "all with one accord in one place".

This inevitably confers a 'heavenly' status onto this octagonal hall as well as onto those who sit within it as part of a 'heavenly council'.

It therefore makes symbolic sense that, in cosmological terms, it seems to have a symbolic association with the Moon as well as the eighth heaven of the fixed stars in which the 12 'zodiacal' knights are seated at the round table of the circulating stars.

A SELECTION OF DIAGRAMS FROM CHAPTER 17

First pyramid triangle

Baseline – 110 lesser feet (5500).
Height – 70 lesser feet (3500).

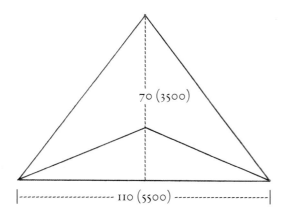

When overlaid, the pyramid and pediment triangles, on the left, govern the underlying design of the east end. The details of this are in the full chapters in the downloadable pdf. The diagram below shows the measurement of 2880 micro-units between the middle axes of the side aisles at both the eastern and western ends of the cathedral. At the eastern end the two measurements of 1440, which together make 2880, are used within a rationalised golden ratio measurement deriving from the pentagram star. This occurs via the fact that 144 is a Fibonacci number. At the western end of the cathedral the number 1440 is used to create an 11/7 relationship via the relationship 3960/2520 which is 360 times greater than 11/7. The number 3960 - the mean radius of the earth in miles - is formed through the addition of 2520 and 1440. The diagram on the page to the right shows the detailed measurements of the east end arising from the pyramid and pediment triangles on the left.

Second pyramid triangle

Baseline – 99 greater feet (5544).
Height – 63 greater feet (3528).

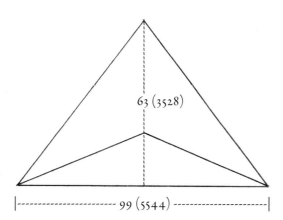

Pediment triangle

Baseline – 105 English feet (5512.5).
Height – see chapter 17 in the pdf for this one.

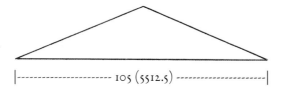

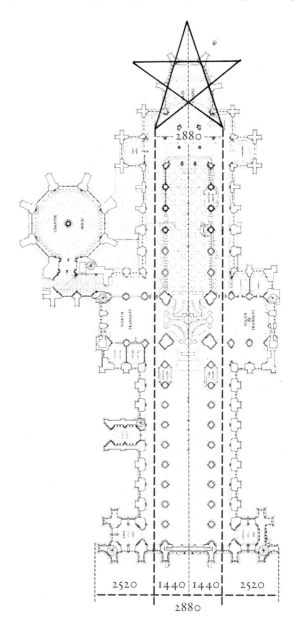

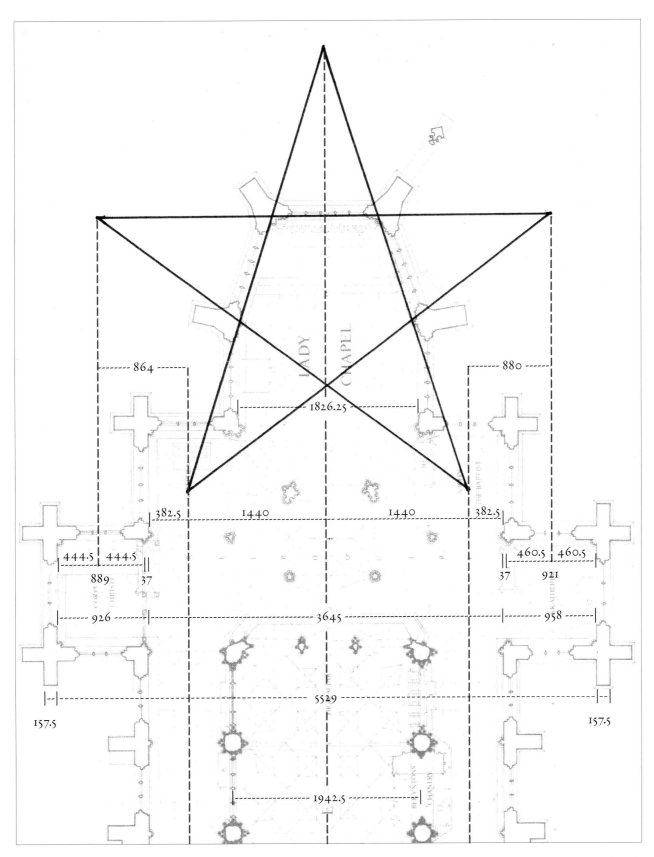

This diagram shows the micro-unit measurements that govern the dimensions of the east-end area of the cathedral. They are all described in more detail within the main text that can be found in the pdf of chapters available online. Note the two 1440 measurements between the feet of the pentagram - as shown in the diagram above - but also at the west entrance of the building as shown in the diagram on the page to the left of this one. These measurements express phi at the east end and pi at the west end.

Part IV

The Cosmos in Stone

and the Initiatic

Journey of the Soul

CHAPTER 18.

The Christian Roots of Freemasonic Symbolism

18.1 THE COSMOLOGICAL DESIGN SYMBOLISM OF WELLS CATHEDRAL AND THE LAYOUT OF A FREEMASON LODGE ROOM

THE PREVIOUS CHAPTERS have slowly unfolded a detailed analysis that demonstrates a mathematically provable and quadrivially integrated theory of design. The measurements of this proposed theory are then reflected within the measureable fabric of the Cathedral building at Wells with a very high degree of accuracy. It is this empirically verifiable accuracy in relation to a coherent and mathematically provable design theory that supports the likelihood that these were the intended measurements used by the person or people who designed Wells Cathedral. The more consistently accurate a theory shows itself to be within a measurable environment, the more difficult it becomes to suggest that the concordances it displays are random and coincidental. Coincidences do happen, and coincidental measurement concordances have certainly happened within the process of this research, but the research trails that such findings led onto would always eventually run dry when they were tested within the wider scheme of measures within the building. So although coincidences do happen within measurement analyses such as these, when apparent concordances begin to show themselves over and over again as part of a definable system of architectural design the theory's threshold of believability is approached, until it is finally reached and passed beyond. As this slow approach takes place it becomes less and less likely that the proposed theory is merely a set of unconnected coincidences, as opposed to a likely theory of the design that was produced and executed by those who devised and built the Cathedral of St Andrew in Wells. Once this threshold has been crossed, the onus passes to the sceptic to demonstrate that the fabric of the Cathedral can be shown to correspond to more than one design theory, also mathematically coherent and empirically accurate when actually measured in-situ.

However, along with mathematical theories and measurements it must also be remembered that the design of Wells Cathedral was produced in 12th-century Western European Christendom, in an era within which there was a learned climate of cosmic Platonist philosophy and theology, whose intention it was to orientate the soul's vision towards the Holy Wisdom. Such Wisdom was itself understood to be a quality of God that the contemplative soul sought to align itself with so as to find the pathway of return leading back to a remembrance of its divine origin. This kind of outlook on the part of the learned 12th-century Christians played just as much of a part in the development of the art and architecture of that time as it did in the thoughts and ideas expressed in spoken and written words. The cathedral schools were renowned for their teaching of the Seven Liberal Arts as a prelude to the study of philosophy and theology, and as shown earlier this was symbolically understood in terms of the ascent of the soul from the material earthly realm back up to a divine origin that lay beyond the embodied world of the senses.

But ultimately it would have been the craft guilds who were enacting and embodying this knowledge within artistic and architectural designs. However, the notion that practitioners of sacred art do not approach any deeper spiritual meaning through their artistic creations has been encouraged within past scholarship. It has been suggested by various art historians, for instance, mainly in the 20th century, that there is no symbolism or spiritual meaning in cathedral design. This quite bizarre notion suggests that such historians had not read much philosophy and theology from the era in question, and were in fact projecting the mental categories of their own atheistic era onto a deeply religious historic past. It is also possible that as non-artists such historians were unaware of the expansive spiritual imagination in which practitioners of sacred art reside. The aesthetic beauty of sacred art is employed to embody the transcendent beauty of God, which it reflects through being ordered and harmonious. Such earthly beauty has the capacity to raise the soul's vision aloft via its longing to remember and return to that which has been forgotten as a result of its fall from the Divine Image.

Medieval artistry was clearly associated with spiritual knowledge and wisdom, as can be seen in depictions of the master mason. The three main characters in medieval images who were depicted with the tools of the mason/geometer are:

1. God the Creator
2. Geometria – (a female personification of geometry as a liberal art)
3. The Master Mason of a cathedral

The first two of these three figures are 'mythical' depictions of Wisdom, whereas the master mason is an actual human character living, as it were, in the mundane day-to-day world. Having said this, the depiction of the master mason could be described as semi-mythical in relation to the symbolic meaning of the tools with which he is depicted.

As to Wisdom herself, she is a quality of God which he brings into play as the Creator when he orders 'all things in measure, number and weight' (Wisdom 11:20).

In the words of Sirach:

'The Lord himself created Wisdom;
he saw her and recognized her value,
and so he filled everything he made with Wisdom.'

Sirach 1:9

God the Geometer - creating the Cosmos from the formless blob of primordial hyle or silva which becomes formed into the perfect circle

Tombstone of Hugues Libergier - Master Mason of Reims Cathedral. The compasses and square are at his feet with the measuring rod in his hand. Spiritual wisdom is implied because he wears the robes of a Doctor of Theology.

This is essentially the symbolic meaning of God's depiction with a pair of compasses or dividers. The eternal forms of number are perpetually known in the Divine Mind, and they come to fruition in the form of the created cosmos both macrocosmically and microcosmically, whereby together they are the larger and smaller images of God. It is no coincidence that two of the four uses of the word 'Wisdom' in the Book of Revelation relate specifically to a capacity of perception that is described as being required for an understanding of number symbolism.[1]

As to Geometria – and more generally the depiction of the Seven Liberal Arts as females who are enacting the arts – this appears to relate to the idea that they are seven aspects of Sophia or Wisdom, to whom they lead in the form of seven steps of ascent.

With this in mind it becomes increasingly difficult to suggest that the depiction of the master mason with the tools of the craft is anything other than an overt symbolic expression of the fact that the artisan was someone who was dealing with spiritual profundity in the form of his art, and that his artistic practice was a kind of sacramental wisdom. After all, geometry is effectively the embodiment or 'incarnation' of the sempiternal truths of number.

Various mentions have been made in this book of ascent symbolism within the design of the Cathedral at Wells. The following sections will now demonstrate this in the form of an ascent symbolism that also happens to closely resemble a cosmological symbolism still existing in the design and use of a modern-day Freemason lodge room. The design of Wells Cathedral long pre-dates the design of a modern-day Freemason lodge room, and along with this a Christian cathedral is inevitably Christ-centred in its death-and-resurrection symbolism, whereas Freemason ritual acts out the symbolic death and resurrection of a mythical figure called Hiram Abiff. But there is an unanswered and perhaps unanswerable question as to whether the enacted story of Hiram Abiff developed within a medieval Christian setting as a kind of initiatic mystery play that reflected the paschal mystery of Christ's death and Resurrection. This may help to explain why a 12th-century cathedral such as the one in Wells would bear such a resemblance to the more recent Freemason lodge rooms in its symbolic layout. But beyond all of this we must not forget a perennial tradition in various different regions of the globe that dates far back into the ancient world, in which a symbolic enactment of death and resurrection formed part of a spiritual initiation in which the soul symbolically died and left the earthly world only to return to it in a transformed state through having been reborn in the Spirit.

In Islamic culture there are contemplative orders known as Tariquas that have their own particular spiritual practice for those Muslims who are orientated towards a deeper engagement with the spiritual mysteries. Those who are initiated into such groups still follow mainstream Islamic practice, as well as participate in the Tariqua's particular form of practice as another way of approaching God. These sorts of groups have existed since the early days of Islam and have been looked upon as acceptable until only very recently, when the very modern phenomenon of Islamic puritanism has led to disapproval of them. Sufism – the name by which this Islamic mysticism is often known – was significant in the Middle East during the medieval era in which the crusades took place. The Jewish tradition also has its own equivalent mystical practice known as the Kabbalah, which flourished in Europe in the 12th-century era of the Crusades. There have also long been Christian practices of a similar sort in the Eastern Orthodox church within a group known as the Hesychasts. They have a particular mode of prayer that is designed to encourage the initiate to turn their focus inward to heighten the experience of union with God.

So with all of this in mind it is reasonable to suggest that medieval Western Christianity also had similar groups to this. Indeed, it would make them uniquely out of the ordinary if they had not. In every era of every

1. See Revelation 13:18 and 17:9.

culture there are inevitably a minority of people orientated towards a more contemplative 'inner' engagement with the Spirit, and this would seem to be a normal facet of any example of human culture at any point in history. In the Western church such groups are generally monastic in form. But should we also consider the craft guilds? Artists are naturally contemplative, and reside within the spiritual imagination along with all of its imaginal forms such as geometry and cosmology.

Bearing in mind that the story of Hiram Abiff is acted out as a drama, such a practice bears a resemblance to the medieval mystery plays that were actually performed by the craft guilds themselves. In this sense Freemasonry looks to have a medieval Christian pedigree, which is something that Freemasonry itself actually claims. This is also clearly present within its various Christo-Masonic symbols, such as the two 'solstitial' Johns – the Baptist and the Evangelist – who will be described briefly in the next section. There is also the emphasis that Freemasonry places on Jerusalem and the Temple of Solomon, which is more reminiscent of 12th/13th-century Crusader Christianity than of the later European culture of the Enlightenment, in which the recognition of Jerusalem and its temple as the centre of the world had receded within the rationalistic movement away from Judeo-Christian symbolism. So to say that Freemasonry only started properly in the 17th/18th century is to not read its language of symbolism in an appropriate manner.

With medieval Christianity in mind, the Freemason storyline of Hiram Abiff does appear to resemble the hagiography of a 10th-century saint called Reinold of Cologne, who is also a patron saint of stonemasons.[2] It is specifically the manner of his death and the discovery of his body that resembles the Masonic legend of Hiram Abiff. But St Reinold was also prominent in the very era in which Wells Cathedral was beginning to be built (late 12th century), through a chanson de geste called 'The four sons of Aymon'. In this long narrative poem there is a character called Renaud de Montauban,

who is clearly based on St Reinold, and again he experiences a death that is similar to St Reinold and Hiram Abiff in which his fellow stonemasons beat him to death with their stone carving tools due to their envy of his piety, knowledge and hard work. A violent death of a holy man at the hands of envious hypocrites reflects the storyline of Christ. Indeed when one takes a close look at the cosmological and Solomonic symbolism of modern-day Freemasonry there are various aspects of it that feel quite 12th-century-Christian in their focus, despite the fact that the decorative appearance of Freemason lodge rooms and the general use of imagery in Freemasonry are far more reminiscent of the early modern era.

What the following sections are designed to reflect is the very interesting possibility that modern-day Freemasonry seems to have preserved certain elements of a kind of 12th-century cosmic Christian initiation symbolism that centres around the death and resurrection of the soul as an initiatic emulation of Christ's paschal mystery in Jerusalem. Such an emulation of Christ's paschal journey is clearly present in the storyline of Dante's *Commedia* in the sense of it being a kind of imaginal drama that begins on Holy Thursday and then runs all the way through and beyond Easter Sunday. Dante's *Commedia* is not the same storyline as Christ's paschal journey, but there is clearly an overt adherence to its basic symbolic framework in the sense that Dante descends into the underworld from Jerusalem on Good Friday and then resurfaces on Easter Sunday having passed through the deathly realm at the centre of the Earth, much as Christ does in his Harrowing of Hell. But there is also a certain resemblance in all of this to Freemason symbolism and ritual, particularly through the emphasis on Jerusalem and a death-and-resurrection symbolism that is cosmologically understood through the age-old symbolism of the rising and setting of the Morning and Evening Star. However, the one thing that isn't present in either Christ's or Dante's journey is an emphasis upon the Temple of Solomon, whereas this lies at the very heart of the Freemason storyline of Hiram Abiff as well as at

2. See Paul Naudon, *The Secret History of Freemasonry,* Inner Traditions, 2005 – the long footnote on page 53.

the heart of the ascent symbolism in the design of Wells Cathedral. As mentioned earlier, the quire is formed of the same basic shape and dimensions as Solomon's Temple. As also described in section 4.2, the design of the Cathedral seemingly emulates a 12th-century Crusader understanding of the topographical layout of the Temple Mount whereby its 'Solomonic' quire appears to symbolically represent the Al-Aqsa Mosque building, which in 12th-century Crusader Jerusalem had been Christianised and was known as the Temple of Solomon.

With all of this in mind, we are left with the question of who would have been the most likely group of medieval Christians to be performing such an initiatic cosmic emulation of the paschal mysteries in a place that symbolically represents the Temple of Solomon on the Temple Mount in the holy city of Jerusalem.

THE WEST DOOR – THE BEGINNING OF THE EQUINOCTIAL/PASCHAL AXIS

IN THE FIRST PART of section 4.2, it was suggested that the double doors, that so commonly characterise the west portal of a Gothic cathedral, would appear to be an image of the two doors on Jerusalem's Golden Gate. Along with this the practice of beginning the Palm Sunday liturgy outside the west door of an English Gothic cathedral is another indication that the west front of Wells Cathedral represents the entryway into Jerusalem and the beginning of the eight-day paschal journey that started on Palm Sunday at the Golden Gate. Such a Palm Sunday procession used to take place in the Crusader culture of 12th-century Jerusalem at the actual Golden Gate, and it still takes place at the west front of Wells Cathedral every year. This entry of Christ into Jerusalem is also a symbolic re-enactment of the coronation of King Solomon, as well as of the arrival of the Jewish Messiah as an image of the Sun rising over the Mount of Olives that lies to the east of Jerusalem.

THE NAVE – THE TROPICS AND THE EQUATOR IN THE POINT-WITHIN-THE-CIRCLE DIAGRAM

THE WEST DOOR LEADS into the nave, which is an image of Planet Earth. The nave is therefore the starting point of the ascent from Earth up to the rising of the Sun and the Bright Morning Star in the east. The north wall and the south wall of the nave geometrically embody the tropics of Cancer and Capricorn, and in this sense the side aisles that they run alongside represent the solstitial pathways. The central axis of the nave is thus the equinoctial axis or the middle path of balance that runs between the solstitial extremes of light and dark. As mentioned earlier, Easter is calculated as the first Sunday after the first full Moon after the spring equinox, and so the paschal and the equinoctial naturally accord within the same middle path of the nave. There is a very interesting correlation between all of this and Freemasonry in relation to one of its most important diagrams – known as *the point within the circle*.

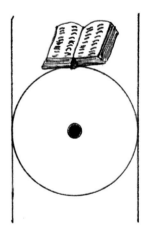

This particular diagram consists of a dot within a circle that is located between a pair of vertical parallel lines. There is also an open book on top of the circle, which is known as the *Volume of the Sacred Law*. Various descriptions have been given of what the diagram symbolises, although all interpretations agree that the two lines are the 'two Johns' – St John the Baptist and St John the Evangelist. These two Christian saints are the patron saints of Freemasonry and in cosmological terms they symbolise the two solstices. This bears a resemblance to the Roman craft guilds, for whom Janus was the patron deity. his two faces symbolise the two solstices, along with various other polarities such as 'past' and 'future'.[3]

3. See René Guénon, *Symbols of Sacred Science,* Sophia Perennis, 2004, chapter 18, 'Some Aspects of the Symbolism of Janus'.

St John the Baptist's feast day on 24 June has long been associated with midsummer, because this was the date of the summer solstice in the old Roman calendar. Nowadays the summer solstice takes place around 20/21 June, but for many hundreds of years St John the Baptist's feast day has been known as Midsummer's Day. In the medieval era there was a big and widely celebrated festival on 'St John's Eve' – the evening before 24 June – to mark the middle of summer. Interestingly, Bishop Reginald de Bohun – who instigated the building of Wells Cathedral – was installed as the Bishop of Bath on St John's Eve in 1174. His installation took place in Saint-Jean-de-Maurienne in France, where the cathedral is dedicated to John the Baptist and claimed to hold the relic of his three 'baptising' fingers. Within a few months of his installation, Bishop de Bohun had set up the Hospital of St John the Baptist next to the ancient Cross Bath bathing pool in his diocesan city of Bath. De Bohun's new diocese was full of famous holy springs such as those at Bath, Wells and Glastonbury, so the Baptist appears to have been an appropriate personal patron. John the Baptist's feast day – itself on 24 June – was also the particular date in the year 1717 when Grand Lodge Freemasonry was instituted. Indeed within Freemason lore the 'proto-lodge' was said to have been instigated in Jerusalem during the era of the 12th-century Crusader Kingdom and was initially known as 'the Lodge of the Holy St John (the Baptist) of Jerusalem'.

In St John's Gospel there are words spoken by John the Baptist in relation to the coming of Christ which have long been understood cosmologically as a symbol of the summer solstice and its association with the Baptist:

> *'He must increase, but I must decrease.'*

> John 3:30

This is John the Baptist's description of Christ superseding him, which is cosmologically symbolised as the decrease of daylight hours from the summer solstice onwards. This is all part of a very old tradition in Christianity, in which the Baptist and Christ were understood to have been born on the two solstices and conceived at the two equinoxes nine months prior to each solstice.[4] However, as already mentioned Freemasonry associates the solstices with the two Johns, and so having now described the Baptist's association with midsummer we will turn to the Evangelist's association with midwinter.

The feast day of St John the Evangelist is on 27 December, which places it close to the winter solstice. However, there is not actually such a prominent Christian association of the Evangelist with midwinter in the way that the Baptist is associated with midsummer. As already mentioned, an earlier Christian tradition associates the winter solstice with the birth of Christ. But around the 15th century John the Evangelist begins to appear as a solstitial saint in written examples of Masonic symbolism in Scotland.[5] However, Wells Cathedral was designed and built a long time before the 15th century, although, as will become clear, the design of Wells appears to involve a similar use of solstitial symbolism associated with Christian saints whose feast days fall around the solstices. But rather than John the Evangelist, the Wells design involves St Stephen, whose feast day is the day before that of John the Evangelist. This naturally places the feast of Stephen on the day that follows the annual commemoration of Christ's birth on 25 December, which was itself the date of the winter solstice in the old Roman calendar.

With cathedral building in mind, and the importance of stonemasonry and craftsmanship, St Stephen is a patron saint of stonemasons due to his martyring through stoning. He does also have a direct association with the winter solstice via his non-biblical patronage of horses. An old Christian tradition on the Feast of Stephen was to bring horses into the church to be blessed. Sometimes horses would be galloped around the churchyard and then ceremonially fed, decorated

---

4. See the 4th-century treatise *On the Solstices and Equinoxes, the Conception and Birth of our Lord Jesus Christ and John the Baptist.*
5. The Freemason 'proto-lodge' is said to have first been dedicated to John the Baptist and then later to John the Evangelist and finally to both of them.

and bled – for what was understood to be their health over the coming year. This bleeding of the horse suggests a Christianised remnant of the very significant and widespread ancient tradition of sacrificing horses at the winter solstice. Indeed such practices were still in existence in some non-Christianised regions of Europe at the time that Wells Cathedral was being built.

Returning to the point-within-the-circle and the design of the nave at Wells, there appears to be a direct correlation between the two in symbolic terms, in the sense that they both represent the moderate middle place existing between two extremes. A common Freemason description looks upon the dot in the circle as symbolising the individual Freemason, whereas the circumference is:

'The boundary line of his duty to God and to man, beyond which a man should not allow his passions, prejudices or interests to betray him.'

This morally orientated definition suggests the need for moderation in one's behaviour, which in turn suggests a middle path of balance. It is clear that such a boundary of moderation is symbolically expressed in cosmological terms by the two parallel lines – 'the two Johns' – that represent the solstitial extremes and thus form the boundaries within which the moderate 'equinoctial' soul resides.[6]

But it is a description of this symbol from a handbook on Freemasonry called *Morals and Dogma* written by the renowned Freemason Albert Pike that bears a particular resemblance to the design of the nave at Wells. He describes the two lines in the diagram as being the tropics of Cancer and Capricorn, and the circle with the point as symbolising the Sun.[7]

'The Solstices, Cancer and Capricorn, the two Gates of Heaven, are the two pillars of Hercules, beyond which he, the sun, never journeyed: and they still appear in our lodges, as the two great columns, Jachin and Boaz, and

also as the two parallel lines that bound the circle, with a point in the centre, emblem of the Sun, between the two tropics of Cancer and Capricorn.'

Chapter 25

This particular interpretation suggests that the parallel lines in the diagram originate from the long edges of either a 7 × 3 or 30 × 13 'tropical' rectangle. Or, put another way, the original version of the diagram could have consisted of those particular dimensions even if more recent versions of the diagram do not. The symbol also has the 'emblem of the Sun' centred on the equinoctial middle axis between the solstitial extremes of Cancer and Capricorn, and this all reflects the geometric design of the nave at Wells. It is after all Christ, symbolised by the Sun, who is reborn around the spring equinox as he rises out of the darkness and death of a winter spent in the dark deathly 'underworld'.

THE CATHEDRAL CROSSING AS THE CENTRE OF THE WORLD

THE CROSSING IN A cathedral is a visible image of 'the central place'. This crossing is located at the centre of the four directions of the compass that the cathedral church embodies through having a nave in the west, a chancel in the east and then two transepts, one in the north and one in the south. In the finished design of Wells Cathedral this central place is the location of the doorway into the quire, which symbolically speaking is the centre or 'heart' of the cathedral. Bearing in mind that the quire at Wells is built with the same dimensions as the Temple of Solomon, this again symbolically suggests 'centrality' in terms of Solomon's Temple being the ancient centre of the holy city of Jerusalem.

The very fact that there is an emulation of Solomon's Temple within the design immediately correlates with Freemasonry, in which the Temple of Solomon is the primary symbolic focus. The building of the physical

---

6. See Ch.7 of Microcosmos in Bernard Sylvestris' *Cosmographia.... "....the sun is content to move between its tropics, and never exceeds these duly established limits."*
7. The symbol of the Sun in alchemy and astrology is also a circle with a dot in the middle.

temple is used as a symbol for the building of the temple 'within the soul', as well as of an ideal society. For this to occur, a great deal of inner work is required which involves hardships and trials. But the reason for building the temple is so that there can be a residing place down here on Earth for the Divine Presence of God, and in this sense the Masonic symbolism of the building of the 'inner' temple becomes similar to the Orthodox Christian aspiration of Theosis, the soul's deification, which is central to the practice of Christian mysticism.

The Temple of Solomon, the spring equinox, computus and Holy Week

The heart of an English cathedral is its quire. This is where the daily offices are sung, and it is both architecturally and ceremonially the focus of the building. The quire at Wells has the same shape and dimensions as the Temple of Solomon. The long rectangular shape of most cathedral quires resembles the ground plan of Solomon's Temple, even if the dimensions are not directly present. A long rectangle that is orientated eastwards is also the characteristic description of a Masonic lodge, and along with this the initiation into the third degree of Freemasonry symbolically takes place within the Temple of Solomon itself. The resurrection of Hiram Abiff also takes place around the time of the spring equinox, which is the day of the year that cosmologically heralds the coming of the paschal season because the date of Easter is calculated according to the spring equinox. The spring equinox is the day on which the sun passes over the equator of the Earth and is thus 'reborn'. As mentioned earlier, in the design of Wells Cathedral there are three symbolic pathways that run from west to east. The two side aisles – one on the north side of the building and the other on the south side – could be said to symbolise the solstitial pathways, and neither of them pass through the quire because they are situated immediately to the north and to the south of it. But the equinoctial middle path passes straight through the middle of the quire and beyond. This naturally shows a cosmological concordance between the paschal storyline of Christ and the Masonic legend of Hiram's death in the Temple of Solomon followed by his resurrection, all taking place around the equinox.

With death and resurrection in mind, the quire and its high altar also symbolically represent the Last Supper on Holy Thursday, which associates it with the body of Christ and his death on the cross the following day. Looking directly above the high altar there is a large Jesse Tree window, which shows Christ's family lineage through the line of King David. In the middle of this green family tree is a depiction of the Crucified Christ himself surrounded by bunches of Eucharistic grapes, because the Tree of Jesse is here depicted as a vine. So the quire's high altar and Jesse window represent Holy Thursday and Good Friday, and this follows in the way that the journey through the cathedral, from west to east, represents the eight days of Easter. If the west door symbolically represents Palm Sunday, then the quire and its Jesse window are in an appropriate location to symbolise Holy Thursday and Good Friday. As they are in the eastward half of the building, spatially this recalls the temporal fact that Thursday and Friday are in the latter half of the eight days of Easter.

Another paschal element to the design is suggested by the position of the 'lunar' chapter house situated to the north of the quire. As a result of the calculation of Easter there is always a full Moon during Holy Week, and indeed it is known as the 'paschal full Moon'. So as the journey through the cathedral progresses from Palm Sunday to Easter Sunday there is a full Moon symbolised by the position of the chapter house, which is partway between the west front/Palm Sunday and the Lady chapel/Easter Sunday. But this calculation of Easter, known as computus – which involves a relationship between the Sun, the Moon and Sunday – is also directly characterised and effectively embodied by the pyramid triangle that governs this area of the cathedral's design. If Easter is the first Sunday after the first full Moon after the spring equinox, we can see all of these cosmological events geometrically marked

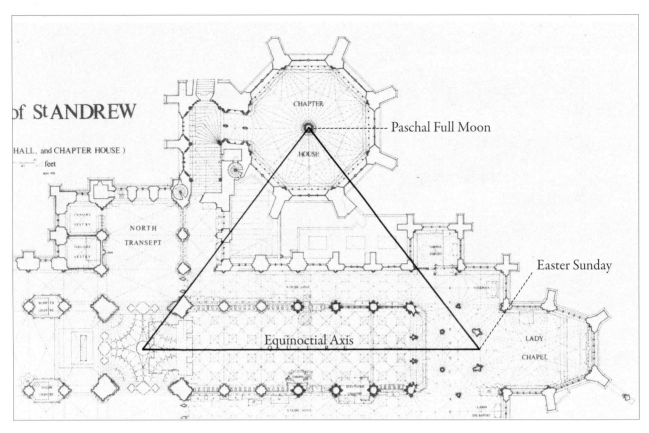

The pyramid triangle marking the three calendrical coordinates used in the calculation of Easter. The equinox is marked by the baseline of the pyramid triangle which runs along the cathedral's equinoctial axis. The chapter house is the Paschal full moon and the Lady chapel is Easter Sunday.

in the positioning of the pyramid triangle. The triangle's baseline runs along the equinoctial middle pathway of the cathedral, its apex coincides with the centre of the 'lunar' chapter house and its bottom right-hand corner coincides with the entrance into the Lady chapel that symbolises Easter Sunday.

The one remaining significant position within this pyramid triangle is its bottom left-hand corner, and this coincides with the centre of the cathedral's crossing – which as already mentioned symbolises the centre of the world in the form of Jerusalem. In the words of the 4th-century St Cyril of Jerusalem:

'He [Christ] stretched out His hands on the Cross, that He might embrace the ends of the world; for this Golgotha is the very centre of the earth. It is not my word, but it is a prophet who has said, "You have wrought salvation in the midst of the earth."'

St Cyril's Catechetical Lecture, 13–28

This central place of Jerusalem is where the paschal story unfolded at what is effectively also the centre of 'Christian-time', because Christ's Passion is the midway crossing-point from the Old Testament era over to the time of the New Testament. This often shows itself in a north–south division of biblical iconography whereby Old Testament scenes will be depicted on one side of a cathedral and New Testament scenes on the other. Such a dual arrangement of iconography naturally places the Passion itself as the middle axis of a cathedral, running as it does between the Old Testament on one side and the New Testament on the other. Another interesting reflection of this in the paschal and cosmological design of Wells Cathedral can be seen in an association made by St Augustine between the Moon and the Sun and the Old and New Testaments. He described the Old Testament as being like the Moon that becomes illuminated and thus fully revealed through the sunlight of the New Testament. This is reflected by the lunar chapter house on the north side of Wells Cathedral, as opposed to the southern sunny side of the building where the Sun passes during the daytime hours. It also reflects the medieval image of Christ's crucifixion, in which there is the Sun on one side of Christ and the Moon on the other. The middle axis between Sun and Moon is thus the Way of the Cross, which again correlates with the paschal middle axis of the cathedral's cruciform ground plan. One could even say that the use of the Sun, Moon and Sunday within the calculation of Easter symbolically expresses the crucifixial middle path of ascent between Sun and Moon as seen in the depictions of Christ on the cross.

However, even though the quire is the heart of the cathedral, it is not the culmination of its eastward ascent. There could be said to be two 'ascents' that begin from the quire at Wells. Being as it is an image of the temple in Jerusalem, the quire is the central place on Earth, and the reaching of this centre is necessary before a symbolically 'vertical' cosmic ascent can begin. These two ascents are both geometrically symbolised by a movement from the baseline of a pyramid triangle up to its apex, and in both cases these triangular apexes coincide with the central point of an architectural space that has a polygonal ground plan.

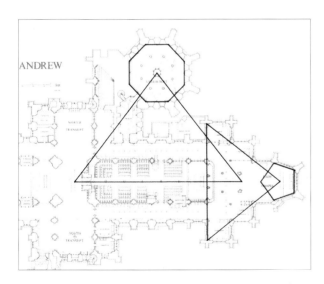

The two pyramid triangles that are 'ascended' to 'heavenly' polygonal places

These two polygonal areas – the only two places in the whole cathedral with regular polygonal ground plans – cosmologically represent heavenly bodies, namely the Morning Star (Lady chapel) and the Moon (chapter house and undercroft). Virtually the whole cathedral ground plan is geometrically composed of rectangles that accordingly symbolise 'the four corners of the Earth'. But the only two places with regular polygon geometry derived from the 'heavenly' circle are the Lady chapel with its conjoined pentagon and octagon ground plan, and the octagonal chapter house area. These 'heavenly' places are the two culminations of the symbolically 'vertical' ascents that begin from the quire. The eastern ascent to Planet Venus – the Morning Star – could be symbolically described as an ascent to Divine Love, whereas the northern ascent to the Moon and the eighth heaven could be described as an ascent to Holy Wisdom. As will become clear a little later, these two ascents also appear to correspond to Dante's journey up Mount Purgatorio towards Eden 'in the east' followed by his 'northward' ascent through the planetary spheres towards and beyond the fixed stars that are themselves centred around the Celestial North Pole.

The eastern 'ascent' begins from the eastern end of the quire and culminates in the centre of the pentagonal east end of the Lady chapel. The northern ascent also begins from the quire and culminates in the centre of the octagonal chapter house/undercroft.

Jachin and Boaz

Bearing in mind the layout of the Temple of Solomon and the cathedral with its 'Solomonic' quire, there is an orientational inversion in the sense that the temple was entered from the east and the progress into it was therefore westward bound.

A Christian church building on the other hand is the opposite to this, whereby entry is in the west and progress is eastward. So if a cathedral quire can be said to symbolise the Temple of Solomon, the entrance to the temple would be, symbolically speaking, up at the eastern end of the cathedral quire. An important characteristic of the doorway to Solomon's Temple was that it was flanked by the two pillars Jachin and Boaz. These two pillars are particularly important in Freemasonry, and have a similar symbolism to that already described as a *middle path between extremes*. In this sense the pillars are understood to represent the extremes, or polar opposites, and the pathway in between that leads into the temple is accordingly the middle way. Two actual pillars representing Jachin and Boaz are an important part of the lodge room furniture, and they are together seen as symbolising various polarities such as the two solstices, Heaven and Earth, and the Sun and Moon, all of which accords with the use of cosmic polar symbolism in the design of Wells Cathedral. In actual fact, at the eastern end of the quire there happen to be two pillars in positions that appropriately reflect the locations of Jachin and Boaz at the door of Solomon's temple. They are located in apparently awkward positions in that they appear to be standing in the middle of what would generally be understood as a processional route leading around the eastern end of the quire. But these pillars are also necessary in practical terms because they support outside buttresses that in turn help to support the eastern end of the building. So it could be said that these pillars have both a practical usefulness and well as a symbolic meaning within the building, and this could have even affected the scope of the design in the sense that their initial symbolic inclusion would naturally lead to a recognition of their weight-bearing potential within that particular area of the building. The two pillars are clearly a symbolically significant area of the cathedral, as it is generally understood that the space between them would have been the location of the tomb of William of March (a former Bishop of Bath and Wells) had he been canonised.

So these pillars are ideally located in relation to the east end of the 'Solomonic' quire, whereby they fit the description of the positions of Jachin and Boaz at the doorway to Solomon's Temple. But along with this they are 9 cubits in height, which is precisely half the height of their biblical description. If they were the full 18 cubits mentioned in the Bible they would be completely out of proportion with their surroundings and would not look right.

Another interesting possibility here can be seen in the fact that these pillars at Wells have a pentagonal cross-

section. However, they are not located in an area that is laid out with five-fold symmetry - which accordingly might also require them to have five-fold symmetry to accord with their surroundings. Indeed, the stone ribs that burst out of the top of the pillars do not continue to exhibit the same five-fold symmetry that runs through the pillar. So we are left with the question of why the designer would make an artistic decision in which the pillars have a pentagonal cross-section for no apparent practical purpose in a cathedral that is generally emphasising the 'fourfoldness' of the Earth. We are again led to the biblical description of the doorway of Solomon's Temple, and to the following description:

'For the entrance to the inner sanctuary he made doors of olivewood; the lintel and the doorposts were five-sided.'

1 Kings 6:31

The pillars beyond the east-end of the quire - symbolising Jachin and Boaz? Their pentagonal cross-section resembles the Temple's five-sided doorposts.

This translation involving 'five-sided' doorposts is a debated one, and it is not always translated with this particular meaning. But the presence of these five-sided pillars at least suggests that this might be the biblical understanding on the part of the designer at Wells. So in short, the two pillars at the east end of the Wells quire appear to symbolise Jachin and Boaz and more generally the doorway to Solomon's Temple. But their existence is also utilised in structural terms by the outside buttresses that help to stabilise the eastern end of the quire.

The solstitial saints and their chapels in the northeast and southeast corners

THE SOLSTITIAL SYMBOLISM that has been described up to now concerns the dimensions of the nave along with the fact that the north and south walls of the nave geometrically embody the tropics of Cancer and Capricorn within the 'Earth circle' that contains the nave rectangle.

This solstitial geometry appears to be confirmed by what occurs at the eastern end of the two 'solstitial' side aisles. As mentioned earlier, the design of Wells Cathedral appears to contain solstitial symbolism relating to Christian saints. This symbolism also appears to be a forerunner of the Freemason use of a similar solstitial symbolism relating to the 'two Johns'. However, in Wells the two saints in question are St John the Baptist and St Stephen. Both have clear associations with the solstices through the position of their feast days within the annual cycle, but also in relation to other aspects of Christian solstitial symbolism that both saints have been associated with for hundreds of years.

The culmination and termination of both side aisles present themselves in the form of chapels, one of which is dedicated to St John the Baptist and the other to St Stephen. These two chapels also happen to flank the three arched entrances that lead into the Lady chapel, whereby entry into the Lady chapel very directly expresses an equinoctial middle way between these two chapels of winter and summer.

However, the symbolism of winter and summer – which accords with darkness and light – brings about an interesting inversion in the position of these chapels of St John and St Stephen within the overall design.

The common understanding of light and dark in a cathedral is that the north is the dark side, whereas the south side is bathed in the light of the Sun because it travels from east to west through the southern sky.

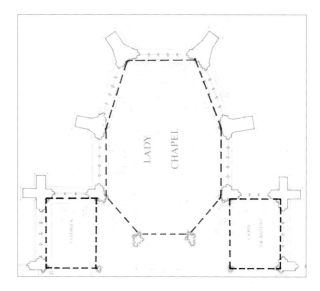

The entrance to the Lady chapel is situated directly between the two 'solstitial' chapels of St Stephen and St John the Baptist

This accords naturally with the idea that the north side of the cathedral is the lunar side relating to the night-time, whereas the south side is the solar side relating to daytime. However, when it comes to the positions of the rising and setting of the Sun on the circular horizon there is a cosmic inversion. At the spring equinox the Sun rises precisely in the east and sets precisely in the west. But then with the move into summer the sunrise and sunset points both begin to move further to the north around the horizon. On the summer solstice the sunrise and sunset points reach the furthest north that they will go and then slowly, day by day, they begin to move back towards the eastern and the western points of the horizon. They return to east and west on the day of the autumn equinox and then proceed inversely to move southward. The equivalent southward movement continues until the winter solstice, and then the Sun turns once again to head back towards the eastern and western points of the horizon for the next spring equinox.

So there is also an association of the north with summer and the south with winter, which is the opposite of what was described above in relation to the northern darkness and southern lightness of the cathedral. As the solstitial symbolism is the most prominent

The dark north quire aisle on a sunny day

The light south quire aisle on a sunny day

within the Wells design rather than merely lightness on one side and darkness on the other, this would appear to give a certain primacy to a design resolution whereby John the Baptist's chapel should be on the north side of the cathedral to reflect the northward movement of the sunrise and sunset horizon points during summer. The opposite should thus apply to St Stephen, whose chapel would then be on the southern side. However, St Stephen's chapel is on the north side and St John's is on the south side. So it would seem as though both of these symbolic seasonal schemas are included within the design in such a way that the presence of solstitial saints implies the solstitial symbolism itself, whereas John in the south implies the summer lightness of the south side and inversely St Stephen in the north implies the wintry darkness of the north. So in this sense the north–south inversion of these solstitial saints incorporates both perceptions of light and dark and summer/winter solstices into the one overall design. This is reminiscent of Chinese Daoist philosophy in the sense of the yin that is in yang and the yang that is in yin.

But there is another very striking symbolism of polarity that associates St John the Baptist with St Stephen, although it is more specifically a biblical symbolism rather than a purely cosmological one. Bearing in the mind that the middle path of the cathedral is associated cosmologically with the equinox, it has also been shown how this relates to the paschal period of time between Palm Sunday and Easter Sunday. So this biblical aspect of the symbolism also correlates with the cosmological symbolism of the equinoxes in relation to the equinoctial calculation of Easter. It is therefore significant that if the middle path of the cathedral is the paschal path, which relates to the Passion of Christ, then the two solstitial chapels, one on either side, are dedicated to the last martyr before the Passion (the Baptist) and the first martyr after the Passion (St Stephen). This again accords with the common feature of locating 'pre-Passion' scenes on one side of a cathedral with 'post-Passion' scenes on the other. The death of the martyrs John and Stephen is architecturally expressed by the right-angular termination of the side aisles formed by these two chapels . But the middle paschal path of Christ – he who is the ultimate Christian martyr – passes in between these two chapels and goes beyond death into Resurrection, as symbolised by the rising of the Bright Morning Star in the east, which presents itself in thc form of the east end Lady chapel.

Again, there is a close reflection of all of this within Freemasonry. But this time the correlation more specifically relates to the occurrence of ritual within the lodge room that is reflected in terms of the particular areas of the room in which the initiations into the three degrees take place. Initiation into the first degree takes place in the lodge room's northeast corner, and symbolically relates to the rising of the Sun on the summer solstice. This northeast corner also symbolically relates to the foundation stone of a new building, and thus the opening initiation for a new Freemason. The second degree then takes place in the southeast corner of the lodge room, and is associated with the rising of the Sun on the winter solstice.

This reflects the locations of the solstitial chapels at Wells, which also form the northeast and southeast corners of the cathedral church building. The enactment of the Masonic 'Third Degree' is then situated along the central east–west axis of the lodge room, which reflects the equinoctial axis of Wells Cathedral. As mentioned earlier, the equinox is the day of the year around which the resurrection story of Hiram Abiff is set – much like Christ's Resurrection, which is commemorated on the first Sunday after the first full Moon after the spring equinox. This leads us to the archetypal storyline of death and resurrection, and to a particularly striking connection between the design of Wells Cathedral and that of a Freemason lodge room: the rising of the Bright Morning Star in the east.

THE RESURRECTION OF THE BRIGHT MORNING STAR IN THE LADY CHAPEL

'Let me now beg you to observe that the Light of a Master Mason is darkness visible, serving only to express that gloom which rests on the prospect of futurity. It is that mysterious veil which the eye of human reason cannot penetrate unless assisted by that Light which is from above. Yet, even by this glimmering ray, you may perceive that you stand on the brink of the grave into which you just figuratively descended, and which, when this transitory life shall have passed away, will again receive you into its cold bosom. Let the emblems of mortality which lie before you lead you to contemplate on your inevitable destiny and guide your reflections to that most interesting of all human studies, the knowledge of yourself. Be careful to perform your allotted task while it is yet day, continue to listen to the voice of Nature, which bears witness that even in this perishable frame resides a vital and immortal principle, which inspires a holy confidence that the Lord of Life will enable us to trample the King of Terrors beneath our feet, and lift our eyes to that bright Morning Star, whose rising brings peace and salvation to the faithful and obedient of the human race.'

THESE ARE THE WORDS addressed to the initiate by the Worshipful Master at the culmination of the Third Degree of initiation. At this particular moment of the enacted drama the lodge room is in complete darkness except for an illuminated pentagram-shaped light on the east wall of the lodge that is situated above the seat of the Worshipful Master.

This pentagram shaped light, with its golden wings and flanking serpents, is known as the Orb of Egypt. It is situated at the east-end of the lodge room at the headquarters of the British federation of Le Droit Humain in London.

This seat is located at the east end of the lodge room and in this sense the Worshipful Master is an image of the rising Sun. So the illuminated pentagram appears to symbolise the rising of the Morning Star in the east, which is also an image of the initiate symbolically resurrecting from their deathly grave.

A great deal was written in chapters 5 and 6 about the cosmological symbolism of both Christ and the Virgin Mary as images of the Morning Star rising in the east. This symbolism centres around the emergence of light and the illumination of the soul in relation to this light. So a Lady chapel at the eastern end of a cathedral church building is naturally the culmination of this eastward movement towards the illuminating light of the rising Sun. In the design of the Lady chapel at Wells, it is its geometric shape that symbolises this emergence of light in the form of a pentagon that is derived from the centre of a pentagram star – much like the illuminated pentagram on the east wall of a Masonic lodge room. This pentagram is a cosmological image of the planet Venus as the Bright Morning Star, which as previously mentioned is itself associated with the archetypal story of death and resurrection over a three-day period. But this emerging pentagram of light is also related to the symbolism of the five-fold rose and to a Masonic symbolism relating to the rosy cross as described by Albert Pike in his book *Morals and Dogma*.

The rose was anciently sacred to Aurora and the Sun. It is a symbol of Dawn, of the resurrection of Light and the renewal of life, and therefore of the dawn of the first day, and more particularly of the resurrection: and the Cross and Rose together are therefore hieroglyphically to be read, the Dawn of Eternal Life which all Nations have hoped for by the advent of a Redeemer.

In Christian terms this paschal Resurrection at dawn into eternal life is also associated with the 'eighth day', which makes Palm Sunday the first of the eight days.

The association of Easter Sunday with the 'eighth day' is a very early Christian calendrical symbolism that was first mentioned in the Epistle of Barnabas:

'Finally He saith to them; "Your new moons and your Sabbaths I cannot stand." Ye see what is His meaning; it is not your present Sabbaths that are acceptable [unto Me], but the Sabbath which I have made, in the which, when I have set all things at rest, I will make the beginning of the eighth day which is the beginning of another world.

Wherefore also we keep the eighth day for rejoicing, in the which also Jesus rose from the dead, and having been manifested ascended into the heavens.'

Barnabas 15:8–9

And in the words of St Augustine:

'When the Lord rose from the dead, he put off the mortality of the flesh; his risen body was still the same body, but it was no longer subject to death. By his resurrection he consecrated Sunday, or the Lord's day. Though the third after his passion, this day is the eighth after the Sabbath, and thus also the first day of the week.'

Sermo 8 in octava Paschae 1, 4; PL 46, 838.841

This eighth day was also associated with the eighth sphere of the fixed stars by some of the Platonist Christians of the early church such as Clement of Alexandria, as described in his description of Plato's *Myth of Er*.

'And the Lord's day Plato prophetically speaks of in the tenth book of the Republic in these words: "And when seven days have passed to each of them in the meadow, on the eighth they are to set out and arrive in four days." By the meadow is to be understood the fixed sphere, as being a mild and genial spot, and the locality of the pious; and by the seven days each motion of the seven planets, and the whole practical art which speeds to the end of rest. But after the wandering orbs the journey leads to heaven, that is, to the eighth motion and day.

The Stromata, Book 5, 14; Book 4, 25: Book 6, 6

So the ascent from Palm Sunday – or day 1 – at the west door of Wells Cathedral to Easter Sunday – day 8 – in the Lady chapel could also be symbolically understood as an ascent through the "seven planetary spheres of Holy Week" to "the eighth sphere of Easter Sunday" and thus Resurrection into eternity in the form of.....

"the one Morning Star who never sets, Christ your Son, who, coming back from death's domain, has shed his peaceful light on humanity, and lives and reigns for ever and ever". (The Exsultet)

Where is the north? One striking difference from a modern-day Freemason lodge room

Great is the Lord, and greatly to be praised in the city of our God, in the mountain of his holiness.

Beautiful for situation, the joy of the whole earth, is mount Zion, on the sides of the north, the city of the great King.

Psalm 48:1-2

BEARING IN MIND the very great similarity between the design of Wells Cathedral and a modern-day Freemason lodge room, it is interesting to note that there is also one quite pronounced difference between them. The difference in question is 'the north'.

In the design of Wells Cathedral its north side is very significant indeed, with its use of the Earth-Moon pyramid diagram along with its very grand octagonal chapter house, with undercroft below, that appear to symbolise both the Moon and the eighth heaven. However, within the symbolism and ritual of a Masonic lodge the 'dark' north is rejected through being associated with the darkness of ignorance as opposed to the solarity of illumination, associated with the eastern and southern sides of the lodge room. So for instance the northeast corner of the lodge room, as already mentioned, is the area used for initiation into the First Degree. This is partly symbolised by the initiate's move from the dark northern side of the room, where all new incomers first sit, towards the illumination of the east – the place of the rising Sun. In such a symbolic schema there doesn't appear to be the positive association with darkness, such as with Wisdom, which is seemingly characterised by the north side of the design at Wells. Here the ascent northwards – through the planetary spheres, as it were – leads to Wisdom in the eighth heaven of the fixed stars, which themselves circulate anticlockwise around the Celestial North Pole, or 'Stella Maris'.

The positive association of darkness with Wisdom can be seen in the symbolism of the wise nocturnal owl – the bird of Minerva/Athena, Goddess of Wisdom.[8] The owl flies around in the darkness of the night where the Wisdom is to be found in the dark hidden places. Its nocturnal vision enables it to see what is hidden in the darkness.

The Platonist mysticism that characterised medieval Christianity spoke of this darkness as the 'unknowing knowing' of God. One expression of this, from Meister Eckhart, suggests that *'To know God really is to know Him as unknowable.'*

In his *De Adhaerendo Deo* Albertus Magnus describes it in the following way:

'When St. John says that God is a Spirit and that He must be worshipped in spirit, he means that the mind must be cleared of images. When thou prayest, shut thy door – that is, the door of thy senses. Keep them barred and bolted against all phantasies and images. Nothing pleases God more than a mind free from all occupations and distractions. Such a mind is in a manner transformed into God, for it can think of nothing, and love nothing, except God; other creatures and itself it only sees in God. He who penetrates into himself, and so transcends himself, ascends truly to God. He whom I love and desire is above all that is sensible, and all that is intelligible; sense and imagination cannot bring us to Him, but only the desire of a pure heart; This brings us into the darkness of the mind, whereby we can ascend to the contemplation even of the mystery of the Trinity.'

The anonymous author of *The Cloud of Unknowing* uses a description of darkness in a similar way:

'And therefore shape thee to bide in this darkness as long as thou mayest, evermore crying after Him that thou lovest. For if ever thou shalt feel Him or see Him, as it may be here, it behoveth always to be in this cloud in this darkness.'

---

8. Bernard Silvestris mentions Minerva in his *Cosmographia* in relation to the character Noys (Nous).

Nicholas of Cusa is even more direct in his description of that which is ultimately beyond all description:

'... *He who is worshipped as Light Inaccessible, is not light that is material, the opposite of which is darkness, but light absolutely simple and infinite in which darkness is infinite light.*'

Nicholas points out the need for *apophatic* 'negative' theology – the 'theology of night-time' to act as a counter-balance for the *cataphatic* or affirmative 'theology of daytime':

'*Negative theology ... is so indispensable to affirmative theology that without it God would be adored, not as the Infinite but rather as a creature, which is idolatry, or giving to an image what is due to Truth alone.*' 9

Returning to the design of Wells Cathedral, another potential association of Wisdom with the 'dark' north side of the building could be said to occur if one is facing eastwards towards the sunrise. In such an instance the left side is to the north, and this naturally also associates Wisdom with the north in the sense of Mother Sophia – who is in the Ogdoad, beyond the seven planetary spheres – being the *Aristera* (the left-handed). This brings to mind the two left-handed dragon slayers on the chapter house staircase on the north side of Wells Cathedral.

But there is also the descent into the darkness of the underworld, as enacted by Christ in his Harrowing of Hell, which is an essential opening stage of the initiatic path. This necessary albeit 'harrowing' stage is associated with a deathly darkness and will be considered in the next chapter.

The Freemasonry of the modern age very much associates itself with the culture of the Enlightenment, and this may help to explain the difference of northern emphasis between the medieval design of Wells Cathedral and the post-Enlightenment understanding of a Freemason lodge room. There was a radical shift within the European soul in the age of the Enlightenment in which, symbolically speaking, there was a clear movement in the direction of the solarity of daytime along with an equivalent movement away from the lunality of night-time. It could be suggested that this has helped to bring about a departure from the middle path that passes between the Sun and the Moon.

Rather than having a positive and a negative symbolism associated with both light and dark, and their relationship with one another, there appears to have developed an unhealthy polarisation in which light symbolises 'good' and dark symbolises 'bad'. This is very much apparent in Mozart's famously Freemasonic opera *The Magic Flute*, in which the 'baddie' is the Queen of the Night – (although she does have the best aria!). The queen is also attended to by a 'lunar threeness' of ladies. It is apparent that this operatic depiction of 'negative' darkness is 'female', and indeed by analogy the feminine archetype could also be said to be associated with the divine darkness of the soul's hidden inner world. This is the feminine *Shekinah* that resides in the darkness of the Holy of Holies in both the Tabernacle and the Temple of Solomon. It is this essential 'inward region' that the so-called Enlightenment appears to have turned its back upon. The social emancipation of women in the 'outer' world may have been encouraged by Enlightenment thinkers, but the feminine archetype – within the soul of every female and male human – has come to be associated with that which is illusory and irrational.

The demonisation of darkness would also seem apparent within the very term 'Enlightenment', in the sense that the Enlightenment was viewed as a glorious move out of the superstitions of the so-called 'Dark Ages', with a progression onwards into the illumination of clear, 'enlightened' rational thought. Symbolically speaking, this modern divergence has ended up placing an

9. Another specifically appropriate example here is Gregory of Nyssa's *Life of Moses* in which he describes Moses' entry into a dark cloud on Mount Sinai. In 16.3 it was described how the pyramid triangle on the north side of Wells can be looked upon as Mount Sinai and the Quire as the Tabernacle. In book 1:46 Gregory writes "... *he boldly approached the very darkness itself and entered the invisible things where he was no longer seen by those watching...he was in company with the Invisible...the one who is going to associate intimately with God must go beyond all that is visible and (lifting up his own mind, as to a mountaintop, to the invisible and incomprehensible)*"

unfortunate emphasis only on that which is empirically seen by the fleshly eye in the light of daytime, while turning its back on the Wisdom that is inwardly known by the soul within the darkness of the night. This is certainly not to say that the symbolism in which 'light overcomes darkness' cannot also be a healthy spiritual symbol. Darkness has both a positive and a negative symbolism in the sense of its relating to an unmanifest or hidden essence, as well as to a more worldly 'absence of the Good'. But without a positive association of any sort with darkness, and an over-emphasis upon the 'goodness' of light, there is the loss of an essential and harmonious counterpoint that is necessary for the orientation of the soul in its attempt to find the middle path of balance between the Sun and the Moon, summer and winter solstices, and commensurable and incommensurable numbers. The loss of this counterpoint has been much to the detriment of our spiritual life in the modern Western world in which, for many, there is currently a hopelessly thick and opaque veil suspended between Heaven and Earth. Indeed many are not even aware of this veil and believe – with a great 'religious' zeal, no less – that there is nothing beyond what can be materially seen with 'earthly' eyes in the light of the daytime. The imaginal world of dreams is now only for those who are asleep, whereas the suggested glory is in waking up 'in a city that never sleeps'.

It is on the threshold between the two states of light and dark that the middle path resides. In terms of cosmological symbolism the short periods of time within the daily cycle in which the Morning and Evening Star can be seen are the threshold times between the night and the day, and the day and the night. It is in the morning period of this time when Plato's Nocturnal Council would meet as described in the *Laws* dialogue. This threshold between light and dark is also the Way of the Cross, as depicted within the medieval images of the Crucifixion of Christ where the Sun is on one side and the Moon is on the other. It is also reflected in the calendrical fact that the feast of Christ's Resurrection is calculated both in relation to the Sun and to

Light and Dark - Stone-carved face on the north side of the chapter house

the Moon. But a worrying fact is that the unhealthy over-emphasis on solarity appears also to have reached the centre of modern-day Christianity, in which there is currently talk of fixing the feast of Easter within the solar calendar whereby it would be on the same date every year.

There is an urgent need in the current time to re-establish the middle path of balance between the soul's inner and outer worlds. Such a mean between extremes always has been, and always will be, the only sustainable way that leads to Truth, Beauty and Goodness – or indeed Faith, Hope and Love – and thus to a true nobility of the soul. The etymology of the word 'noble' is 'to be well known', and if the soul is to regain its nobility it needs to know itself as it is also known.[10] It is within this harmonious inversion of relationship – whereby the solar and lunar faces gaze Knowingly and Lovingly upon one another – that the middle path of initiation is to be found.

10. See 1 Corinthians 13:12.

BOETHIUS

'Hold to the middle way with unshakeable strength. Whatever falls short
or goes beyond, despises happiness but receives no reward for its toil.'

RUMI

'The middle path is the way to wisdom'

GAUTAMA BUDDHA

'Avoiding both these extremes, the Tathagata
(the Perfect one) has realized the Middle Path'

MAIMONIDES

'The right way is the mean in each group of dispositions common
to humanity; namely, that disposition which is equally distant from
the two extremes in its class, not being nearer to the one than to the other.'

PHILOLAUS THE PYTHAGOREAN

'Nature in the world-order was fitted together out of things which are unlimited and
out of things which are limiting, both the world-order as a whole and everything in it.'

CHAPTER 19.

The Middle Path of Initiation

19.1 THE MIDDLE PATH -
A LINEAR EXPRESSION OF CENTRALITY

'... give me neither poverty nor wealth. Feed me with food that I need for today.'

Proverbs 30:8

ONE OF THE MOST fundamental and universal principles found within religious and philosophical ideas the world over is something that could be described as the 'middle way' or 'the ideal mean between extremes'. It is the middle path of Buddhism, the Doctrine of the Mean in Confucianism, the central column of the Kabbalistic Sephirothic tree, as well as the moderate behaviour that characterises the virtuous person according to Aristotle in his *Nicomachean Ethics*. It is the double-edged sword in the Sikh Khanda symbol as well as the Koran's description in the *verse of light* of the olive tree that is neither of the east nor the west. It is also the flight path between the moisture of the sea and the heat of the Sun that was suggested to Icarus by his father Daedalus – which Icarus ignored to his peril. It is the strait gate and narrow way described in the Gospels as well as the third bowl of porridge sampled by Goldilocks that was neither too hot nor too cold. It is also the centre ground on which democratic elections are generally won – albeit only in times of societal comfort and stability, when extremist demagogues are duly ignored.

It is the pathway that opened up to Moses and the Hebrews with the parting of the Red Sea. It is also the third invisible face of the two-faced Janus – his two visible faces looking into the past and the future, and his invisible third face gazing at us in the eternal present. Similarly, it is Shiva's invisible third eye of spiritual perception located above and between his visible right and left eyes which jointly observe the duality of the material world along with the passing of worldly time.

It is the habitable zone within the solar system in which Planet Earth is situated, where life becomes possible.

In terms of Earth's climate it is the temperate zones, one in the northern hemisphere and one in the southern, within which the weather is neither too torrid nor too frigid. In terms of daylight it is the equinoxes in the months of March and September when the Sun is above and below the horizon for equal periods of time, as opposed to the solstices in the cold darkness of midwinter and the warm lightness of midsummer when light and dark are at their greatest disparity.

It is the 'peace-making' central point of a circle, forever equidistant from all diametrically opposed perspectives on the circumference. It is also the middle place between the 'heavenly' compasses and 'earthly' set-square in the renowned Chinese and Freemasonic symbolism concerning the tools of the craft. It is the Vesica Pisces of geometric symbolism as well as the hexagon that results from the overlap of the two opposing triangles in the Star of David. It is the perfect circle that results from the marriage of yin and yang. It is also the radius that flows between the circle's hidden central point and its circumference, which bounds the visible body of the circle. It is of course also the geometer who creates the geometric artform by jointly utilising – and thus uniting – the 'heavenly' compasses with the 'earthly' set-square. In doing so the geometer maieutically facilitates the birth of the 'hidden' eternal form of number into its 'revealed' geometric state.

It was the stick used by Hermes to separate and then reconcile two battling serpents. The serpents eventually coiled together around the stick to become Hermes' caduceus staff. Within Kundalini it is the Sushumna between the two coiled serpents Ida and Pingala. These two serpents are symbolically associated with the Sun and the Moon, and indeed there are various other vertically orientated forms that are depicted between the Sun and the Moon such as the meditating Buddha and the crucified Christ – who is himself also situated between the crosses of the opposing penitent and impenitent thieves. Another dual unity which runs between the Sun and Moon is the ancient Chinese image of Fu Xi and Nu Wa with their half-human and half-serpent bodies. Their serpentine lower halves wrap around one another, resembling the DNA spiral of life – as well as also resembling the inter-coiled serpentine relationship embodied by the caduceus and Kundalini serpents. Nu Wa is generally depicted holding the compasses while Fu Xi holds the set-square.

The pathways of the Sun and Moon during day and night-time actually mirror one another inversely throughout the year as we witness their movements from our Earth-bound perspective. In the winter the Moon takes a higher path through the sky while the Sun takes a lower path. In the summer, vice versa. They follow the same path as one another around the time of the equinoxes – another example of the ideal mean.

The middle path of unity between the duality of Sun and Moon is also suggested within the 41st Surah of the Koran:

'Do not prostrate to the sun and not to the moon, but prostrate to Allah the One Who created them, if you, Him alone, worship.'

It is similarly suggested within the last few paragraphs of the Bible in the description of the Heavenly Jerusalem:

'And the city hath no need of the sun, neither of the moon, to shine upon it: for the glory of God did lighten it, and the lamp thereof is the Lamb.'

The Sun and the Moon are also 'fire and water' (i.e. daylight and tidal motion), although these two elements of fire and water are symbolically reflected as polar opposites in many different storylines within various different traditions.

In mathematics the ideal mean between extremes presents itself as various numerical means located between numerical extremes. Such arithmetically definable means are often associated with Pythagoras. The three classical Pythagorean means are the arithmetic mean, the geometric mean and the harmonic mean. But there are many other mathematical means beyond these three, and together they can be seen as a variety of mathematical ways in which this philosophical principle of the 'ideal balance' can be mathematically expressed. There is even the 'off-centre' golden mean, which reflects the same relationship between its smaller and larger parts as between its larger part to the whole.

In Freemasonry the ideal mean is suggested by the relationship between the two pillars Jachin and Boaz. In Masonic symbolism these two pillars represent various polarities such as the Sun and Moon, Heaven and Earth, and the winter and summer solstices. The ideal mean also features as the day of the equinox around which Hiram Abiff is murdered in the Temple of Solomon – i.e. the day on which there is a balance between the light and the dark of the two solstices. It is also midday – the time of day when Hiram's murder takes place when the Sun is at the midpoint of Heaven, neither ascending nor descending. It is also the third and final blow to Hiram Abiff's head that knocks him dead – the first blow is on his right temple and takes place at the dark northern door, the second is on his left temple and takes place at the sunny southern door. The third is then between his temples directly in the middle of his brow after he has staggered to the eastern door. This is the 'equinoctial' door through which the gentle rays of the Bright Morning Star will shine as Hiram resurrects from his grave. Finally, in relation to Masonic initiation the ideal mean is the middle east–west axis of the lodge room, on which the initiation into the Third Degree takes place. (Initiation into the First Degree takes place in the lodge room's northeast corner, and into the Second Degree in the southeast corner.)

As already mentioned, there are various visual Christian examples of this principle, such as the crucifixion image that depicts the Sun on one side and the Moon on the other, as well as the flanking of the crucified Christ by the penitent and impenitent thieves. But there is also the allegorical understanding of Christ's life and Passion as the period that defines the crossing over from the old covenant to the new. Medieval cathedral designs often display Old Testament iconography on one side of the cathedral with New Testament iconography on the other. The central axis of the cathedral – where these two sides meet – thus marks the eastward movement towards the 'Resurrection' of Christ as the Bright Morning Star, which itself heralds the coming of the illumination of the rising Sun – a cosmological image of Christ, the 'Risen Son'. From a Christian perspective Christ is that 'central' or 'mean' figure in whom everything and everyone meets ...

'For where two or three are gathered together in my name, there am I in the midst of them.'

Matthew 18:20

Another particularly overt Christian example of this middle way can be seen in the Ghent altarpiece in which God the Father, the dove of the Holy Spirit and the Lamb of God all hold the middle position on the upper and lower registers (or levels) of the painted altarpiece. On either side of the lower register there are then groups of people who symbolise various dualities who could be said to meet in Christ. Male martyrs on one side and female martyrs on the other; pre-Christian Jews and pagan philosophers to the left, Christian church figures to the right; establishment figures such as knights and judges on the wing panels to the left, non-establishment figures such as ascetics and pilgrims on the wing panels to the right. In the upper register on the far left and the far right are depictions of Adam (left) and Eve (right). But interestingly, despite being the farthest removed from the centre of the altarpiece when it is opened out, they become united when the altarpiece is closed, and they are also folded directly over the image of God the Father.

So with all of this in mind, it is perhaps of little surprise that the use of means and the 'middle path' is 'central'

to the geometric design of a cathedral such as the one at Wells. The just-ness of the means accordingly informs and embodies the just-ness of this place of worship which, like all places of religious worship, could be described as a meeting place between the 'above' and the 'below' – or the inner and outer worlds – thus embodying an architectural mean or bridge between these two 'regions'.

The ideal mean between extremes could be described as a single idea that becomes embodied or enacted in a host of different ways. The above (long) list of examples may lack moderation in its overly extended length, but this is intended to counter our regular forgetfulness of such principles thus aiding a return to the middle place of remembrance.

The opposite of *re*membering is *dis*membering, and so to *re*member is to re-establish the bridge between the two worlds that have become divided – the world of Spirit and the world of Matter. Henceforth this bridge of remembrance can be looked upon as another example of the ideal mean.

The word *symbol* means to 'throw together', and the opposite of *symbolic* is *diabolic*, which means 'to throw apart'. Symbolism is accordingly another example of the mean in the way it acts as a vehicle by which there can be remembrance of that which has been forgotten.

Finally, the word *religion* means 'to re-bind' – in the sense of re-binding that which has become separated. The *lig* in the word 'religion' is etymologically connected to the word *ligament* – the tissue that joins two bones together. So religion (when practised in moderation) is a 'middle place' in which all can meet – and where remembrance is aided via the re-unifying qualities of symbolism.

19.2 THE MORNING STAR -
BOTH RISEN CHRIST AND FALLEN ANGEL

THE PLANET VENUS, in the form of the Morning Star, is a cosmological symbol in relation to more than one Christian identity. The Risen Christ and the Virgin Mary are two such identities, but so also is John the Baptist. In their own particular ways the Virgin and the Baptist are both seen as heralds of the rising Sun because the rising of the Morning Star immediately precedes the rising of the Sun, which is itself an image of Christ the Risen Son. But Christ is also the Bright Morning Star which symbolically reflects the pre-Christian storyline of Inanna, in which she descends into the underworld – an event that is cosmologically symbolised by the Planet Venus setting below the western horizon as the Evening Star. The story then resolves with a re-ascension out of the underworld, which is symbolised by the rising of the Morning Star in the east. However, within medieval Christian cosmythology there is yet another figure associated with the Morning Star, and that is Lucifer – the Fallen Angel. The name Lucifer is the Roman name for the Morning Star, and it means Light Bearer or Light Bringer because, again, the Morning Star is the herald of the rising Sun and accordingly symbolises the emergence of light. However, the Christian story of Lucifer that developed in the Middle Ages is in many ways the opposite pole to the one of Christ 'the Bright Morning Star' because it begins with the rising of the Morning Star but could then be said to end with the setting of the Evening Star. What's more, the supposed glory suggested by the rising of Lucifer as the 'son of the morning' is associated with his expanding ego and rising hubris rather than a glorious return of the soul to its heavenly origin above, after a harrowing traversal of the underworld.

In chapter 14 of the Book of Isaiah there is a description of Lucifer's rise and fall. It is actually Isaiah's description of the King of Babylon, whose rising hubris causes him to fall down into Sheol, or the deathly underworld. This description accords with the rising and setting symbolism associated with the Morning and Evening Star, despite the fact that the medieval Christian character known as Lucifer – the Fallen Angel – only came to be named after the star of the morning. But Isaiah chides the King of Babylon via a Venusian cosmological symbolism that to some degree resembles the rise-and-fall motif later used by Boethius in relation to the Wheel of Fortune:

'How you are fallen from heaven,
O Lucifer, son of the morning!
How you are cut down to the ground,
You who weakened the nations!
For you have said in your heart:
"I will ascend into heaven,
I will exalt my throne above the stars of God;
I will also sit on the mount of the congregation
On the farthest sides of the north;
I will ascend above the heights of the clouds,
I will be like the Most High."
Yet you shall be brought down to Sheol,
To the lowest depths of the Pit.[1]

So in the medieval Christian myth that arose from what essentially was Isaiah's description of the King of Babylon, the rising of the angel 'Lucifer' as the Morning Star, is an angel's pride-filled attempt to raise his egoic self to the level of deity, only to be struck down by

---

1. The Tower of Babel is another Old Testament example of a hubristic attempt on the part of the human ego to raise itself to the heavens. Again the result is a 'falling down', and in terms of spoken language the collapse of the tower results in a descent from the One (i.e. one language) 'down' into the many (languages) – but worse still a discordant 'many-ness' in which the many nations can no longer communicate with one another. It is like the many organs of the human body no longer working together as one. See 1 Corinthians 12.

God into the deathly underworld of Sheol. It is this fall from Heaven and descent into the underworld by which he then becomes the 'Fallen Angel'.[2]

St Bernard of Clairvaux is again the 12th-century figure to whom we turn in relation to this story of self-destructive pride, as described in one of his sermons:

'Lucifer, who rose brightly as the morning star, because he attempted to usurp a similitude with the Most High, and "it was thought robbery in him to equal himself with God" and equality which was the Son's by right, was cast down from heaven and ruined; for the Father was zealous for the glory of the Son, and seemed by this act to say: "Vengeance is mine, I will repay." And instantly "I saw Satan as lightning falling from heaven." Dust and ashes, why art thou proud? If God spared not pride in His angels, how much less will He tolerate it in thee ... ? ... Fly pride my brethren, I most earnestly beseech you. "Pride is the beginning of all sin," and how quickly did it darken and overshadow with eternal obscurity Lucifer, the most bright and beautiful of the heavenly spirits, and, from not only an angel, but the first of angels, transform him into a hideous devil!' [3]

St Bernard of Clairvaix

There are a few other biblical descriptions that helped to form the story of Lucifer. One of them is the War in Heaven in chapter 12 of the Book of Revelation, which will be looked at a little later on. Another one is in the Book of Ezekiel and concerns the King of Tyre. This story bears a clear resemblance to Isaiah's description of the King of Babylon, along with the hubris that arises from the possession of worldly power and which eventually leads to a downfall.

'... Say to the ruler of Tyre, "This is what the Sovereign LORD says: In the pride of your heart you say",
"I am a god; I sit on the throne of a god in the heart of the seas."
"But you are a mere mortal and not a god, though you think you are as wise as a god ..."
... Therefore this is what the Sovereign Lord says:

"Because you think you are wise, as wise as a god, I am going to bring foreigners against you, the most ruthless of nations; they will draw their swords against your beauty and wisdom and pierce your shining splendour. They will bring you down to the pit ... You were the seal of perfection, full of wisdom and perfect in beauty. You were in Eden, the garden of God; every precious stone adorned you: carnelian, chrysolite and emerald, topaz, onyx and jasper, lapis lazuli, turquoise and beryl. Your settings and mountings were made of gold; on the day you were created they were prepared. You were anointed as a guardian cherub, for so I ordained you. You were on the holy mount of God; you walked among the fiery stones. You were blameless in your ways from the day you were created till wickedness was found in you. Through your widespread trade you were filled with violence, and you sinned. So I drove you in disgrace from the mount of God, and I expelled you, guardian cherub, from among the fiery stones. Your heart became proud on account of your beauty, and you corrupted your wisdom because of your splendour. So I threw you to the earth."'

Ezekiel's description of the precious stones that adorned the King of Tyre appears to be connected to one of the medieval descriptions of Lucifer's appearance. It specifically concerns a gem in Lucifer's crown. In the Grail storyline called Wartburgkrieg it is said that Lucifer originally had an emerald set in his crown that he went

2. The *Jewish Encyclopedia* from 1906 makes the following observation: 'The brilliancy of the morning star, which eclipses all other stars, but is not seen during the night, may easily have given rise to a myth such as was told of Ethana and Zu: he was led by his pride to strive for the highest seat among the star-gods on the northern mountain of the gods (comp. Ezek. xxviii. 14; Ps. xlviii. 3 [A.V. 2]) but was hurled down by the supreme ruler of the Babylonian Olympus. Stars were regarded throughout antiquity as living celestial beings (Job xxxviii. 7).' www.jewishencyclopedia.com/articles/10177-lucifer
The story of Lucifer's pride also bears a certain resemblance to a Jewish story about the angel's adverse reaction to the creation of Adam, which is recounted at the beginning of volume 2 in *Legends of the Jews*. An Islamic equivalent is the story of Iblis, and this one is even more similar to the story of Lucifer in that it focuses on a single angelic entity who falls as a result of his pride.
3. 'Sermon on the Advent of our Lord and its Six Circumstances', from Sermons of Saint Bernard on Advent and Christmas

on to lose as a result of his fall. The 20th-century symbolist René Guénon suggests that the emerald was on Lucifer's brow, and with the design of crowns in mind a singularly prominent gem within a crown is located on the 'brow' of the crown. This would particularly be the case with a diadem, an early form of crown which is essentially a headband. Lucifer's emerald symbolises his angelic capacity for spiritual vision – his 'sense of eternity'[4] – which he loses as a result of falling into Sheol. A story such as this would inevitably be associated with the story of the fall of humankind because Adam and Eve are also situated in Sheol until Christ frees them through his Harrowing of Hell. Wolfram Von Eschenbach makes this association in his Arthurian grail poem, *Parzival*:

> *'When Lucifer and his angels thus*
> *sped on their downward way,*
>
> *To fill their place, a wonder God*
> *wrought from the earth and clay:*
>
> *The son of His hands was Adam,*
> *and from flesh of Adam, Eve*
>
> *He brought, and for Eve's transgression,*
> *I ween, all the world doth grieve'*

However, the difference between the respective falls of the angel Lucifer and the humans Adam and Eve lies in the fact that Lucifer couldn't have fallen as a result of collapsing into any humanly physical senses but rather through collapsing into the lower reaches of the mind, which showed itself in the form of his pride. The descent of the emerald from the angelic level to the human level then presents itself in another part of the storyline whereby when it fell to Earth it landed in the Garden of Eden, and Adam accordingly possessed it before his own fall but was unable to take it with him when he had to leave Eden.[5]

This association of the brow – i.e. from where Lucifer's emerald fell – with a capacity for spiritual vision is also found in other religions such as Hinduism, Buddhism and Daoism in relation to the point on the head known as the 'third eye', or in Sanskrit the 'Ajna chakra'. Part of the symbolism of the third eye on the brow is similar to what was described in the previous section about the 'middle path' between extremes, and this is actually physically embodied through the idea of a third eye being 'above and between' the two visible human eyes. Whereas the two visible eyes observe the passing of time in the world of duality – in which there is both 'past and future' – the third eye has a 'higher view' that sees everything all at once in the eternal present.[6] Returning to Christianity, this is effectively the same capacity of vision described by Boethius in relation to the Eye of Providence – albeit without using the anthropomorphic description of the two human eyes plus an invisible third eye on the brow. But such a physical description does reflect three of the five east end chapels at Wells Cathedral that were described earlier, whereby the two 'solstitial' chapels – of the Baptist and Stephen – bring about a termination of the side aisles whereas the middle path between them leads onwards to the Lady chapel which, like the third eye, is 'above and between' the two solstitial chapels. So to take the middle path between these two 'polar' chapels could be said to restore the spiritual vision of humanity through the Resurrection of Christ, who rises in the east as the Bright Morning Star after his journey through the heart of the Earth.

As mentioned earlier, this middle path is also reflected in Freemason ritual such as with the three locations of the lodge room in which the three degrees of initiation take place – first the northeast corner, then the southeast corner and finally the middle east–west axis that runs between the two eastern corners. The symbolism is also present within the death of Hiram Abiff who is first hit on one side of his head at one of the side doors of the Temple of Solomon, then on the other side of

4. See René Guénon, 'The Sacred Heart and the Legend of the Holy Grail' in *Symbols of Sacred Science*, Sophia Perennis, 2004, page 13 and/or 'The Symbolism of the Grail' in *The King of the World*, Sophia Perennis, 2004, page 28.
5. Ibid.
6. See René Guénon's *Man and His Becoming According to the Vedanta*, chapter 20.

his head at the other side door on the opposite side of the temple, and finally at the front door of the temple in the east, which also runs along the middle east–west axis of the building where he is dealt the final deathly blow to the middle of his brow. As will shortly become clear, this perception of Lucifer and the lost emerald from his brow appears to actually be depicted at a symbolically appropriate location within the nave of Wells Cathedral.

As to the 'lowest depths of the pit' to which Lucifer condemned himself, Sheol is the same deathly underworld to which Christ descends in his Harrowing of Hell. It is also the description that Jonah uses for the inside of the whale, as if it were death itself that had swallowed him up. It was mentioned in section 5.5 that within the stories of Inanna, Jonah and Christ the descent into the underworld is associated with a judgement or condemnation that has led to a deathly state in the deep. But whereas Inanna re-ascends, Jonah is vomited up by the whale and Adam and Eve are freed from Sheol by Christ, Lucifer's condemned state has him remain forever down in the pit, for he is a personification of that which is farthest removed from God. It is perhaps unsurprising that Lucifer has become conflated with Satan in the sense that he is situated at the opposite cosmic pole from the divine realm. Having said this, based on the fact that Lucifer's fall is so closely associated with the fall of Adam and Eve, it would seem reasonable to mythologically extrapolate by suggesting that Christ's Harrowing of Hell also symbolically involves the returning of Lucifer's emerald to his brow, so that he himself can re-ascend out from the darkness into which he caused himself to fall. But such a pathway of return does actually appear to be suggested via the idea that the Holy Grail was carved out of the emerald that fell from Lucifer's crown. So by the very fall of Lucifer and his emerald there becomes the possibility of the soul's return via the Eucharistic mystery of Christ's death, descent and Resurrection. So in this sense, Lucifer's fall is counter-acted and resolved by Christ's descent and Resurrection in which – in the words of the Exsultet – 'Christ breaks the prison-bars of death and rises victorious from the underworld'.

Dante's *Commedia* describes Lucifer as being at the centre of the Earth, and this accords with Isaiah's description of Lucifer's fall to 'the lowest depths of the Pit'. Planet Earth's perceived central position in medieval cosmology meant that it was the furthest sphere removed from the divine realm (the Empyrean) which was out beyond all the planetary spheres as well as the fixed stars and the 'first moved' sphere. However, there is one other place even further removed from the divine realm than the surface of the spherical Earth, and that is the centre of the spherical Earth – and according to Dante this is the frozen deathly place to which Lucifer fell. Such cosmic opposition between the Empyrean and the centre of the Earth is also suggested by Dante's particular description of Lucifer as having three faces, which form an inverted image of the Trinity in that they inversely mirror Dante's geometric description of God's Trinitarian appearance in the Empyrean.[7]

So again the descent into Sheol presents the spectre of a journey of the soul in which it comes into a direct and conscious contact with the Luciferian hubristic lower reaches to which the soul has the capacity to fall. In the Judeo-Christian tradition Babylon is symbolically associated with the corruption of the earthly world in which the soul is in exile from its true heavenly home or 'inner state' (i.e. Jerusalem – the Promised Land). So in this sense the Fallen Angel can also be looked upon as the 'King of Babylon'. Lucifer's hubristic desire for divine glory, as described by Isaiah, results in a descent into the frozen darkness of Sheol. This is because the pride that attempts to elevate the ego to the position of God unwittingly descends into the underworld as a result of beginning its presumed ascent with an inverted

---

7. This Luciferian threeness at the centre of the 'circular/spherical' Earth numerically and visually resembles the Buddhist image of the circular Bhavachakra, at the centre of which are found the 'three roots of evil' that prevent liberation from Samsara. These three roots of evil are symbolically depicted in the form of a pig (ignorance), a serpent (hatred/anger) and a cock (attachment/greed).

view of things in which it puts ego above Spirit. So what is assumed to be an upward movement to glory is actually a descent into Sheol, because before any ascent can occur the soul is required to correctly orientate its vision. This reflects the fact that 'those who exalt themselves will be humbled, and those who humble themselves will be exalted' (Matthew 23:12). But such a re-orientation of the soul's vision can only be effected through first descending into the underworld and coming face to face with the voracious Minotaur that inhabits the soul's deeper recesses. Much like Lucifer, the Minotaur is a personification of the lower traces of the soul, because it was the disobedient pride of King Minos followed by the lustfulness of Queen Pasiphae that led to the Minotaur's conception in the first place. Therefore the Minotaur, much like Lucifer, is condemned to the underworld and the soul is thus required to go down and confront this potential darkness within itself before any ascent can begin.

So the soul's journey of return to its divine origin is one that necessarily begins with a descent into the underworld and a meeting within, followed by a passing beyond, of that which is farthest removed from God.

Dante's journey through Planet Earth forms a straight line from Jerusalem, on one side of the spherical Earth, to the opposite side where the Mountain of Purgatory is situated. But whereas the journey from Jerusalem to the centre of the Earth forms a descent, the journey beyond the centre of the Earth to the mountain of Purgatory on the other side is one of re-ascent. This is because of passing the centre of gravity at the centre of the Earth.[8] So the journey through the underworld helps to re-orientate the soul's vision from its downward focus to an upward focus in preparation for the ascent of the Mountain of Purgatory, followed by cosmic ascent through the planetary spheres to the Empyrean.

Much like Christ's paschal journey, Dante's journey through the underworld begins in Jerusalem on the afternoon of Good Friday and finishes on the morning of Easter Sunday. So the basic co-ordinates of this first part of Dante's journey clearly correspond to Christ's, and it therefore becomes possible to look at the ascent symbolism in the design of Wells Cathedral in relation to Dante's journey. Bearing in mind that the nave at Wells is an image of Planet Earth, it can be suggested that to walk through the nave is to walk 'through' Planet Earth from one side to the other.

This accords with Dante's description of his journey through the Inferno during which, like Christ, he passes through 'the heart of the Earth' (Matthew 12:40). For Dante this is a pivotal point of the storyline, where he stops descending into the Earth and begins to re-ascend back out. This vital transition is also marked by the fact that Lucifer is located at this point, and so to pass beyond the centre of the Earth – the furthest removed point from the divine realm – is to pass beyond the soul's Luciferian potential and begin looking onwards and upwards. In the nave at Wells this is expressed by a movement from the fifth bay to the sixth bay, as it is the midpoint of their dividing line that marks the central point of the nave's ten bays and accordingly the central point of the Earth.

There are marked changes in the passing from the fifth bay to the sixth bay. The carvings on the capitals of the bay pillars become noticeably more frequent, and indeed there begin to be stone carvings of small heads just above the springing points of the nave's arches, which begin from the bay pillars that divide the fifth bay from the sixth bay and carry on up through the rest of the bays moving eastwards. They are in opposite pairs looking directly forwards at one another between the north and south sides.

But perhaps most importantly there is a grand entrance on the north side of the nave which leads into the sixth bay and is traditionally where the canons of the cathedral enter the building. If there is any symbolism in

---

8. See section 49 of Questiones Naturales by Adelard of Bath for a 12th-century description of the centre of gravity at the centre of the Earth: 'Where, if the globe of earth were bored through, a rock thrown into the hole would end up.'

this it would appear to be suggesting that the religious clerics are beyond the centre of the Earth, because they have devoted their life to the risen and ascended Christ and are thus looking upwards and not downwards. This would also associate the canons' doorway with the upward slanting side of the small diagonal bar on the Orthodox cross of St Andrew that was mentioned in section 11.4. There is also a singing gallery up high in the sixth bay, unlike any other bay, and so again there is an emphasis upon 'looking up' within this particular bay that immediately follows the symbolic passing-of-the-centre-of-the-Earth. And there is yet another interesting feature of the sixth bay, although it is no longer possible to see it because of the unfortunate placement of the cathedral's organ in more recent centuries. What follows is a description, imagining that the organ is not there.9

When entering the cathedral at the western entrance the famous Scissor Arch, located at the cathedral's crossing, partially obscures the view of the Jesse window, which is far off above the eastern end of the quire. But as one walks further eastward through the nave, the window slowly becomes less obscured. It is then around the middle of the sixth bay – which coincides with the apex of the nave pyramid triangle – that the Jesse window becomes completely visible through being ideally framed by the Scissor Arch, The dove of the Holy Spirit, positioned at the very apex of the window, comes into view and this accordingly gives an unimpeded view of the heavenly world of golden light10 towards which the soul is now beginning to ascend.

But it is a small stone-carved head that is of particular interest in relation to this transitional point in the nave.

The head is at the top of a bay pillar that marks the-division between the fifth and sixth bay (image on following page). It is technically in the rectangle of the fifth bay, and is actually looking down into the fifth bay itself. So in this sense it is observing the final stages of the soul's descent to the centre of the Earth prior to the transitional crossing over into the sixth bay.

This stone-carved head is of a ghoulish-looking figure with pointy animal ears and a long goatee beard.

But it is the eye-shaped empty hole in the brow of his crown that is the most telling feature, suggesting this is Lucifer himself. Indeed, his crown of serpent-scales is not that dissimilar to the renowned 13th-century image of the devil that appears in the Codex Gigas. This crown of serpent scales also has the appearance of the hood of a rearing cobra, so that the eye-shaped brow hole looks like the cobra's open mouth. There is then a snake-like form running back over the centre of his scaly head.11

As the cathedral's east end Lady chapel appears to embody cosmological symbolism relating to the Risen Christ as the Bright Morning Star, it would naturally follow that Lucifer the Fallen Angel should also be present at the point that symbolises the centre of the Earth. His eventual fall to the lowest point of Sheol is an equivalent opposite of Christ's elevation to the highest point of Heaven. In other words, the angel's fall, as the Evening Star in the west, is subsequently resolved and reversed by Christ's descent into the underworld, followed by his rising and ascending as the Bright Morning Star in the east. More specif-

9. How great it would be if a benefactor paid for a new organ that could be located in a different position so that the view of the Jesse window from the nave could be restored to its original state. The window is effectively the view of heaven - or rather the ascent into heaven - as seen from the earth (i.e. the nave).
10. The Jesse window at Wells is known as the 'golden window' due to its colouring.
11. With the seemingly Egyptian pyramidal emphasis in the geometric design symbolism of Wells Cathedral, this image of Lucifer – minus his green emerald – as a rearing cobra brings to mind Wadjet – the 'Green One'. Wadjet is the Uraeus cobra that rears forth from the brow of the Pharaoh. Interestingly, Wadjet is sometimes associated with Hathor – the ancient Egyptian Venus. But a more obvious Egyptian equivalent to a serpentine Lucifer is the serpent deity Apep who, much like Lucifer, is imprisoned in the underworld and is associated with chaos through his opposition to light and Ma'at. He engages in battle every night with the sun God Re prior to Re's rising in the east.
The association of the cobra with the lowest point of an ascent that leads up towards the light also recalls the Kundalini cobra that is described as being coiled at the base of the spine until awoken and, as it were, 'lifted up [like] the serpent in the wilderness' (see John 3:13–15). Christ's allegorical use of this serpentine ascent symbolism in John, chapter 3 specifically relates to his Resurrection, which is also central to the culmination of the symbolic ascent in Wells Cathedral, in which it could be said that the serpent sheds its skin only so as to be reborn anew. So with the serpentine depiction of Lucifer in mind, such restitution of all of that which is fallen naturally speaks of apokatastasis.

Lucifer as depicted at the centre of the Wells nave i.e. the centre of the Earth. He wears a serpentine crown with a hole in his brow from where an emerald fell.

ically, Christ's descent and re-ascent could also be said to lead the way and beat the path for a similar journey on the part of every human soul. So accordingly, and to this day, Lucifer is still languishing in the depths - and forever will be - until the initiate actively chooses to go down to face him so as to pass beyond his potential.

As mentioned earlier, the brow is a significant point of the body within the understanding of various East/South Asian religions. There appears to be a fascinating correlation between the story of Lucifer's emerald and a Hindu character called Ashwatthama who loses a 'mani' (i.e. a gem) from his brow as a result of his uncontrolled rage that causes him to commit an atrocity. This results in him being given leprosy by Krishna, and then being condemned to wander through the forests in a perpetual state of physical suffering until he is finally freed from this immortal hardship with the coming of Kalki, who re-institutes the golden age or 'Satya Yuga'. Ashwatthama is often understood to resemble a medieval European character who is generally described as 'the Wandering Jew'. This Jewish character is said to have heckled Christ on the road to Golgotha, and as a result of this he was condemned to perpetually wander through[12] the world in a state of suffering until the return of the Messiah. Both Ashwatthama and the Wandering Jew are effectively immortal beings who are eternally experiencing some form of earthly suffering. But alleviation of the suffering eventually comes with the return of the Messianic age, which correlates

12. The Sanskrit word *samsara* also means 'to wander through'.

with the Satya Yuga in Hindu thought.[13] With the Wandering Jew in mind, the carved stone head of Lucifer at Wells does also appear to have a nose that resembles various of the antisemitic depictions of Jews that have existed in European culture for centuries until now. Lucifer himself is yet another character who could be described as in a state of eternal suffering at the lowest point of Sheol before the Messiah 'breaks the prison bars of death' through his Harrowing of Hell. Although it is actually with Christ's second coming that the suffering of the Wandering Jew comes to an end, and likewise in the rendition of Christ's Harrowing of Hell that appears in the Gospel of Nicodemus, it is also with Christ's second coming that Satan is to be dealt with:

'Then the King of glory seized the chief satrap[14] Satan by the head, and delivered him to His angels, and said: With iron chains bind his hands and his feet, and his neck, and his mouth. Then He delivered him to Hades, and said: Take him, and keep him secure till my second appearing.' [15]

Chapter 22

These themes of 'the Jew in a state of perpetual earthly suffering' and indeed 'the Jew in exile from the Promised Land while under the dominion of the "King of Babylon"' all naturally fit together within this apparent depiction of Lucifer the Fallen Angel who perpetually suffers within his imprisonment at the lowest point of Sheol.[16] But perhaps rather tellingly, it is the very demonisation itself of the 'Christ-killing Jew', particularly in more recent centuries, that was used to justify the descent of various sections of European Christian culture to the very lowest depths of the pit in the form of 'sub-human' behaviour towards European Jewry onto whom this very quality of 'sub-humanity' had been projected.

Returning to the nave at Wells, there is another small stone carving directly next to the stone-carved head of Lucifer, which appears again to accord with Lucifer's storyline as well as with the symbolism of transition from the fifth to the sixth bay. It straddles the rectangles in the ground plan that define the fifth and sixth bays, with one of its figures situated in the sixth bay and the other one in the fifth. The figure in the fifth bay is a dragon that is being lanced in the mouth with a 'Trinitarian' trident that is held by a flame-headed winged figure. The precise crossing point between the two bays is where the trident-holding hand of the flame-headed figure is located. His trident is entering the dragon's mouth as if the dragon is being forcibly confined within the fifth bay 'where it belongs', as it were. This fiery flame-headed winged

The War in Heaven depicted directly next to the image of Lucifer - "And the great dragon was cast out, that old serpent, called the Devil, and Satan".

13. The return of the Satya Yuga involves the descent of Vishnu from his celestial abode of Vaikuntha, similar to the descent of the New Jerusalem 'coming down out of heaven from God'. In chapter 7 of his book *Mirror of the Intellect* Titus Burckhardt points out the very great similarity between both the textual and pictorial descriptions of the Vaikuntha mandala and the Heavenly Jerusalem.

14. 'Satrap' is a Persian title for a governor of a particular geographical region; in this particular context the region is clearly Hades. Although in another sense Lucifer is the 'King of Babylon'.

15. This reflects chapter 20 verses 1–3 in Revelation, where Satan is bound for 1000 years.

16. Another interesting connection here is with the Greek character Prometheus, who is also condemned to a life of eternal suffering in which his liver is eaten every day by an eagle, after which it grows back again so it can be devoured yet again the following day. This carries on until he is eventually freed from his suffering by Hercules, who is associated with the re-instituting of the Golden Age in Italy. Prometheus is another character who has been associated with Lucifer in more recent times by the Jewish writer R.J. Zwi Werblowsky.

figure may in some way symbolise St Michael – the Archangel of Fire – who is associated with dragon slaying as well as with the dislodging of the emerald from Lucifer's crown when he fell.[17] These associations with St Michael derive from the description of the War in Heaven in Revelation chapter 12. Indeed, despite being situated at what is symbolically the 'lowest point' of the cathedral, the battle depicted in this stone carving could in some way represent the War in Heaven itself. This is yet another variant of the Lucifer storyline in which 'the dragon' or 'old serpent' is cast out of Heaven and down 'into the earth'. So with this stone-carved depiction of the battle with a dragon being directly next to the serpentine head of Lucifer, it appears to depict the happenings that eventually led to Lucifer's fall.

'And there was war in heaven: Michael and his angels fought against the dragon; and the dragon fought and his angels,

And prevailed not; neither was their place found any more in heaven.

And the great dragon was cast out, that old serpent, called the Devil, and Satan, which deceiveth the whole world: he was cast out into the earth, and his angels were cast out with him.'

Revelation 12:7–9

The angels that were cast out of Heaven along with Satan also seem to be depicted on the same pillar capital, albeit on the diametrically opposite side from the stone-carved head of Lucifer. They have serpentine bodies and the same pointy animal ears and unhappy-looking faces as Lucifer.

These three carvings of Lucifer, the battle with the dragon and the fallen angels, are the only three carvings on the whole of this pillar capital. The pillar itself is also one of the two pillars that is the closest to the centre of the nave – and thus, symbolically, to the centre of the Earth.

The angels that fell with Lucifer - depicted on the Lucifer pillar capital

Returning to the stone heads that were mentioned earlier as being just above the springing points of the nave arches, they also seem to feature directly in the symbolism of these Luciferian carvings. These heads begin from the springing points of the arches on the pillars that divide the fifth bay from the sixth bay and are then located above all the other bay pillars beyond the sixth bay, moving eastwards. They are also on both the north and south pillars of the nave, so they end up in opposite pairs gazing 'face to face' at one another. The only one of them that is not looking directly towards the equivalent head on the opposite side is the one directly above the Luciferian carvings. This particular head is looking to its right, and thus more eastward. It is looking away from the fifth bay as well as also looking upwards, as if to emphasise the new orientation that this part of the cathedral symbolises. As shown in the following photo this head is also looking very much away from the head of Lucifer, who is below and to his left.

There is yet another carving on a pillar capital that looks likely to be a part of this Luciferian symbolism.

---

17. St Michael is also central to the Jewish story mentioned in footnote 2 from *The Legends of the Jews*.

Lucifer on the right, the War in Heaven in the centre and a stone head directly above which is looking upwards and eastwards - i.e. away from Lucifer.

Three carved stone heads looking in different directions. A demonic grimace looks westwards, a benign animal neither east nor westwards. The human looks eastwards.

It also happens to be just one bay further east of the Luciferian carvings, and appears to be acting as a reminder of the choices available to the soul who has just walked beyond the Luciferic centre of the Earth.

These capital carvings are on the north side of the nave, as opposed to the south side on which the Luciferian carvings are based. They consist of three carved stone heads that are all looking in different directions from one another. One is looking more westwards, and thus backwards toward Lucifer at the centre of the nave. This face has a demonic grimace similar to that of Lucifer, and it is rather like an animalised image of a human face. The middle head is looking directly out in neither an easterly nor a westerly direction. This head is of an animal, if rather a benign-looking one. The final face is looking in a more easterly direction and depicts a human.

It is unclear whether these faces are connected to the Luciferian carvings, although they do appear to accord with the associated symbolism in such a way as to remind the soul who has passed the middle of the nave that to 'look back' is effectively to look back 'downwards' now that the ascent out of Earth has begun.[18] This would seem to apply to the westerly-looking face. As for the benign animal who is looking neither to the east nor the west, could this be the soul whose eastern ascent has ground to a halt and will thus not be fully restored as a result of having become stuck? It is only through the continuation of the eastward ascent – the visual orientation of the third 'human' face – that the soul can have any hope of returning to Eden in the far east of the cathedral in the form of the Lady chapel. For it is this chapel, with its associated symbolism of the Bright Morning Star, the rose of divine love and eternal spring, that is the culmination of the equinoctial path.

Finally, bearing in mind that all of this apparent symbolism appears to be based around the idea that the nave at Wells Cathedral is an image of the Earth, and that the centre of the Earth is the place where the soul meets face-to-face with a personification of its lowest traces, there is an interesting correspondence in relation to the French Gothic cathedrals and their famous labyrinths, which are also situated around the centres of their naves. Some of these labyrinths appear to have been directly associated with the ancient Greek Minotaur myth, much like the Roman mosaic labyrinths that usually contained some sort of a depiction of the Minotaur storyline at their centre. The labyrinths at Amiens and Chartres, for instance, are both described in medieval documents as the *House of Daedalus,* and the Chartres labyrinth is also specifically described as having a metal plate at the centre of it bearing an image of the combat that took place between Theseus and the Minotaur in Daedalus' labyrinth.

The particular type of pathway used in both the circular labyrinth at Chartres as well as the octagonal one at Amiens is the same as the one that was used within a small 12th–13th-century circular 'finger labyrinth' that is on the right pier of the portico outside the west front of St Martin's Cathedral in Lucca, Italy.[19] It appears possibly to pre-date the French Gothic nave labyrinths and could thus be considered a kind of prototype of this specific kind of pathway being used for an 'in-situ' ecclesiastical labyrinth.[20] But its connection to the Minotaur storyline is indisputable, as can be understood from the original Latin inscription directly to the right of the labyrinth:

'Hic quem creticus edit. Daedalus est laberinthus. De quo nullus vadere. Quivit qui fuit intus. Ni Theseus gratis Adriane. Stamine jutus.'

18. This idea of 'not looking back' features in various biblical and classical storylines, such as those of Lot escaping Sodom and Gomorrah and Orpheus leading Eurydice out of hell. But of particular interest here is its use by Dante in his *Commedia* as he enters through the gateway of Purgatory itself and is warned not to look back. See *Purgatorio,* Canto 9, verses 130–132.
19. Bearing in mind the 'martial' etymology of the name Martin (quite literally) and the fact that St Martin was famously a soldier who rejected the army to become a 'soldier of Christ', it is interesting that a labyrinth with overt Minotaur symbolism should be on his cathedral in Lucca. Theseus is inevitably martial in his symbolism because of his confrontation with the Minotaur, and more generally in relation to the medieval chivalric/jihadic symbolism of the inner world of the soul as a holy battle ground. See the next chapter which includes a section about what could be described as 'inner chivalry' entitled The War Within the Soul.
20. Diagramatic versions of a labyrinth with this type of pathway appear in various manuscripts going back to the 9th century. See Otfrid of Weissenberg.

(This is the labyrinth built by Daedalus of Crete; all who entered therein were lost, save Theseus, thanks to Ariadne's thread.)

There is another circular example of this particular 'Chartres type' of labyrinth pathway depicted with Theseus and the Minotaur at its centre. It is in a painting from the early 1500s, and is attributed to the Master of the Campana Cassoni. Theseus is depicted as a chivalric Crusader knight with 'alchemical' red and white plumage on his helmet.

Theseus as a Chivalric knight in the 'Chartres type' of labyrinth

Returning to England, there is yet another version of this 'Chartres type' of labyrinth that has an association with the Minotaur storyline. It is on the Mappa Mundi at Hereford Cathedral, which dates back to the very early 1300s. The labyrinth is actually used within the map's depiction of the island of Crete in the Mediterranean Sea. The labyrinth is then labelled:

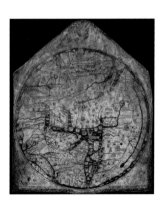

The Hereford Mappa Mundi & detail showing Crete with 'Chartres' labyrinth

'Laborintus id est domus dedali'

('Labyrinth, the house of Daedalus')

Herein appears to lie the most overt correlation between the Christian use of this labyrinth and its direct association with the pre-Christian Minotaur storyline, because this 11-circuit 'Chartres type' of labyrinth was initially developed, and only ever used, in a Christian setting, but here it is directly equated with the island of Crete itself.

Finger labyrinth outside Lucca Cathedral with inscription on right-hand side

The famous labyrinth at Chartres Cathedral

The labyrinth in the nave at Amiens - 'The House of Daedalus'

In classical mythology the labyrinth in Crete is the underworld into which Theseus descends on his way to meeting the Minotaur. As mentioned earlier, this bears a certain resemblance to the story of Lucifer, in that both Lucifer and the Minotaur symbolise the lowest traces of the soul. This lowest level of deathly non-being to which the soul can potentially fall is accordingly condemned to the underworld, although the first part of the soul's journey of return to its origin requires a face-to-face meeting with it, so it can then be recognised and vanquished, to be passed beyond and 'risen above'. This necessarily involves the Minotaur's death, which itself symbolises the death of this potential state of soul within the initiate. The descent into the centre of the womb-like labyrinth is an example of initiatic death followed by rebirth.[21]

So the fact that the French Gothic labyrinths are located around the centres of the naves within which they are situated seems to correspond with the apparent Luciferian symbolism described above as being at the centre of the nave at Wells. Another hint that the Christian labyrinths symbolise the attempts of the soul to rectify its fallenness can be seen in an inscription that is described as having been on a labyrinth that used to be in the church of San Savino in Piacenza.[22]

'The labyrinth represents the world we live in, broad at the entrance, but narrow at the exit, so he who is ensnared by the joys of the world and weighed down by its vices, can regain the doctrines of life only with difficulty.'

Despite the description of 'the world we live in' rather than the 'underworld', the general sentiment expressed is the same. The first stage of the soul's return to its divine origin consists of 'difficulty' in the form of a harrowing of the soul, which thus prepares it for the steep ascent that follows on afterwards and a restoration of spiritual vision through regaining the 'doctrines of life'.

In relation to the Christian use of labyrinths and their apparent associations with pre-Christian storylines, the question could inevitably be asked as to why medieval Christians would use such non-biblical and pre-Christian imagery. A possible answer to this lies again in the open interest that the learned men and women of medieval Christendom took in the ancient world. If a central focus of a religious culture is Wisdom, then such Wisdom could be looked upon as existing wherever it is found. Such an outlook shows itself in the way that learned 12th-century Christians would read Plato, Hermes Trismegistus, Macrobius and Ovid, among others, as well as the Old and New Testaments of the Christian Bible. Such openness particularly shows itself in the wide range of non-Christian characters used by poets such as Bernard Silvestris and Dante in *Cosmographia* and *Commedia*.[23] But if these wider interests of the medieval Christians are looked at in relation to medieval biblical interpretation, we find a theological reason why labyrinth imagery might be used in a Christian setting. In the allegorical aspect of biblical interpretation, the New Testament storylines were seen as having been foreshadowed by stories in the Old Testament. With this in mind it requires only a 'sidestep', as it were, from the Old Testament into other non-Hebrew ancient Wisdom traditions – and herein lies the rationale and the 'validity' of using the descent into the labyrinth and the meeting with the Minotaur as a 'pre-echo' of Christ's Harrowing of Hell and his crossing of paths with Lucifer at the centre of the Earth as described in the Gospel of Nicodemus. But along with this – and looking more generally at the chivalric culture of the Crusader era – the martial nature of the Minotaur storyline might inevitably appeal to such a warrior culture as a symbol of the first stage along the initiatic path – which, like Dante, was walked in emulation of Christ, and is the necessary and harrowing descent into battle before any re-ascent to Eden, or through the heavens, can be embarked upon.

---

21. A cosmological example of this symbolism is present in the Moon's cycle through its death and rebirth once a month. As will be shown in the next chapter, this lunar symbolism appears to be used in the design of the nave at Wells Cathedral.
22. See John James, *The Mystery of the Great Labyrinth at Chartres Cathedral.*
23. In Canto 12 of *Inferno*, Dante even speaks of the Minotaur directly in relation to the leftover traces of Christ's descent into Sheol.

Verily, verily, I say unto thee, Except a man be
born again, he cannot see the kingdom of God.

Nicodemus saith unto him, How can a man
be born when he is old? can he enter the second
time into his mother's womb, and be born?

*   *   *

no man hath ascended up to heaven,
but he that came down from heaven,
even the Son of man which is in heaven.

And as Moses lifted up the serpent
in the wilderness, even so must
the Son of man be lifted up:

That whosoever believeth in him
should not perish, but have eternal life

John 3 : 3-4 & 13-15

CHAPTER 20.

Traces of Medieval Christian Cosmic Initiation

20.1 THE SOUL'S RETURN JOURNEY TO ITSELF

THE WORD 'INITIATION' has been used on several occasions in this book So it is perhaps now necessary to define what the term means within the context of this research.

Initiation usually refers to a formal process involving entry and acceptance into an existing spiritual community. It may be a religious community or a smaller group outside of a religion, albeit with a spiritual orientation. Or it could be a smaller spiritual community that is also a part of a wider religious community. Taking Christianity as a religious example, there can be various different initiatic processes – usually at different stages of life, although the first and most important one of these is baptism. More widely speaking, ritual ablutions – found in various religions – are physically experienceable inwardly realised symbols of a new beginning. In their own way, they reflect a kind of death followed by a resurrection – an ending followed by a new beginning – and such a 'rebirth' is an essential aspect of initiation. But the enacting of such an outer process is specifically designed to awaken the soul to an interior remembrance of the spiritual world. This is why a materialistic or purely empirical outlook, such as that which is actively encouraged in much of the modern educational world, looks with perplexity and bewilderment on any sort of spiritually orientated practice or activity. But to only see an outward enactment that is designed to awaken an inward knowing is to not perceive the entirety of what is taking place. In a similar way, to criticise mythology or fairy tales for not being 'realistic' enough is to miss what such storylines are capable of awakening within the soul through its capacity for spiritual imagination.

It is natural and normal for every human soul to look inwards, towards the realm of Being, and an encouragement towards such a vision is the object of initiation. This is effected through the passing on of a spiritual influence to the initiate. But it could also be said that the soul can spontaneously become initiated through independently waking up to the profundity of Being

So this kind of inner vision can be described as a dormant potential that lies within each soul. Formal initiatic practices are designed to encourage such an inward awakening, leading to *remembrance* – or 'anamnesis' in the words of Plato. However, although every soul in the cosmos could be described as a potential initiate, there are some temperaments of soul more inclined towards such inner journeying.

The aim of initiation is to encourage the opening of a symbolic eye or 'way of seeing' that Plato describes as being worth 10,000 bodily eyes. The number 10,000 is used here as a symbol of 'all things'. This is numerically reflected in the symbolism of the Pythagorean tetraktys in the sense of it having four levels, by which the One moves 'downwards' into the Many first via the number two, then three and finally four. The same numerical symbolism is also used in the Far Eastern tradition in the Daoist writings known as the Dao de Ching.

'The Dao gave birth to the One.

The One gave birth to the Two.

The Two gave birth to the Three.

*And the Three gave birth to the
ten thousand things [i.e. all things].'*

As mentioned earlier, the Pythagorean tetraktys is a geometric image of the number 10 because its four levels together add up to 10:

$$1 + 2 + 3 + 4 = 10$$

The number 10 encompasses 'all things' because all the numbers that are beyond the decad (i.e. the first ten numbers) are made up of numbers from within

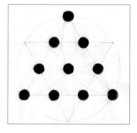

the decad. But ultimately, and most importantly, the number 10 is a multiplicitous image of the One. If this four-fold unfolding of the number 10 is seen through the mathematical use of 'powers', the number 10,000 is reached because ten to the power of four (i.e. 10⁴) is equal to 10,000.[1]

$$10 \times 10 \times 10 \times 10 = 10,000$$

Or, beginning from the number 1:

$$1 \times 10 = 10$$
$$10 \times 10 = 100$$
$$100 \times 10 = 1000$$
$$1000 \times 10 = 10,000$$

In Plato's *Republic* the study of the quadrivial arts is described as being conducive to the opening of this 'Eye of the Soul'. So henceforth geometry is one of the disciplines that is recommended. But again it is worth stressing that this is not just a practical knowledge of geometry, but rather one that very specifically involves a contemplative focus that encourages the soul to spiritually awaken to a remembrance of the Eternal and the Unchanging. Plato criticises the purely practical involvement in geometry whereby it effectively becomes little more than enacted materialism:

'They [i.e. materialistic geometers] *have in view practice only, and are always speaking in a narrow and ridiculous manner, of squaring and extending and applying and the like – they confuse the necessities of geometry with those of daily life; whereas knowledge is the real object of the whole science.*

Certainly, he said.

Then must not a further admission be made?

What admission?

That the knowledge at which geometry aims is knowledge of the eternal, and not of aught perishing and transient.

That, he replied, may be readily allowed, and is true.

Then, my noble friend, geometry will draw the soul towards truth, and create the spirit of philosophy, and raise up that which is now unhappily allowed to fall down.'

As to the eye of the soul itself, Plato is quite direct in his advocating of its importance along with a recognition that, although it is in the capacity of *every* soul, there are those for whom it is not so immediately apparent.

'*... I quite admit the difficulty of believing that in every man there is an eye of the soul which, when by other pursuits lost and dimmed, is by these [the quadrivial arts] purified and re-illumined; and is more precious far than ten thousand bodily eyes, for by it alone is truth seen. Now there are two classes of persons: one class of those who will agree with you and will take your words as a revelation; another class to whom they will be utterly unmeaning, and who will naturally deem them to be idle tales, for they see no sort of profit which is to be obtained from them. And therefore you had better decide at once with which of the two you are proposing to argue.'*

With all of this in mind we can possibly get some sense of the mindset of a 12th-century Christian artist such as the one who designed the cathedral of St Andrew in Wells. The use of practical geometry – and more generally the Quadrivium – in sacred art and architecture has one primary purpose, and that is to remind the soul of That which is Eternal and Unchanging. It is not about the cracking of knowable codes but rather the orientation of the soul's vision towards the unknowable Reality of God.

The specific form of initiation focused on in this book could be described as 'cosmic' in the sense that it involves a journey through the cosmos beginning from the Earth – where we find ourselves in the current life – and then returning back to a heavenly origin, which is symbolically speaking 'above' and beyond physical existence. Different versions of this cosmic pathway are found in various traditions whereby the description

1. See René Guénon, *The Metaphysical Principles of the Infinitesimal Calculus*, chapter 9, final paragraph.

of the journey takes on the 'apparel' that is particular to that tradition. So in one sense these journeys are all particular and different from one another, but in another more overarching sense they are all one-and-the-same journey through which, geometrically speaking, the many aspects of the one reality gather back together into the single dimensionless point from which the original cosmic circle was drawn in the first place. This chapter therefore intends to highlight various examples of apparent traces of a medieval Christian version of this 'cosm-initiatic' storyline. It has already been shown in great detail how similar the ground plan of Wells Cathedral is to a modern-day Freemason lodge room in terms of such cosmological symbolism. This in itself is an example par excellence of such a cosm-initiatic storyline within a medieval Christian setting. Whether this eastward path through the cathedral was ever used within a formal initiatic process is impossible to know, but it is at least one example that demonstrates the apparent medieval Christian pedigree of Freemason cosmological symbolism. It could of course be said that the presence of such an initiatic layout at Wells was incorporated into the building in a more symbolic way, to recognisably reflect a certain anagogical passage through the cathedral, rather than it necessarily being used directly in any formal initiatic pratice. Without written records this shall remain an unknowable mystery, which is perhaps rather fitting considering that unknowable mystery of a more transcendent sort lies at the heart of initiatic practice.

Lack of documentary evidence generally hampers historical investigations. However, a moderate investigation of mythological storylines can sometimes be of use through their capacity to suggest certain themes from the past, rather than recounting direct and literal facts and figures. There are no overt written descriptions of the Templars being involved in the culture of initiation, although it should be stressed that initiatic culture doesn't produce written descriptions of itself for the benefit of future historians. This is to do with the association of initiation with secrecy, or rather that it concerns the inward realisation or 'remembrance' of the hidden 'secret' of the soul's divinity. To completely

dismiss something because there is no written evidence does little to answer the fact that there is a great deal of mythology concerning the Templars and the culture of initiation. The fact that this mythology has seemingly become rather ungrounded and fantastical in more recent times should not be used as a reason to dismiss all Templar mythology – especially when it is Freemasonry itself that makes the mythological connection between Freemasonry and Templar culture.

It has been shown how the design at Wells symbolically suggests the Templar presence on the Temple Mount in Jerusalem. In section 4.2 this was shown in the design's positioning of the quire and the octagonal chapter house, and how they appear to emulate the topographical layout of the 12th-century Christian perception of the Temple Mount. The key to this apparent design symbolism lies in the fact that the Al-Aqsa Mosque, where the Templars were based, was known by the Crusader Kingdom as the 'Temple of Solomon', and the fact that this is then reflected in the Wells design by the quire's ground plan being the same shape and size as Solomon's Temple. There is also the fact that the quire has an octagonal building to the north of it – like the octagonal Dome of the Rock to the north of the Al-Aqsa Mosque. A 12th-century design, in which the Templar headquarters in Jerusalem is so symbolically central, forms a very clear correlation with Freemasonry, for which the Temple of Solomon is also the central symbolic focus. Indeed, the traditional description of a Freemason lodge room is a 'long rectangle orientated eastwards', which is effectively the description of a cathedral quire.

The question here of connections between the Templars and Freemasonry is not to do with a traceable succession of people or families, but rather an ongoing artistic and initiatic use of the same cosmic symbolism-of-passage originating, in its Christian form, within 12th/13th-century Christianity and then eventually passing onwards into the early-modern era of the 18th century. According to writers such as René Guénon the transmission of such symbolism from medieval Christianity into Freemasonry would have taken place via Rosicrucianism.

The Masonic historian Paul Naudon also suggests that the Templars were known to have had many connections to builders' guilds, and one perhaps need look no further than the very large amount of unique Templar architecture that still exists today in various parts of Europe and the Middle East.[2]

So it is not a matter of whether Freemasonry descends 'either' from the Templars 'or' the craft guilds, but rather that it comes from them both.[3] There are also very interesting theories concerning the influence on medieval Crusader Christianity of initiatic groups in the Middle East such as the Druze, who not only have a pentagram star as their primary symbol but also seemingly include 'the building of the Temple of Solomon' as part of their initiatic symbolism.[4]

So as ever it is to the art and architectural forms as well as to the oral arts/literature, such as poetry and storytelling, that we need to look for indications of medieval Christian cosm-initiatic practice. This first leads us to the 12th-century culture of chivalry and courtly love.

The war within the soul

WHAT CAN CERTAINLY be said of the Templars is that they were a very out-of-the-ordinary mixture of both 'consecrated monk' and also 'soldier'. Looking at the biblical accounts of Christ, there is clearly more of an overt pacifism in relation to his teaching as opposed to a warlike one. But having said that, war in spiritual language is always first and foremost connected to a battle that takes place within the soul. This can be seen for instance in Islam, which is more overtly warlike in its symbolism due to the war-torn warrior culture within which this particular revelation came forth. A revelation speaks to its recipients in a language that they will understand, and to preach pacifism to warriors will not be understood. This perhaps also follows in relation to

'warrior monks' in medieval Christianity within the martial era of the Crusades. The suffering and possible death arising from warfare naturally becomes identified with Christ's suffering on the cross, and so to go on a Crusade is to 'take up the cross'. In the light of Matthew's Gospel this would presumably take on a particular relevance in relation to 'holy warfare' and the taking of Jerusalem in a millenarian fervour:

'Then said Jesus unto his disciples, If any man will come after me, let him deny himself, and take up his cross, and follow me.

For whosoever will save his life shall lose it: and whosoever will lose his life for my sake shall find it.

For what is a man profited, if he shall gain the whole world, and lose his own soul? or what shall a man give in exchange for his soul?'

For the Son of man shall come in the glory of his Father with his angels; and then he shall reward every man according to his works.

Verily I say unto you, There be some standing here, which shall not taste of death, till they see the Son of man coming in his kingdom.'

16: 24–28

Holy War or 'Jihad' is seen in Islam as reaching its greatest and most noble form within the war that takes place inside the human soul rather than the one that takes place on the earthly battlefield. The battle is with those aspects of the soul that could be said to prevent it from moving in the direction of a remembrance of its True Self – which in Islamic terms is described as being 'in submission to God''. This inner struggle does show itself within the Christian storyline, but more so in stories such as the temptation of Christ by Satan

---

2. The Scottish writer A.J. Morton has also shown very clearly how the Templar history of the old Royal Burgh of Irvine, along with Kilwinning Abbey close by, appears to present a connection between the Templars and the gradual development of early Freemasonry in Scotland. The oldest Freemason lodge in the world is reputedly at Kilwinning, which is known as the 'Mother Lodge'.
3. See Paul Naudon, *The Secret History of Freemasonry* and A.J. Morton, *The Templars of Medieval Scotland*.
4. See Donna M. Brown, 'The Druze: A Secret Esoteric Sect', *Esoteric Quarterly*, Summer 2017.

during his forty days of fasting in the wilderness, during which both physical appetites and egoic desires are challenged. Other biblical examples of such necessary 'inner work' are suggested by the description in Matthew's Gospel in which the judging of someone's faults will lead to an equivalent judgement in relation to one's own faults. Also the suggestion in John's Gospel that those who are without sin should cast the first stone at those who are accused of sinning. The most challenging war will always be the one that takes place within the soul.

Such inner struggles speak particularly of the earlier stages of the spiritual path, where the physical appetites need to be subdued, followed by the lower aspects of the psyche needing to be raised beyond the lowest levels of ego. So it would appear to be of symbolic significance that the word 'chivalry' relates etymologically to the person who rides and therefore masters the horse.[5] The untamed horse is an image of the untamed human ego along with its unbounded physical appetites. So to ride upon the horse is to be in control of such raw and powerful aspects of the human soul. These unsublimated aspects of the soul are not evil in-and-of themselves, but rather they require a raising and a refining so they do not become the master of the soul, rather than vice versa. In Judeo-Christian terms there is a clear symbolic connection here with the Messiah entering Jerusalem riding on the back of a donkey. This is reflected in a pejorative expression within Jewish culture, in which someone is described as a 'Messiah's donkey' in the sense that they are unwittingly guided into doing the mundane hard work that helps to bring about glory for someone else. In Jewish mysticism the Messiah's donkey symbolises the material world which, again, is not evil in-and-of itself, but needs to be harnessed and orientated towards a heavenly path. This speaks volumes in relation to Christ's riding of a donkey through Jerusalem's Golden Gate on Palm Sunday – the gate of the Jewish temple, no less. It was pointed out in section 4.2 that this biblical storyline was a sig-

nificant focus in both Jerusalem and England during the era of the Kingdom of Jerusalem. Palm Sunday was one of only two days in the whole year when Jerusalem's Golden Gate would be opened up and passed through.

So to be 'riding on the animal' and channelling its strength and energy for a greater purpose is the object of this inner battle. The apparent depiction of the chivalric soul who has risen above their 'untamed energies' is then very commonly shown in medieval Christian art in the form of a knight with an animal of some sort below the soles of his feet. Each animal will often have its own particular meaning, but the position below the feet suggests having 'risen above' or 'mastered' a particular untamed potential within the soul.[6]

Such inner battles again speak of the chivalric knight journeying to the centre of his labyrinthine soul to engage in holy warfare against the voracious Minotaur, whom he must vanquish if his soul is to have any hope of ascending beyond the Earth.

Effigy of William Marshall in Temple Church, London.

5. Chivalry is derived from the Latin word for horseman – *cabalarius*.

6. See the words of the Worshipful Master in the Freemason Third Degree: '... *the Lord of Life will enable us to trample the King of Terrors beneath our feet, and lift our eyes to that bright Morning Star ...*' Dante's *Commedia* also includes similar symbolism in the first half of Canto 12 of *Purgatorio* when Dante-the-pilgrim sees images of various characterisations of human pride below his feet – the first one of them being Lucifer the fallen angel.

Saint Michael and the Dragon - Sienese School of the 14th century

This is, I say, a new kind of knighthood and one unknown to the ages gone by. It ceaselessly wages a twofold war both against flesh and blood and against a spiritual army of evil in the heavens......He is truly a fearless knight and secure on every side, for his soul is protected by the armour of faith just as his body is protected by armour of steel. He is thus doubly armed and need fear neither demons nor men.

Taken from 'In Praise of the New Knighthood' (Liber ad milites Templi: De laude novae militae)
A letter written by St. Bernard of Clairvaux to Hugh de Payens and the Knights Templar.

Saint Michael and the Dragon by anonymous, Spanish (Valencian) Painter

THE PENTAGRAM OF
SOLOMON AND GAWAIN

THE TESTAMENT OF SOLOMON is a text that is thought to date back to the 1st century AD. It contains a storyline recounted by King Solomon himself about demons and the trouble that they cause humanity – as well as how to become free of their malign influence.

The theme of the story is clearly one that could be described as initiatic in the sense that it concerns the transmutation of a lower state of soul into a higher one – or more specifically, that a particular tendency within the soul is redirected away from villainy and towards nobility. The particular tendency in question could be seen as a 'descending' one in the sense of a movement that, symbolically speaking, descends towards the Earth. This is present within the very idea of angels that have fallen from heaven, as described in the Book of Revelation within the description of the War in Heaven.

The story centres around the building of the Temple of Solomon, and the interventions of King Solomon in gaining control over demons, whom he then puts to work in the building of his temple. All of the demons that he traps and gains control over have angelic origins, and Solomon finds this out through questioning each one of them once he gains control over them. The demons also describe to Solomon the various ways in which they cause chaos in the lives of humans through controlling and encouraging them into various destructive behaviours towards themselves and others. These chaotic qualities that the demons cause in human actions can be understood symbolically as downward-moving tendencies that cause the soul to fall downwards 'into the earth', much like Lucifer's descent as the Evening Star when he falls to the 'lowest depths of the pit'. However, Solomon does not attempt to change this downward-moving tendency into an upward-moving one, but rather he transmutes the destructive downward movement into one that becomes constructive. He does this by redirecting the demon's descending energies into building work on the construction of his temple – because 'the devil will find work for idle hands'.

The story of Lucifer the Fallen Angel is clearly present in the Testament of Solomon, although the Luciferian character is called Beelzeboul (Lord of the flies). He describes himself as the exarch of all demons. He also describes how he was originally the highest angel in heaven before he fell down to the Earth, and this is very much a part of the Luciferian storyline. The highest angel is the Seraphim, which – interestingly, with Luciferian symbolism in mind – is derived from the Hebrew word for 'serpent'. The serpent has a dual symbolism in Christianity which is associated both with falling into the underworld and also with ascent into heaven.7 It is generally considered that the Seraphim serpent is in some way connected to the ancient Egyptian Uraeus, who is sometimes associated with Hathor, the Egyptian equivalent of Planet Venus.

The material form of a sacred architectural edifice is inevitably subject to gravity and, much like the descent of the Heavenly Jerusalem, sacred architecture embodies the quality of a movement downwards of the heavenly state on to the Earth. However, rather than sinking downwards into the underworld the architecture establishes itself on the Earth and then becomes a temenos for the divine presence here on Earth. This creates a sacred precinct from which there can then be an upward-moving contemplation that counteracts and balances the downward movement of the material form. Despite the weighty materiality of architectural form, if it is built according to a divine plan it encourages as much of an upward movement – in the sense of encouraging contemplative and prayerful anamnesis in the soul – as it does a downward movement through its material embodiment.

In the storyline King Solomon effectively symbolises the apex of the soul, whose lofty and therefore noble position has the capacity to bring order out of chaos. This essential task is then made possible through the

7. See Revelation 12:9 and John 3:14.

monarch's capacity for Solomonic wisdom – and it is this potential within the soul that initiation aims to bring forth from the outset. The monarch must exert authority over the crown lands to ensure that they are ruled both justly and compassionately, for it is through such a combination of rigour and mercy that the middle path of Wisdom can become apparent. The subduing of self-seeking villainous potential within the soul helps to part the waves and open up the narrow way out of the soul's earthly enslavement to ego and passions, which are swept into the sea and never seen again.[8]

However, the most striking aspect of Solomon's redirection of the demon's energies is that it is effected through the application of the divine language of geometry. Solomon has a ring with a pentagram seal upon it (the Seal of Solomon), and it is through the presentation of this ring to the various demons that they come under his control. In this sense it is through the application of numerical order that chaos is transformed into cosmos. The demons are then put to work building a temple formed of divinely inspired measures that accordingly make it an image of the cosmos.

With the pentagram in mind, it has also been shown in various places within this book that the 1×3 rectangle which forms the measured ground plan of Solomon's temple is generated within the design of the Wells Cathedral quire through the overlapping of two pentagram stars. So in this sense it is truly through the intervention of the pentagram's form that the temple comes into being. The pentagram accordingly marks out a sacred internal place that is safe and protected from hostile demonic forces.

There appears to be a reflection of such themes in the medieval Christian chivalric poem *Sir Gawain and the Green Knight*. Gawain has a golden pentagram on his shield, and when the poem first describes this 'pentangle' it is specifically associated with King Solomon:

'And why the pentangle applies to that prince noble
I intend to tell, though I tarry more than I should.
It is a sign Solomon settled on some while back,
In a token of truth, by the title that it has'

The fact that the pentagram is on a shield associates it with protection from harm, and as already mentioned the inner dimension of chivalry would seem relate to warfare against what could be described as the lower or 'demonic' aspects of the soul. Gawain's success in such inner warfare would also appear to characterise the ongoing suggestion within the poem's description of the pentagram's symbolism:

'For so it accords with this knight and his bright arms,
Forever faithful in five ways, and fives times so,
Gawain was for good known, and, as purified gold,
Void of every villainy, with virtues adorned,
All so'

The 'purified gold' in this description reflects the soul's alchemical transmutation from a lower leaden state of 'villainy' to a higher state of nobility, and this is also reflected in the fact that the shield's pentagram itself is described as being made of gold.

Gawain's golden five-fold soul is then described in the following way:

'First he was found faultless in his five senses,
And then failed never the knight in his five fingers,
And all his trust in the field was in the five wounds
That Christ caught on the cross, as the creed tells.
And wheresoever this man in mêlée was stood,
His first thought was that, over all other things,
All his force in fight he found in the five joys
that holy Heaven's Queen had of her child;
for this cause the knight fittingly had
on the inner half of his shield her image painted,
that when he beheld her his boldness never failed.[9]
The fifth five that I find the Knight used

---

8. Exodus 14:21-30.

9. This boldness, that arises from being reminded of the Virgin Mary – which aids Gawain in his battles against his 'inner adversaries' – is reminiscent of the courage that Dante suddenly gains at the end of the second canto of Inferno, when he hears from Beatrice about how St Lucia and the Virgin Mary have been watching out for him. See Canto 2, 43–142.

Was Free-handedness and Friendship above all things;
his Continence and Courtesy corrupted was never,
and Piety, that surpasses all points – these pure five
were firmer founded in his form that another.'

So the pentagram here symbolically describes various of the inner qualities by which Gawain embodies chivalric nobility.[10] This encompasses his own self-control as well as his noble actions towards his fellow human being. But most importantly his nobility arises out of a devotion to his religious path, which is essentially the path of Love.

The five-foldness of this pentagram symbolism along with the fact that it includes both Christ – the Bright Morning Star – and the Virgin Mary – the Stella Matutina – associates it with the planet Venus, or more specifically the Morning Star rising in the east. The likeness of Beelzeboul to Lucifer in turn associates him and his demonic fallen angels with the Evening Star setting in the west. So again we see the Christian use of the perennial initiatic myth involving the descent and ascent of Venus – the planet who symbolises Love in her Uranic form as well as her Pandemotic form.

It is difficult not to be of the opinion that the designer of Wells Cathedral was aware of this storyline because various aspects of it resonate with the design of the cathedral. However, it would also seem that it must surely be a foundational text for the Solomonic cosm-initiatic symbolism that is practised to this day in Freemasonry. The focus on the building of the temple and the initiatic inner dimension to this work makes it appear very much in keeping with Masonic symbolism, even if there doesn't seem to be much mention of it in the modern Masonic literature that is available to the public.

THE INITIATIC DESCENT OF THE MOON INTO THE EARTH

THE MOON WAS A COSMOLOGICAL symbol of initiation in the ancient world.[11] This is related to the Moon's symbolic descent into the underworld. The descent could be said to lead to the soul's death followed by its rebirth, which is symbolised by the three-day disappearance of the Moon when it changes from being a waning crescent to a waxing crescent.[12] Such underworld lunar symbolism resonates with the lunar numbers that are often associated with the labyrinth in Chartres cathedral.[13] But it could be said that there is a similar lunar association within the design of the Wells Cathedral nave too. This was shown in section 14.1 (p.257), whereby the centre of each bay is effectively the centre of a Moon-square. This symbolic feature occurs as a result of the design's use of the Earth-Moon diagram. So it can be suggested that the initiatic soul, in the form of the Moon, is effectively travelling through the nave from one bay-centre to the next. The point at which the initiate symbolically dies would be at the centre of the fifth bay, so as to be reborn at the centre of the sixth bay having passed beyond the stone-carved head of Lucifer. Indeed, Lucifer is looking more towards the centre of the fifth bay rather than the crossing point of the fifth bay into the sixth bay.

Bearing in mind that there are ten bays, and that the number thirty was one of the numbers of the Moon in the ancient world, such numerics show themselves in the fact that the triforium, which is immediately above the nave's arches, contains thirty of its own small arches on each side. This is because there are three triforium arches directly above each of the ten nave arches.

10. A similar fivefold chivalric nobility appears to be described in Shakespeare's *Twelfth Night* when Cesario (Viola) speaks of his (her) 'fivefold blazon'
11. See Jules Cashford, *The Moon: Symbol of Transformation*.
12. See Eznick of Kolb's commentary on Joel in his *Treatise On God* for an early Christian criticism of magicians who talk about the Moon descending into the Earth.
13. The lunar number associated with the Chartres labyrinth is 28, which is the astrological and 'archetypal' number of the Moon due to it consisting of four seven-day weeks. The two main lunar cycles are actually on either side of the number 28, with the sidereal cycle being 27.32 days and the synodic cycle 29.53 days. As for the Chartres labyrinth, the outer cusps around it have come to be known as 'lunations' partly due to their shape but also because there are 112 of them, which is 28 × 4. There are also 28 semicircular 'half-moon' stones in the labyrinth, by which the soul entirely turns about in the opposite direction – i.e. much like the lunar duality of waxing and waning.

Above each arch in the nave there are three small arches in the Triforium

The number 30 on the clock's lunar dial is on a smaller block and squeezed in between 1 and 29 because a lunar cycle is 29.53 days

So initiatic progress through the nave at Wells involves a passing of thirty triforium arches on either side, which can be looked upon as one full lunar cycle in which the Moon descends to its death and then re-ascends back into light. The association of the Moon with the number thirty is effectively a 'rounding up' of the lunar cycle of 29.53 days, and indeed such a thirty-day lunar cycle is actually depicted on the lunar dial of the medieval clock in Wells Cathedral.

A description of this ancient initiatic lunar symbolism is outlined by the modern-day astrologer Haydn Paul.

'The Underworld journey tends to move from the dark Moon to the full, suggesting that the path to light is first through inner darkness, or that the way to heaven has to pass through hell, reminiscent of the story of Christ enter-

ing the underworld to liberate the prisoners before he was resurrected. The initiation in the depths is cathartic in essence, releasing any repressed dark shadows, potencies, and powers within human nature, destroying the artificially inflated and separative personality, dissolving the false masks and misplaced identifications and thus liberating the real self into light.' [14]

Such symbolism of inner catharsis may explain the existence within the nave's triforium arches of what can effectively be described as 'infernal' Green Men.[15] The only place in the whole of Wells Cathedral where this type of Green Man exists is in the nave, whereas the more standard-looking Green Men are further east within the cathedral, particularly in the transepts. The demonic-looking faces in the nave's triforium arches are seen as being Green Men because they are disgorging

14. *The Astrological Moon: Aspects, Signs, Cycles and the Mythology of the Goddess in Your Chart.* See section entitled 'The Descent into the Underworld'.
15. I am grateful to Mr John Rivere for pointing all these Green Men out to me.

greenery from their mouths, but they also have animal features such as horns. These figures are reminiscent of the aforementioned description of 'repressed dark shadows, potencies, and powers within human nature' which are accordingly released from the soul or 'exorcised', as it were, and this could be said to clear the soul of its negative demons, thus 'liberating the real self into light'.

But another fascinating symbolic possibility here directly accords with the biblical storyline of Judas. In Dante's *Commedia* Judas is with Lucifer at the centre of the Earth because he, along with Brutus and Cassius, is being eternally chewed on by the three mouths of Dante's three-headed Lucifer. Brutus and Cassius meet this grim fate through having betrayed Julius Caesar, whereas for Judas-the-Apostle it is as a result of his betrayal of Christ. The reward received by Judas for his betrayal was the 'lunar' sum of thirty silver pieces. As already mentioned, the number thirty is a lunar number, but along with this silver is the alchemical metal of the Moon. The negative aspect of the Moon can be seen in the fact that it slowly increases, eventually showing a full face for a short period of time, but then recedes and thus turns its face away again. Similarly Judas was at first a follower but then a betrayer of Christ, and so his love for Christ was not constant but transient.

On this lunar journey through the nave at Wells the 'inner Judas' within the initiate must be faced and dealt with, because Judas is also at the Luciferic centre of the Earth where it can be said that the soul's necessary death takes place. So in another sense, the initiatic death of the Christian soul is also the death of Judas himself, or at least the death of this capacity for infidelity that lies within the fallen soul. It is after all only the fallen soul that would put the transient material world ahead of the eternal light of the Sun/Son. As for the soul that

does choose to put the material world first, it dies along with it and accordingly cannot experience resurrection into eternity.[16]

THE INITIATIC CAVE

ONE OF THE VARIOUS Templar myths relates to 'initiatic caves'. There are various caves – such as the one at Royston in hertfordshire and another in the grounds of Caynton Hall in Shropshire – that have come to be mythically associated with the Templars, although it is pointed out by sceptical scholars that the actual direct evidence of this is rather slight. But the fact that such myths persist is still of interest in-and-of-itself, and one might assume that it relates in some way, consciously or not, to the symbolism of descent into the underworld as the first stage of initiation. The word 'myth' is used here in a non-pejorative sense, because mythology could be said to be closer to 'Reality' in comparison to the mundane realities of historical facts and-figures. Mythology engages with perennial spiritual and psychological themes through the vehicle of a storyline that is loosely based around actual historical events. So to dismiss mythology and insist on historical facts is like dismissing the vitamin C from an orange, only be left with its visible material pulp. It could in fact be suggested that the desire to study history is actually unconsciously fired by the soul's longing to look back to 'essence' or 'origin', and this is clearly a spiritual motivation even if the historian is unconscious of this, or indeed even if they are an avowed atheist. Every soul has a natural inbuilt need to remember its origin and, in this sense, to look back into history suggests a desire on the part of the soul to look inwards towards an originating core or essence.

With all of this in mind, let another Templar myth begin its existence here within the following speculation

---

16. The name Judas means 'Jew', and so again it can be seen that an inappropriate externalisation of such initiatic symbolism – which in reality concerns the facing of one's own inner darkness – can very easily descend into a persecution of the Jewish race as some kind of supposed holy warfare. Such a depraved notion appears to have been present within Nazi ideology. These kinds of misperceptions are a very clear example of why initiation must be reserved only for those who are prepared and ready to challenge their own shortcomings rather than project them on to others. It is perhaps unsurprising in this sense how the self-righteous projections that characterise conspiracy theories very often involve a blaming of the Jews in some way for 'the conspiracy', rather than a recognition that there is a conspiracy within each one of us by which our ego attempts to 'keep us from the truth' of remembering the soul's divine origin.

which has no direct historical evidence whatsoever – although it does follow an interesting line of coherent cosm-initiatic symbolism. According to one myth the Templars are said to have spent much time inside the octagonal Dome of the Rock measuring its geometry and dimensions. The possible fruit of such measures has been pointed out in section 16.2 in relation to the pyramid triangle used in the design of the octagonal chapter house/undercroft and Lady chapel at Wells. But on the subject of 'initiatic Templar caves' our attention is immediately drawn to the underground cave in the Dome of the Rock, which is known as the Well of Souls. This cave is directly below the rock around which the shrine is built, and an idea deriving from medieval Islamic legend suggests that the groaning and sighing of the spirits of the deceased can be heard from this cave as they wait for Judgment Day. This legend naturally accords with the idea of souls that are trapped in the underworld prior to Christ's Harrowing of Hell, or indeed prior to his second coming. So in this sense the Well of Souls bears a resemblance to the initiatic cave as a descent into the underworld that is intended to free all that is languishing within the soul in a deathly state waiting for resurrection at 'the end of time'.

It is known that the Well of Souls was extended by the Crusaders, and also that during the Crusader era it came to be looked upon as the place of the annunciation of St John the Baptist's conception, which is described in the first chapter of Luke's Gospel.

As already mentioned, there is an early Christian symbolism that associates the births and conceptions of Christ and St John the Baptist with the solstices and the equinoxes.[17] Whereas Christ's birth is associated with the winter solstice, John the Baptist's is associated with the summer solstice or 'Midsummer's Day'.[18] Their conceptions are then associated with the equinox that took place nine months prior to each particular solstice. The Annunciation of Christ is the spring equinox, whereas the annunciation of the Baptist is the autumn equinox. In terms of seasonal symbolism the autumn equinox is associated with the movement 'downwards', into the dark half of the year dominated by the deathly darkness of winter. In geo-cosmic symbolism this relates to the idea of a movement down below the surface of the Earth. So with the Well of Souls in mind, the autumn equinox seems like an appropriate time to descend into the dark cave via the fifteen 'Freemasonic' steps that lead down to it.[19] So it could be said that to descend into the womb of the Earth on the autumn equinox is to symbolically emulate the Baptist's conception.[20] The point at which an initiate might rise back up to the surface would be on Midsummer's Day itself, when they are born out of the womb of the Earth in emulation of the Baptist's birth. But the mode of this birth has a fascinating symbolic possibility in relation to the Well of Souls. There is a shaft that leads through the rocky ceiling of the cave up to the surface of the rock face above. It is not known for sure who created this shaft, but it is thought most likely to be the Crusaders. Such an initiatic ascent through a vertical ceiling shaft, and the shaft's association with the solstices, and indeed 'initiatic rebirth', is something that René Guénon describes in great detail within a few chapters of his work concerning the 'initiatic cave'.[21] The fact that the Baptist's birth is associated with the summer solstice would mean that this symbolic spell of nine months in the cave would relate to what are known as the 'lesser mysteries'. These are then followed by the 'greater mysteries', which would be associated with the winter solstice and therefore the birth of Christ.[22]

17. See the 4th-century treatise *On the Solstices and Equinoxes, the Conception and Birth of our Lord Jesus Christ and John the Baptist*.

18. 24 June was the summer solstice in the old Roman calendar.

19. The 'fifteen steps' of the temple is central to symbolism in Freemasonry, for which St John the Baptist is also a patron saint. Grand Lodge Freemasonry actually established itself on St John's midsummer feast day in 1717. Freemason mythology also speaks of its proto lodge as being the lodge of St John (the Baptist) of Jerusalem.

20. The other descent into the underworld that is associated with the autumn equinox is that of Lucifer and the Fallen Angels, due to the association of Michaelmas with the autumn equinox.

21. See *Symbols of Sacred Science*, chapters 29–35 – particularly chapter 34.

22. Within the brief 12th-century period of its Christianisation, another interesting initiatic theme that was associated with the Dome of the Rock is Jacob's ladder, which reflects the Islamic Miraj storyline. Both of these storylines could be described as descriptions of the same archetype of ascent through the heavens.

But whether or not a human body could fit through this shaft in the Well of Souls – with its diameter of 1½ feet – is beyond the experiential knowledge of this writer! So it could perhaps also be suggested that the staircase of fifteen steps is another more straightforward way of being 'reborn' out of this cave.23

An overhead head view of the rock in the Dome of the Rock. The hole which forms the ceiling shaft in the Well of Souls can be seen top left.

Another persistent Templar myth suggests that the Templars dug below the Temple Mount and found a treasure of immense value. But rather than material treasure, could this have been treasure of a spiritual kind such as that which is hidden within the soul – below the surface – the type of treasure that is guarded by a sleeping dragon in the underworld?

Returning to the Wells Cathedral nave and its association with descent into the underworld, there is a fasci-

nating symbolic expression of this on the part of an English writer who would appear almost certainly to be associated with initiatic culture, as is quite clear from his poems. The name of this writer is unknown, although he is generally referred to as the 'Gawain poet' because *Sir Gawain and the Green Knight* is his most famous work. But it is actually in one of his lesser-known works – *Patience* – that he makes an overt connection between the doorway into a cathedral nave and the descent into the underworld. The poem is centred around the story of Jonah and the whale, which, as mentioned in secion 5.5, reflects the ancient story of Inanna's descent into the underworld as well as being used by Christ as an allegory of his own Harrowing of Hell. The moment in the storyline at which Jonah enters the whale's mouth is described in the following way:

'He knows that he has gone from the ship into the water and been taken by a whale straight down its throat, like a speck of dust through the door of a great cathedral, so huge was its mouth.'

Regardless of whether or not there is a conscious connection being made here between the intended design of a cathedral nave and a descent into the underworld, the symbolism is clearly one of the soul's utter humiliation – in the positive sense of encouraging humility within the soul. The first stage of the pathway to initiation is for the ego to realise that it is not the central hub about which the cosmos turns, but rather a speck of dust entering through the door of a great cathedral. To enter into a great cathedral in the medieval era, when all other buildings outside of the cathedral were by comparison small and insignificant, must surely have been an awe-inspiring and humbling experience for the average person. But it is surely also this very humiliation that was necessarily experienced by Lucifer when he fell from his self-exalted position as the 'son of the morning' down to the 'lowest depths of the pit' – and as already shown, he fell to the centre of the nave in Wells Cathedral!

23. The notion of 'initiatic rebirth' could be said to be reflected in the words of Nicodemus the Pharisee in chapter 3 of John's Gospel: 'How can a man be born when he is old? Can he enter the second time into his mother's womb, and be born?' Christ's descent into Hades is found within the Gospel of Nicodemus. This Pharisee is also one of the people who prepares Christ's body immediately before His descent into Hades. The name Nicodemus means 'victory to the people', which seems appropriate in relation to the liberation of many people achieved by Christ in His journey through Hades.

Ascent to the heavenly female

The harnessing and re-orientating of the soul brings about the possibility of interaction with the archetype of the heavenly 'Sofianic' female who is so central to the culture of chivalry and courtly love. In the language of medieval Christian symbolism this female is the Virgin Mary, although any female could in a sense be such an image of Divine Love and Wisdom. The way in which this was presented in both sacred and secular medieval musical lyric is described by David J. Rothenberg:

'It is a simple fact that prayers to the Virgin Mary and secular love lyrics of the high and late Middle Ages often sound alike. Though the former are generally in Latin and the latter in the vernacular, the former overtly religious and the latter not, both frequently feature stylised praise of an idealised, impossibly virtuous woman, and both originated within traditions of medieval song – Marian prayer in Gregorian chant, love lyric in the courtly song of the troubadours. The troubadours sang of an elevated and noble type of love, which they called fin'amor (refined love). It is the earliest form of what is now commonly called Courtly Love.' [24]

As shown earlier in chapters 5 and 6, the ascent to this heavenly female presents itself architecturally in the design of Wells Cathedral through an 'ascent' to the Lady chapel up at the east end of the whole building. But as already described, the 'taming of the animal' is an essential prerequisite before this heavenly female can come into view – and likewise, the passage through the 'earthly' nave of Wells Cathedral is an essential stage to pass through before the soul is ready to move towards the quire and then eventually to the 'Edenic' Lady chapel.

The theme of a heavenly female, *fin'amor* and an ascent to Divine Love inevitably speaks of the Italian poet Dante and his poem *Commedia,* in which he is guided through the heavens by the heavenly female figure of Beatrice. It is actually in Eden where Dante first encounters this 'Lady' who had always inspired such an immense love within his soul. In the very final line of the whole work, in which he describes his union with God, Dante speaks of this Divine Love which pervades the whole cosmos. He describes it as:

'... the Love that moves the sun and the other stars'

Beatrice had left Dante's side just before this final moment, but it is only through the intercession of the foremost heavenly female – the Virgin Mary – that Dante is able to reach this absolute pinnacle of finality and union. Dante is another figure who appears to have been associated with Templar culture.[25] As will become clear a little later on, there are various linking themes between Dante and the Templars such as love, the focus upon a heavenly female, and also the number nine.

The subject of Dante also brings us back to the design of Wells Cathedral. The three stages of *Commedia* appear to be reflected in the eastward, and then northward, 'ascent' of the cathedral's ground plan. This is suggested by a few vital details which then inform the overall cosmological design. The measures of the nave clearly reflect the cosmology of Planet Earth, but it is the small, rather missable stone-carved head of Lucifer, between the fifth and sixth bay, that appears to then show how this cosmology of planet Earth is designed to have a similar initiatic meaning to Dante's journey through the Earth. Dante's descent and re-ascent, via the centre of the Earth, is clearly in emulation of Christ's Harrowing of Hell, although it must also be remembered that such a descent is a perennial archetype found in many different initiatic storylines both outside of, and before, Christianity. As mentioned on various occasions, this is not because such a storyline is the invented property of an older religion, but rather that such a storyline recurs perennially because it is an essential opening stage by which the soul becomes able to re-orientate its vision 'upwards' in preparation for an ascent beyond the Earth.

24. David J. Rothenberg, *The Flower of Paradise,* Oxford University Press, 2011, see 'Introduction', page 4.
25. For example see several sections in W Anderson, *Dante, the Maker.*

Dante, the Templars and Love

THE IMAGE OF LUCIFER 'at the centre of the Earth' in the nave at Wells resembles the description of him that is found in Grail literature. Indeed the association of the Templars with initiatic culture appears to be reflected in this particular genre of storyline, which involves medieval knights, initiatic trials and stories of human love in relation to fidelity and betrayal. In Wolfram von Eschenbach's poem *Parzival* there is a group of Grail knights who are actually described as 'Templars' (Templeisen). They live in a castle in the middle of a forest and their symbol is the turtle dove, which is associated with fidelity or pure and faithful love. Fidelity is the quality of the Roman goddess Fides, who is symbolised by the turtle dove. In Greek mythology the turtle dove draws the chariot of Aphrodite, the Goddess of Love. Meanwhile in the Song of Solomon the voice of the turtle dove is the sign of springtime. So again, we see the faithful unending love that is associated with the Eternal Spring, which in this case is associated with a fictional depiction of Christian Templar knights. Moreover, it is interesting to note that when the actual Templars appeared as characters in medieval literature it was very commonly in association with lovers. The Templar expert Helen Nicholson describes it as such:

'It was the Templars who first appeared in literature assisting lovers, and who appeared most often in this role. The literary connection between the Templars and romantic lovers may have originated in the Templars' reputation as an ideal example of Christian love in action. Christian love, caritas or charity, is not the same as romantic love, amor, but in the work of Wolfram von Eschenbach and his contemporaries and later adaptors Christian love for God is paralleled with faithful romantic love between innocent lovers.' [26]

This analogy between faithful romantic love and the soul's faithful love for God may at first appear incongruous with the fact that the Templars were celibate monks who had little or nothing to do with women.

But in actual fact the Templars were very much devoted to a particular Lady, albeit a heavenly one in the form of our 'Our Lady' – the Queen of Heaven to whom they were consecrated and for whom they held a particular loving devotion. But such love was consummated inwardly through prayer and perpetual religious devotion so therefore, symbolically speaking, the relationship of love was more ontological than cosmological. If translated into geometric symbolism this relates to a 'vertical' relationship between Earth and Heaven, which could be described symbolically as a 'pathway to the Holy Land'.

Interestingly, the Templars were originally set up to protect the pathway to the Holy Land. But the fact that there were initially only nine of them makes this responsibility clearly impossible in practical terms within their early years. Along with this they spent their first nine years in Jerusalem rather than on the roads between Western Europe and Palestine. Bearing in mind their circular and polygonal churches which, as pointed out in section 3.2, symbolically reflect a vertical orientation of ascent, it is interesting to note that the cosmic ladder of ascent consists of nine rungs as shown at the very beginning of this book in the image of Lady Philosophy from the north rose window at Laon (see pages 2 and 13). Indeed, the number nine appears to be significant for the Templars as well as for Dante. So does this suggest that in a certain sense the 'pathway to the Holy Land' that the Templars were protecting was the vertical path of ascent traversed by Dante in the third stage of his Commedia – the journey through the seven planetary spheres to the eighth heaven of the stars, circulating around the Stella Maris, and then beyond the eighth to the 'first moved' ninth heaven and finally the Empyrean beyond that? The Marian title Stella Maris (Star of the Sea) is used within the opening invocation of a Templar prayer that was written during their persecutions in the early 14th century:

'May the grace of the Holy Spirit be present with us. May Mary, Star of the Sea, lead us to the harbour of salvation. Amen'

---

26. Helen Nicholson, *Love, War and the Grail*, Brill, 2001, page 49.

Such seafaring symbolism is very much a part of the association with this particular title of the Queen of Heaven. Yet again we turn to the patron of the Knights Templar, St Bernard of Clairvaux, and to one of his sermons on the subject:

> 'If squalls of temptations arise, or thou fall upon the rocks of tribulation, look to the star, call upon Mary.
>
> If thou art tossed by the waves of pride or ambition, detraction or envy, look to the star, call upon Mary.
>
> If anger or avarice or the desires of the flesh dash against the ship of thy soul, turn thine eyes towards Mary.'

As ever, there is an encouragement to look upwards towards the heavenly female guide at the centre of the eighth heaven so as to not be drowned within the worldly waves of perpetual earthly change. When out at sea there are absolutely no visible fixed and unchanging reference points to navigate by except for the North Star 'herself', who helps the pilgrim sailor to cross the 'seven seas' so as to safely arrive at her 'harbour of salvation' in the eighth heaven and then beyond.

In Dante's *Vita Nuova* he associates the number nine with Beatrice – the heavenly female who guides him through the heavens in his *Commedia*. He writes directly about the significance of the number nine in relation to her:

> 'One reason this number was such a good friend of hers could be this: inasmuch as, according to Ptolemy and according to Christian truth, nine are the heavens in motion, and, according to common astrological opinion, the said heavens influence life down here according to their combined disposition, this number was her friend in order to make it understood that all nine motioning heavens utterly, perfectly harmonized with one another at the moment of her conception.

> *This is one reason. But thinking more subtly, and according to infallible truth, she herself was this number – she*

> *bore a resemblance to it – by which I mean the following. The number three is the root of nine, since it makes nine by itself, without any other number, as we see plainly in the fact that three times three makes nine. Therefore, if three by itself is the factor of nine, and the factor of miracles multiplied by itself is three – that is, the Father, the Son, and the Holy Spirit, who are three and one, this woman was accompanied by this number nine to make it understood that she was a nine, a miracle in other words, whose root (the root of the miracle) is none other than the miraculous Trinity.'*

Translated by Andrew Frisardi

At the beginning of *Vita Nuova* – or rather immediately after the initial introduction – the very first word is in fact 'Nine':

> 'Nine times, the heaven of the light had returned to where it was at my birth, almost to the very same point of its orbit, when the glorious lady of my mind first appeared before my eyes.'

Dante then goes on to describe how he first saw Beatrice when he was near the end of his ninth year and she at the beginning of her ninth. The next time he saw her after this was nine years later at the age of eighteen and in the ninth hour of the day.

Such an emphasis upon the number nine is also present in early Templar history. They began as nine knights who were consecrated in Seborga during the ninth month of the eighteenth year of the century. It was, in fact, eighteen years after the crowning of the first King of Jerusalem. They then went on to spend nine years in Jerusalem before returning to Europe in 1127, and this year that they returned was when St Bernard of Clairvaux wrote their Templar Rule. It is suggested through documentary evidence that the Templars already existed, albeit in a proto-form, a few years prior to 1118.[27] If this is so it is interesting that they waited a few years until the eighteenth year of the century before being consecrated as monks.

---

27. This is due to a letter from Ivo of Chartres to Hugh of Champagne, which mentions the possibility of him joining the 'Militia Christi'. See Bulst-Thiele.

Dante guided by the Heavenly light of Beatrice - Illustration by Gustave Doré

Returning to the Dante-esque design of Wells Cathedral, having passed beyond the underworldly nave, the quire is then reached, and this image of Jerusalem's temple is the central place on the Earth as well as being the symbolic heart of the cathedral. It is from this quire that there is an eastward ascent to Eden, which exists in the form of the Lady chapel. It is the Edenic symbolism of the thornless rose and the rising of the Morning Star in the east within the design of the Lady chapel that appears to suggest the second stage of Dante's *Commedia*. Purgatorio is a climb up a mountain, which leads to Eden at its summit. The pyramid triangle that leads from the eastern end of the quire to the Lady chapel could even be seen as Dante's Mountain of Purgatory, although such a direct likeness is not necessarily being suggested here in relation to the *Commedia* and the design of Wells Cathedral – rather a similarity of general cosmic coordinates within the three-stage journey. In both cases there is an ascent that culminates in a return to Eden.

Eden is then the place in the far east where there is an eternal season of spring. When Dante reaches Eden he sees another female - Matilda - whom he associates with Proserpine and the eternal spring in which she resided prior to her abuction into the underworld by Pluto.

THE ETERNAL SPRING IN PARADISE LOST

WITH EDEN, ETERNAL Spring and Earth's cosmology in mind we now briefly move forward by a few hundred years, from when Wells Cathedral was designed, up to the 17th century. There is an interesting use of cosmic symbolism in John Milton's epic poem *Paradise Lost,* which bears a direct resemblance to the Wells design.

Milton's description of Planet Earth is such that prior to the fall of humankind from Eden there was no difference between the orientation of Earth's equator in relation to the ecliptic plane. As shown earlier, it is the 23.4° angle of difference between Earth's equator and the ecliptic which causes the seasonal cycle of fluctuation between the lightness and darkness of the two solstices. But it is at the equinoxes in March and September that the relationship of light and dark is equal, because this is when the equator is the part of Earth that is closest to the Sun. However, whereas the equinoxes are transient moments within an unending seasonal cycle that fluctuates between light and dark, it is possible to see how if there were no angular difference between the equator and the ecliptic there would be a perpetual state of equinox. In symbolic terms this relates both to an Eternal Spring – which as already mentioned is another symbol of Eden – but also 'eternal harvest', i.e. the autumn equinox. In such a state of equilibrium there would no longer be the ascending or descending halves of the year. Even though Milton's description is geo-cosmic, it is a symbolic description of an inner state of soul. Metaphysically speaking, this is a state beyond time in which there is no longer any swing of the pendulum back and forth between light and dark, but rather an eternal state of harmonious balance in which the pendulum remains forever still and orientated in a vertical and timeless state of being. It is much like the linear verticality of a musical string that remains in a motionless ontological silence.

Relating this idea to the cosmic design of Wells Cathedral it is possible to see that the movement both through the quire and then beyond it to the Edenic Lady chapel is effected only through taking the middle 'non-dual' equinoctial path through the 'earthly' nave. The return of the soul to an Edenic state is therefore conditional upon the walking of this 'middle path'. To take a solstitial path (i.e., one of the two side aisles) leads to one of the two chapels dedicated to the death-through-martyring of the Baptist and St Stephen, whereas to walk the middle equinoctial path leads beyond death and onwards to Resurrection in the Lady chapel because the soul has then returned, as a thorn-less rose, to the Garden of Eden in the cathedral's far east. This return to the 'original state' accordingly sees a return to the Divine Love of the Eternal Spring.

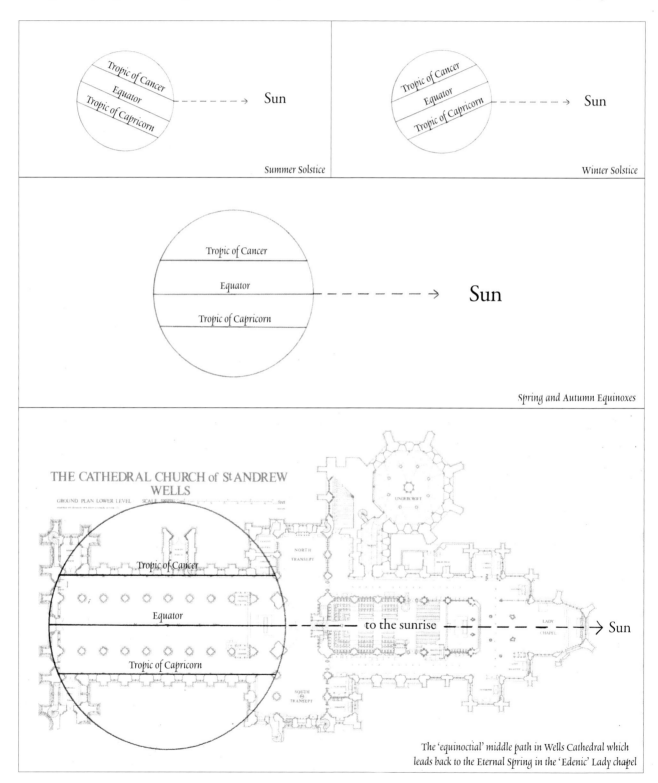

Summer Solstice

Winter Solstice

Spring and Autumn Equinoxes

The 'equinoctial' middle path in Wells Cathedral which leads back to the Eternal Spring in the 'Edenic' Lady chapel

THE MOUNTAIN 'ON THE FARTHEST SIDES OF THE NORTH'

RETURNING AGAIN TO Dante's *Commedia* and the journey through Wells Cathedral, the final stage is the journey 'northwards', as it were, through the heavens in the direction of the Celestial North Pole (the Stella Maris). It is not possible for a cathedral to go further to the east of itself, and the eastern end of the cathedral is indeed its culmination in liturgical terms because it is expressive of the Resurrection through its orientation towards the sunrise in the east. But after his Resurrection Christ remained around in the earthly world for another forty days before his ascent into Heaven.

The Ascension of the initiatic soul through the planetary spheres thus appears in the Wells design to be a northward movement beginning from the quire and symbolically ascending to the octagonal chapter house and undercroft on the north side of the cathedral building.

A great deal was written about the Pentecostal nature of this design symbolism in section 9.5, and so here it is only necessary to point out that the pyramid triangle leading 'upwards' from the quire to the chapter house can be associated with yet another mountain. This particular pyramid triangle has already been associated with Mount Sinai and the Feast of Shavuot, as shown in the section 16.3. But if the symbolism of Lucifer in the nave is now considered, then this northward-pointing pyramid triangle is also the Mount of the Congregation 'on the farthest sides of the north' as described by Isaiah.

When Lucifer rose as the Morning Star, he egoically exclaimed:

> *'I will ascend into heaven,*
> *I will exalt my throne above the stars of God;*
> *I will also sit on the mount of the congregation*
> *On the farthest sides of the north'*

In this sense the northward-pointing pyramid triangle is the highest point towards which Lucifer's pride aspires before it is necessarily humiliated to the lowest depths of the pit. But Dante, in emulation of Christ, takes on this journey of humiliation 'downwards' to vanquish the ego's aspirations so that the soul can slowly begin to remember its True Self, first through the journey eastwards to Eden and then finally northwards through the planetary spheres to the Empyrean.

It is also symbolically interesting that the pyramid triangle leading upwards to the chapter house/undercroft has its two bottom corners with one at the cathedral crossing and the other at the threshold of the Lady chapel. On the one hand the crossing in a cathedral is the centre of the four directions, which is accordingly the symbolic position of the vertical ladder that leads upwards. But also, the fact that the other corner of the triangle is at the threshold of the Lady chapel suggests that this relates in some way to the forty-day period of time between the Resurrection (symbolised by the Lady chapel) and the Ascension (to the chapter house), because the right-hand sloping edge of the pyramid triangle makes a direct connection between these two places. This pyramid triangle does even have a relationship with the number 40 via the Venusian numbers 5 and 8, which was shown in section 14.1

The symbolic idea that the Ascension progresses northwards after forty days also correlates with the idea expressed in section 9.5 of how the octagonal chapter house symbolises the descent of the Holy Spirit after fifty days – i.e. ten days after the Ascension. So therefore the northward ascent of God-the-Son back to God-the-Father eventually leads to the descent of God-the-Holy-Spirit 'down from the north' ten days later. Yet again this associates the chapter house area with the Trinity, and indeed it is Dante's ascent 'northwards' through the heavens that culminates in his meeting with God in Trinitarian form.

There is also the association of the York chapter house with the rose, as was shown in section 9.7, in which it is described as 'the house of houses' in a similar way to the rose being 'the flower of flowers'. This naturally reflects the Celestial Rose that features in the final few cantos of *Commedia*. The centre of the chapter house at Wells also contains the pillar which symbolically equates with the Virgin Mary, and likewise she is also positioned foremost at the centre of Dante's Celestial Rose. In this sense the ascent to the chapter house area can also be symbolically associated with the Assumption of the Virgin Mary into Heaven. The sevenness of the Virgin Mary and Wisdom can even be said to be geometrically embodied by the pyramid triangle itself within its seven units of height – for She is, at the same time, both 'three-fold [and] four-fold blessed'.[28]

Another symbol of northward ascent can be seen in the fact that Dante actually equates Beatrice's chariot with the chariot in Ezekiel's vision. At the very beginning of his vision Ezekiel specifically describes the chariot as descending from the north. So again it is clear that the direction of the (re)ascent is northwards.

Bearing in mind the various symbolic similarities between the design of Wells Cathedral and Dante's *Commedia* perhaps the most interesting dimension of this is the fact that the design of the cathedral building precedes *Commedia* by around 150 years. So the inevitable suggestion is that Dante did not invent the basic overarching coordinates of his journey. This is not to suggest that he copied the design of Wells Cathedral, however. What this does point to is a pre-existing cosm-initiatic path within medieval Christian practice which informed the symbolism of both Wells Cathedral and the *Commedia*. This naturally presents the question of whether there are other examples of this cosmic journey to be found anywhere else in the arts of medieval Christendom.

One can hardly ever be sure of anything in relation to the Templars, but the fact that there appear to be symbolic associations between them and the design of Wells Cathedral as well as to Dante and Freemason

symbolism, and indeed to 'Love', presents another tributary to the great river of mythology about this elusive religious order. It is inevitably of interest that Dante started working on *Commedia* one year after the Templars had begun to be rounded up and arrested through the interventions of King Philip the Fair of France. The less-than-complimentary descriptions of King Philip in *Commedia* leave little to the imagination of what Dante thought of him. In Canto 20 of *Purgatorio* there is an apparent criticism of King Philip's materialistic greed – which is generally recognised as being the actual reason for his mistreatment of the Templars:

> *'And I see the new Pilate, one so cruel*
> *that, still not sated, he, without decree,*
> *carries his greedy sails into the Temple'*

We finish with a particularly intriguing fact in relation to all of this. There was actually a Latin translation of *Commedia* along with a commentary upon it in the Wells Cathedral library from the early 15th century up until the Reformation, when it appears to have gone missing. This was one of the only (if not the one and only) Latin translations in the whole country at the time – although a couple of copies were seemingly made of it, too. It was commissioned by Bishop Bubwith of Bath and Wells along with Bishop Hallum of Salisbury when they spent a few years at a church conference in Constance.[29] They managed to get the Italian Bishop of Fermo, Giovanni Bertoldi da Serravalle, to translate it from Dante's Tuscan dialect into Latin. This presents us with the question of why an English Roman Catholic bishop would be taking an interest in a controversial Italian work that places various popes in hell. Could it be that he recognised aspects of its overarching storyline from what he knew about the design of his own cathedral in Somerset?

---

28. This numerical description of the Virgin's 'sevenness' is written within the pathways of the Abingdon labyrinth.
29. See the article D. Wallace, 'Dante in Somerset', *New Medieval Literatures, Volume III*, Clarendon Press, 1997.

THE DOCTRINE OF CORRESPONDENCES,
THE GOLDEN RATIO
AND THE TETRAKTYS WALK

IN THE PLATONIST understanding of ascent there is a correspondence between each level that the soul passes through. Each rung of the ladder is within reach of the next, and in this sense all the levels are connected through being situated upon the one single ladder of ascent. The climbing of this ladder is a return journey, because the perceived origin is at the top of the ladder. Adrian Snodgrass describes the descent of this ladder:

'... the world comprises a hierarchy of levels, corresponding to the degrees of reality. The series descends from the intelligible to the sensible realms; each realm derives from and is an image of the one above, so that each separate reality at a particular level is the reflection or the expression of a corresponding reality in a higher sphere. The relation existing between phenomena and their equivalents lying at a superior level connects together the entirety of the universe.' [30]

Two of the ways in which this correspondence between different levels can be geometrically symbolised are through the use of the Pythagorean tetraktys and the golden ratio.

It was shown earlier that the Pythagorean tetraktys can be associated with the number 10,000 through the mathematical use of powers. Beginning from the 1, each of the four levels of the tetraktys symbolises sequential multiplications by 10 – which is itself the all-encompassing number of the tetraktys. So the movement from the 1 to the 10,000 is effected through '10-to-the-power-of-4' ... i.e. 10 × 10 × 10 × 10 = 10,000.

Each level corresponds to the level that precedes it, via the number 10, and this correspondence traces itself all the way back to the 1, which is the origin of 'all (i.e. 10,000) things'.

The golden ratio geometrically reflects a correspondence through the fact that its expansion and contraction, through multiplication and division, also accords with the additions and subtractions of these various products and quotients.

If the number 1 is multiplied by 1.618 it produces 1.618.

But if this result of 1.618 is then itself also multiplied by 1.618 it produces 2.618, which happens also to be the sum of 1 and 1.618.

If this result of 2.618 is then multiplied by 1.618 it produces 4.236 and in this particular and unique instance 4.236 is also the sum of 2.618 and 1.618 as well as being their product:

$$2.618 \times 1.618 = 4.236$$

$$2.618 + 1.618 = 4.236$$

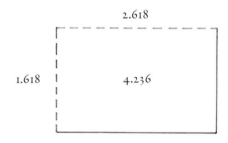

If a line of 4.236 is divided at the golden section it has a shorter segment of 1.618 and a longer segment of 2.618 because 1.618 + 2.618 = 4.236. A golden rectangle with a short edge of 1.618 and a long edge of 2.618 has an area of 4.236 because 1.618 × 2.618 = 4.236

If the above principle is applied to whole numbers, the only one that brings about the same calculated result

30. Adrian Snodgrass, *Architecture, Time and Eternity*, Volume 1, chapter 5.

when added to itself or multiplied by itself is the number 2:

$$2 + 2 = 4$$

$$2 \times 2 = 4$$

This reflects the similar relationship shown above that exists between the numbers 1.618 and 2.618. These two numbers also fall on either side of the number 2, and indeed the number 2 is actually at the golden section of the number line that runs between 1.618 and 2.618.[31]

But this correspondence between golden ratio numbers is also suggestive of the tetraktys. If the number 1 corresponds to the single dot that forms the top level of the tetraktys, then the following numbers 1.618, 2.618 and 4.236 all show an apparent correspondence to the numbers of dots in the second, third and fourth levels:

The nearest whole number to 1.618 is 2 …

the nearest whole number to 2.618 is 3 …

and the nearest whole number to 4.236 is 4.

The numbers 1.618 and 2.618 both fall short of their corresponding tetraktys number by 0.382, whereas 4.236 exceeds its tetraktys number by 0.236.

These two small numbers – 0.382 and 0.236 – together express the golden ratio through their unequal relationship. But perhaps the most interesting thing about these three discrepancies of golden ratio numbers in relation to their corresponding tetraktys numbers is that together they add up to 1:

$$0.382 + 0.382 + 0.236 = 1$$

The number 1 numerically symbolises the origin, which then corresponds ideally to the single dot at the top of the tetraktys. The three following golden ratio numbers all miss their corresponding tetraktys numbers. But even these discrepancies, which make them imperfect reflections of the tetraktys numbers, are together expressive of the One. This is one of the key characteristics of the golden ratio, in that it always brings the soul back to the (number) One.

The Platonist philosophy of Plotinus emphasises an ascent to the One. The tetraktys can also be understood analogously in a particular way that numerically corresponds to Plotinus' description of the three hypostases + nature. The single dot at the top of the tetraktys is again the One. The two dots in the second level then reflect the twoness of Nous (Intelligence) which contemplates the One as well as the contents of its own thoughts. The Soul reflects the threeness of the tetraktys' third level in the sense that the Soul's inherent twoness looks both upwards towards the One (i.e. the 'singular' middle dot of the three looks directly upwards) but also looks down towards the multiple many-ness of the material world (the 'duality' of dots – one on either side of the 'singular' middle dot). The fourth and final level consisting of four dots reflects the fourness of materiality that emanates from the three Hypostases.

An inter-relation between the tetraktys and the golden ratio appears to have been intentionally included within the design of Wells Cathedral in what will here be described as a 'tetraktys walk'. This name is related to the fact that by walking eastwards through the nave and on into the quire there is a gradual revealing of the tetraktys-shaped window, which is far off on the eastern wall of the Lady chapel. This window contains images of nine angels, who are all looking upwards at the levels of the tetraktys situated above them.

31. The raising of phi by its powers is significant within the Lucas sequence, as also is the number 2. When phi is raised by its powers it clearly settles on increasingly rational approximations of Lucas numbers. The Lucas sequence also begins with the number 2. In fact in the raising of phi by its powers the starting point of '1' corresponds to the Lucas starting point of 2. The 1.618 then corresponds to the Lucas number 1. The following paired correspondences are then 2.618 – 3 … 4.236 – 4 … 6.854 – 7 … 11.090 – 11 … 17.944 – 18 … 29.034 – 29 … 46.97 – 47 … 76.013 – 76 … 122.991 – 123 … 199.005 – 199 … and so on.

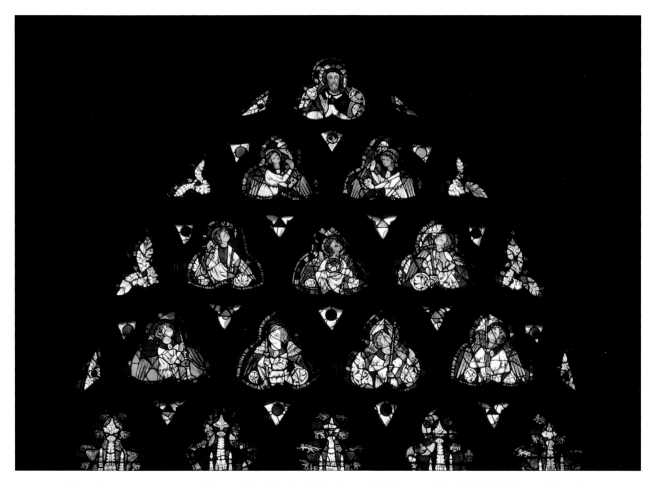

The tetraktys window at the east-end of the Lady chapel and cathedral. Nine angels looking up to the 'One' who is depicted as God the Father.

None of them are looking downwards – but this is the apex of the window that is furthest east in the whole cathedral. By this point in the eastern ascent of the cathedral every gaze is orientated upwards. Such ascent imagery naturally fits the symbolic schema that is being suggested here.

At the top of the tetraktys, in the window that forms the single 'dot', there is an image of a figure who appears to be God-the-Father because he is holding an orb. The gradual revealing of the four levels of this tetraktys window – one by one from bottom to top – occurs as a result of reaching particular golden section thresholds within the ground plan. These thresholds arise from the pyramid triangle master diagram used in the design of the quire/chapter house area.

Apart from the fact that this whole tetraktys walk works in practical terms, a key design feature that suggests intentionality on the part of the designer is that one of these golden section thresholds is formed by the golden section line that passes through the sacristy doorway, which is itself at the golden section of the bay in which it is situated.

This particular golden section line divides the left-hand half of the pyramid triangle's baseline – which measures 72 greater feet – into two segments: one that measures 44.5 feet and the other 27.5 feet. If another golden section line is added, as shown in the following diagram, this further divides the 27.5 feet measurement into 17 feet and 10.5 feet.

This 10.5-foot distance can then be understood to be the single unit from which this series of golden section thresholds spring forth. Owing to the orientation of these linear threshold lines the particular mathematical calculation required here is 2.618 rather than 1.618

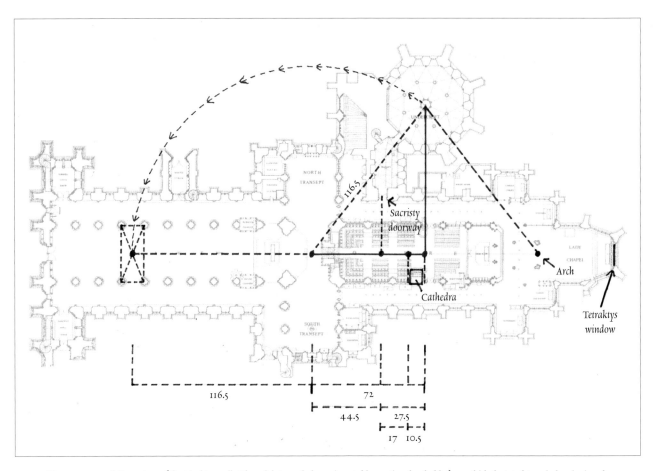

The geometry and dimensions of the tetraktys walk. The red dots mark the various golden section thresholds from which the tetraktys window is viewed. From the first dot - in the middle of the nave's fourth bay - none of the tetraktys is seen. From the second dot two windows in the fourth and lowest level become visible. From the third dot all the windows in the third and fourth levels can be seen. Then from the fourth dot the whole of the second, third and fourth levels become visible. finally, at the fifth dot, the whole of the tetraktys window comes into view. These views of the tetraktys are seen through the archway of the Lady chapel's central entrance.

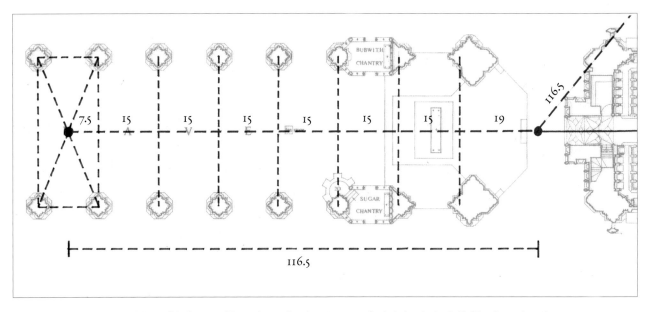

The precise breakdown of the first part of the tetraktys walk. It is 116.5 greater-feet in its length - i.e. half of the Fibonacci number 233. Each bay is 15 greater-feet in its east-west measurement. So the distance from the centre of the fourth bay to the eastern edge of the fourth bay is 7.5 feet. The distance from the end of the tenth and final bay to the centre of the crossing is 19 greater-feet. So therefore 7.5 + 15 + 15 + 15 + 15 + 15 + 15 + 19 = 116.5 greater-feet.

However, it is Fibonacci approximations of 2.618 that are actually used. If 10.5 feet is increased by the Fibonacci ratio 55/21 (2.619), the distance increases to 27.5 feet. This is level with the sacristy doorway. This measurement of 27.5 is then multiplied by the Fibonacci ratio 144/55 (2.61818), which increases 27.5 to 72. This measurement leads to the corner of the pyramid triangle which coincides with the cathedral's crossing. The final measurement sees 72 increased by the Fibonacci ratio 377/144 (2.618), and this leads all the way to the precise mid-point of the fourth bay in the nave, which is 188.5 feet away from the starting point of the 10.5 unit in the middle of the quire. This position in the fourth bay of the nave can accordingly be seen as the beginning point of the tetraktys walk. Its distance can also be defined simply by unfolding the slanting edge of the pyramid triangle so that it reaches from the crossing to the middle of the fourth bay.

From this bay in the nave the tetraktys window lies far away, up at the east end of the cathedral. The fourth bay is not even beyond the symbolic 'centre of the Earth', and so it lies in a dark obscurity and as yet is unable to 'see' any of the tetraktys window at all. The window is actually obscured by a pointed arch that forms the entrance to the Lady chapel. This arch is directly above the point on the floor that marks the bottom right-hand corner of the pyramid triangle. The view of the tetraktys window from the nave also happens to be obscured by the more recent door through the pulpitum into the quire, which has partially obscured what would have been the original view. But as the human eye moves further and further eastwards, the window slowly becomes more and more visible once the angle of view below the pointed arch entrance to the Lady chapel allows this to happen. Having said this, a pointed arch is not an appropriate shape to entirely reveal a whole horizontal line of small glass panels within the tetraktys window. So each new level of the tetraktys could be said to become partly revealed, whereby some of the small windows in each successive line of the tetraktys become fully visible to the eyes of the walker as they reach the appropriate golden section thresholds.

As mentioned above, the beginning point of the tetraktys walk is at the precise mid-point of the fourth

bay of the nave. The end point is then the middle of the pyramid triangle's baseline in the middle of the quire/ presbytery. This is the position from where someone with eyes that are around 5 feet off the ground can see the whole of the tetraktys window through the Lady chapel's arched entrance. As already mentioned this arched entrance actually marks the position of the bottom right-hand corner of the pyramid triangle.

The journey begins from the fourth bay in the nave and, perhaps rather appropriately for such a spiritual embarkation, there is a small young looking face of a particular type of Green Man peering down from the capital of the pillar that divides the fourth and fifth bays. This is the only other human face on a pillar capital looking down towards the nave other than the Lucifer carving and set-of-three faces mentioned in the previous chapter. This type of Green Man is not disgorging greenery but is rather a youthful 'Jack in the green' face peering out from greenery - at the beginning of life's journey.

The young looking Green Man peering down into the fourth bay

Moving off from the nave's fourth bay, the first golden section threshold is 116.5 feet away at the cathedral's crossing. 116.5 is half of the 13th Fibonacci number 233.

This point lies beyond the 'earthly' nave, and indeed a cathedral's crossing symbolises the central place on Earth because it is situated at the centre of the four directions. The transepts are to the north and the south, the nave lies to the west, and the chancel to the east. This point also marks the bottom left-hand corner of the pyramid triangle. It is at this point that it is possible to see the middle area of the lowest line of the tetraktys window. As the image below demonstrates, the middle two windows in the fourth level are now visible.

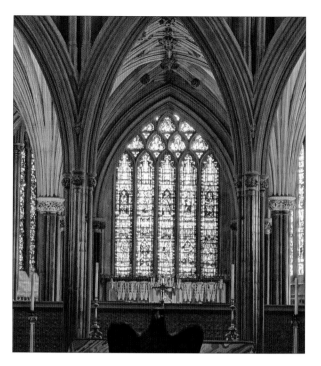

The view that is level with the Sacristy doorway. The middle window from third level of the tetraktys now becomes visible.

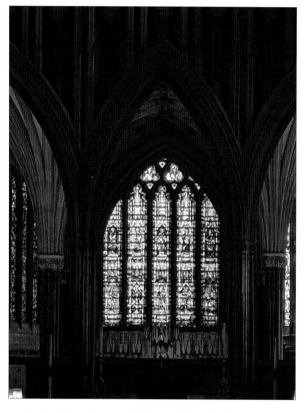

View from the crossing. Two windows on the lowest level become visible.

From here onwards the walker enters the quire. The three remaining golden ratio thresholds could be associated with Plotinus' hypostases, because the walker has symbolically begun their ascent from the central place on the Earth. Proceeding 44.5 feet to the first of these remaining thresholds brings the walker level with the sacristy doorway that is in the north quire aisle. The view of the window at this point now also includes the middle tracery panel from the third line of the tetraktys and the whole of the lowest line. This distance of 44.5 feet is half of the 11th Fibonacci number, 89.

Moving 17 feet onwards to the next threshold, the second level of the tetraktys comes into view. This threshold also brings the walker to the western edge of the bishop's cathedra or throne - which is the very

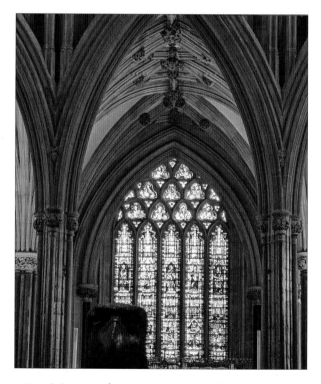

From the beginning of the cathedra. The second, third and fourth levels.

object from which a 'cathedral' gets its name. This distance of 17 feet is half of the 9th Fibonacci number, 34.

The final distance is 10.5 feet which is half of the 7th Fibonacci number, 21. This final distance neatly and fully contains the bishop's cathedra. Once the middle of the pyramid triangle's baseline is reached, through passing the cathedra, the entire tetraktys window comes into view.

the axial ascent symbolism of a bishop's crozier - (which will be touched upon in the following section). These three steps that lead up to the cathedra mean that the fourth step is the ground level of the cathedra itself. So the fact that the cathedra is also located very accurately within the fourth and final stage of the tetraktys walk naturally associates the bishop, who sits on the cathedra, with the one who is in a fully realised or 'ascended' state - the 'Pontiff' (from 'pontifex') or 'builder of the bridge' that runs vertically between Heaven and Earth.

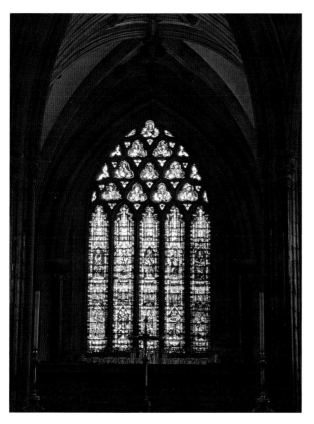

The final view, beyond the cathedra, of the whole tetraktys window.

The Bishop's throne or 'cathedra' - from where a 'cathedral' gets its name

This final threshold is also the point that lies at the bottom of the symbolically 'vertical' axis of the north-ward-pointing pyramid triangle. This is the seven-unit height of the triangle that leads from the quire 'up', as it were, to the octagonal chapter house and undercroft in the 'far north'.

Interestingly a small southward extension of this line also passes directly through the three small steps that lead up to the bishop's cathedra. So in this sense the pyramid triangle's vertical axis also reflects and suggests

Each stage of this golden ratio tetraktys walk reflects the walking of a 'greater part' of a golden ratio relationship. The 'lesser part' that follows on from each greater part is then itself divided into an increasingly smaller golden relationship of greater-to-lesser. So in this sense there is a correspondence between each new level of ascent, in which each new threshold reveals increasingly higher levels of the tetraktys window far off in the east which, by virtue of its east-end location, mediates the light of the Rising Sun as its shines in through the window to awaken the soul for the beginning of a new day.

The sacristy in Wells Cathedral

ANOTHER PLACE IN Wells Cathedral that looks particularly likely to have been some kind of initiatic setting is the sacristy. Much has already been written in this book about the immense number of cosmologically significant measures that there are around the doorway leading into this sacristy, along with the fact that the door itself is positioned at the golden section of the bay in which it is situated. But there are in fact two more significant things that have not yet been described. The first is the position of a gravestone of a renowned medieval bishop in relation to this doorway. The second is the existence of a linear series of seven ceiling bosses in the sacristy itself that can't help but look initiatic, and in some way related to a symbolic alchemical understanding of *fin'amor* as a relationship between Spirit and Soul.

A sacristy is a private place, and the carvings in the Wells sacristy are noticeably different to those found in the rest of the cathedral in the sense of them being a little out-of-the-ordinary and unconventional. So the room naturally feels set apart from the rest of the cathedral, and therefore private and hidden. This makes it a most appropriate place for initiatic practice.

It was also shown in section 15.4 how there is a significant use of the golden ratio within the master diagram in this area, involving the positioning of both the front and back doors of the sacristy at the golden sections of the walls on which they are located. There is accordingly a passage through the sacristy between these golden section doorways that 'ascends' northwards towards the octagonal undercroft, and this route of passage passes directly underneath the seven ceiling bosses.

There is a medieval Bishop of Bath and Glastonbury – as the diocese was then named – who is still very much spoken about in the current time because there is a local dragon legend about him. He is called Bishop Jocelin and was a local figure born in a small village called Launcherley, which is just a couple of miles to the south of Wells. A mile or so from Launcherley, and a few miles to the southeast of Wells, there is a tiny farming hamlet called Worminster which has its own medieval wayside cross. As the name suggests, the hamlet is the centre of a 'worm' legend. The word 'worm' comes from the Anglo Saxon *wyrm*, which also relates to a serpent or a dragon, and this is the origin of this hamlet's name; it is the dragon of Worminster that Bishop Jocelin is said to have slain in the 13th century. The story is still re-enacted once every fifty years in the villages near Worminster, because the legend that has developed over time suggests that if the dragon is not lanced once every fifty years it will return to cause the same trouble that Bishop Jocelin brought to an end when he slew the dragon back in the 13th century.

Jocelin's crozier is still in existence, and on show in Wells Cathedral. It contains a sculpted image of St Michael slaying the serpent during the War in Heaven as described in the Book of Revelation. However, the shepherd's crook shape of the crozier is formed by another larger serpent that is coiling around into a circle.

Bishop Jocelin's serpentine crozier

When croziers are serpentine in form, such as with the caduceus-like croziers found in the Orthodox church, they are generally understood to be an image of the serpent that Moses raised in the wilderness.[32]

32. See the Book of Numbers 21:9.

Jocelin's crozier accordingly forms an interesting polar interplay of symbolism, because Christ himself allegorically associates his Resurrection and Ascension with the serpent that Moses raised in the wilderness:

'No one has ever gone into heaven except the one who came from heaven – the Son of Man. Just as Moses lifted up the snake in the wilderness, so the Son of Man must be lifted up, that everyone who believes may have eternal life in him.'

John 3:13–15

So the two serpents that form Jocelin's crozier are the dragon/serpent that falls to Earth as a result of the War in Heaven, but also the serpent that is raised to eternal life through the Resurrection and Ascension. It should also be noted that the crozier itself is made from copper gilt. Copper is the metal of Aphrodite/Venus, the Morning and Evening Star, who also reflects this dual serpentine movement through first setting in the west and descending into the underworld, much like Lucifer, before re-ascending into Heaven in the east much like the Risen Christ as the Bright Morning Star. The Morning Star is also a herald of the illuminating gilt of the rising Sun, and indeed this theme of copper transformed into gold is prominent in ancient and medieval alchemy.33

Another interesting feature of Jocelin's crozier is that the dragon/serpent, in combat with St Michael, has seven green dots along the length of its body. Could this be the green emerald falling down through the seven planetary spheres from the crown of the serpent? Whereas copper is the metal of Aphrodite/Venus, the emerald is her gemstone. The date of Jocelin's crozier, and various other croziers that are essentially the same as Jocelin's, is the first third of the 13th century, and this is exactly the same time as the grail stories that contain the description of the emerald falling from Lucifer's crown.

Such serpentine imagery along with the local legend of Jocelin-and-the-dragon accords with the symbolism in the Wells Cathedral nave of Lucifer. As already mentioned, he is depicted with the serpentine crown of a cobra's hood which contains an eye-shaped hole from where an emerald fell. It has already been shown that this image of Lucifer is directly next to a stone carving of a dragon that is being lanced in the mouth with a trident.34

But such initiatic symbolism becomes all the more interesting in relation to the position of Bishop Jocelin's gravestone in the middle of the cathedral's quire. When originally put in place, Jocelin's grave was just in front of the position, at that time, of the high altar. But it also happens to be situated in the very same bay as the sacristy doorway that is at the golden section of its bay. This door lies immediately to the north of Jocelin's gravestone. So in this sense Bishop Jocelin could be described as being orientated both eastwards and northwards at the same time. It has already been shown that a golden section line, beginning from the baseline of the pyramid triangle, passes directly through the sacristy doorway. This line also forms the second golden ratio threshold in the tetraktys walk. However, what wasn't mentioned earlier is that the position from where this golden ratio line departs the baseline of the pyramid triangle is actually precisely where Jocelin's gravestone is located.

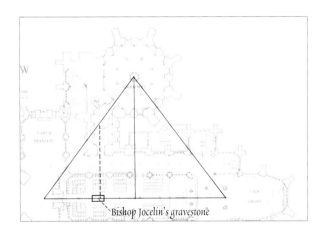

Bishop Jocelin's gravestone

33. For Copper Alchemy see *Hathor's Alchemy* by Alison Roberts. Also the serpent that Moses raises in the wilderness is described as being made of brass, which is itself an alloy formed primarily of copper. It is said that the metal plate at the centre of the Chartres labyrinth was made of copper or brass, and so again the descent into the labyrinthine underworld has an alchemical association with Aphrodite/Venus.

34. The serpentine symbolism of Lucifer is also seemingly apparent in the description of him as once having been the highest angel in Heaven. The highest angel is the Seraphim, and this name derives from a Hebrew word for serpent.

Moving towards the sacristy doorway itself, something that becomes apparent is that halfway up the curves of the arch that cover the doorway there are two faces, one on either side. The face on the left is female and the one on the right is male. Such symbolism of polar opposition in terms of gender must have had a deeper symbolic meaning, because presumably in the medieval era no women would have been passing through this doorway. The celibate clerics who actually were passing through the doorway were inevitably not permitted to be in relationships with women. However, by walking through the doorway, between the two faces, it could be said that one is establishing a relationship between these two 'opposite principles' as it were – the masculine and the feminine. Yet again this denotes a middle path between opposites – much like the doorway to Solomon's Temple that stood between the two pillars Jachin and Boaz.

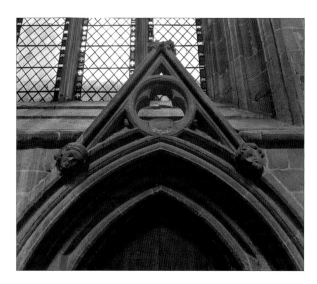

The female and male faces one on either side of the Sacristy doorway

But more directly, the use of a male and female face at a significant doorway brings to mind the image of the Roman god Janus in the form of 'Janus and Jana'. The solstitial association with Janus' two male faces speaks of his solar symbolism – but Jana, the female face that Janus' male face is sometimes paired up with, is actually Diana, the Goddess of the Moon. So to walk between these two faces again suggests the middle path between the Sun and the Moon – much like the vertical axis of Christ's cross flanked by Sun and Moon.

As one walks through the doorway and immediately looks up towards the low vault overhead there is a linear series of seven ceiling bosses running northwards.

The first boss depicts a Green Man disgorging greenery from his mouth. Much has been said by many people about the Green Man, but let it just be suggested here that a Green Man may have something to do with the verdant fertility of the Eternal Spring and is thus an image of 'rebirth' or indeed inward resurrection.

The First of the seven ceiling bosses - a Green Man

There is a stone-carved head in the vestibule that leads into the sacristy depicting a person with very bulging or apparently inflated cheeks. He has three forelocks on his upper forehead (one of which is now missing), and this is the distinguishing feature that suggests he is actually an image of the disgorging Green Man who appears in the first ceiling boss, because he also has these same three forelocks. In this sense the character with bulging cheeks is a kind of 'pre' Green Man, or rather what the Green Man looks like immediately before becoming the Green Man. His bulging cheeks display the *viriditas* of springtime that is welling up and bursting forth from within him. In this sense a disgorging Green Man would appear to depict a state of soul in which there has been an inward experience of wintry death followed by resurrection into the Eternal Spring - a depiction of the soul for whom 'the Morning Star has risen in their heart'.

The emergence of light and the emergence of greenness are intimately connected.

A 'Pre-Green Man' in the short vestibule leading into the Sacristy

The second boss is an image of the Lamb of God holding the 'Resurrection Standard', which is a flag that is effectively the same as a St George's cross.

The Lamb of God in the second boss 35

The association of a 'Templar' red cross on a white background with both St George and also the Resurrection Standard appears to originate from the 12th/13th centuries. There is an interesting possibility: that these two seemingly different depictions of the same cross are symbolically connected to one another via the symbol of 'resurrection'. St George appears to derive from an ancient pre-Christian agrarian cult from the eastern Mediterranean region which is associated with death followed by resurrection, and this is understood through the deathliness of winter being followed by a 'resurrection' that shows itself in the greening of springtime. This ancient agrarian figure is described in mythological storylines as being tortured and killed and then soon after resurrected – sometimes as many as seven times in a row. In Islam this 'Georgic' character is known as 'The one who is green' (Al Khidr). The name George itself literally means 'farmer'. In Judaism the character is known as Elijah, and is often associated with high places such as mountain summits.36

Another interesting point here is that the celebration of this ancient Middle Eastern character is associated with the 'the first lamb of spring'. So both the 'Templar' flag of St George and the Resurrection Standard could appear to hold a similar initiatic symbolism which seems, like the Green Man, to relate to regeneration or resurrection as associated with springtime.

The Middle Eastern feast day of Al Khidr ('Hidirellez', which literally means 'Khidr and Elijah') is on 6 May, which is also the Middle Eastern feast day of St George. This day is the precise midpoint between the spring equinox and the summer solstice, which thus divides the year by 8/5 (from a starting point of the winter solstice). Such Fibonacci numbers and associations with death and resurrection are again reminiscent of the symbolism associated with the planet Venus, the Morning and Evening Star, which descends to death in the west but is then reborn in the east.

35. It so happens that this particular stone carving of the Lamb of God displays a striking resemblance to a medieval stone half-relief on the wall of the atrium of the St. Euphrasius basilica in Poreč, Croatia. Bishop Reginald's nickname 'Lombardus' relates to his Italian connections which may help to explain such a regional connection in artistic style.

36. See the article 'Georgic' Cults and Saints of the Levant' by H.S. Hadad, in Numen, 1 January 1969.

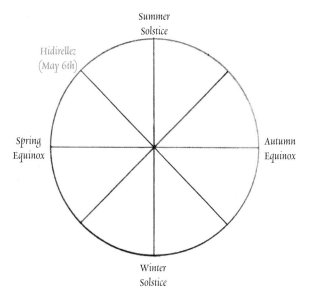

Summer
Solstice

Hidirellez
(May 6th)

Spring
Equinox

Autumn
Equinox

Winter
Solstice

But ultimately this 'Georgic' storyline of a Green Man who experiences torturous death followed by resurrection recalls the green/vegetal Egyptian god Osiris, and such an association again chimes with the Egyptic mythos that appears to be so central to the design of this particular cathedral as well as to the symbolism found both in alchemy and Freemasonry.

The third boss depicts two Green Men who are joined at the crowns of their heads – rather like conjoined twins. They are both disgorging greenery.

The fourth boss appears to be partly missing. From what is left of it there seems to be an image of a child,

although this is not clear. If it is a child, it is tempting to assume that it is Christ, although it is not clear that this is the case either. Two serpentine heads are nibbling this young-looking character – one at the back of his head, and the other at the base of his spine. These dual serpents seem to be a recurring theme in the sacristy and appear on more than one occasion.

The fifth boss depicts a four-legged animal with a tail that makes it look likely to be a cow or bull with horns.

The sixth boss shows two winged serpentine creatures biting their own bodies. Their ouroboric forms are also entwined as two rings linked around one another. This would clearly appear to be an image relating in some way to the uniting of duality. The two serpentine characters also appear to be the two faces that were nibbling the young-looking character in the fourth boss. They also appear to be the double ouroboros at the top of the pillar just inside the sacristy doorway.

The seventh and final boss depicts a male and female character next to one another, which echoes the male and female faces upon the doorway arch in-to the sacristy. But whereas they were on either side of the doorway, like a symbol of Sun and Moon or Spirit and Soul, these two characters are now very much together in *fin'amor*, and the woman is wearing a fillet and barbette headdress rather than a simple headscarf. The two serpentine creatures are again present – they are reaching down from above and nibbling the physical head-crowns of the couple.

But the couple are smiling, so it can't be that bad! An interesting thing about this boss is its orientation. When viewing the boss one has to turn sideways – or face eastwards, as it were – to see it properly, and what this does is to turn the body in such a way that it is almost facing the back door of the sacristy that leads into the octagonal undercroft.

Attempting to interpret the depictions within this sequence of bosses could go in many different directions. A symbolism concerning 'rebirth' and the 'union of opposites' certainly appears to be a recurring theme. But also the fact that there are seven of them, which then appear to usher their viewer into the eight-fold undercroft, displays numbers that are concordant with some sort of symbolic ascent. Various of the bosses do also symbolically chime with the Zodiacal signs that

are in the lighter half of the year – particularly those that fall between the spring equinox and summer solstice. However, they don't follow the usual order of the Zodiac.

1st boss – Green Man – spring equinox?

2nd boss – Lamb of God – Aries

3rd boss – conjoined heads – Gemini (i.e. twins)

4th boss – young child – although the rest of the boss is missing

5th boss – horned cow – Taurus

6th boss – dual ouroboric serpents – summer solstice? (i.e. meeting of descending/ascending halves of the year)

7th boss – male and female – Cancer (i.e. meeting of spiritual with material)

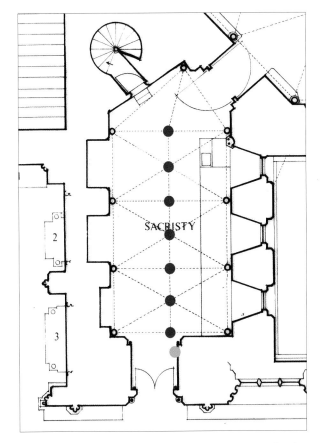

Positions of the seven ceiling bosses (red) and the 'Pre-Green Man' (green)

Whatever the bosses symbolise, their positioning does suggest a symbolic movement or progression of some sort that leads from the baseline of the pyramid triangle up the seven units of its height to its apex. This movement is initiated by the golden ratio line that marks Bishop Jocelin's grave, which itself then passes through the golden section sacristy doorway. There is then the northern ascent via the seven bosses, which finally leads through another golden section doorway towards the central octagonal pillar in the undercroft that marks the peak of the pyramid triangle. This northbound journey through seven stages thus seems to be a physically walkable 'ascent' to the apex of the pyramid triangle. The fact that it is set in a private clerical room appears to be symbolically appropriate to this stage of the soul's journey in the sense that one has to have completely committed oneself to the Trinity to reach this point. But it inevitably also appears to be the third and

final stage of a pathway that first passes through the 'earthly' nave, and which then ascends to the 'Edenic' Lady chapel in the east before the seven-fold ascent northwards towards the 'octagonal' eighth heaven and then beyond.

These various sections of writing have attempted to highlight a few apparent traces of medieval Christian cosm-initiatic culture. It would be interesting to see if there are similar traces elsewhere in the arts of medieval Christendom, although to catch short glimpses of them there is a need to be open to the spiritual imagination as well as to always be 'quadrivially' encouraging an opening of the Eye of the Soul. But ultimately initiation is veiled by secrecy, silence and darkness, and so as ever we are left with mystery which itself points the soul inwards, as if through the sacristy doorway at Wells, towards the apophatic darkness of the north.

The constellation Ursa Major (sometimes known as 'The Plough'). The north Pole Star or 'Polaris' - the current 'Stella Maris' - can be seen top right.

CHAPTER 21.
Final Points

21.1 PALM SUNDAY TO PENTECOST
AND THE SYNODIC PERIOD OF VENUS

THE NUMBERS ASSOCIATED with the synodic cycle, or period of Venus correlate in a symbolically interesting way with the period of time between Palm Sunday and Pentecost.

It was shown in section 5.1 that Planet Venus is the Morning Star for around 263 days. During this time she is on the right-hand side of the Sun as we see her from the Earth, and is visible to us just before sunrise. Then she passes behind the Sun, which makes her invisible to us for 50 days. She then becomes the Evening Star for around 263 days, and appears to the left of the Sun and visible to us just after sunset. After this she disappears again for around 8 days as she passes in front of the Sun before she is 'born again' as the Morning Star. This adds up to a total of 584 days.

The 57-day period of time between Palm Sunday and Pentecost is precisely one-quarter of Venus's orbital period, in that it is during the 57th day that she completes a quarter of her circular journey. A couple of days later Earth and Venus complete 1/10 of their whole synodic cycle. But the various synodic intervals, and their associated movements, also fit in a symbolically interesting way within the Christian storyline of these 57 days, and this shows itself through the paschal number 8 and the Pentecostal number 50, which occur as a result of the alignments between Sun, Venus and Earth.

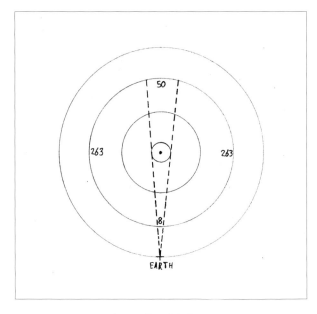

The Synodic Period of Venus

The 8 days between Palm Sunday and Easter Sunday – or when Planet Venus passes in front of the Sun – culminate with the rising of the Morning Star in the east on Easter Sunday. Then at the end of the period of time in which she is the Morning Star there is a 50-day period – like the 50 days of Pentecost – before Venus becomes the Evening Star again, having passed behind the Sun. The descent of the Evening Star, down to the Earth, reflects the descent of the Holy Spirit at Pentecost – 50 days after the rising of the Morning Star.

21.2 THE LATITUDE GEOMETRY OF JERUSALEM AND HERMOPOLIS

IN SECTION 5.6 IT WAS pointed out that one of the etymological theories in relation to the name 'Jerusalem' is that it is formed of the words *Yeru* and *Shalim,* which can be understood to mean 'established by Shalim'. In the Canaanite tradition Shalim is the planet Venus as the Evening Star. His twin brother Shahar is then the Morning Star. So this associates Jerusalem with the planet Venus from a very early period. For this reason, it is of particular interest that the Venusian numbers 5, 8 and 13 feature within the latitude geometry of the Temple Mount.

Below are two Fibonacci rectangles that approximate golden rectangles. The smaller one is 5 × 8. This rectangle also forms part of the second rectangle which is 8 × 13. The diagonals of the two rectangles run at angles very similar to one another, but slightly different. The 5 × 8 rectangle has a diagonal angle that runs at 32.005° whereas in the 8 × 13 rectangle the angle is 31.6075°.

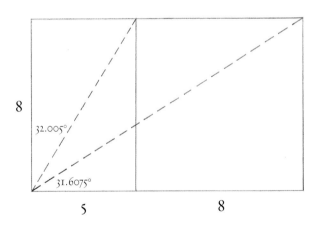

On the surface of the Earth the distance between these two angles of latitude is only around 27½ miles, and so it is interesting to note that the latitude angle of Jerusalem is between these two Fibonacci angles at around 31.77°.

The number 13 is clearly prominent within the Earth-Venus relationship because 8 Earth years are virtually identical to 13 Venus years. However, it can be argued from a sceptical position that this is 'heliocentric knowledge' that wasn't knowable in the ancient world. So we shall concentrate on the angle in the 5 × 8 rectangle, which as mentioned above is 32.005°. The numbers that seem to be used to symbolise Venus in the medieval and ancient world are 5 and 8, and indeed these are the geocentric numbers that we experience in relation to Venus' movements.

The Dome of the Rock on the Temple Mount will be used as the marker for this measurement as being on the presumed ancient sacred centre of the city. The southern edge of the Dome of the Rock building has a latitude of 31.777777°. If the 5 × 8 rectangle latitude angle is rounded down from 32.005° to the simpler 32° the difference between this and 31.777777° is 0.222222°, which is also 800" of latitude.

If this geographical measurement is used to divide the circumference of the Earth it produces 1620 equal parts, which is a phi-friendly number. Dividing 1620 by 1000 produces the phi approximation of 1.62, which is 81/50 (as opposed to 80/50, which is 8/5).

However, the particularly interesting feature of this example of 'geo-metria' is that 32° contains 144 of these geographical units, because:

$$32 \div 0.2222 = 144$$

The number 144 is one of the key numbers of the Heavenly Jerusalem. It is also the 12th Fibonacci number as well as also being the square of 12.

It is the 144th geographical unit itself that stretches between the Temple Mount and the 8/5 latitude that is to the north of it. So it is the presence of Jerusalem's Temple Mount itself, in relation to the 8/5 latitude, that causes the division of Earth's circumference into this particular geographical unit.

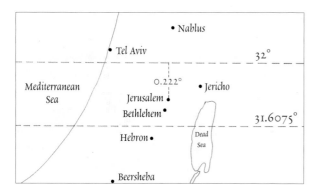

Jerusalem is located between latitude-angles found in the 8/5 and 13/8 rectangles. The Temple Mount is 0.222° south of the 8/5 latitude. There are 1620 of these geographical units in the circumference of the Earth.

This division of the circumference of the Earth via the 81/50 approximation of the golden ratio also shows itself within the latitude of the ancient town of Thoth/Hermes in Egypt. This town was very significant in ancient Egypt, as it was the division point between Upper and Lower Egypt. It used to be called Khemenu, which was a name that referred to the Egyptian Ogdoad – a collection of eight deities. But it was also the primary centre of worship of Thoth, the Egyptian God of Magic, writing and wisdom. The Greeks associated Thoth with their god Hermes, and the town eventually came to be known as Hermopolis. So in a sense, this is also the place of Hermes Trismegistus who is a fusion of Thoth and Hermes.

There was a castle just south of the town, and this was the division point between Upper and Lower Egypt. Today there is a town called El Ashmunein adjoining the southern edge of the archaeological site of Hermopolis, and it is around this area that there is a significant latitude.

This latitude of 27.777777° divides the distance between the equator and the north pole into 81 geographical units. There are 56 of these units between Hermopolis and the north pole, and then 25 units from Hermopolis to the equator.

This division – expressed as 81/25 – is a close approximation of $\sqrt{5} + 1$. In degrees of latitude the geograph-

ical unit is 1.111111°, which is five times larger than the Jerusalem geographical unit of 0.222222°. This 1.111111° unit is also the same as 4000" of latitude. The latitude of Hermopolis itself is 100,000" north of the equator.

The fact that there are 81 geographical units between the equator and pole inevitably means that there are 162 of them between the north and south poles. This accordingly means that the circumference of Earth is divided up into 324 units.

Bearing in mind that 162 can be reduced to 1.62 (81/50), which as described earlier is an approximation of the golden number (i.e. 1.618...), this means that the 324 can be reduced to 3.24 (81/25), which is an approximation of $\sqrt{5} + 1$. (2.236...+ 1) The number 2.24 would then approximate $\sqrt{5}$ itself.

The golden ratio is expressed as $(\sqrt{5} + 1) \div 2$, and this is equal to 1.618033. This can be rationally approximated as $(2.24 + 1) \div 2 = 1.62$.

This means that the position of Hermopolis creates a geographical unit that commensurately expresses the golden ratio formula in relation to the circumference of Planet Earth on its polar axis. The division of the Earth's 3.24 circumference by 2 makes 1.62, and this brings about the division of Earth's circumference into two halves – demarcated as they are by the north and south poles.

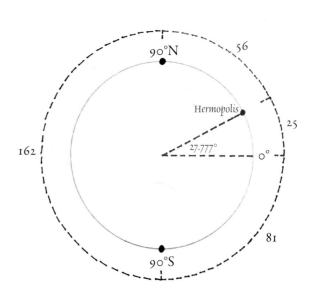

21.3 THE GOLDEN PEDIMENT TRIANGLE IN THE DESIGN OF THE GREAT PYRAMID?

IT WAS SUGGESTED a little earlier that the use of the pediment and pyramid triangles together in the same diagram might have been used in the design of the Great Pyramid as well as the design of Wells Cathedral.

There are an enormous number of geometric and metrological theories about how the Great Pyramid was designed, and what follows here will add yet another to this great plethora.

The pediment triangle which appears to have been used in the Wells design creates an interesting possibility when viewed in relation to the internal design of the Great Pyramid.

It was shown in section 7.2 that if the golden ratio measurements of the two right-angled triangles in this pediment triangle were 'Fibonacci-ised', so that the 1.618 was made into 1.625, it would effectively transmute the right-angled triangles into 5 – 12 – 13 triangles. (see section entitled 'The Golden Pediment Triangle' p.117)

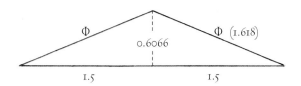

Golden Pediment Triangle - Base of 3, sloping sides of phi, height of 0.6066

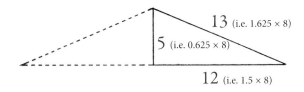

A 'Fibonacci-ised' Golden Pediment Triangle. The sloping sides increase from 1.618 to 1.625. This causes the height of 0.6066 to increase to 0.625. The resulting outcome is that the triangle turns into a fusion of right-handed and left-handed 5 - 12 - 13 triangles via multiplication by 8.

However, it is also possible to use other Fibonacci approximations in relation to this pediment triangle, such as 1.6, which is formed by the ratio 8/5. This is the Fibonacci ratio that immediately precedes 1.625, which is formed by 13/8.

So it is to this version of a pediment triangle, with sloping edges of 1.6, that we will now look in relation to the Great Pyramid, because if a Fibonacci pediment triangle of this sort is projected on to a measured cross-section diagram of the Great Pyramid, the apex of it appears to coincide with the top corner of the Great Step at the top of the Grand Gallery.

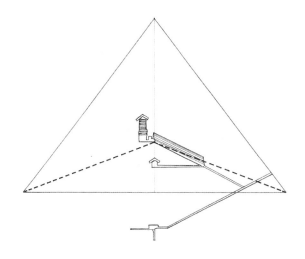

This step is on the same level as the King's Chamber plus its antechamber, and so it can be suggested that this marks a significant height. When this height is calculated in relation to the cubit measurement that appears to be used in the design of the pyramid, it gives a quite precise measure of 81.66 cubits above ground level.

However, this measurement begins to look particularly interesting when the equivalent measurement is taken from the 1.625 version of the pediment triangle, because that yields a result of 91.6666... cubits, which is 'as good as' 10 cubits more than 81.66. This can't help

395

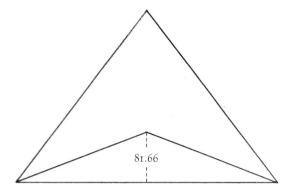

The Great Pyramid with an 8/5 pediment triangle 81.66 cubits in height

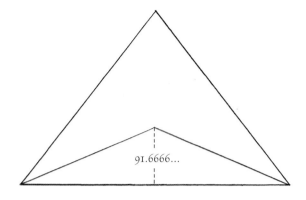

With a 13/8 pediment triangle the height becomes 91.6666... cubits

but seem of interest in relation to the fact that the shorter edge of the King's Chamber's ground plan is itself 10 cubits.

But this becomes even more interesting if a rational measure very close to the golden ratio itself is used to define the measurements of the pediment triangle. It was pointed out earlier that the height of the Golden Pediment Triangle in comparison to the height of the Golden Pyramid Triangle reflects a measurement that closely resembles pi. If the Golden Pediment Triangle has a height of 1, the Golden Pyramid Triangle has a height of 3.1451. So let the 280-cubit height of the Great Pyramid be divided by this pi measurement:

$$280 \div 3.1451 = 89.027$$

The result gives a very close approximation of 89 as the height of the pediment triangle. This is between the previously mentioned cubit measurements of 81.66 and 91.6666. But more to the point, 89 is the eleventh Fibonacci number. So it means that the use of 89 cubits as a height for the pediment triangle would bring about a very close approximation of an actual golden ratio Pediment Triangle.

So let it now be said that the height of the pediment triangle is 89 cubits above ground level. Such a measurement would mean that the sloping side of the pediment triangle would have a measurement that – in terms of the golden ratio – relates to 1.61809. This is the golden ratio expressed correctly to four decimal places.

But the question could be asked as to whether this measure is actually expressed in the Great Pyramid's dimensions in a similar way that the 10-cubit difference between 81.66 and 91.6666 appears to be used for the King's Chamber.

89 is 7.34 cubits higher than the Great Step, which is itself at 81.66.

So this would mean that there would need to be a measurement of 7.34 cubits above the height of the Great Step. There is a very close approximation indeed to this measurement that appears to be present in the height of the antechamber relative to the King's Chamber. According to Flinders Petrie's description:

'The whole chamber is from 149'01 [inches] to 149'65 high, the ceiling being from 152'6 to 153 above the virtual end of the gallery floor.'

7.34 cubits is equal to 151'3", which is as good as the arithmetic mean between these two different measurements given by Petrie.

So in this sense it can be suggested that all three pediment triangles might have been used in the Great Pyramid's design. The fact that the pediment is used along with the pyramid triangle in the design of Wells Cathedral, and that the Wells design's use of the pyramid triangle is fractionally related to the size of the Great Pyramid, suggests a connection between these geometries that characterises the Cosmic Canon.

21.4 BUT WHO DESIGNED WELLS CATHEDRAL?

SUCH A QUESTION is perhaps inevitable when one looks at the brilliance of the design along with its very accurately built dimensions. Since the Renaissance there has increasingly been a focus on the celebrity of a brilliant artist, rather than the more traditional understanding in which one might glory in the fact that the beautiful art form has been brought forth at all. It is after all far more significant in spiritual terms that Wells Cathedral was actually designed and built in the first place, and has been used devotionally ever since, rather than knowing who it actually was that designed it. But one thing that perhaps should be glorified is the fact that whoever designed Wells Cathedral was clearly very skilled in the realm of technical quadrivial knowledge along with being able to theologically shape this knowledge according to the medieval Christian spiritual imagination. It could be suggested that to contemplate the fruit of such artistic brilliance is far more spiritually inspiring than to know the mere historical fact of who this designer was. When a person of faith produces a beautiful work of sacred art they are doing it to encourage the soul who witnesses the art form to be reminded of the all-encompassing God, and not of the individual artist who produced it. As has been said on many an occasion:

'when a sage points at the Moon all that the ignorant see is his finger'.

Having said all of this, we are still left with the question 'Who designed Wells Cathedral?'

From a Christian perspective, the development of such a beautiful and technically coherent design must surely have been guided by the Holy Spirit. On a personal note, as a geometric designer myself, I have little idea how someone would go about producing a design such as this. It continues to act as my teacher. The thing that particularly stands out is the interfusion of so many concordant quadrivial relationships, be they cosmological numbers or geometric and musical relationships,

that all somehow accord with one another, forming a final fixed and mathematically provable design in which several particular relationships all inter-relate as one multi-faceted overarching relationship. As an artist I can revel in awe at such excellence, but am left little the wiser as to how one would embark on producing such a design.

In historical terms, there have been two possible sources for the design that keep returning thematically within this research. One is some kind of Templar-centric person or people associated with the Kingdom of Jerusalem, and the other is the local figure Adelard of Bath. The designer was clearly a highly competent and experienced artist who would presumably have been part of a craft guild. But for such an artist to have had some sort of connection to the Templars and/or Jerusalem and/or Adelard is an interesting possibility.

The reason for looking upon Adelard of Bath as an influence is first of all the fact that he was very local, and also quite uniquely knowledgeable within his era. He was also living in the few decades before Wells Cathedral began to be built. But he also had close royal connections, and is generally assumed to have been the astrologer for Henry II as well as having been his childhood teacher. This astrological and cosmological aspect of Adelard's studies, along with his travels in the Middle East, might explain the sheer profusion of spiritually meaningful cosmology within the design of Wells Cathedral. The solstitial and equinoctial/paschal symbolism within the design requires certain very specific geometric design features which are clearly only present at Wells and no other cathedral. These features include a particular type of 'equator–ecliptic' rectangle for the shape of the nave, the solstitial dedications of the side aisle east end chapels, and the Morning Star geometry that forms the Lady chapel. This is not even to mention the design's use of the Earth-Moon pyramid diagram within the quire/chapter house area – although as shown earlier, this is seemingly also used in the designs of York and Southwell minsters too. Adelard's interest in talismanic astrology seems familiar when looking at a Lady chapel that is formed of Venusian geometry and Rosary numerics. Bearing in mind the association of the planet Venus, and indeed of Lucifer, with the emerald, it is interesting to note that Adelard specifically describes himself as wearing an emerald ring – which for someone such as him in particular would almost certainly have been for reasons of talismanic astrology. For those who believe in talismanic magic – as various medieval church people did – the reason to involve cosmology in an architectural design would be to encourage the descent of a planetary essence which can thus influence the human soul who physically interacts with the 'cosmic' architecture. The 'Venusian' Lady chapel at Wells would presumably therefore embody Divine Love, whereas the 'lunar' chapter house – which also seems to symbolise the eighth heaven of the fixed stars – would presumably be designed to encourage the descent of the Holy Wisdom, which is symbolically associated with the descent of the Holy Spirit.

With Revelation and Adelard's native City of Bath in mind, it is also particularly intriguing that John Michell's book *City of Revelation* - his first book to contain the Earth-Moon diagram - was actually written and researched during what he described as *"almost two years of near total solitude and intense study in Bath".* [1] For Michell to envision this diagram was impressive enough but the fact he was residing in Bath as well...?

As to a Templar-centric influence from the Kingdom of Jerusalem, this looks possible partly because of the apparent connections of Bishop Reginald de Bohun to the culture of the Crusades that were mentioned at the end of chapter 3. But even more so in the Templar-centric aspects of the design such as the topographical emulation of Jerusalem's Temple Mount, as seen in the quire/chapter house area. There is also the pyramid triangle itself in the Wells design, as also in the apparent latitudinal locating of the first two Templar manors at Cressing Temple and Temple Cowley. Along with this, there are the close connections that the Templars appear to have had with building guilds, as well as their mythical association with Freemasonry and also the Dante-esque symbolism of passage in the Wells design.

But in the end, without any definite knowledge of who the designer was, perhaps we should just change our question of 'Who built Wells Cathedral?' to something more like 'Thank God that Wells Cathedral came to be designed and built'.

---

1. See Paul Screeton's biography of John Michell - page 42 (Heart of Albion Press - 2010)

21.5 THE USE OF REVELATION 22:16-17
IN THE DESIGN OF THE EAST END

THE HIGH ALTAR WALL at the east end of the quire at Wells is particularly renowned for its beautiful window depicting the Tree of Jesse, which shows the family line of Christ from Jesse, the father of King David. This window would have originally been visible from the nave, although unfortunately it is now obscured by the organ pipes that sit on the pulpitum at the quire's western end. Below the Jesse window are seven plinths on which seven statues stand, and then below them there are three arches that form the immediate backdrop of the high altar itself. The view through the three arches also affords a glimpse of the Lady chapel which lies beyond the quire up at the east end.

It was mentioned earlier that one of the few design principles known to have been used by Gothic cathedral designers is the practice of having the same architectural diagram in both the horizontal plan as well as the vertical cross-section. It was shown earlier how this appears to happen in relation to a pyramid triangle used in the design of the west front, but which then also 'folds down' on to the nave and produces measurements there too. But this also appears to occur in relation to the high altar wall in the sense that, if it could be laid down horizontally to the east, it would fit very neatly into the retroquire and Lady chapel area. In short, the pointed arch that forms the upper section of the Jesse window would fit nicely into the pentagonal east end of the Lady chapel.

The apparent relationship between this high altar wall and east end ground plan is of biblical interest in relation to the fact that the Jesse window is a visual depiction of Christ's familial connection to King David, and the Lady chapel beyond it an apparent architectural image of the Morning Star.

Bearing in mind that this part of Wells Cathedral is its final eastern culmination we can then look at the final culmination of the Book of Revelation, which also happens to be the final culmination of the Christian New Testament and thus of the whole Bible. The final three verses of Revelation – 18 to 21 – are a warning to anyone who would change the words of the book, and then a final proclamation and blessing to finish off. These feel like an epilogue of sorts that effectively follows on after the closure of the book's very dramatic storyline. So in this sense, the final words from the storyline itself are verses 16 and 17, and they are a proclamation that Christ makes about himself and his

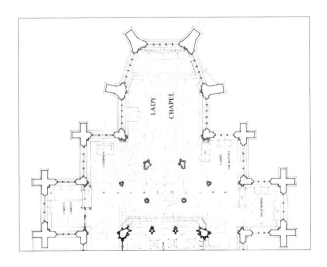

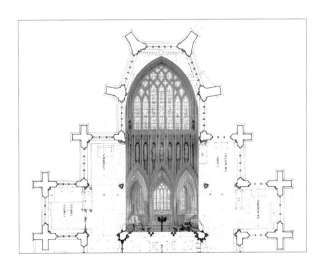

family line and the water of life that flows from the Heavenly City of New Jerusalem:

'16 I Jesus have sent mine angel to testify unto you these things in the churches. I am the root and the offspring of David, and the bright and morning star.

17 And the Spirit and the bride say, Come. And let him that heareth say, Come. And let him that is athirst come. And whosoever will, let him take the water of life freely.

It so happens that all of these themes could be said to be expressed in the cathedral's plan and section relationship mentioned above.

First, looking at the last sentence of verse 16, it begins with Christ's description of himself as *'the root and the offspring of David'*. This is clearly depicted in the Jesse window on the high altar wall because this (family) tree roots out from Jesse the father of King David. If one were to then imagine the high altar wall laid down horizontally eastwards into the Lady chapel, we then get rest of this second sentence in verse 16: *'and the bright morning star'*. Finally, the reference to the *'water of life'* accords with the orientation of the Lady chapel towards the St Andrew's wellspring, which is the holiest of the wells that the city of Wells is named after. Indeed, it is towards this particular well that the old minster church was also orientated, as well as a Roman mausoleum that was found in the Camery garden during archaeological excavations.

So again we are reminded of the Heavenly City of Jerusalem, in which can be found ...

'the river of the water of life, as clear as crystal, flowing from the throne of God and of the Lamb down the middle of the great street of the city"

Revelation 22:1–2

... much like the water from the holy wells of the city of Wells that run down the city's high street to this day.

Epilogue

*What this study suggests in relation to the current climate of
atheistic materialism, environmental destruction and cosmological colonialism.*

AN EPILOGUE concerning 'environmentalism' may at first appear a little incongruous, coming at the end of a book that has spent so much time looking at medieval Christian arts and philosophy. But the fact remains that the designer of Wells Cathedral clearly had a particular way of looking at the natural world and the wider cosmos that is quite different from the one that prevails today.

According to the cathedral's design the created order is viewed as a kind of theophany, or at least a realm by which there can be a remembrance of the transcendent and divine Reality from which creation originates. So therefore it is through a contemplative understanding of the Creation that there can be a remembrance of the Creator. To contemplate and then embody the eternal forms of number within beautiful works of art is to align the human mind with the Divine Mind, and to then act accordingly in relation to the soul's aspiration to remember its origin.

A geometer who wants to locate the 'hidden' centre of a circle needs to use various points on the visible circumference, in relationship with one another, and this then makes possible the discovery of the central point. But, of course, it was this very central point which gave birth to the circumference in the first place, and so the discovery is actually a *re*-covery and a remembrance of that unmanifest, dimensionless and singular point that forever exists at the very heart of the circle as its origin.

In this sense, a spiritually orientated perspective sees this world of material bodies as a perpetual opportunity to remember a transcendent origin. An engagement with the world is then one that reveres and loves the world, because it is through participation in the world that there can be a remembrance of That from which the world originates.

So why have we come to look upon the external world of matter as something 'in and of itself'? Why have we fallen into an existence in which the natural world and the wider cosmos is treated as if only a material object, to be exploited for personal material gain, as opposed to being the most outward and visible part of a soul who is to be loved and revered?

The egoic Luciferian aspiration is increasingly visible in the desire to expand outwards into the material world – and indeed into the wider cosmos beyond Planet Earth, which we have now dragged downward into the material realm within our perceptions. The spiritual ascent into the heavens is in reality a journey 'inward' to the centre of the soul – which is itself coincident with the Spirit. But this is symbolically and mythically depicted as a journey outward/upward through the planetary spheres to a heavenly origin that transcends the material world.

The literal ascent in spaceships, beyond Planet Earth, merely goes to another material realm – albeit one that is inhospitable to the human body, and which seemingly goes on forever. There is no heavenly stopping point or culmination as there would be in a movement inward to a central point, but rather just a perpetual movement outward and away from the centre – fixated upon perpetual growth but ultimately dissipating into nothing. The eternal fiery realm of the Empyrean is, in truth, the eternity of the central point which transcends the bounded spatial realm, rather than just being another material realm 'out there' that increases forever and ever – leading further and further into a dark obscurity.

Yet there is still a deep intuition of the soul's desirous potential for inward ascent, and so modern astronauts are listened to with a hushed reverence. They speak of transformative experiences through having gone into space, and so we dream of following in their exalted footsteps of apparent transcendence. Various modern astronomy programmes on television outwardly profess the usual materialistic atheism of view, but at the same time use imagery and language that is clearly designed to evoke a sense of spiritual awe. There is a genuine desire to transcend the materialism that we are mired in, even if this often shows itself ironically in the excessive use of material resources in an attempt to satiate our desire. But whereas outwardly focused desire moves outward forever and ever and is never satisfied – always wanting more and more, with larger and larger circumferences – the same desire, when focused inwardly to the centre, has the chance of eventually becoming satisfied because the external forms of this world come to be experienced as part of the ladder that leads inwards to a final stopping point and resting place.

So perhaps it is not desire itself that is the problem, but rather misdirected desire that forever increases in its 'radial measurement' rather than decreasing through slowly approaching the centre of the circle. In this sense all desire is ultimately nothing but the desire to remember the soul's Divine Origin ...

... and it is within a relationship ruled by Divine Love that there is the possibility of a marriage between the inner and outer worlds of our Being.

So as we participate in this world, let us look upward (and inward) and begin the ascent.

ACKNOWLEDGEMENTS

In a research project as long as this one it is virtually impossible to remember everyone who needs to be thanked for helping in some way – and I fear naming some names but then missing other names out. So rather than attempting to mention all the names of those who could be thanked – which would surely cover several pages – I would like to express my immense gratitude to all of those who have in some way influenced or aided this long and slow research project. There are some people who would not even be aware of the way in which they helped me along the way and I suspect also various people of whom I'm unaware that helped in the process. But there are many who will also be aware of the help they have given me and I thank each and every person who's had an influence on my perceptions and understanding.

Beyond my ever-developing practical knowledge, and the inevitable study of the written word, much of my learning takes place in the many interesting conversations I have with all sorts of people. It is very often through such conversations – which may even have no direct connection to my research at all – that my understanding of my work takes on new and useful directions. I recall one such random and short conversation with someone at a Christmas bazaar in Wells Town Hall which opened me up to whole new understanding of the journey of the soul through the planetary spheres!

I would like to thank the various members of the Chapter at Wells Cathedral who, over the years, have taken an interest in my research and supported it. Particular thanks also go to the cathedral Virgers who have given me access to various areas of the building for making measurements and taking photographs. I would also like to thank the Prince's Foundation School of Traditional Arts and the Temenos Academy, both of which originate in the work of my teacher Professor Keith Critchlow. A special mention also needs to be made of the 'three Johns' (Michell, Martineau and Neal) whose various researches have been central to the development of this research. I would also like to thank all of the many institutes and organisations who continue to employ me as a teacher and speaker/presenter. It was once I started teaching that my capacity as a researcher really came to fruition. Prof Critchlow would often invoke the exhortation from the Taittiriya Upanishad, about the inextricable connection between learning and teaching, as if to remind any prospective teacher that they are required to remain a student once they take on the role of teacher. Keith would often say "Learn–Teach, Learn–Teach, Learn-Teach!".

A final thanks must go to my wife, Helen and our children, Theo and Miriam who have been in such close proximity to me within this period of my life. Thanks for putting up with my obsession with Wells Cathedral! Also many thanks to my parents Alice and Dan and sisters Katherine and Emma particularly for those formative years being brought up in Muswell Hill.

For the production of this book I'd like to thank Wooden Books/Squeeze Press for publishing it. Thanks to Liz Dalby at Responsive Editing for the edit. For advice/help with my laying out of the book I'd like to thank Ana Maria Giraldo, John Martineau and Emma Bree. Thanks also for the tireless readers of my chapters and the many suggestions for improvement that they offered. In alphabetical order... Jon Allen, Alice and Dan Bree, Emma Clark, Julia Cleave, Leon Conrad, Daniel Docherty, Juliet Faith, Valentin Gerlier, Richard Henry, John Martineau, Julienne McLean, Genevieve Overy, Nicola Raye, Christine Rhone, Safiye Summersgill, Adam Tetlow and Rev David Thomas.

IMAGE CREDITS

All photos and diagram-images by Tom Bree except for,

Images/diagrams that include the Wells Cathedral ground plan - measured and drawn in 1976 by Nick Elkins and Dougal Hunter. Some images show the plan or areas of the plan and some show the plan with Tom Bree's geometric analysis drawn onto it. Plan used with kind permission from the Dean and Chapter of Wells.

In all the following, 'WC' means 'Wikimedia Commons'

Page 1. WC Detail of Madonna and Child enthroned by Bernardo Daddi. Robert Lehman Collection, 1975.
Page 2. WC Rose Nord Cathédrale de Laon. © Vassil, 2008.
Page 3. (top) Detail of Chartres Cathedral south-west portal tympanum. © Daniel Docherty. (bottom) WC See details above for '**Page 1**'. Shows the full image.
Page 4. WC Isis with Horus the Child. Acquired by Henry Walters. Bequeathed to Walters Art Museum.
Page 5. WC Our Lady of Walsingham. © Thorvaldsson. 2008. CC BY 3.0.
Page 7. WC Vitrail Chartres Notre-Dame. © Vassil, 2009.
Page 8. WC Alegoría de la alquimia en Notre-Dame. © Chosovi 2006. CC BY-SA 2.5.
Page 12. (top) WC The Hortus Deliciarum, Philosophy and the seven liberal arts. (bottom) Chartres Cathedral south-west portal tympanum. © Daniel Docherty.
Pages 13 & 14. WC Rose Nord Cathédrale de Laon. p.13 whole window P.14 'Rhetoric'. © Vassil 2008.
Page 15. 'Geometry' from north rose window at Laon. © Painton Cowen. see www.therosewindow.com
Page 16. 'Astronomy' (as above)
Page 17. WC Philosophia-ladder-of-liberal-arts-leipzig. Anon c 1230. Universitats Bibliothek Leipzig.
Page 18. WC Mappa Mundi 2 from Bede, De natura rerum. The Bodleian Libraries, Oxford. CC BY 4.0.
Page 21. WC Virgin's first seven steps. Chora Church. © José Luiz Bernardes Ribeiro / CC BY-SA 3.0
Page 23. WC Meister des Hildegardis. Scivias - c.1165. From the Yorck project. GFDL.
Page 24. WC Ladder of divine ascent. © Pvasiliadis 2007.
Page 25. WC Lambeth Bible - MS3 f6. Lambeth Palace.

Page 27. WC La nouvelle Jérusalem. © Kimon Berlin 2006.
Page 29. Woman Clothed in the Sun. C1255-60. Anon. www.getty.edu/art/collection/object/103S3J
Page 34. WC Samanid Mausoleum. © Faqscl 2012.
Page 35. WC The Kaaba during Hajj. © Adli Wahid 2018.
Page 36. WC (top-left) The Heavenly Jerusalem, 1375-1397. Jacobello Alberegno. State Hermitage Museum, Sanct Petersburg, RF 2016
Page 37. WC (mid-right) Galla Placidia, Ravenna. © Superchilum 2014. CC BY-SA 4.0
Page 38. WC Commentary on the apocalypse C940-45 by Maius. The Morgan Library and Museum.
Page 39. WC (left) Coronation chair by A.D.White (right) Chinese character for 'Wang' © White Whirlwind
Page 41. WC Plan of Jerusalem - Koninklijke Bibliotheek
Page 43. WC (mid-left) Earth © Kevin Gill
Page 44. Manuscript initial image of the Macabees. see www.metmuseum.org/art/collection/search/32832
Page 46. WC (top-right) Temple Church. © Coppins 2007
Page 47. All WC (top-left) Holy Sepulchre rotunda. © Braincricket 2012. (top-right) anastasia floor plan. © Talmoryair 2009 (mid-left) Dome of the Rock floor plan. © Dehio/Von Bezold. (mid-right) Dome of the Rock. © Brian Jeffery Beggerly. 2007. (bot-left) Amiens plan. (bot-mid) Plan of Notre-Dame, Paris. © Viollet-Le-Duc. (bot-right) Plan of Chartres catheral. © JBThomas4 2015
Page 50. WC Fulko melisenda. Anon 13th century.
Page 51. WC Lichfield cathedral. User:Bsou10e01. 2010
Page 53. WC (top-right) Sainte Chapelle. Didier B 2005. (bot-right) Collège des Bernardins. Onyryc 2014
Page 56. WC (top-right) Golden Gate. N Nijaki 2014.
Page 58. WC (mid-left) Dome of the Rock. I Giel 2018.
Page 60. WC Construction du Temple de Jérusalem. Jean Fouquet C1470. Bibliotheque nationale de France.
Page 61. WC (top) Hierosolima 1493. National Library of Israel. (bottom) Notre Dame Paris front facade lower © Benh LIEU SONG, 2007. CC BY-SA 3.0
Page 63. Othea's Epistle (Queen's Manuscript). 'The Influence of Venus'. Christine De Pizan. British Library.
Page 68. WC (bott-right) Cropped version of Kudurru Melishipak. Louvre. © Jastrow 2005

Pages 74 & 76. Neil Bremner www.madeportraits.com.

Page 79. WC Musician angels and the Harrowing of hell. Anon (1290). Walters Art Museum.

Page 81. WC Les Très Riches Heures du duc de Berry octobre. © R.M.N. / R.-G. Ojéda. Musée Condé.

Page 83. 'Venus - rose of the heavens' T & H Bree.

Page 90. WC The Sleeping Beauty by John Collier

Page 92. Rose by Lily Corbett. Venus glyph by Mark Mills

Page 95. WC Rosary with Virgo Lactans. Anon 1480-90. Getty Museum Collection.

Page 97. WC (top-right) Heroic Turkish flag © ATmaCa14 2016. (mid-right) Kudurru Melishipak. Louvre. © Jastrow 2005 (mid-left) Byzantium coin. 1st cent BC - 1st cent AD. Odysses from CNG website.

Page 99. WC (bott-right) Collection of Khamsa. Jewish examples i.e. 'Hand of Miriam'. © Bluewind 2013.

Page 100 and 101. WC Manesse codex 14th century.

Page 107. WC Great Pyramid of Giza. © Barcex 2008

Page 120. Photo of John Michell by Christine Rhone.

Pages 128/130/131. Platonic Solids diagrams from Platonic and Archimedean Solids By Dawud Abu-Asiya.

Page 162. (bottom) Arrol and Snell ground plan of York Minster. Tom Bree's geometric analysis overlaid. Reproduced by kind permission of the Chapter of York.

Page 163. WC Killpack Southwell Minster 1839 Plate Ground plan with Tom Bree's geometric analysis overlaid.

Page 165. WC Full moon in the clouds. © Katsiaιyna Naliuka 2015. CC BY-SA 4.0

Page 171. WC (top-right) woman teaching geometry. © British Library.

Page 174. Arrol and Snell plan of York Chapter House. Reproduced by kind permission of the Chapter of York.

Page 175. WC (mid-left) Killpack Southwell Minster 1839 Plate. Plan with Tom Bree's geometric analysis overlaid.

Page 179. (top-right) Arrol and Snell ground plan with Tom Bree's added red shading. (mid-left) mason's loft doorway. Photographer: Tom Bree. Both images reproduced by kind permission of the Chapter of York.

Page 180. Photographer: Tom Bree. Reproduced by kind permission of the Chapter of York.

Page 184. (top left) Photographer: Tom Bree. Reproduced by kind permission of Salisbury Cathedral. (top right) Photographer: Tom Bree. Reproduced by kind permission of the Chapter of York. (lower three images) WC The Hortus Deliciarum, Philosophy and the seven liberal arts. By Herrad of Landsberg.

Page 189. WC Schwarzes Stundenbuch edit. c 1475. From the workshop of Willem Vrelant.

Page 195. WC (left) Stele with open hand and Tanit sign. 3rd-1st cent BC © Rama. Museum of Fine Arts of Lyon.

Page 196. WC Stefan Lochner Madonna im Rosenhag. Photo - the Yorck Project (2002). Walraf-Richartz Museum.

Page 197. © Painton Cowen. www.therosewindow.com

Page 198. As above

Page 199. (top-left) As above (top-right) WC Killpack Southwell Minster 1839 Plate (bott-right) Arrol and Snell ground plan of York Minster. Reproduced by kind permission of the Chapter of York.

Page 202. WC (bott-left) Lincoln Cathedral, Deans eye window (bott-right) Bishops Eye window, Lincoln Cathedral. © Jules and Jenny (Flikr) 2017 & 2014

Page 205. Display panel from the Wells Bishop's Palace. Used with kind permission from The Palace Trust.

Page 210. Photo by Jason Bryant.

Page 211. WC Earth © Kevin Gill.

Page 221. WC The angel makes St John eat the book, Enoch and Helias. Wellcome images. CC BY 4.0.

Page 319. (bott-left) WC God the Geometer. Anon. c 1220-30 (bott-right) WC Reims Cathedral Hugues Libergier. © Palauenco5 2016. CC BY 4.0.

Page 337. God creating the sun and moon. British Library. See www.bl.uk/catalogues/illuminated manu-scripts/ILLUMIN.ASP?Size=mid&IllID=60211

Page 352. (mid-left) WC Maestro dei cassoni campana, teseo e il minotauro, 1510-15. Sailko 2017 (2 × bott-left) WC Hereford-Karte (lower mid-right) WC Labyrinth at Chartres Cathedral Daderot 2005. CC BY-SA 3.0 (bott-right) WC Labyrinthe de la Cathédrale Notre-Dame d'Amiens. © Jean Robert Thibault 2012 CC BY-SA 2.0

Page 355. From the psalter-hours of Yolande de Soissons. c 1280-1299. Morgan library.

Page 360. WC William Marshall. © Zephyrus27 2018.

Page 361. WC Sienese St Michael and the Dragon. 9gHUaR9XS727lg at Google Cultural Institute.

Page 362. WC St Michael & the dragon. Rogers Fund, 1912.

Page 369. WC The rock of the Dome of the Rock. © G. Eric and Edith Matson Photograph Collection.

Page 373. WC Gustave Doré - Dante Alighieri - Inferno.

Page 384. WC (bott-right) Crozier of the Syriac Orthodox Bishop. © Kokkarani 2015.

INDEX

ablution(s) – 77, 268, 356

Abu Ma'shar – 106

Adam and/or Eve – 78, 80, 84, 340, 342-3, 344

Adelard of Bath – 105, 138, 192-3, 197, 345-ft, 397-8

Aelred (Saint) – 5, 21

agrarian – 81, 387

aisle(s) – 72, 157, 218, 252, 254-5, 301, 306, 309, 322, 329-31, 343, 374, 382, 397

Al – (for Arabic names beginning with 'Al' see initial of name i.e. 'M' for Al-Masudi)

Albert Pike (Freemason) – 324, 332

Alchemy/alchemical – 86-7, 92, 105, 168, 324-ft, 352, 364, 366, 384-6, 388

alien(s) – 104, 107, 205

all-seeing – 184-6, 190, 286

allegorical/allegory – 20, 24, 36, 44, 78, 177, 286, 339, 346-ft, 353, 369, 385

Ambrose (Saint) – 84-8

Amiens Cathedral – 47, 351-2

anagogical(ly) – 24-6, 91, 358

anamnesis – 77, 88, 356, 363

ancient(s) – 4, 15-7, 20-1, 32, 39-40, 70, 77, 88-93, 96-101, 104-8, 120-4, 136-8, 168, 174, 178, 190-5, 205, 229-31, 300, 315, 320, 323-4, 332, 339, 346-ft, 351-3, 363-6, 369, 385-7, 393-4

Andrew the Apostle (Saint) – 50, 54, 136-8, 212-5, 219, 245-6, 258-60, 304, 318, 346, 357, 400

angel(s) – 44, 75, 200, 224, 341, 343-9, 363, 385-ft, 400

Anne (Saint) – Virgin Mary's mother – 21

Annunciation – 66, 100, 223, 368

anticlockwise – 35, 333

antiquity – 24, 68, 342-ft

Aphrodite – 24, 82, 91, 100, 371, 385

apocalypse – 28, 106

apostle(s) – 9, 36, 75, 190-1, 246, 265, 286-7, 367

approximation – 33, 109, 113, 117-18, 122, 133, 152, 155, 222-3, 245, 252, 263, 266-7, 271-77, 283, 289-90, 298, 300-1, 308, 315, 378-ft, 381, 393-6,

(Al)-Aqsa mosque – 46, 57, 59, 322, 358

archbishop – 50, 52, 102, 108

archetype/archetypal – 2, 4, 39, 82, 91, 121, 178, 282, 331-4, 365-ft, 368-ft, 370

Archimedes – 289

Archytas - 231

Aristotle – 14, 192, 338

arithmetic(al)-(ly) – 11, 14-6, 19, 62, 110, 119, 140, 143, 148, 168-9, 182, 192, 220, 224-5, 229, 245, 248, 276, 297, 299, 309-10, 314-5, 339

arithmetic mean – 167-8, 234, 237, 248, 252, 256, 264, 267, 268-ft, 271, 293, 299, 306, 308, 310, 339, 396

artist(ic) – 15, 32, 52, 55, 120, 174, 181, 200, 260, 265, 318-21, 328, 357-8, 397

ascension – 42, 59, 66, 77, 171, 191, 218, 265, 341, 375, 385

ascent – 2, 3, 17, 19-26, 40, 42-3, 47-8, 54, 80-1, 91, 100, 107, 124, 159, 185, 190-ft, 191, 216-9, 234, 291, 318-22, 327, 332-3, 344, 346-ft, 347, 351, 353, 363, 365, 368, 370-1, 373-83, 389-90, 401-3

Asclepius – 15, 106, 124, 192, 224-ft

Ashwatthama - 347

astrology/astrological – 19, 92-3, 104-6, 171-3, 192-3, 212, 324-ft, 365-ft, 366, 372, 397-8

Athanasius (Saint) – 21, 75

Athelstan (King) - 212

Augustine (Saint) – 4, 16, 22-3, 91, 286-9, 326, 332

Aurora – 89-90, 332

autumn – 56-ft, 66-ft, 214, 329, 368, 373-4, 388

Avebury – 134-5

axial tilt of Earth – 168, 213-7, 234

axis/axial(ity) etc – 9, 30, 32, 46-8, 50-ft, 71, 134, 138, 150, 178, 181, 191, 206, 214, 215-ft, 216-8, 232, 236-7, 251-4, 271-3, 277, 280, 286, 309, 322, 324-7, 331, 339-40, 343-4, 383, 386, 394

Babylon(ian) – 28, 68, 97-9, 104-6, 192-4, 341-4, 348,

baptism – 77, 356

Barnabas (Saint) - 332

Basil (Saint) – 84-8,

bay – 47, 57, 144, 159, 169-71, 181, 235-8, 248, 255-7, 262, 269-74, 303-4, 345-51, 365, 370, 379-81, 384-5,

Bayt al-Hikma (House of Wisdom) – 106, 192

Beatrice – 101-ft, 160, 364-ft, 370-76

beauty/beautiful etc – 6, 22, 40, 54, 75, 85-90, 100, 121, 126, 160, 166, 222-4, 232, 237, 260, 319, 333-5, 342, 397-401

Beelzeboul – 363-5

Bernard of Chartres - 104

Bernard of Clairvaux (Saint) – 5, 22, 25, 52, 80, 85-8, 342, 372

Bernard Silvestris – 24, 294, 324-ft, 333-ft 353

Bible/Biblical – 2, 5, 21, 22-ft, 24-5, 28, 48, 56-9, 75, 81, 98, 178, 186, 262, 265-8, 287, 323, 326-30, 339, 342, 351-ft, 353, 359-60, 367, 399

Bishop(ric) – 50, 155, 164, 184-7, 200-2, 283, 376, 382-4

Bishops -
- Beckynton of Bath and Wells – 56
- Bertoldi da Serravalle - 376
- Bubwith of Bath and Wells – 376
- Hallum of Salisbury - 376
- Hugh (Saint) of Lincoln – 202-3
- Hugh of Wells (Bishop of Lincoln) – 203
- Jocelin of Bath – 384-90
- John Drokensford of Bath and Wells – 145
- Reginald de Bohun of Bath – 50, 203, 323, 398
- William of March (Bishop of Wells) - 328

Bishop's Palace – 62, 201-10, 245, 313,

Boethius – 2-5, 9, 14, 16, 22, 81, 185-6, 192, 336, 341, 343

bounded (peiron) – 112, 222-4, 402

boundless (apeiron) – 222-4

bride – 38, 400

Bright Morning Star (see 'Morning Star')

Buddhist/Buddhism – 59, 338, 343, 344-ft

Burckhardt (Titus) – 35-6, 55, 348-ft

buttresses – 52, 328

Caduceus – 338-9, 384

Cancer – 217-9 322-4, 329, 374, 389

canon's door – 159, 219, 255, 345-6

Canterbury – 42, 50, 53, 67

Carthage - 194

Capricorn – 217-9, 322-4, 329, 374

cathedra (Bishop's throne) – 382-3

cathedral – 2-4, 7, 11-3, 17, 22, 26, 44-7, 50-62, 66-7, 70-6, 81, 85-6, 91, 96, 100, 106-9, 112-9, 123, 128, 132-3, 136-49, 152, 155-9, 162-9, 173-8, 181-3, 186, 190-213, 216-20, 224-5, 231-47, 252-5, 258-65, 269, 281, 284-7, 291, 296-8, 303-13, 318-34, 339-40, 343-6, 349-53, 357-8, 364-6, 369-70, 373-85, 388, 395-401

cave(s) – 367-9

celestial – 17, 23, 26, 93, 98, 106, 160, 294, 342-ft, 348-ft, 376

Celestial North Pole – 21, 29, 35, 138, 190-1, 194, 327, 333, 375

centre(d)/central(ity) – 4, 9, 14, 17, 25-6 30-7, 40-49, 58-9, 64, 68, 72-6, 80, 88, 95, 98-ft, 108, 116, 123-4, 128, 136, 138, 140-8, 159, 169, 174, 184-6, 190-4, 197, 203, 208-9, 214, 218-9, 223, 237, 246, 252, 255-7, 284-5, 301, 306, 313-4, 320-1, 324-7, 332, 335 338-40, 344-53, 360 363-72, 375-6, 380-85, 393-4, 401-2

chapel (also see Lady chapel) – 11, 53-ft, 56, 67, 72, 137, 141, 174, 208-9, 215, 219, 298-9, 303-4, 306, 308-12, 329-31, 343, 373, 397

chapter house – 57-8, 72, 144-52, 161-8, 173-202, 220, 243-6, 249, 262, 279-87, 292-3, 325-7, 333-5, 358, 368, 375-6, 383, 397

Chartres Cathedral and school – 3-4, 7, 12-4, 24-5, 47-8, 104, 351-2, 353-ft, 365, 372-ft, 385-ft,

Chinese – 32, 39, 168, 173, 330, 338-9

chivalry/chivalric – 84, 87, 100, 351-ft, 352-3, 359-63, 370

Christ – 3-5, 9, 13, 21-2, 25, 29, 40-9, 56, 60, 64, 66-7, 73-80, 86-7, 95, 124, 177, 198, 218-9, 223, 240, 287, 312, 321-7, 331-5, 338-47, 359-60, 364-9, 375, 385, 399

Christian/Christianity – 2-5, 10-11, 14-6, 19-30, 35, 40-5, 48, 52, 55-9, 66-7, 75-81, 84, 87-8, 91-4, 98-100, 104-6, 109, 124, 136, 177-81, 186, 190-ft, 192-3, 205, 217-8, 223, 260, 265, 286, 291, 294, 316-35, 339-41, 344, 348, 352-3, 355-60 363-72, 376, 387, 390, 392, 397-401

chromatic scale – 230-1

church(es) etc – 2-4, 16, 21-2, 24-6, 28, 31, 42, 46-50, 54, 58-9, 75, 93-4, 98, 134-7, 140, 143, 149, 163-4, 174, 177, 197, 213, 219, 320-4, 327, 332, 340, 353, 360, 369, 376, 384, 398, 400

churchmen and women – 15, 19, 93, 104, 192

circle(s) – 9, 18, 28, 30-3, 36, 39-40, 43, 47, 64, 69, 72, 88-9, 92, 95, 98, 112-6, 120-4, 134-5, 140-3, 147-8, 182, 185, 190-1, 194, 206-7, 214, 217, 222-3, 229, 247, 258-9, 265-6, 267-8-ft, 281-9, 291-3, 301-9, 312-4, 319, 322-4, 327, 329, 338, 358, 384, 401-2

circumference – 33, 40, 43, 113-4, 122-3, 134, 182, 223, 247-8, 258-9, 268, 282-5, 304, 324, 338, 393-4, 401-2

Cistercian – 5, 22, 25, 53,

Clement of Alexandria (Saint) – 30, 332

climb(ed) – 2, 21, 24-6, 29, 42-3, 80, 91, 100, 166-71, 286, 373, 377

408

clockwise – 116, 182

cobra – 346, 385

commensurable – 222-3, 249-50, 289, 335

compasses – 32-3, 110, 113, 123, 180, 223, 320, 338-9

Confucius/Confucianism – 32, 338

conjunction – 65, 69

Consolation of Philosophy – 2, 8-9, 17, 22, 24, 81, 185, 190

conspiracy theories – 107-8, 190, 367-ft

Constantine the Great – 212, 215

constellations – 6, 29, 37, 390

contemplating/contemplation etc – 2-3, 10, 11, 15, 16, 32, 42-3, 91, 92, 101, 107, 124, 181, 195, 223-4, 232, 260, 313, 318, 320-1, 331, 333, 357, 363, 378, 397, 401

Convivio – 19, 185

copper – 385

Corinthians (two Biblical books) – 25, 40, 335-ft

corner(s) – 4, 28, 30-7, 45-7, 110-1, 124, 128, 141, 143, 146, 152, 157, 162-4, 208, 214, 235, 249, 275, 313, 326-9, 331, 333, 339, 343, 375, 381-82, 395

coronation – 39-40-2, 49-50, 59, 66, 322

correspondence(s) – 13, 14, 36, 93, 287, 351, 377-8, 383

corrupt(ion) – 3, 15, 20-2, 50, 342, 344, 365

cosmic(ally) – 17, 24-5, 29, 37, 43, 48, 50-ft, 56-ft, 68, 82, 96, 97, 98, 105, 108, 120-1, 123, 130, 132, 143, 148, 185, 195, 225, 232, 238-40, 245, 249, 260, 296, 305-6, 308, 318, 321, 327-9, 344-5, 357-8, 371, 373, 376, 396

cosmic canon of measures – 130, 224, 249, 296, 396

cosm-initiatic - 358-9, 365, 368, 376, 390

cosmos – 22, 25, 43, 108, 120-1, 222, 316, 319-20, 356-7, 364, 369-70, 401

Cosmographia – 24, 294, 324-ft, 333-ft, 353

cosmology/cosmological – 14, 16-21, 26, 29, 38, 47-8, 64-70, 73-8, 82, 87-ft, 93, 96-100, 104-5, 108, 118-20, 132, 134, 142, 148, 163, 167-8, 174, 178, 190, 193-4, 205, 212-3, 216-8, 224-5, 230-6, 239-40, 244, 282-3, 294, 304-5, 318-27, 330-32, 335, 340-1, 344-6, 353-ft, 358, 365, 370-73, 384, 397-8, 401

cosmythology – 77, 341

courtly love – 87, 101, 217, 359, 370

covenant – 42, 190, 287, 339

craft guild(s) – 177-8, 318, 321, 359, 397

Creation – 16, 23, 25, 84, 93, 318, 342-ft, 401

Creator – 16, 22-3, 39-ft, 93, 180, 319, 401

crescent (moon) – 65, 97, 286, 365

Cressing Temple – 49, 134-8, 194, 398

cross – 30-1, 37, 40-6, 92, 124, 212-9, 325-7, 332, 335, 339, 346, 359, 364, 384-7

crown(ed) etc – 29, 39-40, 49, 53-ft, 67, 73-4, 80, 84, 100, 124, 185, 200, 312, 342-9, 364, 372, 385, 388-9

crozier – 383-5

crucified/crucifixion etc – 22, 42, 46, 74, 92, 212, 219, 325, 327, 335, 338-40,

cruciform – 37, 219, 256, 327

Crusader(s) – 18, 42-5, 48-50, 55-8, 135, 157, 193, 322-3, 352-3, 358-9, 368

Crusades – 44-5, 50-2, 99, 320, 359, 398

cube/cubic/cuboid – 29-37, 39-40, 55, 128-30, 224

cubit(s) – 35, 57, 106, 112, 119-20, 143, 148, 206-9, 223-5, 228-9, 242-56, 262-8, 271-5, 292-7, 312-3, 328, 395-6

culmination – 46-8, 88, 200, 327-32, 346-ft, 351, 375, 399, 401

Daedalus – 81-ft, 338, 351-2,

Dante – 18-19, 25, 80-1, 86-ft, 88-9, 93, 98-ft, 101-ft, 160, 185, 190-ft, 200, 219, 291, 321, 327, 344-5, 351-ft, 353, 360-ft, 364-ft, 367, 370-76, 398

Dao(ist)(ism) – 330, 342, 356

dark/darkness etc – 4-5, 21, 26, 66-ft, 70, 75-7, 80-ft, 86-ft, 101, 108, 202-3, 218-9, 322-4, 329-35, 338-9, 342-5, 366-8, 373, 381, 390, 402

dawn – 5, 44, 65, 75, 85, 89-90, 332

dean – 145, 186-8, 202, 283

death(ly) etc – 23, 28, 38, 40-ft, 42, 74-82, 87, 93, 157, 173, 203, 218, 257, 320-1, 324-5, 331-4, 341-4, 348, 353, 356, 359, 365-8, 374, 386-8

decad – 10-1, 94, 126, 356

decagon – 112-7, 262, 267, 268-ft, 283-ft

decagram (star) – 58, 114, 152-4, 262-3, 266-7

decimal – 112, 194, 222, 231, 245, 252, 255, 266-7, 276-7, 300, 305, 308-9, 312, 396

degrees (Freemason initiation) – 81, 177, 325, 331-3, 339, 343, 360-ft,

degrees (see appropriate number) – 42, 128-31, 135-8, 163, 182, 215, 248, 259, 314-5, 394

Demiurge – 20-2

demon(s) etc – 154, 350-1, 362-364, 367

descend(ing)/Descent etc – 9, 21, 25-7, 32, 40, 42, 44, 48, 64, 75-82, 86, 91, 101, 107, 191, 193, 218-9, 223, 234, 265, 286-7, 321, 331, 334, 339, 341-8, 353, 359, 363-70,

373-7, 385, 387, 389, 392, 398

Devil – 44, 202, 342-9, 363

diabolical – 22, 340

diagonal(ly) – 111, 138, 141, 151, 169, 182, 212-9, 222, 234-5, 277, 280-1, 291-3, 346, 393

Dialectic – 14, 19

diatonic scale – 230, 231-ft, 311-2,

dimension(al) – 30-4, 37, 59, 66, 82, 89, 105, 136, 148, 152, 177, 181, 205-6, 209, 215-ft, 223, 229, 242, 245, 262, 266-7, 277, 289, 296, 305-7, 310, 313, 322-5, 329, 364-5, 368, 376, 380, 396-7

dimensionless – 33-4, 43, 358, 401

Dionysius (Saint) – 16, 26

Divine Comedy/Commedia – 19, 25, 80, 86-ft, 88, 98-ft, 190-ft, 200, 291, 321, 344, 351-ft, 353, 360-ft, 367, 370-76

Divine Mind – 107, 121, 124, 232, 237, 260, 320, 401

divorce(d) – 23, 88, 223

doctrine – 4, 16, 338, 353, 377

dome – 31, 34, 47, 61, 73-4, 80,

Dome of the Rock – 25, 46-8, 57-8, 61, 284, 358, 368-9, 393

donkey – 44, 58-9, 360

door(s) – 3, 8, 13, 21, 26, 44, 46, 54-9, 66, 157-9, 162, 177-83, 186-ft, 193, 234, 250-5, 269-70, 276-78, 309, 322, 325, 328, 332-3, 339, 343, 369, 381, 384-5, 389

doorway(s) – 5, 13, 36, 56, 59, 133, 159, 163, 167, 171, 175-87, 190, 209, 219, 251-4, 269-277, 286, 292, 324, 327-9, 346, 369, 379-90

dove – 21, 223, 340, 371

Dowry of Mary – 4-5, 87

dragon – 28, 44, 169, 170, 334, 348-9, 369, 384-5

Druze – 359

duality – 33, 222, 338-9, 343, 365-ft, 378, 388

Earth (planet) – 5, 9, 17-8, 20-3, 26, 31-7, 39-40, 43, 45-6, 64-70, 80, 87, 91, 93, 96, 102, 108, 120-8, 134-5, 148, 162, 167-8, 174-7, 206-7, 211-9, 222-3, 229-ft, 232-8, 242-6, 258-60, 296-7, 304, 308, 313-5, 322, 325, 338, 343-6, 351-3, 357, 363, 365, 367-71, 373, 382, 385, 392-4

Earth-Moon diagram – 120-1, 124-31, 148-9, 155, 162-4, 173-4, 191, 194-5, 206, 220 241-7, 256-9, 265, 276, 280-1, 286, 293, 296, 313-5, 333, 365, 398

Earth-square – 122, 126-30, 162, 173, 247,

east/eastern etc – 5, 21, 36-7, 42-3, 47-8, 52-4, 56-ft, 57-9,

64, 66-7, 71, 75-80, 85-6, 91, 99-100, 106, 134, 138, 142-6, 152, 155, 159, 174, 178, 180-1, 187, 191, 193, 208, 212-9, 237, 248, 255-7, 262, 265, 273, 283, 312, 320-34, 339-46, 349-51, 356-9, 365, 370, 373-5, 378-92, 397-400

east end – 26, 55, 66-7, 71-4, 85, 114, 140-5, 149, 152-4, 197-203, 216, 234, 262-3, 269, 284, 296-301, 307-9, 312, 327-9, 331-2, 343, 346, 370, 373-5, 379-83, 399

Easter – 9, 22-3, 75, 78, 86, 217-8, 286, 321-2, 325-7, 330-2, 335, 345, 392

ecliptic – 18, 175, 212-3, 216, 219, 234-6, 373, 397

Eden(ic) – 45, 66, 80, 84-92, 100, 197, 312, 327, 342-3, 351-3, 370, 373-5, 390

education(al) – 11, 16, 19, 22, 106, 197, 356

Egypt/Egyptian etc – 4, 24, 31, 53, 102-9, 112, 123, 136, 192, 204-6, 242-4, 249-50, 287, 297, 331, 346-ft, 363, 388, 394

Egyptian Royal Cubit – 206, 242-4, 249-50

eight – 30, 33-4, 37, 68-71, 74, 96, 101, 169, 193, 218, 285, 325, 332, 394

eighth heaven – 17, 21, 37, 62, 161, 185, 190-1, 200, 230, 282, 287, 327, 333, 371-72, 390, 398

elements (i.e. four earthly) – 6, 34, 128, 339,

eleven – 49, 113, 125, 128, 170, 297, 314-5, 396

Elijah - 387

emanation – 6, 20

embody(ing) etc – 33, 43, 46-8, 61, 72, 77, 85-ft, 94-5, 98, 100, 109-10, 119, 122, 164-68, 174, 177, 186, 200, 205, 216, 223-5, 230-2, 240, 260-2, 294, 297, 300-1, 304, 318-9, 322, 329, 340, 346, 398, 401

emerald – 342-4, 346-ft, 347-9, 385, 398

empirical(ly) – 107, 120, 140, 180, 209, 285, 318, 334, 356

Empyrean – 25, 80, 344-5, 371, 375, 402

end of time – 24, 28, 37-8, 44, 55, 157, 368

England/English etc – 4-5, 18-9, 39, 42-4, 49-54, 58, 62, 66-7, 73, 87, 95, 106-8, 135-7, 143, 174, 186, 192-3, 197, 203, 212, 220, 225, 322, 325, 352, 360, 369, 376

English foot/feet – 120, 125, 130, 182, 225-31, 235-6, 240, 249-51, 255-6, 264, 285, 294-300, 303, 308, 311-2,

Enlightenment – 91, 107-8, 136, 180-1, 321, 334

epic – 25, 373

equal(ly)/equality etc – 21, 29-35, 68, 86-ft, 89, 92, 116-7, 123-4, 134, 158, 234, 239, 247, 265-8, 273, 283-5, 297, 305, 336-8, 342, 357, 373, 393-6

equator – 18, 134-8, 175, 212-9, 234-6, 248, 258-9, 314, 322, 325, 373-4, 394, 397 equinox(es) – 4-ft, 22, 36-7, 56-ft, 66, 86, 138, 213-4, 218, 322-6, 329-31, 338-9, 368, 373-4, 387-9

Ernest McClain – 128, 231, 247-8, 264

eschatological – 28, 44, 48, 157

eternal(ly) – 6, 15, 55, 86, 124, 160, 177, 185, 195, 200, 260, 313, 332, 338, 342-3, 347-8, 354, 357, 367, 371, 373-4, 385-6

eternal forms of number – 223, 232, 320, 401

Eternal Spring – 85-6, 101, 351, 373-4, 386

Eucharistic – 22, 325, 344

Evening Star – 64-5, 68, 71, 74, 77, 82, 91, 321, 341, 346, 363-4, 385-7, 392-3

evil – 6, 20-2, 93, 99, 108, 344-ft, 360

Exsultet – 75, 78, 332, 344

external – 30-2, 52, 124, 209, 266-7, 401-2

extreme(s) – 43-6, 81, 106, 116, 163, 168, 214-5, 218, 234, 251-2, 322-4, 328, 335-40, 343

Eye of Providence – 184-6, 190-1, 286, 343

Eye of the Soul – 357, 390

Ezekiel – 5, 21, 25, 35-7, 42, 66, 157, 342, 376

fairy tales – 88, 356

fall (The) – 20, 78, 85-8, 319, 341-6, 353, 357, 363, 372-3

Fallen Angel – 341-9

Fatimah Zahra – 84-ft, 87-ft, 89-ft, 98-9

feet (human anatomy) – 9, 29, 34, 42, 46, 71, 309, 319-ft, 331, 348, 360,

female(s) – 2, 4, 11-4, 22, 29, 84, 87-92, 141, 181, 184, 319-20, 334, 340, 370-73, 386, 388

Fibonacci – 68, 71, 92-ft, 112-3, 117-9, 128-33, 150, 155, 168, 193, 222-3, 243-6, 250, 263, 266-7, 271, 276-7, 280, 283, 293, 303-ft, 305, 309-13, 380-83, 387, 393-6

Fibonacci Pyramid Triangle – 119, 245

Fin'amor – 37, 384, 389

fire/fiery 2, 15, 34, 89, 128, 349

fire and water – 81-ft, 106, 339

five – 11, 31, 34, 45-6, 50, 68, 71, 74, 80, 84-6, 91-5, 98-101, 114, 147, 162, 169-70, 176-8, 181, 193, 200, 231, 237, 252, 255, 284, 287, 292, 309, 328, 332, 343, 364-5 394

five wounds – 46, 73-4, 80, 84, 124, 364

focal(ity) – 42-3, 46-8, 98, 126, 136, 146

foot/ feet (human anatomy) – 9, 29, 34, 42, 46, 71, 120-1 309, 319-ft, 331, 348, 360,

foot/feet (measurement unit) – 112, 120-1, 136, 143, 147-8, 174, 194, 209 225-8, 231, 234-40, 249-51, 255-6,

264, 271-85, 293-4, 298-304, 308, 311-2, 369, 379-83

foundation stone – 35, 39, 331

four – 9, 13-6, 24-37, 42, 45-6, 52, 94-6, 123-4, 128, 131-2, 141, 145, 168-9, 177-8, 187, 190-2, 214-5, 225, 229, 256, 265, 283, 292-4, 315, 320-1, 324, 327-8, 332, 356-7, 365-ft, 375, 377-9, 382,

fourteen – 25, 289

fraction(al) – 164, 168, 204-6, 222, 225, 236, 240, 244, 311, 396

Freemason(ry) etc – 32, 81, 136, 167-8, 173-ft, 177, 180-1, 190, 193, 215, 316-34, 338-9, 343, 358-9, 360-ft, 365, 368, 376, 388, 398

Fu Xi and Nu Wa - 339

Fulk (King of Jerusalem) – 49-50, 135

Gawain – 84, 92-ft, 99, 363-5, 369

gaze – 30, 43, 100, 101-ft, 160, 335, 379

Genesis – 25, 40, 84-5, 90-ft

geo-cosmic – 207, 314, 368, 373

geo-metria – 102 108, 171, 248, 258, 319-20,

geocentric – 64, 68-70, 96, 308

Geoffrey Chaucer – 135-6, 137

geometer – 32, 43, 89, 119, 124, 128, 169, 314, 319, 338, 357, 401

geometry/geometric – 11, 14-6, 19, 29-33, 39-40, 43-8, 58, 62, 68, 70-2, 88, 92-4, 97, 102-13, 116-21, 124, 132-44, 147-8, 152-5, 157, 164, 169, 173-6, 180-2, 190-5, 200, 204-6, 210, 213-4, 218, 222-4, 229-31, 234-6, 244-6, 258, 262-3, 267-9, 273, 277, 287, 291, 298, 303-5, 310, 313-4, 319-29, 332, 338-40, 344, 346-ft, 356-8, 364, 368, 371, 376-7, 380, 393-8

George (Saint) – 31, 387

Glastonbury – 323, 384

gnomon – 138, 168-73,

Gnostic – 3, 19-24, 193

God – 2, 5, 6, 15-6, 21-6, 28-30, 38-42, 48-9, 59, 75-80, 84-8, 89-ft, 93, 97-8, 105, 108, 121, 124, 135, 145, 157, 160, 177-80, 185-6, 190-4, 200, 223, 229-ft, 232, 286, 294, 318-20, 324-5, 333-4, 339-48, 354, 357-9, 365-6, 370-2, 375, 379, 386-90, 394, 397-400

Goddess – 89, 91, 97, 194, 333, 366-ft, 371, 386

Godhead - 20

Golden Gate – 55-9, 322, 360

golden number – 109, 112, 117, 133, 263, 273, 276, 394

Golden Pediment Triangle – 117-8, 132, 140-1, 147, 284,

298-305, 308-9, 395-6

Golden Pyramid Triangle – 109-17, 135-41, 147-8, 151, 183, 276, 284, 287, 298-300, 396

golden ratio – 68, 72, 109-18, 135, 142, 149, 157, 164, 181-3, 222-3, 250-2, 256, 268-9, 278-81, 298, 309-10, 377-8, 382-5, 390, 394-6

golden section – 110-2, 133, 149-51, 155-9, 175, 178, 181-2, 250-2, 269-80, 310, 377-81, 384-5, 390

Goldilocks - 338

Golgotha – 40, 326, 347

good(ness) – 6, 16, 81, 84, 91, 92-ft, 93, 121, 125, 237, 252, 277, 334-5, 364, 372, 396

Good Friday – 78-80, 321, 325, 345

Gospel – 45, 75-8, 157, 285-9, 323, 338, 348, 353, 359-60, 368, 369-ft

Gothic – 5, 22, 26, 47, 50-62, 66-7, 72-3, 106-8, 139, 143, 163, 177, 193, 197, 220, 322, 351-3, 399

Grail – 342-4, 371, 385

Grammar – 14, 19

Great Pyramid – 104-9, 112, 127, 136, 164, 204-10, 220, 241-4, 296-300, 313-5, 395-6

Greek – 2-3, 8, 14, 17, 24, 28, 81, 91, 96, 99, 104-5, 120, 174, 192, 348-ft, 351, 371, 394

green(ness) – 22-3, 80, 101, 325, 346-ft, 367, 381, 385, 387-8

Green Man/Men – 22, 366, 381, 386-9

Green Knight – 84, 92-ft, 364, 369

Gregory the Great (Saint) – 285-9

grid – 109-11, 119, 126, 159, 218, 232-9, 262, 296, 308-10

ground plan – 37, 45-7, 53-ft, 54, 71, 116, 140, 144-7, 154-5, 162, 174, 190, 197-8, 203-5, 209-10, 219, 225, 232-4, 238-40, 245, 256, 259, 262-6, 272, 284, 298-9, 302, 309, 312-3, 325-7, 358, 364, 370, 379, 396, 399

Guenon (Rene) – 30, 39-ft, 81, 185, 215-ft, 322-ft, 343, 357-ft, 358, 368

guild(s) – 177-8, 318, 321-2, 359, 397-8

Hades – 265, 348, 369-ft

harmony/harmonious – 15, 23, 55, 93, 98, 222-4, 232, 260, 273, 278, 293, 313, 319, 335, 373

Harran(ian) - 25, 105-6, 192-4, 229

harrow(ing) – 48, 75, 78-81, 265, 321, 334, 341-4, 348, 353, 368-70

Hathor – 346-ft, 363, 385

heart – 11, 16, 30, 40, 46-8, 59-60, 75, 78-80, 84, 90-3,

124, 195, 248, 287, 312, 321-7, 333, 341-5, 358, 373, 387, 401

heaven(ly) – 2, 3-4, 9, 14-5, 17, 19-26, 29-40, 44, 47-8, 55, 62, 70, 73-4, 77-80, 89-93, 97-100, 101-ft, 102, 107-8, 123-4, 160, 177, 185, 190-1, 195, 200-2, 212, 218-9, 222, 223, 230, 237, 260, 282, 286, 294, 312, 324, 327-8, 332, 335, 338-46, 353-4, 357, 360-6, 368-ft, 371-76, 385, 401

heavenly female – 84, 87, 100 370-72

Heavenly Jerusalem/City – 26-30, 35-8, 44, 48, 54-6, 59, 61, 157, 203, 224, 246, 252, 265, 310, 313 339, 348-ft, 363, 393, 400

Hebrew(s) – 14, 37-ft, 78, 106, 266-8, 338, 353, 363, 385-ft,

heliocentric – 68-70, 393

Hell – 28, 48, 75-80, 203, 219, 265, 321, 334, 343-4, 348, 351-ft, 353, 366-70, 376

hemisphere/hemispherical – 30, 218, 338

Herald(ing) – 5, 64, 66-ft, 85, 192, 325, 340-1, 385

Heresies/heretical – 20-2

Hermes – 105-6, 192-3, 338, 394

Hermes Trismegistus/Hermetic – 4, 15-6, 93, 105 6, 121, 124, 192, 224-ft, 353, 394

Hermopolis – 138, 393-4

hierarchy – 19, 377

high altar – 146, 150-2, 263, 273, 325, 385, 399-400

Hildegard of Bingen (Saint) – 23

Hindu(ism) – 59, 343, 347-8

Hipparchus - 174

Hiram Abiff – 320-1, 325, 331, 339, 343

historian – 104, 193, 318, 359

history/historical – 13-4, 21, 24, 49-ft, 50, 52-ft, 55, 66, 87, 91, 106, 108, 144, 168, 225, 231, 284, 319, 321, 358, 359-ft, 367-8, 372, 397

Holy Land – 50-5, 99, 157, 174, 371

holy of holies – 35, 59, 334

Holy Sepulchre – 46-9, 82

Holy Spirit – 9, 19-21, 66, 81, 85, 100, 185, 190-1, 202, 223, 283, 286-7, 340, 371-72, 392, 397-8

Holy Thursday – 321, 325

Holy Week – 218, 325, 332

horizon – 5, 40-2, 56-ft, 64, 214-5, 240, 329-30, 338, 341

horizontal(ly) – 32-3, 38-9, 59-ft, 138, 157-9, 169, 173-ft, 212, 215-ft, 219, 242-3, 249, 252, 255, 272, 293, 381, 399-400

hortus – 12-3, 85, 90, 184-5

Horus - 4

hubris – 77-8, 80-ft, 341-4

Hugh of St Victor – 4-ft, 17, 93, 104

humanity – 9, 20, 42, 66, 75, 78-80, 85, 88, 107, 190, 232-3, 336, 343, 348, 363

hypostases – 378-82

Iamblichus – 11, 168, 192

Icarus – 81-ft, 338

Icon/Iconographical etc – 9, 42, 84, 97, 186, 326, 340

illumination – 12-4, 48, 75-7, 80-1, 87-ft, 100, 181, 332-4, 340

imaginal – 60, 181, 275, 321, 335

imagination – 89, 107, 194, 265, 319-21, 333, 356, 376, 390, 397

Imperial (measurement units) – 120-1, 125, 148, 205, 225

Inanna – 67, 77-81, 89, 99, 341, 344, 369

incarnate/Incarnation etc – 4, 9, 21, 29, 43, 185, 222-3, 237, 313, 320

inches – 112, 225, 284-ft, 396

inclination (of the Moon) – 174-82

incommensurable – 109, 112, 122-3, 222-3, 263, 284-5, 308, 335

Inferno – 80-1, 345, 353-ft, 364-ft

initiatic – 77, 80, 136, 320-2, 334, 353, 356-9, 363-71, 375, 384-90

initiation – 11, 77, 81, 177, 316, 320-1, 325, 331-9, 343, 355-8, 364-9, 390

intellect – 14, 36, 124, 194, 348-ft

intelligible – 3, 15, 124, 333, 377

Intercessor/intercession – 20, 25, 66, 85, 88, 370

internal – 30-2, 209, 252, 266-7, 306-8, 364, 395

inverse(ly)/inversion – 31-2, 50-ft, 59, 119, 124, 126, 164, 218, 252-3, 296, 327-30, 335, 339, 344

inward(s) or (ly) – 2, 26, 32, 35, 40, 43, 48, 50-ft, 59, 75-7, 85, 89-90, 100, 176-7, 186, 260, 320, 334-5, 344, 356-8, 367, 371, 386, 390, 401-2

Irenaeus (Saint) – 19, 20

irrational – 109, 112, 117, 123, 152, 222-3, 263, 293, 334

Isaiah – 9-10, 48, 341-4, 375

Ishtar – 68, 73, 97-9

Isidore of Seville (Saint) – 102, 108, 123, 222

Isis – 4, 21, 88

Islam(ic) – 25, 35, 45-6, 52, 58-60, 85-ft, 96-9, 105-6, 124, 168, 173, 192-3, 205, 239, 320, 342-ft, 359, 368, 387

Israel(ism) – 5, 35-6, 42, 59, 106, 157, 265

Jachin and Boaz – 5, 324, 327-8, 339, 386

Jacob's ladder – 21, 25-6, 39-40, 48, 368-ft

Janus – 177-8, 185-6, 322, 338, 386

Jerusalem – 18, 20, 25, 30, 35, 40, 42-61, 80, 82, 135, 138, 157, 218, 266, 284, 310, 321-7, 344-5, 358-60, 368-ft, 371-3, 393-4, 397-8

Jesse – 9, 325, 346, 399-400

Jesus – 3-4, 20, 49, 59, 75, 87, 219, 323-ft, 332, 359, 368-ft, 400

Jew/Jewish/Judaism etc – 5-6, 20, 30, 35, 40-4, 58-60, 64, 99, 106, 168, 219, 286, 287-ft, 320-2, 340, 342-ft, 347-8, 349-ft, 360, 367-ft

John Martineau – 68-ft

John Michell – 119-20, 124-5, 130, 134, 148, 155, 194, 207, 231, 265, 289-ft, 296, 300, 314-5, 398

John Neal – 231, 296-7, 300, 315

John of Salisbury – 93, 104

John the Baptist (Saint) – 4, 66, 141, 145, 193, 306, 321-4, 329-30, 341-3, 368, 374

John the Divine (Saint) – 26, 28, 265

John the Evangelist (Saint) – 81-ft, 177-ft, 285-7, 322-4, 333, 346-ft, 354, 360, 363-ft 369, 385

Jonah – 77-81, 344, 369

journey(ing) etc – 17, 24-6, 31, 33, 37, 43-6, 54, 78-81, 88-90, 108, 167, 213, 218-9, 234, 257, 286, 291, 294, 321-7, 332, 343-7, 353, 356-60, 366-77, 381, 390, 392, 401

Judas – 365

Judeo-Christian – 20, 40-ft, 42, 78, 105, 321, 344, 360

Just intonation – 231, 302, 303-ft,

Kaaba – 35, 40

Kabbalah/Kabbalistic – 320, 338

kenosis – 81, 85

Kepler Triangle – 110, 116

Khanda (Sikh symbol) - 338

king(ship) – 4-6, 18, 23, 39, 42, 49, 59, 68, 80, 90, 97, 121, 193, 212, 219, 331, 348, 360, 372, 376

King David (of Israel) – 5, 42, 49, 59-60, 64, 75, 325, 338, 399-400

King Fulk (of Jerusalem) – 49-50, 135

King Henry II (of England) – 49, 135, 193, 397

King of Babylon – 341-4, 348

King Richard 1st (Lionheart) – 18-9, 50

King Solomon (of Israel) – 5, 42, 58-9, 84, 191, 322, 363-4

King Stephen (of England) – 49, 135

Kingdom of Jerusalem (Crusader) – 25, 40-52, 56-9, 135, 157, 323, 358-60, 397-8

knight – 44, 101, 340, 352, 360-2, 364 371-72

Knights Templar – 46, 49, 52, 57-9, 135, 215

knowledge(able) – 4, 6, 9-10, 14-7, 19-ft, 20, 68-70, 77, 84, 90, 96, 104-8, 124, 128, 136-7, 148, 164, 174, 185, 192, 195, 205, 210, 229, 244, 265, 300, 315, 318-21, 331, 357, 369, 393, 397-8

Koran – 85-ft, 338-9,

Krishna - 347

Kubera Kolam – 173

Kundalini – 40, 338-9, 346-ft

labyrinth(ine) – 9, 80-ft, 351-3, 360, 365, 376-ft, 385-ft

ladder – 2-3, 8-9, 14, 17-26, 29, 39-42, 48, 91, 100, 107, 185, 191, 286, 368-ft, 371, 375-7, 402

Lady – 5, 87, 100-1, 160, 370-2

Lady chapel, 11, 62-3, 66-7, 70-4, 76, 80, 85, 91, 94-5, 100, 140-7, 152, 164, 200, 209-10, 218, 220, 234, 262-3, 269, 295, 298, 305-8, 312-3, 325-32, 343, 346, 351, 368-70, 373-5, 378-81, 390, 398-400

Lady Philosophy – 2-5, 8, 14, 17, 22, 24, 107, 185, 190, 197, 371

Lamb of God – 28, 340, 387-9, 400

Lambda – 312,

Laon – 2, 12-6, 197-200

law(s) – 16, 78, 93, 190, 322, 401

Laws (Plato's written work) - 126-8, 231, 247, 264-5, 335,

Latin – 14-5, 39, 47, 104-ft, 120, 180, 192-3, 219, 265, 351, 360-ft, 370, 376

latitude – 134-8, 174, 194, 215, 245-6, 258-60, 304, 310-ft, 314-5, 393-4

Latitude Geometry – 134-8 194, 258, 324, 393

light(est)/(ness) etc – 4-6, 16, 23-6, 29, 43-4, 48, 52, 56-ft, 64-7, 70, 75, 80, 85-9, 93-6, 100, 106-8, 157, 160, 182-3, 193, 203, 212, 218-9, 223, 252-4, 322-3, 326, 329-35, 338-41, 346, 366-7, 372-3, 383, 387, 389

Lily – 15, 85-6

Lincoln – 50, 202-3, 283-ft

literal/literally etc – 20, 22-ft, 24-6, 35, 67, 78-ft, 80-1, 107, 181, 351, 387, 401

liturgy/liturgical etc – 48, 55-8, 86, 144-6, 260, 322, 375

Lo Shu - 170

lodge room (Freemason) – 181, 193, 215, 318-34, 343, 358,

359-ft, 368-ft

love – 3, 6, 15-6, 22-4, 85, 88-93, 97, 100-1, 190-ft, 287, 327, 333-5, 351, 359, 365-7, 370-1, 376, 398, 401, 402

lover – 23, 371

loving(ly) – 2, 6, 17, 22, 87, 335, 371

Lucifer(ian) – 265, 341-53, 360-ft, 363-7, 368-ft, 369-71, 375, 381, 385, 398, 401

Lunar – 96-8, 118, 132-3, 148, 163, 166-7, 170, 173-8, 181-2, 192-4, 239-40, 257, 276, 281-3, 289-94, 325-6, 329, 334-5, 353-ft, 365-7, 398

Lunation Triangle – 173, 275-6, 291-4

macrocosm(ic) – 14, 40, 93, 121, 320

magic – 84-ft, 92, 104-6, 169 -173, 193-ft, 286-7, 292, 365-ft, 394, 398

Magic Flute (Mozart opera) - 334

magic square – 166-73, 193, 286-7

Magnesia – 128, 231, 247-8, 262-5

magnitude – 14-5, 121-3, 222-3

Mandeans - 193

Mappa Mundi – 18, 45, 352

Marian – 4-5, 9, 20-1, 29, 66-7, 80, 84-7, 190, 370-1

marriage – 6, 14, 23-4, 38, 39-ft, 338, 402

Mars – 17, 19, 194, 229-ft

martial – 351-ft, 353, 359

martyr – 67, 190, 212-3, 323, 330-1, 340, 374

marvel comma (musical interval) – 231, 247,

mason's loft (York Minster) – 178-82

Master diagram – 119, 140, 143, 220, 241-50, 258, 262-3, 293, 298-300, 304, 309, 379, 384

Master Mason – 32, 148, 174, 180, 210, 263, 319-20

(Al-)Masudi – 193

material – 15, 20-1, 89, 94, 124, 177, 232, 251, 318, 338, 360, 363, 367, 369, 378, 401-2

materialist/materialism – 16, 32, 106-8, 124, 136, 190, 223-4, 308, 356-7, 376-8, 401-2

maternal – 20-2,

mathematics/mathematical etc – 4-ft, 10, 14-6, 30-3, 88, 105, 109, 120-1, 124, 132, 135, 140, 148, 155-7, 231-2, 244-5, 260, 278, 286-8, 296, 299, 302, 313, 318, 339, 357, 377, 379, 397

Matilda of Boulogne – 49, 135-8

Matilda (Dante's character in Eden) – 86-ft, 373

Matthew ('s Gospel) – 77-8, 157, 340, 345, 359-60

measurement(s) – 15, 28, 33, 54, 57, 60, 73, 106-13,

116-38, 143, 147-51, 154-9, 168, 173, 182, 205-9, 220-5, 230-9, 242-68, 271-315, 318, 379-81, 393-6, 399, 402

measuring rod – 224-8, 319

Medieval – 2-4, 11, 21, 25-6, 39-40, 42-5, 50-2, 58-60, 66, 70, 75, 80-ft, 84-7, 92-4, 98-100, 104-9, 123, 128, 134-8, 168, 171, 174, 177, 180-1, 185, 192-5, 202-5, 209, 212, 215, 222, 243, 260, 264, 294, 316, 319-23, 327, 333-5, 339-4, 347, 351-5, 358-71, 376, 384-7, 390, 393, 397-8, 401

Mediatrix – 20, 100

Megacosm(os) – 25, 294

Mercury – 14, 17-9, 24, 64, 194, 281

Messiah(ship) – 42, 44, 58-60, 64, 218, 322, 347-8, 360

metaphysic(s)-(al) etc – 19, 48, 185, 282, 357-ft, 373

Metonic Cycle – 96, 173-ft

metrology – 120, 143, 147, 205, 223-5, 231, 250, 300

Michael(mas) (Archangel Saint) – 349, 368-ft, 384-5

micro-unit – 143, 148, 225-312

micro-variation (variated) etc – 232, 244-ft, 247-51, 256-7, 265, 271, 281-3, 297-301, 308, 312-3

microcosm(ic)(ally) etc – 14, 25, 34, 40, 46, 93, 121, 185, 320, 324-ft

middle way/path – 81, 217-8, 224, 316, 322-30, 334-40, 343, 364, 374, 386

midst – 40, 42, 326, 340

Midsummer ('s Day) – 323, 338, 368

mile(s)(age) – 120-1, 125-31, 136-7, 148, 173-ft, 193, 223, 240, 244, 256, 263, 281-3, 293, 296-7, 311-5, 384, 393

millenarian – 44, 48, 359

Minos and Pasiphae – 80-ft, 345

Minotaur – 80, 81-ft, 345, 351-3, 360

moat walls (Wells Bishop's Palace) – 203-9, 245, 313

Molten Sea - 268

monarch(y) – 39-40, 44, 49, 364

month(s) – 6, 21, 36, 44, 132, 173, 177, 217-8, 265, 290-1, 323, 338, 353-ft, 368, 372

Moon – 17, 19, 22-3, 29, 62, 65, 77, 89, 96-8, 101-ft, 102, 120-7, 130-3, 148-51, 155, 160-75, 182, 190-5, 206-7, 216, 218, 220, 229-ft, 239-47, 256-60, 265, 275-6, 280-3, 286, 290-3, 296-7, 313-5, 322, 325-8, 331-5, 338-9, 353-ft, 365-7, 386, 389, 397-8

Moon-square – 151, 162, 164, 173-4, 194, 256-7, 280-3, 293

moral – 19, 24, 50, 84, 324, 332

Morning Star – 5, 48, 62-82, 84-92, 100-1, 143, 327, 332, 339-42, 365, 373-5, 385-6, 392

- 'Bright' Morning Star – 5, 26, 64, 66-ft, 75, 80, 101, 142, 181, 216, 218, 322, 331-2, 339, 341-3, 346, 351, 360-ft, 385, 400

Moses – 99, 338, 354, 384-5

mother(hood) – 4-ft, 6, 11, 19-21, 50, 67, 87, 89, 98, 104, 200, 215, 334, 354, 359-ft, 369-ft

Mother of God – 87, 200, 223

mountain – 25, 28, 32, 43, 47, 80, 101, 106, 190, 219, 287, 333, 342-ft, 345, 373, 375, 387

Mount of Olives – 44, 55-8

music(al) – 14-6, 19, 23, 31, 34, 79, 86-7, 143, 173, 192, 220, 230-3, 247-8, 262-5, 271, 301-2, 310-12, 370, 373, 397

musical ratios – 128, 143, 224-7, 230-2, 235, 247, 262-5, 270-1, 273, 301-2, 310-14

musicologist – 86, 128, 231, 264

Muslim(s) – 35, 40, 55, 87-ft, 98, 229, 320

mystic(al)(ism) – 16, 24, 55, 84, 320, 325, 333, 360

myth(ology)/mythical… etc – 11, 77, 78-ft, 88-9, 101, 105-8, 121, 181, 192, 205, 212-3, 218, 231, 247, 283, 319-20, 341, 342-ft, 344, 351-3, 356, 358, 365, 366-ft, 367-71, 376, 387-8, 398, 401

Myth of Er – 19, 24, 332

(Al-)Nadim – 193

natural world – 22, 401

nature/Natura – 6, 9, 15, 18-9, 22-3, 25-6, 31, 55, 93, 104, 108, 121, 124, 130, 173, 177, 181, 186, 222, 225, 232, 294, 331, 336, 345-ft, 353, 356, 366-7, 375, 378, 401

Naudon (Paul) – 321-ft, 359,

nave – 57, 62, 144-ft, 155, 159, 203, 211, 213, 216-20, 232-240, 243-5, 249, 252, 255-7, 305, 308-10, 322-4, 329, 344-53, 365-7, 369-71, 373-5, 378, 380-2, 385, 390, 397, 399

Neckam (Alexander) – 18-9

Neolithic – 134, 174

New Testament – 20, 24-5, 28, 75, 223, 286, 326, 340, 399

Nicholas of Cusa – 16, 334

Nicodemus (and his gospel) – 75, 348, 353-4, 369-ft

nine – 16, 62, 80, 105, 168, 298, 314, 323, 368, 370-2, 378-9

ninety-nine – 89-ft, 96-8

north/northern etc – 2, 12, 14-6, 36-7, 45, 57, 66-ft, 134-8, 146, 149-50, 159, 162, 166, 169-ft, 174, 179-80, 183, 191-4, 197-203, 208-9, 214-9, 237-40, 249, 253, 255,

258-9, 263-6, 278, 285-7, 291, 299, 305-10, 314-5, 322, 324-35, 338-9, 341, 342-ft, 345, 349, 351, 358, 370-72, 375-6, 382-6, 390, 393-4

north pole – 134-8, 314, 394

northeast corner – 329-33, 339, 343

Notre-Dame – 7-8

number(s) – 9-11, 14-6, 28-35, 43, 68, 74, 78, 81, 84, 91-102, 107-9, 112-3, 117-133, 136, 148, 152, 157, 166-173, 182-3, 193-5, 200, 206, 220-36, 239-252, 255-8, 263-7, 272-7, 280-97, 300, 303-ft, 304-15, 319-20, 335, 338, 356-7, 365-7, 370-2, 375-84, 387-9, 392-7, 401

(for small numbers see the initial letter i.e. 'o' for one)

1.618 – 68, 72, 109-14, 117, 157-8, 222, 252, 263, 269, 273, 276, 377-8, 381, 394-6

$\sqrt{2}$ – 33, 222, 276-7, 281

2.618 – 263-4, 267, 293, 305, 377-81

2:1 (musical ratio) – 14, 34, 270-3, 311, 314

$\sqrt{3}$ – 33-4, 222, 289-90

3:2 (musical ratio) – 14, 34, 270-3, 311, 314

$\sqrt{4}$ – 33-4, 129

5, 15, 17, 28 and 45 (3 x 3 magic square) – 168-73

$\sqrt{5}$ – 157-8, 164, 222, 394

16:15 (Just diatonic semitone) – 226-8, 231, 235, 302-3, 312

17 – 168-73, 285-8, 290-1, 379-83

21:20 (Septimal Chromatic semitone) – 227-8, 231, 303

33 – 98-9, 240, 251, 254-5, 311

44 – 122-3, 250, 259, 267, 281-3, 300, 315

55 – 92, 113, 119, 128-30, 222, 239, 245, 255, 258, 263, 266, 280-1, 381

56 – 119, 192, 226-8, 236-7, 240, 243-6, 249-50, 255, 258, 263-4, 273-5, 280-2, 293, 394

56:55 (difference between 8:5 and 11:7) – 245-6, 249-50, 254-5, 258, 313

88 – 119, 243-6, 250, 254, 258-9, 311-2

144 – 128-30, 224, 247, 252, 256, 263-7, 271, 280, 310, 313, 393

153 – 285-92, 312, 396

225:224 ('Marvel' musical comma) – 231, 247-8, 264-5, 271

360 – 31, 128, 134, 182, 247, 248, 257, 265, 304

440:441 – 244-ft, 296-7, 314-5

720 – 126-30, 296

1080 – 125, 293

2160 – 130-1, 173-ft, 256-7, 281-3

3960 – 125, 251, 254, 314

5040 – 126-7, 148, 244-6, 255, 263-4, 296-7, 313

5280 (feet in a mile)– 120, 125, 130, 240

7920 – 127-9, 148, 244-6, 249-50, 254-5, 296-7, 315

10,000 – 356-7, 377

55,440 – 127, 206, 296-7, 300-ft, 314

numerical(ly) – 9, 11, 16, 21, 28, 31, 34, 74, 78-ft, 84, 92-4, 98, 101, 106-9, 112, 120-30, 150, 167, 171-3, 222-4, 229, 231-2, 235-9, 244-5, 260, 268, 285-7, 291-3, 296, 301, 308, 339, 344, 356, 364, 376-ft, 378

oblate (planet Earth) – 300, 314-5

octagon(al) – 46-7, 57-8, 62, 71-3, 143, 146-51, 161-4, 174-6, 181-4, 190-4, 197-200, 209, 220, 256, 269, 274-87, 291, 301, 305, 308, 313, 327, 333, 351, 358, 368, 375, 383-4, 389-90

octagram star – 68-73, 96-7, 143, 147-8, 181-2, 274-6, 284-5, 301-8, 312

octave (music) – 34, 230, 311-2

Óengus mac Fergusa - 212

off-centre – 162-3, 175, 177-8, 181, 208, 269, 271, 276, 339

Ogdoad – 19-21, 191, 200, 334, 394

Old Testament – 20, 24-5 42, 48, 78, 84, 248, 326, 341-ft, 353

one – 2-6, 9, 13-8, 21-33, 36, 39-50, 54-8, 64-6, 69-81, 85-100, 106-12, 116-34, 137-8, 145-8, 158, 167-70, 173-87, 190, 193-4, 197, 202-4, 209, 212, 215-9, 222-5, 228-39, 243-6, 249-59, 262-74, 277, 280-7, 290-94, 297-9, 303-5, 309-15, 318-30, 333-51, 356-79, 383-90, 393, 397-401

ontological – 32, 38-9, 48, 50-ft, 286, 371, 373

orbit(s)(ing)(al) – 43, 64-5, 68-9, 93, 96, 125, 167, 174-5, 213, 216, 229, 234-6, 308, 372, 392

orientate(d)/orientation(al) – 2, 30, 37, 42-43, 46-8, 59, 66, 71, 85, 91, 105, 146, 151, 162-3, 174-7, 180, 181, 203-5, 318, 320-1, 324-7, 335, 338, 345, 349, 351, 356-60, 371-75, 379, 385, 389, 400-1

origin(s)(al)(ate) etc – 4-5, 20-2, 24-6, 30, 33, 39, 40-ft, 43, 45-7, 56, 58-9, 80-2, 84, 86-ft, 87-8, 97-9, 101-2, 104-5, 107-8, 123, 136-7, 140-2, 144-5, 152-4, 157, 190-1, 193, 203, 205, 207, 210, 218, 223, 245, 249, 252, 263, 287, 318, 324, 341, 343-5, 346-ft, 351-3, 357-8, 363, 367, 370-1, 374, 377, 381, 384-7, 399-402

Orthodox(y) – 20, 84, 130, 212, 219, 320, 325, 346, 384

Osiris – 173, 388

Our Lady of Walsingham – 5, 9, 13,

Our Lady of the Rosary – 87, 291

ouroboros/ouroboric – 275, 388-9

Oxford – 49, 134-8, 259

Pagan(ism) – 91, 186, 340

Palm Sunday – 44, 55-6, 218, 322, 325, 330-2, 360, 392

Paradise/Paradiso – 19, 25, 80-ft, 81, 89, 101-ft, 160, 291, 370

Paradise Lost – 86, 373

Parzival – 343, 371

Paschal – 23, 74-7, 80, 86, 218-9, 320-2, 325-7, 330-2, 345, 392, 397

passion(s) – 30, 80-ft, 82, 84, 90, 324, 326, 330-2, 339, 364

path(way) – 9-ft, 14-6, 43, 59, 64, 69, 81, 86, 113, 180, 190, 212, 218, 224, 316-8, 322-31, 334-40, 343-4, 347, 351-3, 357-66, 369, 371, 374-6, 386, 390

Patmos - 28

Paul (Saint) – 25, 78, 286,

penitent and impenitent thieves – 219, 339

pentagon(al) – 71-3, 112-4, 140-3, 148, 203, 222, 255, 269, 298, 301, 305-9, 327-8, 332, 399

pentagram/pentangle (star) – 58, 68-73, 84-6, 92-ft, 96-9, 114-7, 140-2, 147-8, 152-4, 181, 255, 262, 284, 287, 298, 301-12, 331-2, 359, 363-5

Pentecost(al) – 9, 186, 189-91, 286-7, 375, 392

perennial – 4, 77, 91, 320, 365, 367, 370

periphery – 33-4, 222, 247, 267-ft, 281

perpetual(ly) – 15, 38, 40, 43, 66, 85, 93, 177, 320, 347-8, 371

personification – 66, 85, 319, 344-5, 351

phi (see also 1.618) – 109, 137, 148, 245, 258, 266-7, 276, 313, 378-ft, 393

Philolaus the Pythagorean – 222, 336

Philosophia/Philia-Sophia – 13, 184-5, 191

philosophy – 2-4, 15-9, 22, 26, 32, 93, 126, 180, 185, 190-2, 197, 318, 330, 357, 378, 401

physics – 19, 185

pi – 28, 33, 109-13, 119, 122-4, 135-8, 148, 151, 222-3, 245, 258, 266-8, 281-3, 298, 300-1, 304, 309, 313-5, 396

Pi Pyramid Triangle – 111-3, 119, 122, 135-8, 148, 151, 258, 281, 284, 208, 301, 313, 396

piety – 10, 15, 84, 98, 321, 365

pillar(s) – 5, 8-9, 12-3, 21-2, 46, 140-1, 175, 178, 186-7, 190, 232, 235-8, 246, 256-7, 264, 269, 272-5, 286, 304,

324, 327-8, 339, 345-6, 349, 375, 381, 386, 388, 390

plane(s) – 30-4, 174-5, 213, 216, 229, 234, 280

planet(s)(ary) – 5, 14, 17-21, 24, 29, 43, 62-8, 71, 75-8, 82-4, 91-3, 97-9, 101, 107, 121, 134-5, 152, 173, 193-4, 211, 216-8, 220, 232-9, 245, 258, 281, 294, 296, 304-5, 308, 314-5, 322, 327, 332, 338, 341, 344-5, 363-5, 370, 373, 387, 392-4, 398, 401

planetary spheres – 17-22, 25, 29, 35, 40, 48, 80, 93, 160, 185, 191, 193, 230, 327, 332-4, 344-5, 371, 375, 385, 401

Plato/Platonist/Platonism etc – 2-4, 13, 16-9, 22-5, 34, 77, 85-8, 91, 101-ft, 104, 126-30, 181, 185-6, 192-3, 224, 231, 247-8, 264-5, 312, 318, 332-5, 353, 356-7, 377-8

Platonic Solids – 34, 128-31

Pleroma - 20

Plotinus – 22, 378, 382

Plutarch – 173, 182

Pluto – 86-ft, 265, 373

point-within-the-circle (Freemason diagram) – 322-4

pointed arch – 52-4, 381, 399

polar(ity) etc – 32, 81, 134, 177-8, 185, 190, 193, 216, 219, 222, 287, 297, 314, 322, 328, 330, 334, 339, 343, 385-6, 400

pole(s) – 21, 29, 35, 134-8, 190-4, 217, 248, 258-9, 314-5, 327, 333, 341, 344, 375, 390, 394

pole (north) star – 190, 193-4, 390

polygon(al) – 31, 34, 46-7, 58, 68, 71, 112-3, 117, 128, 182, 186, 197, 209, 222-4, 262, 283-ft, 327, 371

portal – 12, 59, 61, 187, 322

precentor – 50, 186-7, 283

prison(ers) – 2, 20-2, 75, 78, 344, 348, 366

Proserpine – 86-ft

Protoevangelium of (St) James – 21, 90

Proverbs (Book of) – 5, 9, 12, 14, 20-1, 338

Psalm(s) – 20, 78, 333

Ptolemy – 14, 231, 372

Purgatory/Purgatorio (in Commedia) – 25, 80-1, 93, 219, 327, 345, 351-ft, 360-ft 373, 376

pyramid(al) – 105-6, 109, 120-1, 124, 127, 134-8, 147, 190, 276, 281, 297, 300, 303, 314, 333, 346, 395-6, 398

pyramid geometry – 58, 62, 72, 103, 108, 116-8, 136, 139-40, 144, 204, 210, 244, 313

Pyramid Rhomb – 114-6, 152-4, 262-3, 266-7, 287

Pyramid Triangle – 58, 109-13, 116-9, 122, 125-7, 135-49, 151-9, 162-4, 181-3, 190-1, 203-10, 242-58, 262-4, 267, 269-76, 280-1, 284, 287, 296, 298-305, 308-13, 315, 325-7, 346, 368, 373, 375-6, 379, 381-83, 385, 390, 395-6, 398-9

Pyramidology – 105-6

Pythagoras – 10, 14-6, 34, 104-6, 192, 283, 339

Pythagorean(s) – 10-1, 94, 104, 110, 118, 125-6, 132, 169, 194, 222, 230-1, 294, 303-ft, 310, 336, 339, 356, 377

quadrilateral(s) – 214-5, 234-5, 292

Quadrivium/quadrivial – 13-22, 54, 104-8, 136, 181, 192, 195, 205, 224, 229, 231-2, 318, 357, 390, 397

Queen of Heaven – 66, 364, 371-72

quincuncial – 45-6, 124

quire – 53, 57-9, 116, 144-54, 164, 191, 220, 246-8, 261-6, 271-3, 287, 291, 298, 304-6, 312, 322-30, 358, 364, 370, 373-5, 378, 397-9

radial – 110-3, 246

radius – 33, 72, 111, 116, 122, 125, 223, 247, 258, 267-ft, 284-5, 293, 297, 302-9, 312-4, 338

ratio (also see Golden 'ratio') – 34, 116, 167, 206, 226-7, 231-8, 245-6, 249-52, 255-9, 262, 267, 270, 277-8, 281-5, 289, 297, 299-305, 308-15,

rational(ised)(ising) etc – 109, 112, 117-8, 122-4, 132, 152, 222-4, 239, 245, 250, 252, 263, 267, 277, 280-5, 290, 293, 298, 308, 334, 378, 394, 396

rationale – 121, 140, 144, 230, 252, 287, 304, 353

rationalism/rationalistic – 136, 180, 321

rebirth – 353, 356, 365, 368, 369-ft, 386, 389

rectangle – 58, 114, 145, 152-4, 157, 181, 213-8, 225, 234-7, 250-1, 255-6, 262-8, 271, 287, 289-90, 293, 324-9, 346-8, 358, 364, 377, 393-4, 397

reflect(s)(ing)/reflection etc – 5-6, 9, 17, 19-21, 24, 30-40, 43, 48, 56, 64, 66, 77, 84, 86-ft, 88-93, 97, 100, 112, 116, 121-4, 128, 143, 150, 157, 177, 186, 190-1, 206, 212, 219, 222-4, 231-2, 235, 237-9, 242, 245, 247-52, 265-7, 280, 285, 287, 296, 298, 300, 303-15 319-21, 324-31, 335, 339, 341-5, 348-ft, 356-64, 368-ft, 369-71, 375-8, 383-5, 392, 396, 401

Reginald De Bohun - Bishop of Bath – 50, 203, 323, 398

Regulus (Saint) - 213

Reinold of Cologne (Saint) - 321

relationship(s) – 5, 11, 14, 23, 31-4, 39, 49, 58, 66-72, 85, 96, 109-13, 118-9, 122-6, 130, 150, 164, 167, 173, 177, 181, 186, 205-6, 209, 213, 219, 222-32, 235-36, 242, 245, 247, 254-7, 260, 263, 267-70, 275-7, 281, 283, 285, 289, 297, 300-5 308-13, 325, 334-5, 339, 371, 373, 375, 378, 383-6, 393, 397-402

remember(ed)(ing) – 26, 32, 77, 108, 224, 260, 281, 318-9, 340, 367, 370, 375, 401-2

remembrance – 55, 85, 88, 108, 177, 224, 286, 318, 340, 356-9, 401

re-orientate – 24, 345, 370

Republic (Plato's written work) – 332, 357

resemble(s)/resemblance/resembling etc – 4-5, 20-2, 29, 32, 35, 40, 4, 53-ft, 57-60, 78, 87-ft, 88, 92, 98, 119-21, 124, 133, 171, 180, 185-6, 190-4, 198-ft, 205, 212, 225, 232, 287, 290-1, 312, 320-5, 339, 341-2, 344-ft, 347-8, 353, 368, 371-73, 387-ft, 396

Resurrection – 22-3, 30, 42, 46, 74-80, 86, 157, 173, 218, 257, 265, 287, 320-1, 325, 331-2, 335, 340, 343-4, 346-ft, 356, 367-8, 374-5, 385-8

retroquire – 140-1, 144-7, 150, 220, 263, 269, 295, 298, 302-3, 399

Revelation (Book of) – 5, 26-9, 35, 37-8, 44, 56, 64, 75, 80, 224, 246, 320, 342, 348-ft, 349, 363, 384, 398-400

revere(d)(nce) – 15, 56, 98, 401-402

Rhetoric – 14, 19

ribbed vault – 22, 52, 169-70, 174, 177

Richard (Ist/Lionheart) – 18-9, 50

right-angled triangle – 110-7, 132, 216-7, 234, 292, 395

ritual(istic) – 39, 42, 77, 181, 260, 320-1, 331-3, 343, 356

Roman – 2, 48-9, 66, 82, 87, 89, 91, 106, 177-8, 185, 322-3, 341, 351, 368-ft, 371, 386, 400

Roman Catholic(ism) – 22, 75, 84, 99, 376

Romanesque – 52, 163

Rome – 4, 42, 49, 212, 287-ft,

Rosary – 87, 92-5, 98-9, 291, 398

rose/rosa (flower) – 62, 83-92, 95, 98-100, 180-1, 196-200, 332, 351, 373-6

rose (window) – 2, 12-6, 197-8, 202, 371

ruler – 32, 49, 123, 135, 342

rung(s) – 17-9, 311, 371, 377

sacred – 9, 42, 46, 81-ft, 85-6, 124, 177, 185, 215-ft, 224, 232, 318-9, 322, 332, 343, 357, 363-4, 368, 370, 393, 397

sacred geometry – 32, 72-ft, 180

sacristy – 182-3, 270, 275-8, 286, 384-9

sacristy doorway – 133, 159, 181-3, 269-78, 286, 379-90

Saints – look under initial of first name

Saint Andrews, Scotland – 136-8, 213, 245-6, 258-60, 304

Salisbury cathedral chapter house – 178, 184-6, 190

saltire – 212-5, 219

Samsara – 344-ft, 347-ft

Sanskrit – 223-ft, 343, 347

(Al-)Sarakhsi - 229

Satan – 44, 342-4, 348-9, 359

Saturn – 17, 19, 173, 194

Satya Yuga – 347-8

science(s) – 15-6, 19, 81-ft, 93, 106, 124, 185, 192, 215-ft, 322-ft, 343-ft, 357, 368-ft

Scotland – 53, 106, 136-8, 212-5, 245-6, 258-9, 304, 323, 359-ft

Scottish – 39, 212-5, 359-ft

scripture – 22-ft, 24-5

sea – 81-ft, 87, 96, 166, 268, 338, 364, 372

seal(ed) – 28, 44-5, 84-5, 212, 342, 364

Second Coming – 48, 348, 368

secret(ly) – 6, 17, 30, 136, 243-ft, 294, 321, 358, 359-ft

Sedes Sapientiae – 3-5, 198

Seked - 242

semitone (musical interval) – 227, 230-1, 235, 302-3, 312

senses/sensible – 3, 84, 124, 318, 333, 343, 364, 401

sensible – 124, 333, 377

Seraphim – 363, 385-ft

serpent(ine) – 339, 346-ft, 347, 349, 384-5, 388-9

set-square – 32, 169-71, 174, 178-80, 338-9

seven(ness) – 9-11, 17, 19-22, 28, 30-1, 35, 37, 40, 58, 77, 84, 100, 123-4, 134, 169-ft, 180, 185-7, 190-1, 203, 229, 278, 287, 297, 312, 314-5, 320, 332, 365-ft, 372, 376, 383-90, 399

Seven Gifts of the Holy Spirit – 9, 19, 21, 185, 190-1, 286-7

Seven Liberal Arts – 11-4, 17-9, 22, 184-5, 197, 318, 320

seven-limit musical tuning – 231, 247, 264

seven planetary spheres – 17-22, 24-5, 29, 35, 40, 124, 185, 191, 193, 230, 332, 334, 371, 385

shadow – 138, 169, 353, 366-7

Shalim – 82, 393

Shavuot – 286-7, 375

Sheol – 48, 78, 82, 341-8, 353-ft

side (west) doors – 157, 251-5

side aisle – 72, 252-5, 301, 309, 322, 325, 329, 330, 343, 374, 397

sidereal – 96, 167, 282, 365-ft

Sinai, 24, 286-7, 375

Sirach – 20, 319

six – 16, 21, 30-1, 34, 37, 57, 84-5, 159, 182, 194. 215, 248,

255, 262, 272-5, 281, 289, 303-4, 308, 311-4, 342-ft, 345-9, 365, 370, 388

skew – 162-3, 174-9, 182, 186-ft

sky – 2, 5, 8, 17, 40, 50-ft, 64-5, 80, 85, 102, 107, 212, 329, 339

Sleeping Beauty – 89-90

Socrates – 13, 185

solar(ity) – 5, 64-6, 80, 121, 130, 173-ft, 181, 212-3, 239-40, 291-2, 329, 333-5, 338, 386

solid – 34, 91, 128-31, 229

Solomon/Solomonic etc – 5-6, 42-4, 57-9 84, 154, 191, 262, 287, 321-2, 363-5

   - Song of – 85, 371

   - Testament of – 84, 154, 363

solstice(s)/solstitial – 4, 6, 36-7, 86-ft, 141, 177, 213-5, 218-9, 306, 321-5, 328-31, 335, 338-9, 343, 368, 373-4, 386-9, 397

son – 5, 9, 20-1, 49, 59, 66, 78, 121, 223, 341-3, 354, 359, 385

Sophia/Sofianic – 2-3, 13-4, 17-9, 20-3, 169, 184-5, 190-ft, 191, 200, 320, 334

soul – 2-3, 6, 14-26, 32, 38-40, 43-4, 48, 55, 59, 66, 75-81, 84-93, 100, 107-8, 124, 159, 177, 180, 185, 190-1, 194, 197, 203, 218, 223-4, 229, 260, 294, 318-21, 324-5, 332-5, 341, 344-7, 351-3, 356-78, 384-90, 397-8, 401-2

south/southern etc – 3, 12-3, 36-7, 52, 57, 66-ft, 123, 128, 136-8, 162, 174, 179-80, 193, 202-5, 208-9, 214-9, 237-40, 249, 253, 258, 263-6, 299, 305-10, 313-5, 322-33, 338-9, 343-5, 347, 349-51, 382-4, 393-4

southeast corner – 329, 331, 339, 343, 384

Southwell Minster – 128, 162-4, 174-8, 194, 197-9, 398

sphere/spherical – 30-4, 36-7, 40, 43, 55, 121, 134, 245, 294, 314, 344-5, 377

spine – 32, 40, 286, 346-ft, 388

spirit(s) (see also Holy Spirit)- 6, 9, 15-6, 28, 40, 42, 77-8, 180, 320-1, 333, 340, 342, 345, 357, 368, 384, 389, 400-1

spiritual(ly) – 10-1, 14, 20, 22, 40, 43-4, 48, 75, 81, 90-1, 98, 99, 105-6, 108-9, 157, 159, 177-80, 190, 260, 318-20, 335, 338,

343, 353, 356-7, 359-60, 367, 369, 381, 389, 397, 401-2

Spiritual Imagination – 107, 194, 318, 321, 356, 390, 397

Spouse of the Holy Spirit – 9

spring(time) – 22-3, 56-ft, 85-6, 101, 217, 371, 373, 379, 386-7 spring equinox – 22, 37, 66, 86, 214, 218, 322-5, 329-31, 368, 387-9

square(ish)(d) – 16, 31-9, 46, 89, 109, 122-6, 128-30, 137-8, 140-1, 144, 151, 157, 168-9, 194, 203, 214-5, 222-4, 234-5, 242, 247, 249-51, 256, 258, 266-7, 276-7, 280-3, 289, 291, 296, 314, 319, 393

square root – 33, 129, 222-3, 277, 292

square roots (see appropriate number)

squaring-of-the-circle – 30-2, 35, 88/89, 123-4, 222, 247, 281, 283

staircase – 2, 149-50, 166-73, 176, 179-80, 183, 286-7, 292-4, 334, 369

star(s)(ry) – 6, 14, 17, 19-25, 28-9, 31, 35-7, 64, 68, 70, 76, 80, 87, 89, 93, 97, 106, 108, 112, 121, 160, 182, 185, 190-1, 194, 230, 282, 287, 294, 327, 332-3, 338, 342, 344, 370-72, 375, 398

Stella Maris – 21, 29, 190-1, 287, 333, 371, 375, 390

Stella Matutina – 5, 62, 66-7, 83-4, 100, 365

step(s) – 2, 8-9, 17, 19-21, 28, 124, 166-72, 185-6, 191, 292-4, 320, 353, 368-9, 383, 395-6, 402

Stephen (Saint) – 52-3, 141, 306, 312, 323, 329-30, 343, 374

story – 21-2, 25, 30, 40-ft, 44, 48, 75, 77-80, 81-ft, 87-90, 98, 106, 128, 140, 212, 218, 265, 287, 289, 320-1, 326, 331-2, 341-3, 347, 349-ft, 353, 359, 363, 366, 369, 384

storyline(s) – 2, 4, 21-2, 24-6, 28, 40, 59, 77-80, 88-9, 101, 106, 124, 154, 231, 291, 321, 325, 331, 339, 341-5, 348-9, 351-3, 356, 358-63, 365, 367, 368-ft, 369-71, 376, 387-8, 392, 399

student – 14-5, 22

subject(s) – 14, 19, 22, 24, 92-ft, 93, 99, 104, 108, 120, 134, 140, 185, 190, 192, 222, 232, 363, 368, 370, 372

Sumerian – 67, 77, 89, 97, 99

summer – 66, 214, 218-9, 306, 323, 329-31, 335, 338-9, 359-ft, 368, 374, 387-9

summit – 32, 34, 43, 47, 59, 66, 80, 100, 190, 373, 387

Sun – 5-6, 17, 19, 23, 26, 29, 40, 44, 47, 56-ft, 64-6, 77, 86-7, 89, 96-7, 100, 138, 173-ft, 175, 181, 186, 193-4, 212-4, 215-ft, 217-8, 236, 240, 322, 324-ft, 325-31, 334-5, 338-41, 346-ft, 370, 383, 386, 389, 392

Sunday – 9, 22, 44, 55-6, 75, 78, 218, 286, 321-2, 325-7, 330-2, 345, 360, 392

supernal – 5, 44, 64, 66

symbol(s)(ise)/symbolic – 4-5, 11, 13, 16-40, 40-ft, 45-48, 50-ft, 53-ft, 54-61, 64-67, 73-101, 106, 109, 123-4,

148, 159, 163, 166, 169-86, 190-203, 212-9, 222-3, 229, 232-4, 252, 257, 264-5, 269, 282-3, 286-91, 306-8, 312, 316-35, 338-53, 356-93, 397-8, 401

Symposium (Plato's written work) – 24, 91

synodic – 64, 68, 96, 98, 132-3, 167, 173-ft, 229, 239, 275-6, 282, 290-4, 308, 365-ft, 392

syntonic comma (musical interval) – 231, 302, 303-ft

Tabernacle – 36, 38, 154, 265-8, 287, 334

talisman(ic) – 92-3, 99, 105, 193, 398

Tanit – 194-5

Tantric - 40

teacher(s) – 17, 19, 22, 104, 106, 116, 193, 197, 397

Templar(s) – 46, 49-53, 57-9, 135-8, 141, 194, 197, 215, 358-9, 367-72, 376, 387, 397-8

temple – 25, 30, 35, 40, 44, 46, 57-61, 66, 82, 106, 177, 191-4, 266, 321, 325, 327, 331, 339, 344, 360, 364-5, 368-ft, 373-ft, 376

Temple Cowley – 49, 134, 138, 398

Temple Mount – 25, 30, 35, 40, 57-60, 310-ft, 322, 358, 369, 393-4, 398

Temple of Solomon – 5, 21, 35, 46, 57-61, 66, 106, 116, 148, 154, 177, 181, 191, 206, 248, 262-8, 287, 321-2, 324-8, 334, 339, 343, 358-9, 363-4, 373-ft, 386

temporal – 55, 185, 214, 240, 265, 325

ten – 6, 11, 19, 58, 92, 94-5, 113, 235, 287, 315, 356-7, 365, 375

Ten Commandments – 286-7

Testament of Solomon – 84, 154, 363

Tetraktys – 10-1, 34, 94-5, 312, 356, 375-83

Thabbit ibn Qurra - 193

theology/theological etc – 4-ft, 11, 16-9, 22, 25, 86, 168, 180, 265, 286, 318-9, 334, 353, 397

Theoria(l) – 2-3, 22, 232

Theseus – 80-ft, 351-3

Thierry of Chartres – 14, 25

third eye – 338, 343

thirteen - 68

thirty – 28, 203, 365-7

thirty-three – 98,

thorn(s)(less) – 84-90, 100, 373-4

Thoth – 182, 192, 394

three – 9, 12-21, 30, 33-6, 39, 56, 61, 71, 77-81, 88-9, 98, 101, 106, 110-1, 119, 125, 128, 130, 132, 141, 143-6, 157, 162-4, 169, 178, 183-7, 190, 193, 198-200, 208, 223-31,

244-6, 250, 265, 268, 285-92, 296, 299-301, 308-10, 319, 323-6, 331-2, 339-40, 343-4, 349-51, 356, 365-7, 370-73, 378, 381-83, 386, 396, 399

three-fold – 31, 81, 186, 190-2, 286, 291, 376

threeness – 186, 190-ft, 286-7, 289, 334, 344-ft, 378

three dimensions/-dimensional – 30-1, 34, 37, 59, 215, 229

throne (and enthroned) – 1-6, 9, 11-3, 22, 49, 50-ft, 135, 184, 198-200, 341-2, 375, 382-3, 400

Timaeus (Plato's written work) – 17, 22, 34, 85-ft

tone(s) (musical interval) – 230-1, 311-2

tradition(al)(s) etc – 3-5, 14, 19-22, 25, 30, 34-42, 48, 56-8, 77-8, 82-4, 91-3, 105, 121, 124, 168, 177, 180, 186, 192, 223, 312, 320-4, 339, 344-5, 353, 356-8, 370, 393, 397

transcend(s)(ent) – 40, 107, 124, 224, 319, 333, 358, 401-2

transmute/transmutation etc – 30-1, 37, 90, 117, 147, 152, 159, 247, 263, 363-4, 395

transept – 72, 162, 166, 202, 219, 298-9, 303-4, 308-12, 324, 366, 382

transform(ed)(ation) etc – 32, 77, 88, 173-ft, 177, 320, 333, 342, 364, 365-ft, 385, 402

transition(al) – 40, 59, 77, 98-ft, 177, 345-6, 348

tree(s) – 22-3, 36, 84, 208, 325, 338, 399-400

triangle(s)/triangular – 31, 58, 109-119, 122, 125-28, 132-59, 162-4, 173, 181-3, 186, 190-1, 194, 203-10, 216-7, 222, 229, 234, 242-58, 262-4, 267-76, 280-1, 284, 287, 291-305, 308-15, 325-7, 338, 346, 368, 373-76, 379-85, 390, 395-9

tribe(s) – 36, 106, 265

triforium – 365-6

Trinity/Trinitarian – 81, 88, 186, 223, 285-7, 291, 333, 344, 348, 372, 375

Trivium – 13-4, 17-9, 22

tropic(s) – 217-8, 232, 322-4, 329, 374

troubadour(s) – 87, 100, 370

true – 5-6, 15-6, 93, 138, 180, 185-6, 190, 209, 263, 267, 344, 357

True Identity/Image/nobility (of the soul) – 26, 77, 100, 108, 177, 200

True Self – 81, 88, 108, 197, 359, 375

truncated – 152, 263

truth(s) – 10, 15-7, 108, 181, 320, 334-5, 357, 364, 367-ft, 372, 402

Tudor – 87-8

turtle dove - 371

twelfth century/12th Century – 2-5, 11-8, 21-6, 40-4, 48-52, 55-9, 84, 93, 99, 104-5, 137, 148, 168, 178, 181, 192-3, 197, 203, 216, 283, 318-23, 342, 345-ft, 351-3, 357-9, 368-ft, 372

twelve – 9, 29, 34-6, 170, 190-2, 229, 239, 265, 287, 292

twenty-two – 28, 192

two – 2-5, 8-14, 19-24, 28-35, 38-42, 46-49, 55-60, 64, 68-72, 75, 78, 81, 86, 91, 94-6, 109-18, 121, 124-37, 140-8, 151-2, 157-8, 166-7, 170-1, 174-8, 182-7, 192-4, 200-9, 213-9, 222-5, 230-1, 234-9, 242, 245-6, 250-8, 262-4, 267-9, 272-7, 280-7, 290-305, 308-11, 314-5, 319-31, 334-43, 348-9, 356-7, 364-5, 374-5, 378-89, 393-8

two-dimensional – 31, 34

tympanum – 3, 12-3

undercroft (or treasury) – 57, 146-8, 181-3, 220, 269, 273-9, 281, 284-7, 305, 327, 333, 368, 375, 383-4, 389-90

Underworld – 37, 75-82, 257, 321, 324, 334, 341-6, 353, 363-9, 373, 385

unequal – 269, 378

unity – 9, 26, 30-3, 81, 190, 223-4, 283, 291, 339

Uraeus – 346-ft, 363

veil(ed) – 28, 331, 335, 390

Venus – 5, 17-9, 64-71, 75-78, 82-4, 91-2, 96-101, 117, 142, 229-ft, 308, 327, 332, 341, 365, 392-3

Venusian – 68, 92, 96-101, 193, 243, 341, 375, 393, 398

verdant – 22, 85, 386

vertical(ly)(ity) – 26, 32, 37-9, 48, 59-ft, 86, 110-1, 133, 138-40, 150-1, 155-7, 162, 169, 175, 181, 212, 215-ft, 219, 230, 238, 243, 249-52, 263-4, 272, 277, 280, 293, 303, 309, 322, 327, 338, 368, 371, 373-5, 383, 386, 399

Vesica Pisces – 72, 289, 338

Vespers – 20-1

vestibule – 167, 174-9, 182, 186-ft, 386-7

vine – 22, 101

Virgil - 16

virgin(ity) – 81, 85-7

virgin (i.e. the number 7) – 10-1

Virgin Mary/Marian etc – 2-5, 9-10, 13, 20-2, 25, 29, 62-7, 70, 73-4, 80, 83-91, 95, 98-100, 136-7, 141, 164, 186, 190, 197-200, 223, 287, 291, 312, 332, 341, 364-ft, 365, 370, 376

viriditas – 23, 386

vision – 2, 24-8, 43, 55, 64-6, 91, 104, 138, 185-6, 190, 212, 265, 318-9, 333, 343-5, 356, 370, 376

walled garden – 66, 100
Walsingham – 4, 9, 13, 42
wander(er)(ing) – 17, 90, 92, 190, 332, 347-8
war – 39, 359-60, 371
War in Heaven – 342, 348-50, 363, 384-5
Wartburgkrieg - 342
waxing and waning (of the moon) – 77, 286, 365
Well of Souls, 368
Wells – 50, 54, 56, 62, 201-4, 207, 323, 400
Wells Cathedral – 11, 46, 50-60, 70-6, 81, 85-6, 94-6, 100, 108-9, 112-9, 123, 128, 132, 140, 144, 148, 155-6, 162-6, 176-8, 181-3, 186, 190-3, 197-8, 203-4, 208-10, 212-3, 216-20, 224-5, 228, 231-325, 318-34, 343-5, 346-ft, 347-53, 358, 365-78, 384-5, 395-401
west/western etc – 36-7, 40, 45-52, 57-9, 64, 66-ft, 71, 75-7, 82, 91, 99, 134, 143-8, 157, 163, 178, 181, 191-3, 208, 212-8, 238-40, 248, 252-5, 257, 262, 265, 303, 308-9, 318-21, 324-32, 335, 338-46, 350-1, 365, 371, 380-2, 385-7, 399
west door – 3, 8, 26, 44, 54-9, 158, 234, 250-1, 254, 322, 325

west front – 26, 54, 61, 155-9, 218, 243-5, 249-56, 309, 322, 325, 351, 399
whale – 78-80, 344, 369
window(s) – 2, 11-6, 36, 52, 66, 86-7, 94-5, 157, 162, 169, 197-8, 202, 209, 223, 252-5, 273-4, 280, 286, 309, 312, 325, 346, 371, 378-83, 399-400
winter – 4, 23, 66-ft, 177, 214, 218-9, 306, 323-4, 329-31, 335, 338-9, 368, 374, 387-8
Wisdom – 1-6, 9-17, 20-3, 28, 32, 43, 62, 86, 97, 104-ft, 105-6, 161, 180, 184-6, 190-5, 198-200, 205, 283, 318-20, 327, 333-6, 342, 353, 364, 370, 376, 394, 398
wise – 5-6, 16, 102, 185, 191, 333, 342, 397
world(s)(ly) etc – 2-6, 9, 15-8, 20-6, 28-30, 34-5, 38-46, 49, 54-5, 59, 66-7, 75-7, 84-93, 96-8, 104-8, 121, 124, 136-8, 159, 168, 174, 177-81, 190-5, 205, 223-4, 229-31, 260, 289-ft, 318-21, 324-6, 332-40, 342-9, 351-ft, 353, 356, 359-60, 365-7, 372, 375-8, 383, 393, 401-2

Yin/Yang – 39, 50-ft, 330, 338
York Minster   128, 162-4, 174, 176-86, 194, 197-200, 283-ft, 375, 398

Zodiac(al) – 29, 36-7, 190-1, 217, 230, 287, 389